The Hebrew Bible: A Contemporary Introduction to the Christian Old Testament and the Jewish Tanakh

THE HEBREW BIBLE

SECOND EDITION

A CONTEMPORARY INTRODUCTION TO THE CHRISTIAN OLD TESTAMENT AND THE JEWISH TANAKH

DAVID M. CARR

WILEY Blackwell

This edition first published 2021
© 2021 David M. Carr

All rights reserved. No part of this publication may be reproduced, stored in a retrieval system, or transmitted, in any form or by any means, electronic, mechanical, photocopying, recording or otherwise, except as permitted by law. Advice on how to obtain permission to reuse material from this title is available at http://www.wiley.com/go/permissions.

The right of David M. Carr to be identified as the author of this work has been asserted in accordance with law.

Registered Offices
John Wiley & Sons Ltd, The Atrium, Southern Gate, Chichester, West Sussex, PO19 8SQ, UK
John Wiley & Sons, Inc., 111 River Street, Hoboken, NJ 07030, USA

Editorial Office
The Atrium, Southern Gate, Chichester, West Sussex, PO19 8SQ, UK

For details of our global editorial offices, customer services, and more information about Wiley products visit us at www.wiley.com.

Wiley also publishes its books in a variety of electronic formats and by print-on-demand. Some content that appears in standard print versions of this book may not be available in other formats.

Limit of Liability/Disclaimer of Warranty
While the publisher and authors have used their best efforts in preparing this work, they make no representations or warranties with respect to the accuracy or completeness of the contents of this work and specifically disclaim all warranties, including without limitation any implied warranties of merchantability or fitness for a particular purpose. No warranty may be created or extended by sales representatives, written sales materials or promotional statements for this work. The fact that an organization, website, or product is referred to in this work as a citation and/or potential source of further information does not mean that the publisher and authors endorse the information or services the organization, website, or product may provide or recommendations it may make. This work is sold with the understanding that the publisher is not engaged in rendering professional services. The advice and strategies contained herein may not be suitable for your situation. You should consult with a specialist where appropriate. Further, readers should be aware that websites listed in this work may have changed or disappeared between when this work was written and when it is read. Neither the publisher nor authors shall be liable for any loss of profit or any other commercial damages, including but not limited to special, incidental, consequential, or other damages.

Library of Congress Cataloging-in-Publication Data
Names: Carr, David McLain, 1961– author.
Title: The Hebrew Bible: A Contemporary Introduction to the
   Christian Old Testament and the Jewish Tanakh/ David M. Carr.
Other titles: Introduction to the Old Testament
Description: Second edition. | Hoboken : Wiley, 2021. | Includes index.
Identifiers: LCCN 2020039756 (print) | LCCN 2020039757 (ebook) | ISBN
   9781119636670 (paperback) | ISBN 9781119636663 (adobe pdf) | ISBN
   9781119636687 (epub)
Subjects: LCSH: Bible. Old Testament--History. | Bible. Old
   Testament–History of contemporary events. | Bible. Old
   Testament–Introductions.
Classification: LCC BS1130 .C37 2020 (print) | LCC BS1130 (ebook) | DDC
   221.9/5–dc23
LC record available at https://lccn.loc.gov/2020039756
LC ebook record available at https://lccn.loc.gov/2020039757

Cover Design: Wiley
Cover Image: © Historical Picture Archive/Contributor/Getty Images

A catalogue record for this book is available from the British Library.

Set in 9.5/12pt STIX Two Text by SPi Global, Pondicherry, India

10 9 8 7 6 5 4 3 2 1

Contents

List of Figures	vii
List of Maps	ix
Main Discussions/Outlines of Biblical Books	x
Preface	xiv
Acknowledgments	xvii
List of Abbreviations	xix
Overview of the Historical Period	xx
Timeline	xxii
Prologue: Multiple Bibles, Versions, and Translations	1
1 Studying the Bible in its Ancient Context(s)	19
2 The Emergence of Ancient Israel and its First Oral Traditions	35
3 Beginnings of the Monarchy and Royal and Zion Texts	59
4 Interlude: Echoes of Past Empires in Biblical Wisdom, Love Poetry, Law, and Narrative	77
5 Narrative and Prophecy Amidst the Rise and Fall of The Northern Kingdom	101
6 Micah, Isaiah, and the Southern Prophetic Encounter with Assyria	123
7 Torah and History in the Wake of the Assyrian Empire	139
8 Prophecy in the Transition from Assyrian to Babylonian Domination	165
9 Laments, History, and Prophecies after the Destruction of Jerusalem	177
10 Torah and Trauma	199
11 The Torah, the Psalms, and the Persian-Sponsored Rebuilding of Judah	227
12 Other Texts Formed in the Crucible of Post-Exilic Rebuilding	249
13 Hellenistic Empires and the Formation of Multiple Scriptures	265
Glossary	287
Index	301

FIGURES

0.1 Scholarly edition of the same text as in Figure 0.2.   7
0.2 One of our earliest manuscripts of the book of Isaiah.   12
1.1 Ancient visitors to Egypt from the East (Canaanites?)   26
2.1 Part of the hill country of central Israel.   37
2.2 Typical pillared house of the Israelites.   38
2.3 Tablet containing a letter from Abdi-heba.   40
2.4 Stela listing Egyptian conquests.   43
2.5 Animals feeding on trees.   46
3.1 Artist's reconstruction of Solomon's Jerusalem.   61
3.2 Scribe standing before the king of a small neighboring kingdom.   67
3.3 Student exercise tablet.   68
3.4 Letters inscribed into the surface of a stone.   69
3.5 The "Gezer Calendar."   70
4.1 Copy of the Egyptian Instruction of Amenemope.   83
4.2 The Hammurabi stela.   86
4.3 Tablet of the Gilgamesh Epic containing the flood narrative.   91
4.4 Titian's painting of Adam and Eve taking the apple.   93
5.1 One of the ivory carvings found in Samaria.   106
5.2 Detail from a wall-sized panorama of the defeat of the town of Lachish in Judah.   107
5.3 Panel from the Black Obelisk of the Assyrian king Shalmaneser III.   108
5.4 Ivory spoon found at Hazor.   115

5.5 Pillar figurines of a sort common in archaeological remains of the eighth century.   117

5.6 Drawing and inscription found at a desert trading post called Kuntillet Adjrud used by eighth-century Israelites.   118

6.1 The Sennacherib prism.   125

6.2 Judean seals from the time of Isaiah and Micah.   132

7.1 Seals and other images from the late seventh century.   143

9.1 Ashes and arrowheads left from the Babylonian attack on Jerusalem.   179

9.2 Reproduction of part of the magnificent temple of Ishtar.   181

10.1 The exilic L source or Lay source is much like this conglomerate rock.   203

10.2 Silver amulet, dating to just before the fall of Jerusalem.   218

11.1 Relief from the Persian capital of Persepolis.   228

11.2 The Cyrus cylinder.   230

13.1 Copy of the Hebrew book of Ben Sira found near the Dead Sea.   268

13.2 Coin from the time of the Hasmoneans.   276

Maps

0.1 The ancient Near East.   xxiv
1.1 The land of Israel and its surroundings.   24
1.2 The major routes of the ancient Near East.   27
1.3 The reach of three of the major empires that dominated Israel and/or Judah.   29
2.1 Areas of the hill country occupied by the Israelites and Judeans.   44
5.1 The neighboring kingdoms of Israel and Judah.   103
7.1 The Judean kingdom after the fall of the north.   141
9.1 The journey to Babylon.   180
11.1 Judah as a province of the Persian empire.   231
13.1 The expanding kingdom of the Hasmoneans.   275

Main Discussions/Outlines of Biblical Books

Where to Find Basic Information on Biblical Books

Below is a list of where you can find basic discussions of books (or major parts of books) in the Hebrew scriptures, with the books listed here in the order that they appear in the Jewish Tanakh (//Hebrew Bible), followed by some deutero-canonical books. The page given in **bold number(s)** indicates where you can find a "Basics Box" that provides major information about a biblical book. This includes an outline, information about the time(s) in which the book was written, and (usually) a discussion of a major issue in interpretation of the book or text. In addition, some other pages are provided where you can find more information on different biblical books.

Book	Pages
Genesis	**52–3, 237**; cf. 49–51, 88-97
Exodus	**238–9**; cf. 54–6
Leviticus	**214**
Numbers	**239**
Deuteronomy	**150**; cf. 145–50
Joshua	**153**; cf. 145–50
Judges	**154**; cf. 153–4
1–2 Samuel	**155**; cf. 65–6, 154–6
1–2 Kings	**157**; cf. 156–7
Isaiah	**191, 257–8**; cf. 130–7, 190–6, 257–61
Jeremiah	**172**; cf. 168–74
Ezekiel	**188**; cf. 186–9
Hosea	**116**; cf. 113–21
Amos	**112**; cf. 110–13
Jonah	**255**; cf. 255–6
Micah	**129–30**; cf. 126–30
Nahum	**166**; cf. 166–7
Zephaniah	**168**; cf. 167–8
Haggai	**250**; cf. 250–1
Zechariah	**251**; cf. 251–3

Main Discussions/Outlines of Biblical Books   xi

Psalms	**73, 243–4**; cf. 70–4; 241–6
Job	**254**
Proverbs	**84**; cf. 82–6
Ruth	**256**
Song of Songs/Solomon, Canticles	**79**; cf. 78–80, 280
Ecclesiastes/Qoheleth	**82**; cf. 80–5, 280
Lamentations	**183**; cf. 182–3
Esther	**279**
Daniel	**272**; cf. 270–2
Ezra-Nehemiah	**278–9**; cf. 252–3; 277–9
1–2 Chronicles	**277**
2 Maccabees	**274**
Ben Sira/Sirach	**269–70**
Enoch	**268–9**
Judith	**274**

What is a More on Method Box?

These boxes give a brief introduction to methods used to interpret the Hebrew Bible. They detail the sorts of questions that each method attempts to answer, give an example of how the method has been applied, and include a reference to an article or book with more information about the method under discussion.

Textual Criticism	6
Tradition History and Transmission History	41
African American Biblical Interpretation	55
Poetic Analysis	75
Afrocentric and Womanist Interpretation of the Bible	80
Source and Redaction Criticism	89
Feminist Criticism and History of Interpretation/Biblical Reception	93
Comparison with Non-Biblical Texts	96
The Joseph Story and Literary Approaches	105

Postcolonial Criticism	148
Trauma Studies and the Bible	184
(Study of) Intertextuality	193
Insights from History of Religions	219
Ecological Biblical Criticism	220
Form Criticism and Genre	242

What is in Special Topics Boxes?

These boxes offer extra information relevant to the broader discussion. Some pull together relevant dates for a period, while others show parallels between texts, or summarize information on a theme or question that relates to the topic at hand. This information is not optional or superfluous. Instead, these boxes highlight topics that are worth focused attention.

Contents of the Hebrew Bible/Tanakh/Old Testament	4
Bible Abbreviations, Chapters, and Verses	11
The Origins of Chapters and Verses	12
Overview: Order of Main Discussions of Biblical Books	21
Visualizing (the Possible Ancestors of) Ancient Israelites	26
AD, BC, BCE, and CE	28
The Name of Israel's God: Yahweh/the LORD	31
What Was Earliest "Israel" and Who Were "Judges"?	39
History and the Books of Joshua and Judges	40
The Name "Israel"	46
Labels (e.g. "Psalm of David"): What They (Don't) Tell Us	69
Contrasts and Parallels between Biblical and Mesopotamian Flood Narratives	90
Significant Dates: The Northern Kingdom ("Israel")	108
Hosea and the "Book of the Twelve Prophets"	120
Significant Dates: Judah under Assyrian Domination	124
A View from the Assyrian Imperial Court: The Annals of Sennacherib	126
Isaiah 6 and the "Call Narrative"	133
Comparison: The Covenant Code and Deuteronomy	145
Overview: The Three Pilgrimage Festivals in the Covenant Code and Deuteronomy	146
Proverbs and Deuteronomy	147
The Conquest and Ancient Holy War	152
Forced Labor for Exiles Under Nebuchadnezzar	181
The Divine Council	190

Traditions that Moses Wrote the Pentateuch	201
The Story of Jacob at Bethel as an Example of the Addition of Promise to an Older Story	205
J (the "Yahwistic Source"), E (the "Elohistic Source") and the Documentary Hypothesis	211
Which Texts Were Part of the P Source?	215
Significant Dates: The Persian-Sponsored Restoration of Judah	235
The Emergence of "Judaism"	267
Significant Dates: The Rise of the Hasmonean Kingdom	273
The Dead Sea Scrolls	282

Preface to the First Edition

This book introduces students to the books of the Hebrew Bible as shaped in the crucible of the history of Israel and Judah, as well as in the varied interpretations of later Jewish and Christian communities. A prominent theme throughout is the way the books of the Bible reflect quite different sorts of interaction with past and present empires that dominated the ancient Near East. At first both students and professors may find this approach jarring, since I do not begin with Genesis and do not proceed through biblical books in order. The group of texts introduced early on in this textbook is quite different from the Bible they now know. Moreover, this textbook incorporates advances in Pentateuchal criticism over the past decades that are unfamiliar to both students and many professors. Yet I can say on the basis of my and others' experience teaching this approach that the picture of the Bible's development comes into focus as the narrative of its formation unfolds. At the outset, I highly encourage readers to consult the charts at the beginning of this introduction (pp. xx–xxiii) that provide an overview of major periods in Israelite history and texts connected to those periods. By the end of the process, students should find meaning in aspects of the Bible that they once overlooked, even as they also understand that much of the power of the Bible has been its capability to transcend the original contexts in which it was written. Moreover, through discussion of the history of Jewish and Christian interpretation of "Focus texts" at the end of each chapter, students will gain a taste of how faith communities have used the Bible in creative, inspired, and sometimes death-dealing ways to guide and make sense of their lives.

I have been helped by many people in writing this textbook, first and foremost my wife, Colleen Conway. Versions of these chapters were originally written for a combined introduction to the Old and New Testaments that is co-authored with her, *Introduction to the Bible: Sacred Texts and Imperial Contexts* (also published by Wiley-Blackwell), and so she has read multiple versions of them, taught them in her courses, and offered many suggestions for improvement. Several colleagues – Benjamin Sommer, Kent Reynolds, Mark Smith, and Marvin Sweeney – went way beyond the call of duty to read and suggest revisions to excerpts from the manuscript relating to areas of their expertise. I cannot say that I incorporated all of their suggestions, but I can affirm that this book is much stronger thanks to their gracious help. In addition, my students over the past two years have read earlier drafts of this textbook and suggested corrections. Some students and teaching assistants who have offered a particularly large volume of helpful corrections are Mary Ellen Kris, Candice Olson, Lizzie Berne-DeGear, Laurel Koepf, Meagan Manas, and Todd Kennedy. My thanks to all for their generous help in this project.

The date framework given in this textbook follows that of Anson Rainey and Steven Notley's *The Sacred Bridge: Carta's Atlas of the Biblical World*

(Jerusalem: Carta, 2005). In many cases specific dates are uncertain, but Rainey and Notley provide a recent, solid framework to start from on an introductory level. Unless otherwise indicated, the Hebrew and Aramaic translations of biblical and additional texts here are my own.

As with any such textbook, there is plenty of room for improvement. In particular, I am acutely conscious of the multiple ways in which virtually everything that is written here could be footnoted, qualified, and balanced with other perspectives. At particular points, such as my treatment of Pentateuchal source criticism, I explicitly summarize alternative perspectives that students may encounter when reading other resources. But inclusion of all alternative perspectives would have turned this into quite a different book, and one – I suggest – that would be much less suited for introducing students to academic study of the Bible. This introduction provides one general outline of the Hebrew Bible, which students can then supplement, correct, and balance in their future studies. All that said, I certainly invite all possible suggestions for correction and improvement so that any future edition of this textbook will be better.

DAVID CARR
NEW YORK

PREFACE TO THE SECOND EDITION

I am happy to have this opportunity to update and revise this *Introduction* after using and receiving feedback on the first edition over the past decade. This new edition includes corrections and a number of updates to reflect developments in recent scholarship. These revisions are too numerous to mention, but are illustrated by the inclusion of several new "More on Methods" boxes that discuss African American Biblical Interpretation, Afrocentric and Womanist Interpretation of the Bible, Feminist Criticism and History of Interpretation/Biblical Reception, Trauma Studies and the Bible, and Ecological Biblical Criticism. This list reflects my ever-increasing consciousness of the importance for white male scholars like myself to recognize the impact of my social location on my writing and how I and my students must learn from the work and insights of colleagues of color. Readers are particularly encouraged to read those scholars' work directly, and I have provided some initial suggestions of resources to do so.

One of the primary aims of the first edition of the *Introduction* was to provide a relatively concise textbook so that students would have more time to read biblical texts as well. Though this revision includes substantial new material, I have worked to keep the overall book compact. In addition, users should note some new exercises and chapter review questions that focus on analysis of the Bible itself, including a series of questions oriented to the discussion of "Focus texts" featured in most chapters. Overall, I have endeavored to cite biblical passages by the numbers that appear in widely used English translations (e.g. NRSV, NIV; though note that some important English translations, e.g. the New Jerusalem or New Jewish Publication Society versions, follow the Hebrew versification, which diverges slightly for some biblical passages). Also, users of this book are encouraged to consult my own website, www.davidmcarr.com, for links to some non-biblical texts discussed in this book, explanatory videos, and other materials related to this textbook.

Overall, I hope to have provided a "Contemporary" Introduction to the Hebrew Bible and highlighted this in the revised title of the book. Moreover, the main title was revised to focus on "Hebrew Bible" rather than just "Old Testament" in order to reflect the way that this book emphasizes academic study of the Bible and not just one (Christian) confessional approach to its subject matter. It should be emphasized, however, that this second edition preserves a focus on the impact of successive empires on the Hebrew Bible/Old Testament/Tanakh, even though it no longer includes the previous subtitle "sacred texts and imperial contexts."

Finally, I have been profoundly helped in this revision by the feedback provided by colleagues and numerous classes of students at my institution, Union Theological Seminary in New York City, especially the Fall 2019 section of my Introduction to the Old Testament. I want to offer specific thanks to several colleagues for sharing bibliography and/or reading drafts of sections and suggesting revisions, including Charles Carter, Thomas Dozeman, Esther Hamori, Mahri Leonard-Fleckman, Robert Rezetko, Jerusha Rhodes, William Schniedewind, and my wife (and fellow biblical scholar) Colleen Conway. I dedicate this revision to my beloved parents, Adrienne and John Carr, both of them teachers and lifelong learners, even as I now mourn the loss of my father two years ago.

DAVID CARR

NEW YORK

Acknowledgments

The author and publisher gratefully acknowledge the permission granted to reproduce the copyrighted material in this book:

Figure 0.1	Biblia Hebraica Stuttgartensia, edited by Karl Elliger and Wilhelm Rudolph, Fifth Revised Edition, edited by Adrian Schenker, © 1977 and 1997 Deutsche Bibelgesellschaft, Stuttgart. Used by permission.
Figure 0.2	Israel Talby/Israel images/Alamy Stock Photo
Figure 1.1	FALKENSTEINFOTO/Alamy Stock Photo
Figure 2.1	Zev Radovan/BibleLandPictures/Alamy Stock Photo
Figure 2.2	Redrawn from Philip J. King and Lawrence E. Stager, *Life in Biblical Israel*. Louisville, KY: Westminster John Knox Press, 2001, page 29.
Figure 2.3	bpk/Vorderasiatisches Museum, SMB/Gudrun Stenzel
Figure 2.4	Jürgen Liepe
Figure 2.5	Redrawn from Othmar Keel and Christoph Uehlinger, *Göttinnen, Götter und Gottessymbole: neue Erkenntnisse zur Religionsgeschichte Kanaans und Israels aufgrund bislang unerschlossener ikonographischer Quellen* (Quaestiones disputatae). Freiburg im Breisgau: Herder, 1992, page 134.
Figure 3.1	Lloyd K. Townsend
Figure 3.2	William Schniedewind
Figure 3.3	akg images/Erich Lessing
Figure 3.4	Courtesy of R. E. Tappy and The Zeitah Excavations Photograph by B. Zuckerman and M. Lundberg Overlay by P. K. McCarter, Jr.
Figure 3.5	Zev Radovan/BibleLandPictures/Alamy Stock Photo
Figure 4.1	© The Trustees of the British Museum. All rights reserved.
Figure 4.2	www.BibleLandPictures.com/Alamy Stock Photo
Figure 4.3	akg-images.
Figure 4.4	Francis G. Mayer/Getty Images
Figure 5.1	Zev Radovan/BibleLandPictures/Alamy Images
Figure 5.2	akg-images/Erich Lessing
Figure 5.3	Zev Radovan/BibleLandPictures/Alamy Images
Figure 5.4	Stiftung BIBEL+ORIENT.
Figure 5.5	akg-images/Fototeca Gilardi
Figure 5.6	Stiftung BIBEL+ORIENT.
Figure 6.1	AP Images/NAM Y HUH
Figure 6.2	Stiftung BIBEL+ORIENT.
Figure 7.1	Stiftung BIBEL+ORIENT.
Figure 9.1	Zev Radovan/BibleLandPictures/Alamy Stock Photo
Figure 9.2	akg-images/Erich Lessing

Figure 10.1	Puddingstone/Natural History Museum, London, UK/Bridgeman Images
Figure 10.2	Stiftung BIBEL+ORIENT.
Figure 11.1	Prisma by Dukas Presseagentur GmbH/Alamy Stock Photo
Figure 11.2	akg-images/Erich Lessing
Figure 13.1	Photo © The Israel Museum, Jerusalem
Figure 13.2	Courtesy of Carta, Jerusalem

The Pharaoh Merneptah hymn in Chapter 3, pages 70–71, and the Cyrus cylinder text in Chapter 11, page 229: PRITCHARD, JAMES; *ANCIENT NEAR EASTERN TEXTS RELATING TO THE OLD TESTAMENT – THIRD EDITION WITH SUPPLEMENT.* © 1950, 1955, 1969, renewed 1978 by Princeton University Press. Reprinted by permission of Princeton University Press.

At points throughout the book extracts have been used from the Revised Standard Version of the Bible: Revised Standard Version of the Bible, copyright 1952 [2nd edition, 1971] by the Division of Christian Education of the National Council of the Churches of Christ in the United States of America. Used by permission. All rights reserved.

The publisher apologizes for any errors or omissions in the above list and would be grateful if notified of any corrections that should be incorporated in future reprints or editions of this book.

ABBREVIATIONS

ANET	James Pritchard (ed.), *Ancient Near Eastern Texts Relating to the Old Testament with Supplement*. Princeton: Princeton University Press, 1969.
George	Andrew George, *The Babylonian Gilgamesh Epic: Introduction, Critical Edition and Cuneiform Texts*. New York: Oxford University Press, 2003.
Livingstone	Alasdair Livingstone (ed.), *Court Poetry and Literary Miscellanea*. State Archives of Assyria, 3. Helsinki: Helsinki University Press, 1989.
NJPS	*The New Jewish Publication Society Tanakh Translation*. Philadelphia: Jewish Publication Society, 1985.
NRSV	*The New Revised Standard Version of the Bible*. New York: National Council of Churches, 1989.
NT	New Testament
OT	Old Testament
OT Parallels	Victor Matthews and Don Benjamin, *Old Testament Parallels: Laws and Stories from the Ancient Near East* (3rd revised and expanded edition). Mahwah, NJ: Paulist Press, 2007.

For Bible abbreviations, see the box on "Bible Abbreviations, Chapters, and Verses," in the Prologue, p. 11.

Asterisks after Bible citations, e.g. "Genesis 12–50*," indicate that only parts of the cited texts are included.

// indicate that the texts before and after the slashes are parallel to each other.

Overview of the Historical Period

This shows major periods and corresponding texts covered in this book.

Dates	1250–1000 BCE (13th–11th centuries)	1000–930 (10th century)	930–800 (10th–9th centuries)	800–700 (8th century)	700–586 (7th and early 6th centuries)	586–538 (6th century)	538–332 (6th–4th centuries)	332–63 (4th–1st centuries)
Chapter	2	3 and 4	5	5 and 6	7 and 8	9 and 10	11 and 12	12 and 13
Major Events (in Chronological Order)	Spread of villages in hill country Tribal "Israel" emerge Saul's chieftainship	Formation of Davidic monarchy Jerusalem taken as capital of Judah/Israel David and Solomon	Formation of northern kingdom of "Israel" Rise and fall of Omride dynasty	Domination and destruction of northern "Israel" by Assyria Domination of Judah by Assyria	Eventual decline of Assyrian power Enactment of Josiah's "reform" Decline of Judah into domination by Babylon First wave of exile	Destruction of Jerusalem and its Temple Second and third waves of exile of elites to Babylon	Persian victory, waves of return, rebuilding of Temple Nehemiah's rebuilding of the wall Divorce of foreign wives under Ezra and elevation of Torah	Hellenistic rule Hellenizing crisis Hasmonean kingdom

MAJOR WRITINGS (AND ORAL TRADITIONS)	(No writings, but oral traditions about exodus, Trickster ancestors)	(start of writing) Royal and Zion psalms (some) Proverbs ?Non-P primeval history	Jacob narrative Joseph narrative Exodus – wilderness story Song of Deborah	Prophecy to the north by Amos and Hosea Prophecy to the south by Micah and Isaiah	Formation of Deuteronomy and following historical books Nahum Zephaniah Early prophecies from Jeremiah	Exilic additions to biblical books Lamentations Ezekiel and Second Isaiah Non-P (L) narrative of early Israel P counter-narrative of early Israel	Haggai Zechariah Nehemiah memoir Narratives of Temple rebuilding and of Ezra Third Isaiah Combined P and non-P (L) Pentateuch Psalter	Early parts of Enoch Ben Sira Ezra-Nehemiah Esther 1–2 Chronicles Daniel 1–2 Maccabees, Judith
MAJOR NEW IDEAS AND THEMES	Election theology	Royal/Zion theology			Exclusive devotion to Yahweh enforced (briefly) by Josiah	Monotheism	Dual Temple–Torah focus	Judaism

Timeline

Important texts are noted in **boldface**.

BCE	SOUTH (Judah)	NORTH ("Israel" in narrower sense)
1300	(Waning Egyptian domination of Canaan)	
		Spread of villages in Israelite hill county
		Merneptah Stela mention of "Israel"
1200		Battles of hill-country Israelites with neighbors
		Oral exodus traditions
		Oral ancestral traditions
1100		**Oral victory traditions**
	Saul's "chieftainship"	
	David (Hebron; 1010–1002)	
1000	David (Jerusalem; 1002–970)	
	Royal psalms, Zion psalms	
	Solomon (Jerusalem; 970–930)	
	Proverb collections	
	(early form??) **Non-P primeval narrative**	
	Rehoboam (Jerusalem)	Jeroboam founds northern monarchy
900		(early form of written) **Jacob narrative, Joseph novella, and exodus-Moses narrative**
		Song of Deborah (written form)
		Omride dynasty (880–841)
		Jehu's coup (841)
800		Jeroboam II (782–753)
		Amos
	Isaiah (early prophecy) Assyrian domination of Israel begins (745–)	
	Syro-Ephraimite war (735–734)	**Hosea**
	Assyrian domination of Judah (734–)	
	Micah, Isaiah (later prophecy)	
		Assyrian destruction of Israel (722)
	Hezekiah (715–686)	
	Hezekiah's rebellion and reform (705)	
700	Sennacherib's attack and mysterious withdrawal (701)	
	Manasseh (686–642)	
	Amon (642–640)	(Waning of Assyrian power)
	Josiah (640–609)	
	Zephaniah	
	Josiah's reform (623)	
	Josianic edition of Deuteronomy, 2 Kings, etc.	
		(Fall of Nineveh, Assyria's capital)
	Nahum	
	Jeremiah	

Domination of Judah by Babylonia
600   First wave of exiles (597)
                  Ezekiel's early prophecy
          Destruction of Jerusalem and second wave of exiles (586)
                  Lamentations and Psalm 137
                  Ezekiel's later prophecy
          Third wave of exiles (582)
                  Exilic additions to Deuteronomy, 2 Kings, and other Books

                  Non-P/L Pentateuchal source (incorporating exilic-modified forms of older non-P primeval history, Jacob-Joseph story, exodus-Moses story, and Deuteronomy)

                  Priestly Pentateuchal source

                  Second Isaiah
          Persian conquering of Babylonian empire (539)
              First wave of returnees (~538)
              Another wave, beginning of Temple restoration (532)
                  Another wave with Zerubbabel, completion of Temple rebuilding (520–515)
                  Haggai and Zechariah (1–9)
500   Nehemiah's return and governorships (445–425)
              (rebuilding wall, purification of priesthood)
              Nehemiah memoir
400   Return with Ezra, divorce of foreign wives, elevation of Torah (397–)
                  Combined (P and non-P/L) Pentateuch
                  Narratives of Temple-rebuilding and Ezra
                  Third Isaiah
                  Psalter (final, Torah-oriented version of the book)
          Greek conquering of Persian empire (332)

300   (Shifting domination of Palestine by Greek Ptolemies
          (Egypt) and Seleucids (Mesopotamia); 332–142)
                  Early parts of Enoch

                  1–2 Chronicles

                  Wisdom of Ben Sira (Sirach)

200   Jason purchase of high priesthood, attempt to Hellenize Jerusalem (174)

          Menelaus purchase of high priesthood (171) and Judean rebellion against him
                  Daniel

          Antiochus Epiphanes IV campaign to eradicate observant Judaism and beginning of
              Hasmonean-led rebellion against Hellenistic rule (167–)
          Purification and rededication of Temple (164)

          Hasmonean independence and rule (142–63)
                  Ezra-Nehemiah, Esther

                  1–2 Maccabees, Judith

100
CE   Roman takeover of Palestine (63)
          Destruction of the Second Temple (70)

MAP 0.1
The ancient Near East. Redrawn from Adrian Curtis (ed.), *Oxford Bible Atlas* (4th edition). Oxford, New York: Oxford University Press, 2007, page 67.

Prologue: Multiple Bibles, Versions, and Translations

The Bible as a Complex Product of Many Hands

The Different Scriptures of Judaism and Christianity

Becoming an Informed User of a Contemporary Bible Translation

Bible Abbreviations, Chapters, and Verses

Conclusion on Critically Analyzing a Page of Your Own Bible

Chapter Review

Resources for Further Study

Appendix 1: Translation and Paraphrase Comparison of Isa 52:13–15

Appendix 2: Characteristics of Select English Translations of the Bible

CHAPTER OVERVIEW

This prologue helps you learn the basic characteristics and background of the Bible that you will use across the course. As you will see, not all Bibles are the same. Judaism and different forms of Christianity include different books in their Bibles. Also, ancient manuscripts of the Bible diverge from one another, and contemporary translations follow different manuscript readings and translation practices. By the end of this chapter you should know the differences between the Bibles of Judaism and Christianity, as well as the relationship of the Islamic Qur'an to both sets of scriptures. You will also learn about how study of different readings of ancient manuscripts of the Bible, "textual criticism," and advances in knowledge of ancient languages have led to major progress in translation of the Bible since the King James Version was completed in 1611. Finally, you will learn some basic things to keep in mind in choosing and using an up-to-date English translation of the Bible.

The Hebrew Bible: A Contemporary Introduction to the Christian Old Testament and the Jewish Tanakh, Second Edition. David M. Carr.
© 2021 David M. Carr. Published 2021 by John Wiley & Sons Ltd.

EXERCISES

1) Using the parallels provided at the end of the chapter in Appendix 1, compare the translations (and paraphrase) of Isa 52:13–15. What differences do you notice?
2) Take a look at two pages of a biblical book in your Bible. Make a list of *all* types of elements on those pages aside from the actual text of the Bible. Using the discussions in this chapter, identify where those elements came from

The Bible as a Complex Product of Many Hands

We start here with your Bible – the book that you hold in your hands. A major aim of this chapter, and this introduction as a whole, is to give you a deeper appreciation of the way this seeming simple book is actually the complex product of centuries of human work. The last stages of that work are already obvious when you take a closer look at a Bible you hold in your hands. Notice the type of cover it is packaged in (unless you are working with a digital copy!). Take a look at the typeface used for the biblical text and various aids that are provided for you as a reader (depending on your particular Bible): paragraph divisions, headings for different Bible passages, and maybe some cross-references to other Bible passages or brief explanatory notes. None of these aspects come from ancient manuscripts. They are aids that the publisher of your Bible provides to you as a reader.

These parts of your Bible, however, are just the first set of ways that your Bible has been worked into the form you have it now. Take, for example, the chapter and verse numbers in your Bible. None appear in ancient manuscripts. They were added to the text over a thousand years after it was written. Or consider the translation in your Bible. The biblical texts were originally written in Hebrew, Aramaic (an ancient language similar to Hebrew), and Greek. We will see in this prologue how every translation of these ancient texts involves significant style decisions, reasoned guesses, and compromises. In addition, we have multiple handwritten copies of ancient biblical manuscripts. These ancient copies disagree with each other. As a result, a translator must not just decide how to translate a given biblical verse. She or he also must choose which manuscript reading to translate in the first place. And all this does not even get into the centuries-long process that produced these ancient Hebrew, Aramaic, and Greek biblical texts, or how they were collected into specific scriptural collections by Jews and Christians. That long process will be the focus of much of the rest of this introduction.

For now we are focusing on some of the elements that were added to those texts in the Bible before you, many of which distinguish one Bible that you might find from another. These include what books are included and in what order, what kind of translation is used, and how translators chose, for a given phrase or word, to follow a reading in one ancient manuscript versus another. This prologue discusses these elements in turn, aiming to help you be a more informed user of your Bible.

The Different Scriptures of Judaism and Christianity

To begin, it is important to recognize that the Bibles of different faith communities contain somewhat different books, put those books in different order, and call their Bibles different things. Your Bible reflects one of those collections or a mix of them. These are often referred to as different "canons" of the Bible, with "**canon**" meaning a collection of books that are recognized as divinely inspired scripture by a given religious community. Such books are recognized as "**canonical**."

In Judaism, the scriptures are called the "**Tanakh**" (with the kh pronounced like the ch in Bach). Tanakh is a word formed out of the first letters of the Hebrew names of the three main parts of the Jewish Bible: *Torah* (Genesis, Exodus, Leviticus, Numbers, and Deuteronomy), *Neviim* ("prophets"), and *Ketuvim* ("writings"). See the box on p. 4 for an overview of the contents of each of these three parts. Judaism focuses particularly on the **Torah**, otherwise known as the **Pentateuch**, with most synagogues reading the Torah's five books all across the year, starting with Genesis at the outset of the Fall (the Jewish New Year) and concluding with Deuteronomy 12 months later. Jews certainly read other parts of the Tanakh, for example singing psalms (part of the "Writings") and reading portions of the "Prophets" to accompany the Torah reading. Nevertheless, the Torah takes pride of place within the Jewish Bible, while other parts of the Tanakh are often seen as commentary on it.

The Christian version of these scriptures, the "Old Testament" (OT), is part of a two-part Bible that also includes specifically Christian scriptures, the New Testament (NT). The Christian Old Testament is organized differently from the Jewish Tanakh. Though both the Tanakh and the Christian Old Testament start with the biblical narrative-historical books of Genesis to 2 Kings, the Christian Old Testament follows those books with the parallel narration of that history in Chronicles, Ezra, and Nehemiah. It then sequences the other biblical books in the order of their traditional authors, starting with the book of Job (an early Edomite sage), and moving through Psalms (David as traditional author), Proverbs, Ecclesiastes, and Song of Songs (Solomon as traditional author), and on to the major (Isaiah, Jeremiah, Ezekiel) and minor (Hosea, etc.) prophets. As in the case of the Jewish Tanakh, the ending of the Christian Old Testament is revealing. It concludes with the last chapter of Malachi, a prediction of the second coming of Elijah (Mal 4:5). This ending leads nicely into the first book of the New Testament, the Gospel of Matthew, which describes the coming of John the Baptist, who is clothed like Elijah and prophesies the coming of Jesus (Matt 3:1–6).

Contents of the Hebrew Bible/Tanakh/Old Testament

Jewish Tanakh	Protestant OT	Roman Catholic OT (*italics* = not in Tanakh)	Eastern Orthodox OT (*italics* = not in Tanakh)
Torah	**(Pentateuch)**	**(Pentateuch)**	**(Pentateuch)**
Genesis, Exodus, Leviticus, Numbers, Deuteronomy	Genesis, Exodus, Leviticus, Numbers, Deuteronomy	Genesis, Exodus, Leviticus, Numbers, Deuteronomy	Genesis, Exodus, Leviticus, Numbers, Deuteronomy
Prophets (Nevi'im)	**(Historical Books)**	**(Historical Books)**	**(Historical Books)**
Former prophets Joshua, Judges	Joshua, Judges, Ruth	Joshua, Judges, Ruth	Joshua, Judges, Ruth
1–2 Samuel	1–2 Samuel	1–2 Samuel	1–2 Samuel
1–2 Kings	1–2 Kings	1–2 Kings	1–2 Kings
	1–2 Chronicles	1–2 Chronicles	1–2 Chronicles
Latter prophets	Ezra-Nehemiah	Ezra-Nehemiah	Ezra-Nehemiah
			1 Esdras (2 Esdras in Russian Orthodox)
Major prophets			
		Tobit	*Tobit*
Isaiah		*Judith*	*Judith*
Jeremiah	Esther	Esther *(with additions)*	Esther *(with additions)*
Ezekiel		*1–2 Maccabees*	*1–3 Maccabees*
Minor prophets/ book of the twelve	**(Poetical Books)**	**(Poetical Books)**	**(Poetical Books)**
	Job	Job	Job
Hosea, Joel, Amos, Obadiah, Jonah, Micah, Nahum, Habakkuk, Zephaniah, Haggai, Zechariah, Malachi	Psalms	Psalms	Psalms (with Psalm 151)
	Proverbs	Proverbs	Proverbs
	Ecclesiastes	Ecclesiastes	Ecclesiastes
	Song of Solomon	Song of Solomon	Song of Solomon
		Wisdom of Solomon	*Wisdom of Solomon*
		Sirach	*Sirach*
Writings (Ketuvim)	**(Prophets)**	**(Prophets)**	**(Prophets)**
Psalms	Isaiah	Isaiah	Isaiah
Proverbs	Jeremiah	Jeremiah	Jeremiah
Job	Lamentations	Lamentations	Lamentations
Five festal scrolls		*Baruch*	*Baruch*
Song of Songs		*Letter of Jeremiah*	*Letter of Jeremiah*
Ruth	Ezekiel	Ezekiel	Ezekiel
Lamentations	Daniel	Daniel *(with additions)*	Daniel *(with additions)*
Ecclesiastes	Hosea, Joel, Amos, Obadiah, Jonah, Micah, Nahum, Habakkuk, Zephaniah, Haggai, Zechariah, Malachi	Hosea, Joel, Amos, Obadiah, Jonah, Micah, Nahum, Habakkuk, Zephaniah, Haggai, Zechariah, Malachi	Hosea, Joel, Amos, Obadiah, Jonah, Micah, Nahum, Habakkuk, Zephaniah, Haggai, Zechariah, Malachi
Esther			
Daniel			
Ezra-Nehemiah			
1–2 Chronicles			*4 Maccabees* (appendix)

You also should know that there are differences between the books included in different Christian Old Testament collections. The Protestant Old Testament contains the same books as the Jewish Tanakh, though in the above-noted different order leading up to the New Testament. The Roman Catholic Old Testament includes some additional books such as 1 and 2 Maccabees, Sirach, and the Wisdom of Solomon. The Ethiopic church recognizes the book of Enoch as part of its Old Testament, and various forms of Orthodox Christianity likewise recognize slightly different groups of additional books. For Roman Catholics, such additional books (not in the Jewish Tanakh) are "**deuterocanonical**," which means that they belong to a "second canon." For Protestants, such books not in the Jewish Tanakh are not considered true scripture, but "**apocrypha**," which means "books hidden away." I will not hide such books away in this textbook, but neither will I discuss them at length. Instead, I briefly discuss a sampling of them: Ben Sira/Sirach, Enoch, and Judith. In addition, toward the end of this introduction I will return to discuss how Jewish and Christian communities ended up with these slightly different collections of scriptural books.

"**Hebrew Bible**" is yet another term that is often used to designate the scriptures shared by Jews and Christians. Many teachers and scholars prefer the expression "Hebrew Bible" because it avoids the pejorative connotations that the term "Old Testament" has assumed in some Christian circles. The terms "Old" and "New Testament" derive from Greek and Latin terms that have been used by Christians to contrast an old covenant (with Israel) and new covenant (through Jesus Christ). Often this has been part of a Christian **supersessionist** assumption that God's covenant with the world through Christ superseded any prior covenant that God made with Israel. For Christians who subscribe to this idea, the Old Testament is often treated as the *old* and superseded Testament. It is negatively cast as the outdated book of the "law," as opposed to the New Testament, which is understood to be the truly scriptural word about Jesus, love, and grace. Such views reflect a lack of close reading of both the Old and New Testament, but they are widespread and influential. This is why many people avoid the term "Old Testament," with its possible implications of **supersessionism**, and use terms such as "Hebrew Bible" or "First Testament" instead. Others, however, find these terms odd and/or inaccurate (for example, several chapters in the Tanakh/Old Testament are not in Hebrew, but Aramaic). They prefer sticking with the Christian term "Old Testament," at least within specifically Christian contexts, but emphasize the more ancient understanding of "Old" as implying something good, rather than the more contemporary idea of "Old" being something that is outdated.

The important thing for academic study of the Bible is to understand the meanings of these different terms for the Tanakh/Old Testament/Hebrew scriptures and the slight differences in contents and order of these otherwise similar collections. These differences reflect the fact that these scriptures have come to belong to multiple faith communities. In addition, Islamic tradition sees the scriptures of Judaism and Christianity as possessing a secondary authority to that of its central text, the Qur'an. From the Muslim perspective, the Qur'an represents the final part of a long line of Divine revelations to human communities, including the Jewish Tanakh and Christian Old and New Testaments. This Qur'an is quite different in contents and form from the Tanakh/Old Testament, containing 114 chapters (surahs) of primarily ethical and theological exhortations that were communicated by Prophet Muhammad. It is not a parallel "Old Testament" or "Tanakh." Nevertheless, parts of the Qur'an reflect post-biblical Jewish traditions about history up to Moses (e.g. about Abraham, Ishmael, Mary), and other Muslim traditions (e.g. the biography and example of the prophet Muhammad).

From this discussion, we can see that there is no one "Bible," not even one "Hebrew Bible," shared by Judaism and Christianity, let alone Islam. Even if we focus on the overlapping contents of the Jewish Tanakh and Christian Old Testament, there are significant differences in order and (occasionally) content as well. This is an initial indicator of the quite different readings that Christians and Jews give to the texts they hold in common. We will see others along the way. Moreover, this diversity of Jewish and Christian Bibles is preceded by a diversity of perspectives and voices found within the Hebrew scriptures themselves. In the following chapters, we will see this diversity in texts written at different times and even in texts offering different perspectives on the same time.

Becoming an Informed User of a Contemporary Bible Translation

So let us assume that you have in your hands a Jewish Tanakh or some contemporary version of a Christian Old Testament. Unless you read Hebrew fluently, you will be working with an English translation of the Bible. Let us prepare for this study of the Hebrew scriptures by looking at the different components that go into this Bible above).

First, as discussed above, every translation builds on a number of decisions about which Hebrew text to translate. There is no single authoritative ancient copy of the Hebrew scriptures, even in the original Hebrew. Instead, we have several different sorts of ancient Hebrew manuscripts and ancient translations that used old Hebrew manuscripts, all of which are the products of centuries of hand-copying and occasional miscopying. Scholars preparing to do translation must engage in the practice of **"textual criticism"** or (more often) build on textual criticism by text-critical experts (see box). Biblical verses are preserved differently in the different ancient manuscripts, and it is not always easy to decide which manuscript reading of a given section to translate. Nevertheless, such decisions must be made, for each verse and chapter, in order to even begin the process of producing the translation you now have.

More on Method: Textual Criticism

"Textual criticism" is not general study of a text. Instead, textual criticism studies the diverse ancient manuscript *copies* of biblical texts, analyzing their development and providing data that can be used to choose which reading of a biblical text to follow. Over the centuries, scribes have introduced tens of thousands of minor changes into biblical texts as they have copied them by hand. Some changes were introduced by accident, as when a scribe might accidentally copy a given line twice. Other changes seem more intentional, where a scribe seems to have added a clarification of a place name or a theological correction or expansion. The ancient copies are often termed **manuscript witnesses** because they "witness" to diverse forms of these hand-copied texts.

ישעיהו

וַיַּרְאֵם אֶת־כָּל־בֵּית נְכֹתֹה אֶת־הַכֶּסֶף וְאֶת־הַזָּהָב וְאֶת־הַבְּשָׂמִים ׀ וְאֵת
הַשֶּׁמֶן הַטּוֹב וְאֵת כָּל־בֵּית כֵּלָיו וְאֵת כָּל־אֲשֶׁר נִמְצָא בְּאֹצְרֹתָיו
לֹא־הָיָה דָבָר אֲשֶׁר לֹא־הֶרְאָם חִזְקִיָּהוּ בְּבֵיתוֹ וּבְכָל־מֶמְשַׁלְתּוֹ׃
3 וַיָּבֹא יְשַׁעְיָהוּ הַנָּבִיא אֶל־הַמֶּלֶךְ חִזְקִיָּהוּ וַיֹּאמֶר אֵלָיו מָה אָמְרוּ ׀
הָאֲנָשִׁים הָאֵלֶּה וּמֵאַיִן יָבֹאוּ אֵלֶיךָ וַיֹּאמֶר חִזְקִיָּהוּ מֵאֶרֶץ רְחוֹקָה
בָּאוּ אֵלַי מִבָּבֶל׃ 4 וַיֹּאמֶר מָה רָאוּ בְּבֵיתֶךָ וַיֹּאמֶר חִזְקִיָּהוּ אֶת כָּל־
אֲשֶׁר בְּבֵיתִי רָאוּ לֹא־הָיָה דָבָר אֲשֶׁר לֹא־הִרְאִיתִים בְּאוֹצְרֹתָי׃
5 וַיֹּאמֶר יְשַׁעְיָהוּ אֶל־חִזְקִיָּהוּ שְׁמַע דְּבַר־יְהוָה צְבָאוֹת׃ 6 הִנֵּה יָמִים
בָּאִים וְנִשָּׂא ׀ כָּל־אֲשֶׁר בְּבֵיתֶךָ וַאֲשֶׁר אָצְרוּ אֲבֹתֶיךָ עַד־הַיּוֹם הַזֶּה
בָּבֶלָה לֹא־יִוָּתֵר דָּבָר אָמַר יְהוָה׃ 7 וּמִבָּנֶיךָ אֲשֶׁר יֵצְאוּ מִמְּךָ אֲשֶׁר
תּוֹלִיד יִקָּחוּ וְהָיוּ סָרִיסִים בְּהֵיכַל מֶלֶךְ בָּבֶל׃ 8 וַיֹּאמֶר חִזְקִיָּהוּ אֶל־
יְשַׁעְיָהוּ טוֹב דְּבַר־יְהוָה אֲשֶׁר דִּבַּרְתָּ וַיֹּאמֶר כִּי יִהְיֶה שָׁלוֹם וֶאֱמֶת
בְּיָמָי׃

40 1 נַחֲמוּ נַחֲמוּ עַמִּי יֹאמַר אֱלֹהֵיכֶם׃
2 דַּבְּרוּ עַל־לֵב יְרוּשָׁלִַם וְקִרְאוּ אֵלֶיהָ
כִּי מָלְאָה צְבָאָהּ כִּי נִרְצָה עֲוֺנָהּ
כִּי לָקְחָה מִיַּד יְהוָה כִּפְלַיִם בְּכָל־חַטֹּאתֶיהָ׃
3 קוֹל קוֹרֵא
בַּמִּדְבָּר פַּנּוּ דֶּרֶךְ יְהוָה
יַשְּׁרוּ בָּעֲרָבָה מְסִלָּה לֵאלֹהֵינוּ׃
4 כָּל־גֶּיא יִנָּשֵׂא וְכָל־הַר וְגִבְעָה יִשְׁפָּלוּ
וְהָיָה הֶעָקֹב לְמִישׁוֹר וְהָרְכָסִים לְבִקְעָה׃
5 וְנִגְלָה כְּבוֹד יְהוָה וְרָאוּ כָל־בָּשָׂר יַחְדָּו כִּי פִּי יְהוָה
6 קוֹל אֹמֵר קְרָא וְאָמַר מָה אֶקְרָא׃

FIGURE 0.1
Scholarly edition of the same text as in Figure 0.2, below. In contrast to that early manuscript this edition has chapter and verse numbers along with scholarly notes at the bottom about alternative Hebrew readings to the ones given in the body of the text.

In search of the best reading

A translator or translation committee often needs to decide word by word whether to follow a reading in one manuscript tradition or another. To do this, most scholars use "critical editions" prepared by textual critics that gather and compare the readings found in ancient biblical manuscripts (see Figure 0.1). For the Hebrew Bible, the usual comparison point is the **Masoretic text** (**MT**), the authoritative version of the Hebrew text that was produced by Jewish scribes in the medieval period. Most critical editions feature a high quality version of the Masoretic text as the main section of each page. Notes in the critical edition then provide an overview of variant readings from other important manuscript witnesses for the Hebrew Bible, such as the biblical manuscripts found at the Dead Sea (Qumran), the Pentateuch preserved by the Samaritan community (around Samaria in the north), and very early translations of early Hebrew manuscripts, especially the **Septuagint (LXX)**, an ancient set of translations of various biblical books into Greek. Drawing on this data, a translator then must decide on which ancient manuscript reading to follow and translate, often determining that some ancient readings are errors, while other manuscripts witness to an earlier, better reading, at least for a given verse or phrase.

On occasion, a biblical scholar may judge that all of the manuscript witnesses preserve an error. In such cases, that scholar may propose a reading that is not preserved in any manuscript. This second method of correction is called **conjectural emendation**.

Second, each contemporary translation must build on its translators' **philological** knowledge of Hebrew, Greek, or (in a few cases) Aramaic. None of these languages is spoken today in the form in which it is found in the Bible, and scholars often must depend on comparisons of biblical expressions with similar expressions in related languages. For example, medieval Jewish scholars such as Ibn Ezra made much progress in understanding certain aspects of Hebrew through comparing rare Hebrew expressions with similar words and grammatical formations in Arabic. Then, in the past one hundred fifty years, scholars of biblical Hebrew began benefiting from analysis of more ancient languages similar to Hebrew, such as Akkadian and Ugaritic, as texts in these languages were discovered, deciphered, and analyzed. Insights from comparison with these latter languages are not reflected in older translations, but they are incorporated to varying extents in many recent ones.

These advances in knowledge about the text and language of the Bible mean that academic study of the Bible requires use of an up-to-date biblical translation. The **King James Version** (also known as the KJV or "Authorized Version"), though beautiful and cherished by many, is not up to date. It was completed four hundred years ago. Scholars then knew far less about Hebrew and Greek than they do now. Moreover, the KJV translation is based on unusually corrupt manuscripts with more errors and expansions than the higher quality manuscripts used for translations today. This is why you need to acquire and use a more recent translation of the Bible for this introduction to the Hebrew Bible/Old Testament, rather than the King James Version.

Translations also vary in religious perspective. The New Jewish Publication Society translation (NJPS) obviously comes out of a tradition of Jewish interpretation of the Tanakh. The New Jerusalem Bible (NJB) and New American Bible (NAB) were produced by Catholic scholars. The New Revised Standard Version (NRSV; preceded by the Revised Standard Version – RSV) aims to be an ecumenical translation, but it is part of a line of Protestant revisions of the King James Version. The New International Version (NIV; now available in updated form as Today's New International Version) is also Protestant and was conceived as an evangelical alternative to the RSV/NRSV.

Translations also vary in style: whether they aim to stay as close to the biblical languages as possible or whether they aim for maximum readability. **Formal correspondence** translations, while still containing interpretation on the part of translators, aim to stay as close as possible to word-for-word translation of the Hebrew, Aramaic, or Greek text. This can make them good tools for study, but it also makes them more difficult to understand. Translations that tend toward formal correspondence include the NRSV, NIV, and the New American Standard Bible (NASB). Other translations tend toward **dynamic equivalence**, which aims for equivalent meaning but not a word-for-word translation. This results in translations that are more readable but also may contain some more interpretation on the part of translators. Examples of translations that tend toward dynamic equivalence include the NJB, NAB, and several other translations produced by Protestant groups, such as the Good News Translation (GNT; also known as the "Good News Bible" and as TEV – Today's English Version) and the Contemporary English Version (CEV). These translations should be distinguished from resources such as the Living Bible or the Amplified Bible. The latter are not direct translations of the Hebrew and Greek texts, but paraphrases or expansions of other translations. For example, the Living Bible is a paraphrase of the nineteenth-century American Standard Version. Such paraphrase subtly adds yet another level of interpretation between the reader and the Hebrew text and is not helpful for academic work on the Bible. This becomes evident, for example, in cases like the one given at the end of this chapter in Appendix 1, where the Living Bible adds a long section to Isa 52:15 (anticipating Jesus) that has no parallel in the Hebrew text.

One more way that contemporary Bible translations vary is in the extent to which they aim to use gender-neutral language, such as "humanity" instead of "mankind." Though older writing conventions endorsed the use of "man" for "human" or "he" for "he or she," many now argue that general use of such male-focused language reinforces male domination of women. This has led to two levels of revision of older translations that used such male-specific language. In some cases, past English translators had used male-specific words to translate Hebrew or Greek expressions that were gender neutral. The recent revision of the NIV translation, Today's New International Version (TNIV), aims to correct such mistranslations to what is termed "gender-accurate" English expressions. For example, where the King James Version and some other versions render the first part of Gen 1:26 as "Let us make man in our image," versions like the TNIV more accurately reflect the gender neutrality of the Hebrew word for "humanity" that is used here, e.g. "let us make human beings in our image."

Some other translations go yet further, revising other references to human beings toward gender-neutral English terms, even in cases where the original biblical languages use masculine nouns. Examples of such translations include the NRSV, NJB, and the Contemporary Torah, a "gender-sensitive" revision of the NJPS. I generally follow that policy in this *Introduction*, using "God" rather than "he" or "him" and preferring gender-neutral references to human beings. Nevertheless, the Bible was formed in a culture that privileged masculinity and conceived its God in largely masculine terms, and this is reflected at points in the translations included in this textbook.

Finally, readers should recognize that all these translations are published in different editions, each with its own perspective and added resources. For example, the *New Oxford Annotated Bible with Apocrypha* and the *HarperCollins Study Bible* are not different translations, but different editions of the NRSV. Each one has a different introductory essay, introductions to the biblical books, and brief commentary on the biblical text written by biblical scholars commissioned by the publisher. Indeed, whenever you use a given translation, it usually includes many other elements that were added by the publisher of that particular edition: headings for different sections of the biblical text, marginal references to other biblical passages, maps, and other additions. These can be helpful resources. Nevertheless, users of such editions should be aware of how these additional elements – none of which is actually part of the Bible per se – can subtly influence how one reads a given biblical passage. They should be used critically.

In the end, there is no one contemporary translation that scholars agree is decisively best. Arguments can be made for a variety of the contemporary translations that are listed in Appendix 2 of this chapter. Also, if your work focuses on a particular passage, you can get a good sense of particular translation issues in it by comparing multiple up-to-date translations with each other. Some like to use online resources for this, such as Bible Study Tools (www.biblestudytools.com\compare-translations) or the Bible Gateway (www.biblegateway.com). It should be noted, however, that these resources contain a number of out-of-date translations and neglect Jewish translations (e.g. the NJPS). If you use these sites, be sure to select up-to-date translations on the Christian comparison sites (e.g. NRSV, NIV) and compare those with the Jewish NJPS translation which can be purchased in book form or accessed online at www.sefaria.org. Alternatively, you can greatly benefit from using a Bible software tool (such as Accordance) and purchasing multiple recent Christian (e.g. NRSV, NJV) and Jewish (e.g. NJPS) translations for it that you then can compare with each other. Such comparison can reveal major differences between translations, and the more one finds such differences, the more one wonders how to decide between the alternatives. This is ideally solved by learning biblical languages! Many students, however, lack time and/or interest in going that far with biblical studies. For those lacking knowledge of biblical languages it is important to know where a given translation is only one possible rendering in English of a phrase in Hebrew, Aramaic, or Greek that could also be rendered, perhaps better, in another way. Comparison of Bible translations shows this.

Bible Abbreviations, Chapters, and Verses

When books and articles cite biblical passages by chapter and verse, they usually follow this order: abbreviation for the biblical book, followed by the chapter number, followed by the verse. An example is Isa 44:28 (chapter 44, verse 28). If more than one verse is cited, dashes and commas can be used: Isa 44:20, 28 or Isa 44:10–13, 28. When scholars want to refer to the bulk of a passage without detailing specific verses left out, they will add an asterisk to indicate that some verses are not meant to be included in the reference, e.g. Genesis 28*. Occasionally, you will also see scholars refer to half-verses, e.g. 2:4a or 2:4b, following accent divisions found in their Hebrew Bibles. Such notations will be sparingly used in this book only to label citations that begin or end in a half-verse.

Here are some standard abbreviations for biblical books shared by Jewish and Christian Bibles (given in the order followed by most Christian Bibles). Sometimes these are further shortened through just giving the first two letters (e.g. Ex instead of Exod) or removing a vowel (e.g. Jdg for Judges):

Gen = Genesis
Exod = Exodus
Lev = Leviticus
Num = Numbers
Deut = Deuteronomy
Josh = Joshua
Judg = Judges
Ruth = Ruth
Sam = Samuel
Kgs = Kings
Chr = Chronicles
Ezra = Ezra
Neh = Nehemiah
Esth = Esther
Job = Job
Ps or Pss (for plural) = Psalms
Prov = Proverbs
Eccl (or Qoh) = Ecclesiastes
   (Hebrew Qohelet)

Song (or Cant) = Song of Songs
   (Canticles)
Isa = Isaiah
Jer = Jeremiah
Lam = Lamentations
Ezek = Ezekiel
Dan = Daniel
Hos = Hosea
Joel = Joel
Amos = Amos
Ob = Obadiah
Jon = Jonah
Mic = Micah
Nah = Nahum
Hab = Habakkuk
Zeph = Zephaniah
Hag = Haggai
Zech = Zechariah

The Origins of Chapters and Verses

The earliest Hebrew and Greek manuscripts of the Bible lack any chapter or verse numberings (see Figure 0.2). The Hebrew Bible/Old Testament was divided into sections for reading in the synagogue, and the Greek New Testament was divided into sections as well, but there were no numbers in these early manuscripts.

Verse divisions were first added into the Hebrew Bible (without numbers) by the Masoretes, a group of Jewish scholars who worked in the seventh to tenth centuries ce and produced the standard edition of the Hebrew Bible now used in Judaism. The chapter divisions we now have were developed in 1205 by Stephen Langton, a professor in Paris and eventually an archbishop of the Church of England. He introduced them into his edition of the Latin Vulgate translation of the Bible, and these divisions were later adopted by Jewish scholars as they became popular means to refer to biblical passages.

The first Old Testament and New Testament Bible with numbered verses was produced in 1555 by a Parisian book seller, Robert Estienne (also known as Stephanus). He is reported to have divided a copy of his New Testament into the present 7,959 verses while riding on horseback from Paris to Lyon. He also numbered the chapters and verses of both the Old and New Testament. Now these verses are found in scholarly editions of the Hebrew Bible (see Figure 0.1) and in translations of the Bible.

FIGURE 0.2
One of our earliest manuscripts of the book of Isaiah, dated to the early first century bce. Note how the letters are hung from lines on the parchment and a scribe has added a verse into the middle.

Conclusion on Critically Analyzing a Page of Your Own Bible

This chapter just starts to indicate how every page of your Bible, whether a Jewish Tanakh or a particular Christian Bible, is the product of an intense process of textual criticism, analysis of the original language of biblical passages, and packaging of the particular translation of such passages through elements like chapter and verse numbers. Ancient manuscripts often were divided into longer, unnumbered reading sections (for use in worship), and they sometimes included marginal comments or additional verses here or there (see Figure 0.2). Nevertheless, they did not have the numbering, headings, or the reader-guides now in the Bible before you. Take note of every element on a given page of your contemporary Bible that helps frame the biblical text and present it to you. Your first step as a critical reader of the Bible is to become more conscious of these elements and more familiar with their characteristics.

CHAPTER REVIEW

For Review

1. Know the meaning and significance of the following terms discussed in this chapter:
   - apocrypha
   - canon and canonical
   - conjectural emendation
   - deuterocanonical books
   - dynamic equivalence translation
   - formal correspondence translation
   - Hebrew Bible
   - King James Version
   - Qur'an
   - LXX
   - manuscript witness
   - Masoretic text
   - MT
   - Old Testament
   - Pentateuch
   - Septuagint
   - supersessionism
   - Tanakh
   - textual criticism
   - Torah
2. What are the main differences between the Christian Old Testament and the Jewish Tanakh?
3. How is the Muslim Qur'an related to the Jewish and Christian Bibles?

RESOURCES FOR FURTHER STUDY

Editions of translations

The first edition listed provides an overview of several translations; some good editions follow.

The New Jerusalem Bible. New York: Doubleday, 1985. This is the NJB.

The New Oxford Annotated Bible with Apocrypha (5th edition), eds. Michael Coogan et al. New York: Oxford University Press, 2018. This contains the NRSV.

The Jewish Study Bible, eds. A. Berlin et al. New York: Oxford University Press, 2004. This contains the NJPS.

The HarperCollins Study Bible (fully revised and updated), eds. Harold W. Attridge et al. San Francisco: HarperSanFrancisco, 2006. This contains the NRSV.

One-volume commentaries

Mays, James L., ed. *HarperCollin's Bible Commentary* (revised edition). San Francisco: Harper & Row, 2000.

Newsom, Carol A., and Ringe, Sharon H., *The Women's Bible Commentary* (3rd edition). Louisville, KY: Westminster John Knox Press, 2012.

Technological Resources

Bible Software: Accordance Bible Software. It is recommended that you purchase the NRSV, NJB, or another up-to-date translation. As of the writing of this introduction, you are given the King James Version (outdated for academic study of the Bible) as part of the initial package.

Useful websites for translation comparison

The Bible Gateway (mostly Christian translations) – www.biblegateway.com

Bible Study Tools (mostly Christian translations) – https://www.biblestudytools.com/compare-translations

Sefaria (access to the New Jewish Publication Society/NJPS version and other Jewish texts) – www.sefaria.org

APPENDIX 1: TRANSLATION AND PARAPHRASE COMPARISON OF ISA 52:13-15

ISA Chapter and Verse	Revised Standard Version	New American Standard Version	New International Version	Today's English Version (Good News Bible)
52:13	Behold my servant shall prosper, he shall be exalted and lifted up, and shall be very high.	Behold my servant will prosper, He will be high and lifted up, and greatly exalted.	See, my servant will act wisely; he will be raised and lifted up and highly exalted.	The Lord says, My servant will succeed in his task; he will be highly honored.
52:14	As many were astonished at him – his appearance was so marred, beyond human semblance, and his form beyond that of the sons of men –	Just as many were astonished at you, *My People*, so His appearance was marred more than any man, And his form more than the sons of men.	Just as there were many who were appalled at him – his appearance was so disfigured beyond that of any man and his form marred beyond human likeness –	Many people were shocked when they saw him; he was so disfigured that he hardly looked human.
52:15	so shall he startle many nations; kings shall shut their mouths because of him; for that which has not been told them they shall see, and that which they have not heard they shall understand.	Thus he will sprinkle many nations, Kings will shut their mouths on account of Him; For what had not been told them they will see, And what they had not heard they will understand.	so will he sprinkle many nations, and kings will shut their mouths because of him. For what they were not told, they will see, and what they have not heard, they will understand.	But now many nations will marvel at him, and kings will be speechless with amazement. They will see and understand something they had never known.

(continued)

ISA Chapter and Verse	New English Bible	Living Bible	Tanakh	New Jerusalem Bible
52:13	Behold, my servant shall prosper, he shall be lifted up, exalted to the heights.	See, my Servant shall prosper; he shall be highly exalted.	Indeed, My servant shall prosper, be exalted and raised to great heights.	Look, my servant will prosper, will grow great, will rise to great heights.
52:14	Time was when many were aghast at you, my people;	Yet many shall be amazed when they see him – yes, even far-off foreign nations and their kings; [See the end of 52:15 for the rest]	Just as the many were appalled at him – So marred was his appearance, unlike that of man, His form, beyond human semblance –	As many people were aghast at him – he was so inhumanly disfigured that he no longer looked like a man –
52:15	... so now many nations recoil at the sight of him, and kings curl their lips in disgust. For they see what they had never been told and things unheard before fill their thoughts.	... they shall stand dumbfounded, speechless in his presence. For they shall see and understand what they had not been told before. They shall see my Servant beaten and bloodied, so disfigured one would scarcely know it was a person standing there. So shall he cleanse many nations.	Just so he shall startle many nations. Kings shall be silenced because of him, For they shall see what has not been told them, Shall behold what they never have heard.	so many nations will be astonished and kings will stay tightlipped before him, seeing what had never been told them, learning what they had not heard before.

APPENDIX 2: CHARACTERISTICS OF SELECT ENGLISH TRANSLATIONS OF THE BIBLE

Translation	Background	Style	Use of MT (Masoretic text, with translation of Isa 7:14 as indicator of theological leanings)	Gender language
NJPS (1985)	Jewish Publication Society	Formal correspondence, colloquial	No deviation from MT and uses Jewish chapter/verse numbering	Aims at "gender accuracy" (Note: 2006 JPS *Contemporary Torah* with more changes)
NRSV (1989)	Protestant, National Council of Churches	Formal correspondence, literary	Some deviation from MT in light of Dead Sea Scrolls and LXX	Modest move toward inclusive language
NIV (1978)	Protestant Evangelical, International Bible Society	Formal correspondence, literary	Very modest deviation from MT, mostly in notes. Modifies Hebrew of Isa 7:14 to match Matthew	
Today's NIV (TNIV) (2005)	Protestant Evangelical, International Bible Society	Formal correspondence, literary	Very modest deviation from MT, mostly in notes. Modifies Hebrew of Isa 7:14 to match Matthew	Modest move toward "gender-accurate" language
NASB (1971)	Protestant Evangelical, Lockman Foundation	Formal correspondence, quite literal and often awkward	Little revision of MT. Modifies Hebrew of Isa 7:14 to match Matthew	
GNT (formerly TEV) (1992)	Protestant, American Bible Society (particularly for missionaries)	Dynamic equivalence, colloquial and simple vocabulary	Little deviation from MT	Includes revisions toward gender-inclusive language
CEV (1999)	Protestant, American Bible Society	Dynamic equivalence, colloquial, yet more simple vocabulary and syntax	Little deviation from MT. Modifies Hebrew of Isa 7:14 to match Matthew	Moves toward gender-inclusive language for humans

(continued)

Translation	Background	Style	Use of MT (Masoretic text, with translation of Isa 7:14 as indicator of theological leanings)	Gender language
REB (1989), revision of NEB (1970)	British Protestant and Roman Catholic churches	Dynamic equivalence, literary	Substantial deviations from MT	Moves in 1989 revision toward gender-inclusive language
NJB (1985)	European Roman Catholic	Dynamic equivalence, but literary	Some substantial deviations from the MT	Very modest moves toward gender-inclusive language
NAB (1991)	United States Roman Catholic	Mix of dynamic equivalence and formal correspondence (the latter especially in NT)	Some substantial deviations from the MT. Modifies Hebrew of Isa 7:14 to match Matthew	Modest moves toward gender-inclusive language in NT and Psalms

Studying the Bible in its Ancient Context(s)

1

Chapter Overview

Academic Study of the Bible

The Geography and Major Characters of the Biblical Drama

Major Periods in the Biblical Drama

Multiple Contexts, Multiple Methods

Conclusion

Chapter One Review

Resources for Further Study

Appendix: Israel's History and Empires

CHAPTER OVERVIEW

This chapter introduces the basic orientation of the textbook and sets the stage for what follows with three overviews: geographical, historical, and methodological. The beginning of the chapter answers the questions "What makes academic study of the Bible different from typical 'Bible study'?" and "Why is such academic study important?" We will briefly compare the general outline of the biblical story with the history of Israel that will structure this textbook. Next you gain a bird's-eye view of the major regions of the land of Israel, the periods of Israel's history, and some methods used by scholars to analyze the Bible. Your future study will be helped in particular by learning the location of the two major regions of ancient Israel – the heartland of tribal Israel to the north and the area of David's clan, Judah, to the south (with the famous city of Jerusalem between these two areas) – and by memorizing the dates of the major periods in the history of Israel (see the appendix to this chapter).

The Hebrew Bible: A Contemporary Introduction to the Christian Old Testament and the Jewish Tanakh, Second Edition. David M. Carr.
© 2021 David M. Carr. Published 2021 by John Wiley & Sons Ltd.

EXERCISE Write a half-page to one-page statement or mini-autobiography of your past encounters with the Bible. Which parts of it have been most central in such encounters? Have you studied the Bible in an academic context before? Have you had unusually positive or negative experiences with the Bible or people citing it?

Academic Study of the Bible

At first glance, the Bible is one of the most familiar of books. Most families own a copy. Every weekend, Jews and Christians read from it at worship. There are echoes of the Bible in all kinds of music, from Handel's *Messiah* to reggae and hip hop. Popular expressions, such as "Thou shalt not" or "Love thy neighbor as thyself," come from the Bible. Movies are often filled with biblical allusions. And you still can find a copy of the Bible, or at least the New Testament and Psalms, in many hotels.

At second glance, the Bible is one of the most foreign of books. Its language, even in English translation, is often difficult to understand, especially if you are reading the King James Translation (1611), with its beautiful, but often obscure, seventeenth-century cadences and words. Moreover, the Hebrew texts that are the basis of all translations are thousands of years old, dating to a span of centuries from 1000 BCE to around 164 BCE. These texts reflect ancient origins, in many ways, and this can make them difficult to understand. If someone sees a reference to "Cyrus" in Isa 44:28 and 45:1, that person likely will have few associations with who "Cyrus" was and what he meant to the writer of this text. Most readers have even fewer associations with places and empires mentioned in the Bible, such as "Ephraim" or "Assyria." Usually, their only acquaintance with "Egypt" or "Babylonia" is a brief discussion in a world history class. Furthermore, certain types of writing mean little or nothing to contemporary readers, for example the long genealogies of Genesis or the detailed instructions for sacrificing animals in Leviticus. As a result of all this unfamiliarity, few people who try to read the Bible from beginning to end actually get very far, and those who do often fail to make much sense out of what they have read.

The goal of this book is to give you keys to understand the Bible, including its more obscure parts. Names (e.g. Cyrus), events (e.g. the liberation from Babylonian captivity), and general perspectives in the Bible that previously you might have skipped past or not noticed should come into focus and make sense. For many, the experience of reading the Bible in historical context is much like finally getting to see a movie in color that beforehand had only been available in black and white. It is not at all that the meaning of the Bible can or should be limited to the settings in which it was originally composed. On the contrary: along the way we will see how the Bible is an important document now thanks to the fact that it has been radically *re*interpreted over centuries, first by successive communities of ancient Israelites and later by Jewish and Christian communities who cherished the Bible. Still, learning to see scriptures in relation to ancient history and culture can make previously bland or puzzling biblical texts come alive.

To pursue this historical approach, we will not read the Bible from beginning to end. Instead, we will look at biblical texts in relationship to when they were written. This means that, rather than starting with the creation stories of Genesis 1–3, this book starts with remnants of Israel's earliest oral traditions. These are songs and sagas from the time when Israel had no cities and was still a purely tribal people. Our next stop will be texts from the rise of Israel's first monarchies, particularly certain "royal" psalms that celebrate God's choice of Jerusalem and anointing of kings there. Overall, as we move through Israelite history, we will see how biblical texts reflect the influences of successive world empires: the Mesopotamian empires of Assyria and Babylonia, and then the Persian and Hellenistic (Greek) empires. The common thread will be historical, and this will mean starting most chapters with some discussion of the historical and cultural context of the biblical texts to be discussed there.

Overview: Order of Main Discussions of Biblical Books

Steps in the Bible's own story	This textbook's discussion of biblical texts and traditions in the order they were created
Creation, flood, and other materials about the origins of the world (Genesis 1–11)	[See below, discussed later in the textbook]
Stories of Israel's patriarchs and matriarchs (e.g. Abraham and Sarah, Jacob, Joseph; Genesis 12–50)	[See below, discussed later in the textbook, since few or no identifiable traditions in the Bible are clearly datable to these periods]
The growth of the people of Israel and their exodus from Egypt (Exodus 1–15)	
40 years in the wilderness, gift of law at Sinai (Exodus 16–40; Leviticus, Numbers, Deuteronomy)	[See below, discussed later in the textbook]
Israel's conquest of Canaan (Joshua) Tribal life under various leaders (Judges)	*Period of the Judges: Chapter 2.* Oral traditions in Genesis 12–35, Exodus, and Judges 5. *Early monarchy/David and Solomon: Chapters 3 and 4.*
The establishment of Saul and then David's monarchy (1–2 Samuel)	1–2 Samuel, Proverbs, and ancient stories of primeval families in Genesis 2–4 and 9. *Later northern and southern monarchies: Chapters 5 and 6.*
The kings of Jerusalem and Israel (1–2 Kings 17 also 1 Chronicles 10–2 Chronicles 28)	Amos, Hosea, Micah, and early parts of Isaiah (along with possible northern traditions in Exodus, Genesis 25–35, etc.).

(continued)

Steps in the Bible's own story	This textbook's discussion of biblical texts and traditions in the order they were created
The later kingship in Jerusalem (after destruction of the kingdom of Israel (2 Kings 18–25//2 Chronicles 29–36)) [The Bible lacks narratives directly of this time (the book of Daniel is a much later legend)] Rebuilding of a temple-focused community under Persian rulership (Ezra-Nehemiah) Deuterocanonical/Apocryphal books of 1–4 Maccabees	*Twilight of the monarchy in Jerusalem: Chapters 7 and 8.* Deuteronomy through 2 Kings, Jeremiah, Nahum, and Zephaniah. *Exile of Judeans to Babylonia: Chapters 9 and 10.* **Lamentations, Ezekiel, Isaiah 40–55, and exilic parts of Genesis through Numbers (such as the creation account in Genesis 1 and laws in Leviticus).** *Return of exiles and rebuilding: Chapters 11 and 12.* **Haggai, Zechariah, Isaiah 56–66, Jonah, Ruth, Job, and the book of Psalms (along with parts of Ezra-Nehemiah and Genesis through Numbers).** *The Hellenistic empires and crisis: Chapter 13.* **Sirach, Enoch, Daniel, Ezra-Nehemiah, 1–2 Chronicles, Esther, and questions about the final formation of the Hebrew Bible (along with some on Ecclesiastes and Song of Songs).**

At first this approach may be disorienting, since it involves placing familiar biblical texts in a different order and in new contexts. Take the example of the story of creation in Gen 1:1–2:3. It seems straightforward enough as it is. Why wait to talk much about this opening story of the Bible until Chapter 10 of this *Introduction*? As we will see, one reason is that reading Gen 1:1–2:3 in relation to the Judeans' experience of forced exile in Babylonia (the focus of Chapter 10) explains the major emphasis in this text on the Sabbath. This is an aspect of the text that many people, especially non-Jews, completely miss, since it has little meaning for them. But the whole seven-day structure of the story is meant to lead up to one thing: God's rest on the seventh day and blessing of it (Gen 2:1–3). Reading this text in relation to the Babylonian exile highlights this important feature and makes sense of other aspects of the creation story as well.

This is just one way in which academic study of the Bible is quite a different thing from study of the Bible in Sunday school or even high school religion classes in parochial schools. Many people come to a university or seminary class on the Bible expecting a summary of the contents of the Bible or indoctrination into biblical theologies or values. Others expect a devotional approach that they have learned in church Bible studies where the Bible often is read as a lesson book for life. All these approaches have their value and place, but they differ from the academic approach of a college or seminary course. Moreover, they are misleading indicators of what to expect out of such a course. Where a student might expect to work hard in a history or organic chemistry class, study of the "Bible" – especially if it's imagined on the basis of earlier experience with religious education – promises to be easy. Yet an *academic* course on the Bible offers its own set of challenges, somewhat similar to those of a good course in history or English literature. Indeed, some students find academic study of the Bible especially difficult because it offers alternatives to their past interpretations of biblical texts that they cherish. These students not only must learn the course material about the Bible, but must integrate this knowledge with their beliefs and values.

The benefits of such study are substantial. Familiar texts offer new meanings. Difficult biblical texts start to make better sense when placed in their original historical contexts. Where once the Bible might have seemed a monolithic, ancient set of rules, it becomes a rich variety of different perspectives that have stood the test of time. I encourage you to be open to this approach, *frequently consult* the historical timeline and overview charts at the outset of the introduction to orient yourself (see pp. xx–xxiv), and learn for yourself what this way of studying the Bible has to offer.

The Geography and Major Characters of the Biblical Drama

Let us start by setting the scene for the drama of biblical history, looking at the geography of the biblical world, major nations, and major historical periods. This information is important, because it will orient you to the quite different world in which the Bible was created.

Asked to picture the land of Israel, many would conjure up images from TV specials or popular movies where biblical events occur amidst sand dunes, palm trees, and small villages. The reality is that the area of Israel encompasses sharp contrasts in topography, rainfall, and vegetation. Imagine Map 1.1 as divided into four narrow strips running up and down. The strip to the left is the *coastal plain* along the Mediterranean Sea. It is low, flat, and fertile and receives relatively regular rainfall. Non-Israelites lived here through most of Israelite history, and it was ruled from Jerusalem only for short periods. The next strip is the *central hill country* and runs down the middle of the map, encompassing the hill country of Judah, hill country of Ephraim (Israel), and Galilee. This is an area of rocky hills (starting with a strip of lower foothills, the "Shephelah"), that eventually rise up to 3,000 feet. This hill country is where most of Israelite history took place. It is drier and less accessible than the coastal plain to the west. The third strip is the *Jordan Valley*, encompassing the Dead Sea, Jordan River, and Sea of Galilee (from south to north). This is one of the lowest places on earth, about 1,000 feet below sea level, and – aside from some oases – it is very dry and barren. The fourth strip is the *Transjordanian Plateau*, including Edom, Moab, Ammon, and the Gilead region (where Israelites settled). This plateau, now in the contemporary nation of Jordan, has similar characteristics to the central highlands of Israel. To the east of it (and off the map) lies the desert.

MAP 1.1
The land of Israel and its surroundings. Redrawn and adapted from Adrian Curtis (ed.), *Oxford Bible Atlas* (4th edition). Oxford, New York: Oxford University Press, 2007.

As you start study of the Bible, it is particularly important to get an understanding of the different parts of the land of Israel and the peoples who lived there. Though people often apply the term "Israel" to this entire area, this term often refers more narrowly to the peoples who settled in the *northern* highlands described above ("Hill Country of Ephraim/Israel" on Map 1.1, with Shechem at its center) along with parts of the Gilead of the Transjordan. For much of biblical history, this area and this people are to be distinguished from "Judah," which is located in the *southern* highlands of the map ("Hill Country of Judah;" Hebron is a Judean city). Note that Jerusalem lay between Israel and Judah and was not "Israelite"/"Judean" until David conquered it by stealth at the outset of his monarchy. This distinction between "Judah" in the south and "Israel" in the north is important for much of Israel's early history. Later on, the term "Israel" came to encompass Judah as well, and the narratives of the Hebrew Bible – many of them written later – project that picture onto the earliest history of the people. Therefore, the word "**Israel**" has at least two major meanings in the Bible: a narrow sense referring to the ancient tribal groups settled in the northern highlands and a broader sense referring to Judah along with those other tribal groups. When people refer to the "land of Israel" or the "people of Israel," they usually are using the word "Israel" in the broader sense, but there will be numerous times in this *Introduction* when it will be important to remember the narrower sense of "Israel" (in the north) as opposed to "Judah" (in the south).

Those are the scholarly terms for the region and its inhabitants. As we move forward, it is important to distinguish such terms from contemporary designations for the land. In particular, it is important not to confuse the word "**Israelite**," which refers to ancient inhabitants of the land of Israel, and the word "Israeli," which is a modern term referring to citizens of the contemporary state of Israel. Note also the use of the term "**Palestine**" to refer to the same area from the Roman period onward. This term is now used by **Palestinians** and many others to refer to the same land area that Jews and others refer to as "Israel."

The "land of Israel" where most biblical events take place is actually relatively small. As you can see on Map 1.1, the Sea of Galilee is only 30 miles from the Mediterranean Sea, and the Dead Sea is only 60 miles away. The distance from the area around Shechem in the north to Beersheba in the south is about 90 miles. This means that the main setting of biblical history, the area of the central highlands (thus excluding the non-Israelite coastal plains), is about 40 miles by 90 miles – not much bigger than many large metropolitan areas. This tiny area is the site where texts and religious ideas were formed that would change world history. Notably, this highland area also encompasses many areas most in dispute in the contemporary Middle East, areas that are variously designated as "the West Bank," "occupied territories," and "Judea and Samaria." Before 1967 these regions were not part of the modern nation of Israel, but they were seized by Israel from Jordan during the 1967 war, and their status is one major issue in the ongoing Middle East conflict.

Visualizing (the Possible Ancestors of) Ancient Israelites

These ancient Israelites were different in important ways from all contemporary peoples, including Israelis. Unfortunately, we do not have contemporary representations of ancient Israelites. The best we can do are images like Figure 1.1 (a relief painting from an official's tomb at Beni Hasan), which is an Egyptian depiction of visitors to Egypt from the east, perhaps from the region of Canaan. As we will see in the next chapter, the Israelites likely descended from Canaanite peoples, and so this representation gives us an image of what the ancestors of ancient Israelites (or their near-neighbors) looked like.

On the far right of the picture, there is a clean-shaven Egyptian with darker brown skin. The visitors from the east (Canaan?) are the six figures to the left of him. They have lighter brown skin, beards, and some colorful tunics. One thing such images make clear is that the people who dwelled east of Egypt looked more like the contemporary inhabitants of the Middle East and Africa than the light-skinned inhabitants of North America and Europe. Indeed, not only were ancient Israelites non-white, but the ancient world lacked an exact correlate to modern concepts of race.

FIGURE 1.1
Ancient visitors to Egypt from the East (Canaanites?).

This conflict is the latest chapter in thousands of years of struggles between different groups for control of this narrow strip of land. In ancient times, the land of Israel occupied a strategic location along the "Fertile Crescent" extending from Egypt in the southwest to the Mesopotamian empires of Assyria and Babylonia in the northeast. Because much of the area east of Israel was impassable desert, the major roads between Egypt and Mesopotamia had to cross the narrow strip of land between the Mediterranean Sea and the desert (see Map 1.2). Israel lay right along those roads and often got run over by the armies of its more powerful neighbors. The various empires of the ancient Near East were almost always laying claim to Israel and the surrounding areas, and the peoples of Israel got caught in the middle.

MAP 1.2
The major routes of the ancient Near East. Note how the major routes move from Egypt on the left through Judah/Israel near the Mediterranean to Syria and Mesopotamia to the northeast and east. Redrawn from Yohanan Aharoni and Michael Avi-Yonah, *The Macmillan Bible Atlas* (revised edition). New York, Macmillan, 1977, map 9.

Major Periods in the Biblical Drama

The major turns in biblical history can be seen in this context. The Egyptian empire dominated the area of ancient Israel from around 1450 to 1200 BCE, the years when most scholars think the biblical exodus may have happened. Then a series of catastrophes ended Egyptian rule over the area and inaugurated a power vacuum in the land of Israel. This is when we first see identifiable archaeological evidence of a "people of Israel." This people

AD, BC, BCE, and CE

The older expressions for dates, BC and AD, are explicitly Christian in orientation. BC comes from "Before Christ," and AD comes from the Latin *anno Domini*, which means "in the year of the Lord."

Over the past decades, scholarly works have tended to use the more neutral terms BCE and CE, which refer to "Before the Common Era" and "Common Era," respectively. The year references are the same, but the labels are not specifically Christian.

This *Introduction* uses the standard scholarly BCE and CE abbreviations.

settled in small villages in the hill country of Judah and Israel during the **pre-state tribal period** (1250–1000 BCE, including the time of the chieftain, Saul). At the outset of the first millennium, the figures David and Solomon establish what might be termed a **proto-monarchy** in Jerusalem that rules Israelite tribes for several decades (around 1000–930 BCE). In the later ninth century, the tribes of Israel form a monarchy of their own, and we see a period of **neighboring monarchies** where there are two kingdoms in broader Israel: a kingdom of Israel in the north, and a kingdom of Judah in the south (930–722 BCE).

This window of freedom from imperial domination, however, was not to last. Especially in the late eighth century (745 BCE and onward), the Assyrian empire, based in what is now northern Iraq, gained control of both Israel and (later) Judah (see Map 1.3). This empire completely destroyed the kingdom of Israel in 722 BCE and dominated the kingdom of Judah for decades. Indeed, from 745 to 586 BCE, Israel and Judah were dominated by a series of brutal empires – Assyria, Egypt (for a couple of years), and Babylonia (based in middle Iraq). Though Judah enjoyed brief independence between domination by the Assyrians and the Egyptians, the nation was dominated and eventually destroyed by the Babylonian empire, which reduced Jerusalem, along with its Temple, to rubble in 586 BCE (**destruction of Jerusalem**, ending a period of **Judah alone**, 722–586 BCE). Thus began one of the most important periods of biblical history, the **Babylonian exile** (586–538 BCE). At the outset of this period, most of the elite who had lived in Judah were forcibly deported to Babylon, and in many cases neither they nor their children ever returned. The Hebrew Bible is a collection of documents from the perspective of these deportees and their children, such that biblical history is now usually defined (from their point of view) in terms of "pre-exile" and "exile."

The story of Israel and empires, however, was not over. Just decades later, the Persian ruler, Cyrus, conquered the Babylonian empire, ushering in a period of Persian rule of Judah that lasted from 538 to 332 BCE (the **Persian period**, the beginning of the **post-exilic period**, starting in 538 BCE). The Bible records a number of ways in which Cyrus and his successors helped former exiles in Babylonia rebuild the Temple and rebuild their community. Later, Alexander the Great conquered the area in 333 BCE, beginning a period of Hellenistic rule, and it appears that he and his successors generally continued the Persian

MAP 1.3
The reach of three of the major empires that dominated Israel and/or Judah: the Assyrian, Babylonian, and Persian empires. Redrawn from Successive World Kingdoms: Persia, Babylon, Assyria 640–500 BC, www.bible.ca, Abingdon Press, 1994.

policies of support of Jerusalem and its leadership during their rule of Judah and Jerusalem (**Hellenistic period**, 332–167 BCE). Nevertheless, in the late second century (starting in 167 BCE), there was a major crisis in Judah, precipitated by the efforts of some elite Judeans to turn the city of Jerusalem into a Greek city. This crisis eventually led to the formation, for a brief period, of another monarchy in Judah, this one led by a priestly family called the **Hasmoneans** (also known as the **Maccabees**). This **Hasmonean monarchy** continued from 142 to 63 BCE, when the Romans took control of the area, which they named "Palestine" and put under control of a series of governors. The year 63 BCE represents the **beginning of the Roman period** in Palestine.

With this, "Palestine" joined much of the surrounding world as part of the Roman empire. This is the time when Jesus lived, the early church formed in the wake of his crucifixion by the Romans, and the Christian movement spread across the Mediterranean Sea to cities around the Roman empire. This was also the time of multiple Judean revolts against Roman control that eventually led to the destruction in 70 CE of the Jerusalem temple (**destruction of the Second Temple** [earlier rebuilt under the Persians]) and the complete destruction of Jewish Jerusalem in 135 CE. Thus the Jewish temple state was completely destroyed. The main form of Jewish life to survive this catastrophe was rabbinic Judaism, which grew out of the scholarship and leadership of the earlier, popular movement of the Pharisees.

Later chapters of this *Introduction* will give details about these historical periods, correlating each of them with biblical texts. The aim here is to give a sense of how much Israelite history was shaped by relationships with various empires. Though "Israel" (and "Judah") emerged as recognizable peoples and states during an imperial power vacuum (1200–745 BCE), the books of the Bible were largely written during the periods of imperial domination by Assyrian, Babylonian, Persian, Hellenistic, and Roman empires. We gain a deeper understanding of the Hebrew Bible the more we see how diverse biblical pictures of the "empire of God" were formed in response to domination by these powerful empires in the ancient world.

Multiple Contexts, Multiple Methods

Reading biblical texts in relation to their original contexts can make many aspects of them come alive, but the reason such texts are read now is that they have remained meaningful to diverse communities in much later contexts. These texts are in the Bible because they have transcended their origins. This *Introduction* will discuss both aspects of the Bible: its origins in the ancient Near East and its later interpretation by Jewish and Christian communities today. Knowing more about the Bible's early contexts gives some perspective on contemporary differences in interpretation. The more you know about the antiquity of the Bible, the more you may appreciate both the care and the creativity with which it has been read and reread over time by different communities.

This can be illustrated through a brief look at how different methods of biblical criticism might look at Israel's "exodus," the story of **Yahweh**'s (see box on p. 31) liberation of the people from Egypt that is now found in the first chapters of the book of Exodus (Exodus 1–15). To start, some scholars try to reconstruct whether and when this exodus actually happened. Such academic study of the history of Israel uses biblical texts as one among multiple sources for the reconstruction of "what probably happened." So far, the results of such study have been inconclusive. On the one hand, many scholars believe some sort of exodus out of Egypt happened, probably during the centuries just before the emergence of the people of "Israel" as a distinct group in the highlands of Canaan. On the other hand, most academic scholars of the Bible also believe that the written texts of the Bible are so far removed from the events that they describe that they are not useful for precise retelling of what actually happened back then: who said what, how many and who were involved, etc. The biblical texts are not reliable for such details because they have been filtered by centuries of oral retelling and written expansions by later Israelites. Imagine a game of "telephone" where hundreds of people over a period of five hundred years retell a story important to them (e.g. of the exodus from Egypt), each one to different members of the next generation, and then imagine trying to use the end result of this complex process for historical analysis. Because biblical texts are so shaped by time, scholars studying the history of Israel attempt to reconstruct what happened through analyzing them and comparing them – where possible – with archaeological records and non-biblical historical sources.

> ## The Name of Israel's God: Yahweh/the LORD
>
> The name of Israel's God in Hebrew is Yahweh, but you will not see this name written out in most English translations of the Bible. Instead, most translations have "the LORD" where the Hebrew manuscripts have a strange combination of the consonants for Yahweh (YHWH) and the vowels for the Hebrew word "lord." Why this combination?
>
> The consonants are earlier, since the earliest Hebrew Bible manuscripts were written in all consonants. When Jewish scholars started producing manuscripts with vowels, the divine name Yahweh had become so holy that they did not pronounce it out loud (this is still true for many Jews). Therefore, they added the vowels for "lord" in every place where the consonants for Yahweh occurred so that readers would say "lord" rather than the holy name. English translations reflect this combination when they put "lord" in all capital letters (LORD), indicating that this particular "lord" is Yahweh. (Note "Jehovah" is the word that is produced when you simply pronounce the consonants of YHWH with the vowels for the Hebrew word for "lord.")
>
> We will be focusing here on the state of the Bible before such prohibitions on pronouncing the divine name existed. So there will be occasions where it will be helpful to refer to Israel's God by the name Yahweh.

Historical criticism is a family of historical methods that analyzes how and where the biblical texts (and oral traditions in them) were composed. "Criticism" in this case does not mean that historical critics find fault with the biblical texts that they study, but that they use academically critical analysis to arrive at their conclusions rather than starting on the basis of faith assumptions. Through **tradition criticism**, for example, biblical scholars attempt to identify early oral traditions standing behind the biblical text. For example, past tradition critics have supposed that the following song of Miriam may be one of the earliest traditions in the Bible to speak of the defeat of the Egyptian army at the Red sea:

> Sing to Yahweh, for he has been victorious
> Horse and rider, he has thrown into the sea.
> (Exod 15:21)

The next chapter will discuss places where other texts of the Bible, though being later written texts, still reflect the general outlines of earlier oral traditions.

Many scholars, however, focus not on how the Bible was formed, but on what it means and has meant to generations of readers of the Bible. For example, **literary criticism** has drawn on methods in the study of modern literature to study the plot, characterization, pacing, and shape of biblical texts. Scholars employing such criticism have examined Exodus 1–15 as if it were a novel, looking at *how* the story is artfully told: how is Moses introduced and characterized? How does this contrast with the characterization of the Egyptians and their leaders? What does the reader expect and learn as the narrative unfolds? Such study of the poetic and narrative dynamics of biblical texts is distinct from study of how such texts have been interpreted by later readers, which is the **history of interpretation**. Historians of interpretation study how the story of the exodus became central to Judaism and Christianity in different ways. For example, the exodus story is the centerpiece of the Jewish celebration of Passover and is a founding story for the Christian practices of baptism and Eucharist.

Finally, various forms of **ideological criticism** analyze ways that the exodus story can be, has been, and should be read in the midst of systematic structures of power. For example, early **feminist criticism** lifted up the importance of the story of the midwives in the lead-up to the exodus (Exod 1:15–21), and later feminist critics have raised questions about the male (androcentric) focus of the exodus story and most other parts of the Bible.

This is just a sampling of some of the different types of academic research that are used to investigate the Bible and its readings. Across this introduction numerous other forms of biblical criticism will be introduced.

Conclusion

This chapter has given an overview which will be filled in by the following chapters. It may be disorienting to encounter so many terms and dates at once. Nevertheless, it is important to get this larger picture in order to understand the details of what follows. The remaining chapters of this *Introduction* will unfold the story of the Bible's formation. This story moves from discussion of oral traditions in pre-literate Israel all the way through to the writing of the latest books of the Bible during the Hasmonean period. Though the first chapters will uncover a strange and different ancient Israel unfamiliar to many readers, this historical approach will illuminate many aspects of the Bible that otherwise make little sense. In addition, it will provide a starting point for engaging other scholarly methods of looking at biblical texts in new ways.

Of course, the analysis of the formation of the Bible and its texts is always in flux. Within the space of this brief *Introduction* I will only be able to touch on a few of the major debates. Nevertheless, scholars have been doing this kind of historical analysis of the Bible for about three hundred years, and these efforts have produced some interesting and important results. This textbook draws on the breadth of that scholarship in giving a historical orientation to the Bible that can be a starting point for further study, questioning, and correction. For now, use this textbook as your initial guide, rather than doing internet searches on Bible-related topics (websites on the internet are particularly variable in quality). Each chapter concludes with some recommended written resources, and this chapter concludes with some websites that also provide high quality resources for further study.

CHAPTER ONE REVIEW

For Review

1. Know the meaning and significance of the following terms discussed in this chapter:
   - Israel [two meanings]
   - Israelite (know the difference from "Israeli")
   - Yahweh
   - literary criticism
   - tradition criticism
   - historical criticism

2. Be able to identify the following areas on a map and describe their general characteristics:
   - coastal plain
   - central hill country
   - Jordan Valley
   - Judah
   - Transjordan

3. Know the dates and basic significance of the following overall periods of history:
   - pre-state tribal period
   - proto-monarchy
   - neighboring monarchies
   - Judah alone
   - destruction of Jerusalem
   - Babylonian exile
   - Persian period
   - post-exilic period
   - Hellenistic period
   - Hasmonean (Maccabean) monarchy
   - beginning of the Roman period
   - destruction of the Second Temple

4. Know the order in which the following empires dominated Israel and Judah:
   - Assyrian
   - Babylonian
   - Persian
   - Hellenistic (or Greek)
   - Roman

RESOURCES FOR FURTHER STUDY

Overviews of the history of Israel

Miller, J. Maxwell. *The History of Israel: An Essential Guide*. Nashville: Abingdon, 1997.

Schipper, Bernd. *A Concise History of Ancient Israel: From the Beginnings Through the Hellenistic Era*, trans. Michael J. Lesley. University Park, PA: Eisenbrauns, 2019.

Shanks, Hershel. *Ancient Israel: From Abraham to the Roman Destruction of the Temple* (2nd edition). Washington, DC: Biblical Archaeology Society, 1999.

Geography of lands and places featured in the Bible

Atlas of the Bible Lands (revised edition). Maplewood, NJ: Hammond, 1990.

Rainey, Anson F., and Notley, R. Steven. *The Sacred Bridge: Carta's Atlas of the Biblical World*. Jerusalem: Carta, 2006. Detailed. Much focus on reconstructing history.

Rogerson, John. *The New Atlas of the Bible*. London: McDonald, 1985. Organized not by historical periods, but by regions. Excellent photographs and art.

Especially good internet resources

The Bible Odyssey (by the Society of Biblical Literature): www.bibleodyssey.org.

http://www.TheTorah.com A non-profit website run by Jewish scholars with accessible articles on Tanakh/Bible

Discussions of methods in biblical interpretation

McKenzie, Steven L., and Haynes, Stephen R. *To Each Its Own Meaning: An Introduction to Biblical Criticisms and Their Application* (2nd edition). Louisville, KY: Westminster John Knox Press, 1999.

McKenzie, Steven L., and Kaltner, John, eds. *New Meanings for Ancient Texts: Recent Approaches to Biblical Criticisms and Their Applications*. Louisville, KY: Westminster John Knox Press, 2013.

APPENDIX: ISRAEL'S HISTORY AND EMPIRES

(Prehistory of Israel: domination of Canaan by Egypt, 1450–1200 BCE)

Emergence of "Israel" in imperial power vacuum
Appearance of Israelite villages in unsettled hill country (approximately 1250–1000 BCE)
David and Solomon's proto-monarchy in Jerusalem (approximately 1000–930 BCE)
Neighboring monarchies: (Southern) Judah and (Northern) Israel (approximately 930–722 BCE)

Oppression by successive empires: Assyria, Egypt, and Babylonia (745–586 BCE)
Fall of northern kingdom (722 BCE)
Destruction of Jerusalem and exile of its leadership (586 BCE; also other waves of exile)

Imperial sponsorship of (formerly exiled) Judeans: post-exilic period (starting 538 BCE)
Persian-sponsored rebuilding and rule of Judah (538–332 BCE)
Hellenistic continuation of Persian policies until Hellenistic crisis (332–167 BCE)
Hellenistic crisis and emergence of Hasmonean/Maccabean monarchy (167–63 BCE)

Roman rule (starting 63 bce with different dates of end)
Destruction of the Second Temple (70 CE)
Total destruction of Jerusalem (135 CE)

The Emergence of Ancient Israel and its First Oral Traditions

2

Chapter Overview

Imagining Early Israel

Problems in Reconstructing Early Israel

Traces of the Most Ancient Israelite Oral Traditions in the Bible

Focus Text: The Song of Deborah

Ancient Israel and Israelites

The Oral Background of Genesis

Exodus

The Creation of "Israel" Through Cultural Memory of Resistance to Domination

Chapter Two Review

Resources for Further Study

CHAPTER OVERVIEW

This chapter addresses the questions "How did the earliest Israelites live?" and "What were some of Israel's most ancient traditions?" You will learn about ancient Israelite tribal life and how that form of social organization is distinguished from two other forms of social life important in later chapters of Israel's history: the monarchal city-state and the empire. The chapter discusses some unique characteristics of the kind of oral tradition typical of such tribal groups, and it finds evidence of such oral traditions embedded in biblical texts about Jacob, the exodus from Egypt, and Deborah's victory over the armies of Hazor. In their early oral form (no longer available to us), these stories and poems, often celebrating devious "tricksters" who triumph over all odds, formed part of a "collective memory" that helped distinguish the tribal-culture Israelites from the Canaanites surrounding them. At the same time, despite these differences in social organization and tribal tradition, you will also discover in this chapter ways that early Israel was more "Canaanite" in its religion and culture than you previously thought. Read both for ways ancient Israel was different from its neighbors and for ways it was similar.

Imagining Early Israel

Let us begin with a look at the stories and songs treasured by Israel at the outset of its history. More than anywhere else in this book, this requires a lot of imagination, since we have no Israelite writings from this period. Therefore, we must piece together a picture of Israel based on a combination of archaeology, some material from neighboring cultures, and distant echoes of early Israel in the much later writings now found in our Bible.

So we start with imagination – a creative reconstruction of the kind of village where Israel's first oral traditions might have developed. It is a journey back to the time described in the Bible in the books of Joshua and Judges. Nevertheless, there are major contrasts between what these books say about this "period of the Judges" and what historians reconstruct of it. Chapter 7 will discuss the later writing of the books of Joshua and Judges. For now, however, the focus is not on the written books of the Bible, but on the oral culture that produced Israel's first traditions. Here is a picture based on archaeology and careful analysis of the Bible and non-biblical texts.

If we were to take a time machine back to Israel's beginnings, the journey probably would take us to one of the hilltop villages in the hill country that existed in the late second millennium (1250–1000 BCE) between the coastal plains and Jordan Valley (see Figure 2.1). The early Israelites in the **village** lived on a subsistence level, surviving largely on the crops that they grew. Generally, there were two main seasons: a dry summer–fall season and a rainy winter–spring season culminating in the harvest of barley, then wheat and other crops. The rain on which they depended was fickle. They would store water from the rainy season in sealed underground holes, "cisterns." They used large pottery jars to store food produced from the harvest. Nevertheless, about every three or four years there would be too little rain for crops. Life would be especially hard then, with families struggling to keep from starving until another year, a better rainy season, and the first harvests from that next year's crop. In such times, they might sacrifice and eat one of their precious animals in order to survive. Otherwise, animals were primarily sources of milk and clothing (wool or skins).

Our village would have only a few homes, housing a handful of clans, settled in separate households where extended families lived together (see Figure 2.2 for an image of a typical house): grandparents, their sons and sons' wives, unmarried daughters, and dependents. Only about 50–200 people would have lived in each such village, and their lives were short and hard (as everywhere else in the ancient world). Though a few lucky individuals lived much longer, most males who survived early childhood typically lived into their mid-thirties,

FIGURE 2.1
Part of the hill country of central Israel. Notice the ancient terraces cut into the limestone hills to help in farming them.

while most women died as early as their late twenties, half of them in childbirth. They were vulnerable to starvation, diseases, warfare, and (for women) the hazards of childbirth.

Because a village lacked a wall or many men of fighting age, it was vulnerable to raids from other areas or attacks by the organized armies of the city-states in the coastal areas and lowlands. Their only hope of defense was divine help, along with assistance from banding together with other villages in their tribe (e.g. Ephraim, Manasseh, Asher). In times of particular crisis, the villages of multiple tribes might join together in a temporary military alliance led by a charismatic individual. As we will see in the Song of Deborah, it was not always easy to pull together these scattered tribes and villages into a coordinated defense. Such texts show that – contrary to some other biblical portrayals – earliest "Israel" was a very loosely organized whole. Villages and tribes bonded together to counter the unpredictabilities of military or agricultural catastrophe. Still, the primary social reality for most people in early Israel would have been their village and its clans. They would have spent the vast bulk of their lives living and working within the confines of the village itself and the surrounding hills.

This way of life contrasted with that of non-Israelite **monarchal city-states** near Israel. Ancient Near Eastern city-states were territories controlled by a city, generally cities ruled by kings. Such cities could amass resources and achieve levels of organization that were impossible in more decentralized

FIGURE 2.2
Typical pillared house of the Israelites. The bottom floor had stables for animals, a cistern for water, and areas for cooking and food preparation. The top floor was where the family slept, dined, and entertained.

systems such as tribal Israel. The walls around cities gave them immense defensive advantages over forces attacking with superior numbers. City-states often had a professional army, whose training and equipment gave them an advantage over more disorganized voluntary forces like those of Israel. Their greater military power and social organization allowed them to dominate surrounding areas, requiring peasants under their domination to help build fortifications in the city and provide regular deliveries of a certain amount of their produce. Even though the stories of the book of Judges come from a later time, we can read between the lines to see signs of struggle by Israelites against the attempts of surrounding city-states (e.g. Hazor) to dominate them. These threats, along with raids from groups such as the Midianites and Amalekites, created the need for charismatic leaders in crisis, "judges" such as Deborah or Samson, to rally disparate villages and tribes together, pooling their resources to repel a common enemy.

One enemy these Israelites did not have to face – in stark contrast to later periods in the history of Israel – was the might of a major ancient Near Eastern **empire** such as Egypt or Babylonia. The most this village culture would have known of such superpowers would have been distant echoes of Egyptian influence in some of the cities against which the villages had to fight for survival. Before the Israelite settlements emerged, Egypt had dominated the area for about two hundred years, subduing and demanding allegiance from the rulers of its major cities (for an Egyptian text about this, see the Merneptah stela

What Was Earliest "Israel" and Who Were "Judges"?

Though the Bible portrays "Israel" as a coherent group of 12 tribes descended from Jacob, most scholars now agree that this is not an accurate historical portrayal. Instead, as we will see later (in our look at Judges 5), earliest "Israel" was loosely organized. It was a group of tribes who shared a way of life (in villages) and helped in each other's military defense. Anthropologists use the term "**segmentary society**" to describe the kind of decentralized social grouping that was early Israel.

One distinctive element of such segmentary societies is the lack of a permanent power structure, such as a kingship. Instead, the villages and larger groupings were guided in their day-to-day life by elders. In times of great need, charismatic leaders, such as Deborah, would arise to unite the different groups of "Israel" into a common army. They are referred to in English biblical translations as "judges," but a better – though awkward – translation probably would be "temporary leaders."

below). We even have letters sent to and from the Pharaoh's scribes and rulers of city-states in Palestine such as Jerusalem, Shechem, and Megiddo. Jerusalem at this time was not inhabited by Israelites, but by Jebusites, and its king, Abdi-heba, writes the Pharaoh as his "servant" and pronounces that he falls "at the feet of my lord, the king, seven times" (see Figure 2.3). Later he predicts that, if he is not sent enough troops, "The lands of the king are lost." It does turn out that Egypt lost control of the area. Nevertheless, Egyptian influence continued for centuries in major coastal cities such as Byblos, and elsewhere in Palestine.

Unlike the scribes who once wrote letters for king Abdi-heba of (pre-Israelite) Jerusalem, our hilltop villagers did not have much use for writing. We know from both comparative and archaeological evidence that writing – when it occurs – is primarily connected to centralized and hierarchical urban forms of social organization (e.g. Jerusalem). Nevertheless, like other small groups throughout time, our early Israelite villagers would have had a rich and varied cultural life. Rather than writing texts, they passed on traditions orally from one generation to another. These traditions would have included genealogical trees organizing clans and villages into tribal groups and sub-groups, stories of cultural heroes such as Jacob, and songs of deliverance about the exodus or the victory under Deborah.

These **oral traditions** were in flux, as they were sung and told from year to year amidst constantly cycling generations. At one time, scholars used to think that non-literate cultures, such as the early Israelites, had unusual powers of memory that allowed them to memorize and precisely recite oral traditions over hundreds of years. Careful study of such cultures, however, has revealed that people who memorize traditions through purely oral means change those traditions constantly and substantially. To be sure, some elements may be preserved because they are anchored in a name, topographical feature, or ongoing cultural practice. Nevertheless, the singers of oral cultures regularly adapt the traditions they receive – telling versions of the same story about different

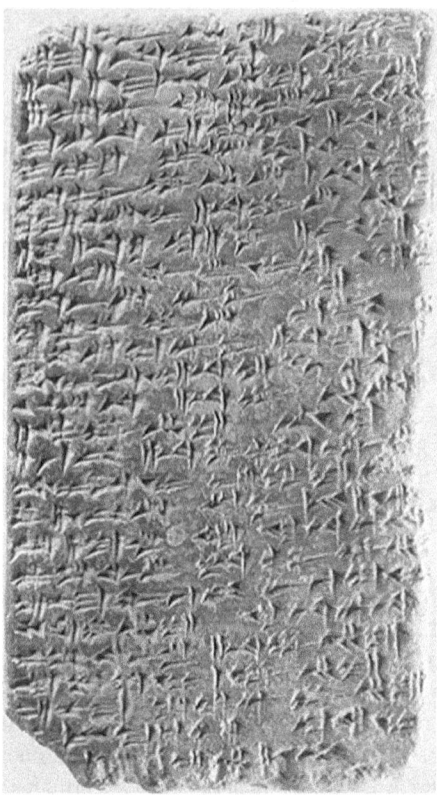

FIGURE 2.3
Tablet containing a letter from Abdi-heba, the ruler of Jerusalem while it was still a Jebusite city, before David captured it. In it the ruler reports on the area to his overlords in Egypt.

figures and/or in different settings, revising what those figures say, conforming the story over time to certain broader types of tales (e.g. adding trickster themes), etc.

This means that the early traditions of ancient Israel, whatever they were, evolved in their journey across the centuries of the late second and early first

History and the Books of Joshua and Judges

At this point we are discussing Israel's earliest history in the land. This is the time when Israel lived in villages and did not yet have a king, a period described in the biblical books of Joshua and Judges. These books, however, date from around 600 BCE at the earliest, at least five hundred years after the events they describe. They are different from each other, and each builds on diverse oral and written traditions to tell its stories. For example, the books tell up to three different stories of the conquest of several cities: e.g. Hebron in Josh 10:36–37, 15:13–14, and Judg 1:10 or Debir in Josh 10:38–39, 15:15–17, and Judg 1:11. Because of problems like these, historians of ancient Israel are ever more careful about how they use information from Joshua and Judges. Also, the discipline of archaeology has provided an important control for helping such historians evaluate the historical usefulness of biblical traditions. Later in this *Introduction* we will return to look at the books of Joshua and Judges as theological texts addressed to the people of the seventh century.

millennia, passing from one set of lips to another. A name such as "Moses" might stick, even the name of a long-abandoned Egyptian city – "Rameses" – but the story of the Israelites' exodus out of Egypt would evolve as they faced new enemies and challenges in later centuries. In the process of oral telling and retelling, the "Moses" of the story might start to resemble leaders or liberators at the time of retelling, and the "Egypt" of the retold story might resemble later enemies. Similarly, the story of Jacob wrestling God at the Jabbok (now in Gen 32:22–32) explains the place name "Penuel," and because the place name implies a divine encounter (Penuel is interpreted as Hebrew for "face of God"), that part of the story may have stayed stable over time while other details changed in the retelling process.

One characteristic appears to have been remarkably frequent, particularly in Israel's early traditions: the **trickster** – that is, a character whose ability to survive through trickery and even lawbreaking is celebrated in religion, literature, or another part of culture. As we will see below, the Bible features both male and female versions of such characters, such as the figure of Jacob in Genesis, along with his mother, Rebecca, and his second wife, Rachel. Anthropologists have long noted that many cultures, particularly cultures of more vulnerable groups, celebrate such tricksters who survive against difficult odds through cunning and sometimes deceptive behavior. Figures such as the Plains Indian Coyote demonstrate to their people how one can survive in a hostile environment where the rules are stacked against you. Throughout time people in vulnerable circumstances have celebrated such tricksters, who are often heroes within their own group. In home rituals, agricultural celebrations, weddings and other rites of passage, and other events, they would tell and sing stories of how their ancestors had triumphed against all odds, often tricking and defeating their more powerful opponents. Oral stories about figures like Jacob, Rebecca, and Rachel may have served similar functions in early Israel.

More on Method: Tradition History and Transmission History

Though traditions can be written as well as oral, many scholars use the term "**tradition history**" to refer to the history of oral traditions that existed before and alongside the written texts now in the Bible. Different versions of an oral tradition can be recognized by the combination of thematic or plot parallels on the one hand and variation in characters, setting, and especially wording on the other. Take the example of the parallel stories of Abraham and Sarah at Philistine Gerar with King Abimelech (Gen 20:1–18, 21:22–34) and Isaac and Rebekah at the same place and with the same king (Gen 26:6–33). Look at the similarities and differences! Though the two sets of stories are remarkably parallel, they diverge enough from each other that many believe them to be oral variants of the same tales. The same is likely true of different versions of the story of Hagar in the wilderness (Gen 16:1–14; 21:8–19) or three different versions of stories where a patriarch (whether Abraham or Isaac) endangers his wife in the process of trying to protect himself (Gen 12:10–20; 20:1–18; 26:6–11).

The more you compare these texts with each other, the more you should realize just how fluid oral tradition really is. This means we need to move away from concepts of verbatim repetition of traditions and toward a focus on the complex process of *transmission* (including revision) of traditions, both oral *and* written! Scholars often use the term "**transmission history**" to refer more broadly to the history of the transmission of oral *and* written biblical traditions. Later in this *Introduction* we will discuss numerous examples of the growth of written texts through combination with or expansion of earlier sources.

Problems in Reconstructing Early Israel

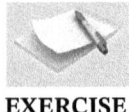

EXERCISE

Read Joshua 11. What impression do you get from this chapter of the Israelites' military accomplishments? How does this compare with the picture of these as summarized in Judges 1? As was discussed in the above textbox on History and the Books of Joshua (p. 40), both these narratives about Israel's origins were written centuries after the events they describe and are historically problematic. As will be discussed below, the Song of Deborah probably provides a better glimpse at "Israel" in a time before kingship and the growth of scribalism associated with it.

The village imagined above is forever lost for us, if it ever existed in anything like that form. At the most, we have fragments of its existence. Archaeological surveys have uncovered the remains of hundreds of settlements in the northern hill country of Israel that suddenly sprang up in unusual numbers around 1250 BCE. Strikingly, this also happens to be around the time when we see the first mention of the name "Israel" in a datable ancient document. A stone monument set up by Pharaoh Merneptah (see Figure 2.4) celebrates his army's victory over cities and other groups in Syria-Palestine, saying:

> Canaan is plundered, Ashkelon is carried off, and Gezer is captured. Yenoam [a town near the sea of Galilee] is made into non-existence; Israel is wasted, its seed [offspring] is no more; and Hurru [a term for Syria] has become a widow because of Egypt.
>
> (Translation adapted from that by James Hoffmeier in *Hallo, Context of Scripture*, vol. 2, p. 41)

The stela commemorates an Egyptian campaign carried out sometime around 1220 BCE. Interestingly, the Egyptian writing system clearly indicates that this "Israel" is a tribal people, not a territory. The next securely datable mention of anything specifically Israelite comes four hundred years later. So this mention

FIGURE 2.4
The Merneptah stela, including a list of Egyptian conquests and dating to around 1200 BCE. It contains the earliest mention of "Israel" outside the Bible.

of a people, "Israel," in the Merneptah stela of 1207 is a precious clue. It helps us interpret the village settlements across the hill country in 1250–1000 BCE as the earliest remains of "Israel," the people who would later create the Hebrew Bible.

The earlier history of this people cannot be recovered. This is as far back as we can go using academic methods of historical reconstruction. Through a combination of archaeological evidence for early hilltop villages and the Merneptah stela, we have good reason to think that some kind of village culture "Israel" already lived in the hill country of Palestine from around 1300 BCE onward (see Map 2.1 on the next page). Nevertheless, we do not have the kind of secure written or other sources that historians would typically rely on to tell us where these people came from or how they got there.

To be sure, the Bible tells a story of how this people was formed from ancestors of Jacob's sons, who went down into Egypt, emerged in the exodus, and wandered in the wilderness, before entering Canaan through a triumphant military conquest of all of the area and destruction of all its inhabitants. Scholars once thought that archaeological remains confirmed this picture of external origins and total conquest, since there are destruction layers in many Canaanite towns in the late second millennium. Some thought these destruction layers were evidence of an Israelite onslaught. Nevertheless, others have rightly argued that the cities where destruction layers were found are not

MAP 2.1

Areas of the hill country occupied by the Israelites and Judeans, and where the tribes are said to have been located in the pre-state period. Redrawn from Norman Gottwald, *The Hebrew Bible: A Socio-Literary Introduction.* Minneapolis: Fortress, 1985, page 133.

generally cities mentioned in the Bible. Moreover, their destructions apparently occurred over a period of over one hundred years rather than in a single conquest as related in the book of Joshua. This calls into question the idea that they are the result of a coordinated Israelite conquest of the sort described in Joshua. Instead, many of these cities probably disappeared as part of a more widespread destruction of major urban centers that occurred toward the end of the second millennium, a destruction caused by a combination of environmental catastrophe and invasions of "sea peoples" from the Western Mediterranean. In sum, the archaeological evidence, if anything, contradicts rather than confirms the picture of total destruction of the Canaanite people given in Joshua (and somewhat concurs with the picture of decentralized tribal life in the book of Judges). Chapter 7 of this textbook will return to the story of total conquest written in the book of Joshua and how that story was crafted to address the humiliation and trauma of later Israel.

All this leads us back to the origins of the Israelite people and their culture – *in* Canaan. Our evidence shows every sign that the vast bulk of the earliest Israelites came from Canaan and shared its language, its material culture, and – to some extent – its religion. To be sure, there may have been a "Moses group," themselves of Canaanite extraction, who experienced slavery and liberation from Egypt, but most scholars believe that such a group – if it existed – was only a small minority in early Israel, even though their story came to be claimed by all. The rest of the early Israelites did not come from outside the land through conquest or gradual settlement. The architecture and pottery of early Israelite settlements show close connections to pre-Israelite, "Canaanite," architecture and pottery. Prior attempts to identify a distinctively different Israelite pottery, house type, or other feature have failed. The Hebrew language, including its more ancient forms, is so closely related to neighboring languages that a student who learns Hebrew is well on his or her way to reading Phoenician, Moabite, Ammonite, etc.

Finally, both archaeological remains and the much later evidence from the Hebrew Bible indicate that the oldest forms of Israelite religion were not as distinct from non-Israelite, "Canaanite" religion as scholars once thought. The Canaanites worshipped various gods, such as the creator and father god **El**, his wife **Asherah**, the storm god **Baal**, and the goddess of love and war Anat. Anat is not particularly prominent in biblical traditions, but the other three all appear to have played significant roles in early Israel, alongside Israelite worship of a non-Canaanite God, "Yahweh." For example, ancient Israelites often expressed their theology by giving their children pious sentence names. The Bible records that Saul, one of Israel's earliest leaders, had descendants named "Ishbaal" (Hebrew for "man of Baal") and "Mephibaal" ("from the mouth of Baal"). In this case, these names of Saul's descendants probably indicate reverence for Baal in his family. The name "El" is yet more prominent in biblical tradition, forming part of the name "Isra*el*," and of several important place names (e.g. Bethel – "house of El"). One biblical text even uses a frequent epithet of El, "the Most High," to describe how El assigned Yahweh to Israel:

> When the Most High assigned the nations,
> when he divided humankind,
> He determined the boundaries of the peoples
> according to the number of the gods.
> Yahweh's own portion was his people,
> Jacob was his assigned share.
>
> (Deut 32:8–9)

Israel's worship probably was not confined to male deities such as Baal, El, or Yahweh. Archaeologists have found remains in early Israelite settlements both of female figurines and of early Israelite depictions of trees, a frequent symbol in ancient Canaan of female reproductive power (see Figure 2.5). Many scholars think these early images of trees/women were representations of the goddess Asherah, the wife of the creator god El. Worship of Asherah appears to have been widespread in earliest Israel. Each ancient village probably had its own hilltop sanctuary, a raised platform for sacrifice, featuring both a pillar to symbolize male deity and a tree to symbolize divine female power. Asherah, whose symbol is the tree, was the probable focus of the tree symbolism.

The Name "Israel"

The name "Israel," like most ancient Hebrew names, is a sentence. It is formed from the divine name "El," and may mean "El rules" or "May El prove his rulership." It reflects the potential focus in earliest Israel on El's role in helping early tribal groups resist the "rulership" of surrounding cities and their armies.

FIGURE 2.5
Animals feeding on trees, an early Israelite reflection of a yet earlier artistic pattern seen in pre-Israelite remains where the same animals were fed by a goddess figure, possibly Asherah.

READING

Judges 5 (note that this potentially early poem is different from the later account in Judges 4).

The Song of Deborah (Judges 5) as a Window to Ancient Tribal Israel

FOCUS TEXT

Because a tribal society like early Israel did not produce extended literary texts, the Bible does not contain many traditions from this early period. Instead, the Bible, even parts that talk of Israel's early history, is a corpus of texts written down centuries later. Nevertheless, these ancient villages had their own oral traditions, passed down by word of mouth from generation to generation. These traditions, constantly evolving to fit the hopes and fears of the performers and their audiences, expressed the deepest values of their community.

The Song of Deborah in Judges 5 is the one of the best candidates for at least echoing some such ancient oral traditions. It is a poem celebrating Israel's triumph over the Canaanite king Sisera, and its poetic – and perhaps sung – form may preserve, at least in part, early oral traditions of the Israelite tribes. In addition, the song contains archaic elements of Hebrew language, and the list of tribes and other groups in Judges 5 only partially overlaps with later lists of tribes that made up early Israel. Judges 5 does not even mention some of the southern tribes, and it mentions other names not typically found in 12-tribe lists (e.g. Machir = Manasseh; and Meroz). These are among some of our first clues that this text may reflect a very early poem. Open up your Bible to Judges 5 and let us use this text as an evocative window to a time long before texts of our Bible began to be written down.

5:2–5: The song opens with a hymn of praise describing Yahweh's triumphant appearance from the southern desert regions of Seir and Edom (5:4–5). It is one of several potentially early texts that locate Sinai and Yahweh's origins in the desert regions south of Palestine (Deut 33:2; Hab 3:3; Ps 68:7–9). Our ancient text envisions Yahweh as a powerful storm god, whose arrival is marked by earthquakes and torrential floods. Yet there is also a focus here and throughout the poem on the people. The first verse of the poem celebrates the way leaders took the lead and the people responded willingly (5:2), and the second verse (5:3) calls on the powerful "kings and princes" of the world to hear this "song" about the triumph of a kingless group of tribal villagers.

5:6–12: The next section of the poem celebrates the emergence of leadership in this otherwise disorganized group: the rise of Deborah. Beforehand, trails had become unsafe, settlements were defenseless, and the people had no weapons (5:6–7a). But then Deborah arose "as a mother in Israel." The poem then again calls on those who volunteered in the effort to offer praise (5:9), along with other groups (5:10–11), and Deborah and Barak themselves (5:12).

5:13–18 and 5:23: The poem then details which tribal groups answered the call to battle willingly, and which did not. Six tribes came when called: Ephraim, Benjamin, Machir (related to Manasseh; Num 26:29), Zebulun, Issachar, and Naphtali. Four did not: Reuben, Gilead (perhaps in place of Gad in the standard lists of tribes), Dan, and Asher. Two southern tribes are not even mentioned: Judah and Simeon. Apparently, at the time the Song was written, they were not even envisioned as potential partners in this kind of military effort. Even the northern groups that appear here are clearly not unified. Only six out of ten answered the call to battle. Indeed, from the initial call to praise those who volunteered (5:2) to the contrast of those who volunteered and those who did not (5:13–18), much of Deborah's song seems aimed at encouraging the separate tribes to affirm their common destiny. It calls on villagers to sing praises to God for a victory where six tribes joined together to defeat – with God's help – the mighty forces of Sisera. And it soon calls on them to curse "Meroz," an unknown group who failed to answer the call (5:23).

5:19–22: The actual description of the battle occurs only in these four verses. They move beyond the conflict between Israel and Sisera to juxtapose the "kings of Canaan" and their horses, on the one hand, with the cosmic powers of Yahweh, on the other. The kings may have the superior military technology, but they have no chance against the power of stars fighting from heaven and the force of the Kishon River (5:19–21). Soon the once powerful stallions were fleeing (5:22).

5:24–31: In two scenes, 5:24–27 and 28–30, the poet concludes with vignettes about the aftermath of the battle. The first blesses Jael, of the Kenites, for aiding in the effort by cleverly tricking Sisera into enjoying her hospitality and then killing him with a mallet (5:24–27). Again, there is an element of the trickster here, since hospitality is otherwise celebrated as a profound value, not just in surrounding cultures, but in Israelite traditions as well. Nevertheless, Jael welcomes Sisera into her tent and feeds him, before killing him. Like a slow-motion movie, the poetry uses repetition to focus in on the moment.

> Between her feet he sank, he fell, he lay
> Between her feet he sank, he fell
> Where he sank, there he fell, destroyed.

Meanwhile, in 5:28–30 the poet offers another vision featuring a woman, this time the mother of Sisera, waiting for him to return triumphant from battle, not knowing of his recent death. As she wonders at his delay, her "wise women" speculate that he is probably delayed by dividing spoil: a few Israelite maidens for each warrior and some nice cloth to bring back to the women at home.

In this way, "Deborah's song" uses two scenes involving women to illustrate the contrast between the destinies of Yahweh's friends and enemies. Yahweh's enemies will perish and their women (like Sisera's mother) will mourn, but those who join in the effort to fight, like Jael, will be "like the sun when it rises with all its might" (5:31).

This belief in the triumph of the people that God chooses is an early form of what is often termed "**election theology**" – that is, the idea that God has chosen a particular people to care for and defend. This idea is present in the affirmation of the exodus tradition that Yahweh delivered Israel from Egypt. And it is implicit in the stories of God's protection and provision for Israel's trickster ancestor, Jacob, and his family. In all these traditions, God chooses not a place, nor a territorial nation, but a people, and protects them against seemingly impossible odds. This belief in God's choosing of a particular people, rooted in tribal traditions like the Song of Deborah and the exodus story, is a fundamental bedrock of later Israelite theology, especially in the northern part of Israel. Moreover, this idea of the distinctiveness and chosenness of a *people*, election theology, may have distinguished early Israel from some of the monarchal nation states that surrounded it. Those states were more focused on how their gods chose a particular city and/or royal-priestly dynasty.

Ancient Israel and Israelites

A variety of data thus suggest that ancient Israel was quite different from the "Israel" that many people imagine. Whereas the later state of Israel came to control cities like Jerusalem, earliest tribal Israel was confined to more sparsely settled northern and eastern hills. This is where we see settlements start to appear in the early Israelite period. And these hills are the regions associated with known tribes that appear in the song of Deborah. If you look at Map 2.1, you can see that Deborah only called upon tribes associated with the upper thirds of the map (e.g. Naphtali, Issachar, Manasseh [related to Machir] and Ephraim), while the southernmost tribes are not mentioned (e.g. Judah, Simeon). This song, like some other biblical texts, is working with a concept of "Israel" that refers more narrowly to these northern tribes and their land. This northern hill country was the most ancient "Israel," and its people were distinguished from the inhabitants of "Judah," which is located in the *southern* highlands of the map.

The Oral Background of Genesis

We turn now to look at how stories in the first book of the Bible, Genesis, are built on oral traditions, including some trickster elements. Notably, the stories we will discuss here do not come from the first chapters of Genesis, narratives of primeval beginnings (creation, etc.) found in Genesis 1–11. We will discuss those chapters once we come to the development of writing in later Israel.

READING

Stories of the Endangerment of the Matriarch: compare Gen 12:10–20; 20:1–18; 26:6–11.
Abraham and Lot Cycle of Stories: Genesis 13, 18–19.
Stories of Hagar and Ishmael: compare Gen 16:1–14 and 21:8–19.
Stories about Rebecca, Jacob, and his family: Genesis 27–35.

Rather, the parts of Genesis that most reflect oral origins are narratives about Israel's ancestors in Genesis 12–50 – Abraham, Isaac, Jacob, and their families.

Of course, the written biblical text contains no such oral tradition in pure form. The often-repeated idea that people in oral cultures perfectly remember and repeat their traditions was long ago shown to be untrue (see box on pp. 41–42). That said, blurry forms of ancient Israelite traditions can be seen in biblical texts, especially in ways that those texts feature one or more accounts of how such figures survived by means of deception and trickery. Take, for example, the multiple accounts of how a patriarch worked to avoid being killed by a king because of his beautiful wife by telling the king that she actually was his sister. The Bible preserves two versions of this story about Abraham (Gen 12:10–20 and 20:1–18) and one version about Isaac (Gen 26:6–11). At least one biblical author seems to have found Abraham's lying on this point problematic, since the second version of this story (in Genesis 20) has Abraham claiming that she was his half-sister (Gen 20:12). Nevertheless, the Bible's own narrative says nothing of the sort about her (see Gen 11:29–30), and this additional part of Abraham's speech is probably evidence of the discomfort that some later authors had with the trickster traditions that they adapted.

As we move to the section of Genesis focused on Jacob (Genesis 25–35), we see more places where the Bible's written text preserves echoes of earlier trickster traditions. In Genesis 25, Jacob cleverly gets a hungry Esau to sell his birthright for a pot of lentil stew. Then, in Genesis 27, Rebekah, Jacob's mother, develops a tricky ruse to get Jacob's father, Isaac, to give Jacob the superior blessing that he meant to give to Esau. At Rebekah's urging, Jacob flees to escape Esau's plan to murder him, and he gets a taste of his own medicine in Haran, where his father-in-law, Laban, gets him to work seven years to marry Rachel, but then slips Leah into Jacob's marriage bed instead (Genesis 29). Soon Jacob turns the tables on Laban, using magical means to outwit Laban's plan to deprive Jacob of his wages in livestock (Genesis 30) and later escaping with Laban's daughters without Laban's knowledge (Genesis 31). In the process, Rachel shows her own capacity for trickery, stealing her father's household gods and then preventing him from finding them by sitting on them and then telling her father that she cannot get up because she has her period ("the way of woman is on me"; Gen 31:35). In these ways and others, the story depicts Jacob and his closest family as crafty tricksters, able to survive and flourish in the face of difficult odds. Not only is he himself a trickster, but his mother helped get him started, and he worked 14 years to marry a woman, Rachel, who continues the tradition.

These traditions of trickery are not the sort of thing typically focused on in sermons and Sunday school lessons. Many within dominant cultures are not used to celebrations of such culture heroes – figures who trick and even lie to get their way. Nevertheless, such stories can be encouraging to people who feel that they will inevitably perish if they play by "the rules" of their social context. Whether Native American or ancient Israelite, vulnerable people often gain empowerment through celebrating ancestors who made their way in the world through using cleverness to overcome impossible odds. For people on top, such trickster stories can appear to be embarrassing elements in an otherwise tidy Bible. For people on the bottom, such stories can be a major way of gaining hope and resisting domination.

That said, none of the texts in the Bible, including Genesis, are transcripts of early oral traditions. Rather these are later literary texts where earlier oral traditions have been radically reshaped to fit into a broader narrative. This means that we must distinguish between the present *written* level of the biblical text and faint outlines of oral traditions standing behind that text. The written text develops a new picture of Abraham as a recipient of God's promises and even adds the idea of God making a covenant with him. This picture of Abraham and focus on God's promise to him and his descendants developed as a response to Israel's trauma under later empires. Meanwhile, another set of stories about Israel's ancestors looms behind this picture: older oral stories of how some of Israel's ancestors successfully fended for themselves.

(Echoes of) earlier oral traditions in Genesis	Elements specific to the present written text of Genesis 12–50
A focus on how both men (e.g. Abraham, Jacob) and women (e.g. Rebekah, Rachel) survived and flourished through their wits	A focus on how God promised the patriarchs of Israel (Abraham, Isaac, Jacob) to make them a great people, bless them, and give them the land of Canaan
Traditions about these figures circulate in one or more cycles of stories about each figure (e.g. Abraham, Isaac, Jacob, Hagar), with some of the same stories told about different figures (e.g. wife endangerment by Abraham in Gen 20:1–18 and 21:22–34; Isaac in Gen 26:6–33)	The reshaping and connection of originally separate traditions so that they are linked with new themes of blessing and promise that spoke to the despair of later Israelites
A celebration of deception if it ensures the success of the underdog trickster	Introduction of divine speeches to early ancestors (Abraham, Jacob, Isaac, and also Hagar) and focus on their need to trust in God's covenant with them and provision for them

> **Basics**
>
> ## The Written Version of the Ancestral Story (Genesis 12–50)
>
> Though this chapter focuses on reconstructing ancient Israel's oral traditions, it can be helpful to contrast such speculation about now lost oral traditions with a look at the written text that we actually have. In the case of Israel's ancestors, we start with the written text of Genesis 12–50, one that is thoroughly shaped by the above-noted, later written themes of promise and covenant.
>
> ### Outline: the three major parts of Genesis 12–50
>
> | | | |
> |---|---|---|
> | I | Abraham: God's promises of blessing and land to Abraham and his descendants | 11:27–25:11 |
> | | [Interlude: genealogy of the descendants of Ishmael | 25:12–18] |
> | II. | Jacob: transfer of promises to Isaac and Jacob; also stories of Rebekah, Esau, Rachel 25:19–35:29 | |
> | | [Interlude: genealogy of the descendants of Esau | 36:1–43] |
> | II. | Joseph and other sons of Jacob: division among brothers and eventual reconciliation | 37–50 |
>
> ### Key themes
>
> An overarching theme for this section is God's gift of promises of blessing and land to Abraham (Gen 12:1–7) and covenant with him (Genesis 15 and 17), promises that are then passed on to his heirs Isaac (Gen 26:2–5, 24) and Jacob (Gen 28:13–14; 35:9–15).
>
> Much of the Abraham story is particularly oriented toward these promises. It tells of how Abraham is protected by God in Egypt and in Gerar when he leaves Israel because of famine (Gen 12:10–20; 20:1–18), how God eventually makes covenants with him sealed by sacrifice (Genesis 15) and the sign of male circumcision (Genesis 17), and how God provides him a son through Sarah to inherit the promise, Isaac (Genesis 18; 21:1–7), alongside his son Ishmael, whom he fathers through Sarah's slave, Hagar (Gen 16; 21:8–21).
>
> The theme of promise continues in the Jacob story (Genesis 25–35), especially in an initial digression focused on Isaac (Gen 26:1–33). Nevertheless, most of this part of Genesis focuses on Jacob's journey away from home, fleeing the wrath of his brother, Esau, caused by Jacob's trickery (Gen 25:29–34; 27:1–45). Jacob travels to stay with Abraham's relatives in Haran and acquires family and flocks there, including fathering the ancestors of the 12 tribes of Israel (Genesis 28–30). The story concludes with Jacob's return to the land, wrestling with God (Gen 32:22–32) just before reconciling with his brother Esau (Genesis 33).

The Joseph story in Genesis 37–50 is even more focused on the theme of division among brothers. Joseph's brothers sell him into slavery at the outset (Genesis 37), but he rises to power in Egypt (Genesis 39–41), and he then is able to provide for his father and brothers when they flee to Egypt because of another famine in Israel (42–50).

Women in Israel's ancestral stories

There are some important stories focusing on women among Israel's ancestors. On the one hand, we see biblical matriarchs exerting a limited form of power in the household sphere, whether through using slaves as sexual surrogates (Sarah using Hagar in Genesis 16; Rachel and Leah, using Bilhah and Zilpah in Gen 30:3–13) or using their wits to promote their favored son (Rebekah in Genesis 27) or protect their husband from a vengeful father-in-law (Rachel in Gen 31:26–35). On the other hand, the stories of Dinah and Tamar show the extreme vulnerability of women in the Israelite world. Tamar exposes her body and risks death in the process of trying to secure a lineage for her father-in-law, Judah (Genesis 38), and Dinah is raped and revenged amidst a power struggle between her brothers and the inhabitants of Shechem (Genesis 34).

Further reading

Try reading through Genesis 12–50 now with this background. These are some of the most famous stories in the Bible, particularly because three major world faiths – Judaism, Christianity, and Islam – focus on Abraham and God's promises to him and his heirs. We will return to these texts later in this introduction, but this is a good time to initially familiarize yourself with them.

Your reading of texts like Genesis becomes more nuanced when you are attuned to the fact that it contains such earlier oral traditions. Rather than trying to explain away or excuse strategies like Jacob's tricking of Esau out of his father's blessing (Genesis 27), you can see such elements as part of the Bible's complex mix. Not only does the Bible describe God's promises to and covenants with Israel's great patriarchs (e.g. Genesis 15 and 17), but it includes adaptations of these stories of ancestral trickery and self-reliance.

Finally, it should be stressed that these earlier oral traditions are adaptations themselves of centuries of earlier oral traditions. As stories about Abraham and Jacob, Rebekah and Rachel were told and retold in the vulnerable unwalled villages of Israel, they were selected and reshaped to encourage early Israelites. Those Israelites faced challenges in securing their livelihood and defending themselves against kings like Sisera. Generations of Israelite storytellers selected certain stories and reshaped them for their hearers. Some tales fell by the wayside while others gained new elements. And this complex oral storytelling process produced uncanny elements in Israel's ancestral narratives that readers often overlook.

READING

Exodus 2, 5–10, and the potential early song of Miriam in Exod 15:20–21.

Exodus

The book of Exodus, like Genesis, is a complex mix. In Chapter 10 of this introduction, I will discuss how major parts of Exodus – such as the stories of God's delay of the exodus to inflict plagues on Egypt – were shaped in relation to later Israel's experiences of imperial trauma. That does not mean, however, that later storytellers completely made up the figure of Moses and the exodus event. Rather, key parts of the exodus story would never have been invented by later writers, such as Moses having an Egyptian name (consider, for example, the famous Pharaoh Thut*mose*) or Moses having foreign wives from Midian (Exodus 2) and Cush (Numbers 12). And these are just two initial indicators that *some kind of* story of the exodus circulated in ancient Israel from a very early period. At the start, such a story may well have been the property of a sub-group in Israel, perhaps an "exodus group" of prisoners who had escaped from Egypt who then joined others living in hill-country villages and told their story of liberation from Pharaoh under the leadership of Moses.

Yet, even assuming that some sort of exodus from Egypt occurred historically, the story about it would not have survived if it had not also spoken an important new word to the people living in the hill-country villages. And there are good reasons to think it did. For these village-culture Israelites had "pharaohs" of their own day, the rulers of the city-states surrounding them, whom they needed to resist. As we have seen, the Song of Deborah in Judges 5 (and the later accompanying story in Judges 4) vividly describes the kind of threat posed by such cities, with their professional armies and chariots. Furthermore, it is likely that some such formerly Egyptian-dominated cities, such as Jerusalem or Shechem, preserved remnants of the Egyptian culture. At the least, these former outposts of Egyptian domination of Canaan would have been perceived by villagers as the closest oppressive counterpart to the Egypt that had once dominated the area.

The story of Yahweh's deliverance of slaves from Egypt would have served as a powerful rallying cry for villagers now fighting for survival against such city-states. The story became the property of all "Israel," not just former slaves and their descendants. We see this sort of community claiming of an older story today, for example, in the way later African Americans have claimed the stories of the Bible for themselves. In his March 2008 speech on race, "A More Perfect Union," Barack Obama drew on his autobiography to describe how he found hope in the merging of biblical stories and contemporary lives in the black church:

People began to shout, to rise from their seats and clap and cry out, a forceful wind carrying the reverend's voice up into the rafters . . . And in that single note – hope! – I heard something else; at the foot of that cross, inside the thousands of churches across the city, I imagined the stories of ordinary black people merging with the stories of David and Goliath, Moses and Pharaoh, the Christians in the lion's den, Ezekiel's field of dry bones. Those stories – of survival, and freedom, and hope – became our story, my story; the blood that had spilled was our blood, the tears our tears; until this black church, on this bright day, seemed once more a vessel carrying the story of a people into future generations and into a larger world. Our trials and triumphs became at once unique and universal, black and more than black; in chronicling our journey, the stories and songs gave us a means to reclaim memories that we didn't need to feel shame about . . . memories that all people might study and cherish – and with which we could start to rebuild.

This claiming of older stories by new groups is hardly limited to the black church. Much as many Americans now claim for themselves the story of the *Mayflower* and the Puritan holiday of thanksgiving, despite the fact that many descend from immigrants of the twentieth century, so also Israelite villagers of varied origins claimed the exodus story as their own. That story celebrated the god, Yahweh, who had liberated "them" from Egypt, and it expressed their confidence that this exodus God would also fight on their behalf against their contemporary "pharaohs," the local city-states.

More on Method: African American Biblical Interpretation

The above-quoted speech by President Obama connects with a complicated history of African Americans and the Bible. On the one hand, African Americans have seen the Bible used against them. In particular, slaveholders reinterpreted the story of Noah's curse of Ham (Gen 9:20–27) as an eternal curse of Africans to slavery, and they noted that slavery is assumed as an ongoing reality in a number of biblical writings (e.g. Lev 25:44–46). On the other hand, African Americans also have found encouragement in the Bible's story of God's liberation of slaves from Egypt, calls for justice in prophets like Amos, and the Bible's picture of Jesus.

African American scholars have engaged in multiple ways with this complicated history. To start, a number of scholars highlighted the presence of African characters in the Bible and countered racist interpretations of stories like the curse of Ham. More recently, a number of studies have analyzed the diverse ways that the Bible, especially elements like the story of exodus from Egyptian slavery, have functioned in African American religion and culture. For one survey of the broader field of critical African American Interpretation see Mitzi J. Smith, *Insights from African American Interpretation* (Minneapolis: Fortress, 2017). We will return to themes of African American interpretation in the next chapter's discussion of Afrocentric and Womanist interpretation and the biblical Song of Songs.

Yet again we must remember that the exodus story (or stories) that ancient Israelites claimed was not identical with the story found in the Bible in Exodus 1–15. No one would have been writing such texts in the villages of early Israel. Moreover, there are numerous signs – to be discussed elsewhere in this book – that these stories in the book of Exodus were shaped into their present form by much later Israelites rereading the story of exodus in relation to ever new "pharaohs": the "pharaoh" of Solomon and his kingdom, the "pharaoh" of Assyrian and Babylonian superpowers, etc. This process of merging of stories described by Barack Obama has been going on a very long time.

That said, there are some trickster elements in the biblical exodus story that may point to a few early oral elements lying in some form behind the text in Exodus 1–15. Take, for example, the tale of the tricky midwives, Shiphrah and Puah (Exod 1:15–22), who disobey Pharaoh's command to kill all male Israelite babies, claiming "Hebrew women are not like Egyptian women; they are so strong that they give birth before the midwife has a chance to get to them." Later on, fully intending to depart for good, Moses nevertheless tries to get the Israelites free by asking Pharaoh for a three-day vacation in the wilderness so they can fulfill God's command to worship there (Exod 5:1–5). Later, when Pharaoh agrees to let the Israelites have a three-day festival in Egypt rather than going away, Moses claims that they cannot do so because the Israelite sacrifices would be too distasteful to the Egyptians (8:21–23). When the plagues finally persuade Pharaoh to let the male Israelites go on their supposed worship pilgrimage, Moses slyly insists that the men cannot adequately observe this particular festival without all of their families and livestock along (10:7–10). These elements are now found in later, written biblical texts (some composed amidst later contexts of cultural resistance). Nevertheless, these stories about the exodus reflect a tone of trickery particularly characteristic of early oral traditions.

Conclusion: The Creation of "Israel" Through Cultural Memory of Resistance to Domination

All this is a prelude to the gradual creation of the Hebrew Bible. At this point in the history of Israel no books, not even chapters, had been written. "Israel" was only a very loose association of village-tribal groups. These villages shared, however, a common way of life. They aided each other in times of famine, and charismatic leaders such as Deborah rose up in times of crisis to fight common enemies. Whatever their diverse origins, these village dwellers came to claim a common story of liberation from Egypt. They claimed a common ancestor, Jacob, along with the rest of his trickster family. And through poems like the Song of Deborah, they celebrated those occasions where they joined together to experience Yahweh's deliverance against the more powerful city-states around them.

Some scholars, such as Maurice Halbwachs (*On Collective Memory* [Chicago: University of Chicago Press, 1992]) and Jan Assmann (*Religion and Cultural Memory* [Stanford: University of Stanford Press, 2005]), have argued persuasively that such common memories are what form groups of people. Such

Conclusion: The Creation of "Israel" Through Cultural Memory of Resistance to Domination

cultural memory is reinforced through parental teaching, schools, festivals, and other practices in which people in groups recite or act out their common heritage. For example, national holidays, such as July 4 in the US, are occasions when national identity is reinforced through various festivities, in this case marking the day when the nation was born. New citizens are required to learn the common story before they can become "Americans." Similarly, the worship year in Jewish synagogues and Christian churches continually reminds those communities of their stories, having them relive the events of the Torah (for synagogues) or the life of Jesus (for churches) and reinforce their sense of a particular religious identity. You become a "Jew" or "Christian" partly through learning the story of that group and claiming it as your own.

We do not know exactly how the oral versions of the texts about exodus, Jacob's family, and Deborah's victory were used, but they appear to have served a similar purpose in helping to create and reinforce a sense of common "Israelite" identity out of varied groups. Whether taught to children, recited at clan worship, sung at festivals, or used in some other way, the ancient oral traditions discussed in this chapter helped turn the people living in the hill country of Syria-Palestine into the "Israelites" who would create the later Bible.

The shared oral memories discussed in this chapter made for a particular kind of community: one that celebrated powerful work by God on the one hand and the clever action of tricksters on the other. In the midst of the pluralistic Canaanite religious environment, these traditions praise the liberative work of Yahweh, a god known from the southern deserts. Yet they also celebrate Israelite resourcefulness and wit. In particular, they empower people living on the margins by celebrating clever underdogs such as Jacob or Jael. Women are quite prominent in these traditions, as mothers, tricksters, and even military leaders (Deborah). Meanwhile, "kings" and their representatives are the opponents in these village-culture traditions, whether Pharaoh or Hazor's general Sisera.

Even when Israel developed writing, the stories of these oral traditions – in highly varied forms – continued to be told and sung among Israelites, many of whom never learned to write. We must keep in mind that our written Bible is but the tip of the iceberg of a largely lost oral tradition in ancient Israel. The process started not with writing, but with telling tales of Israelite liberation, survival, and victory.

CHAPTER TWO REVIEW

For Review

1 Know the meaning and significance of the following terms discussed in this chapter:
   - Asherah
   - Baal
   - cultural memory
   - El
   - election theology
   - empire
   - monarchal city-state

- oral traditions
- segmentary society
- trickster
- village

2. Know the main differences between the following three ancient forms of social organization:
   - empire
   - monarchal city-state
   - village

3. What is "tradition history," and what is an example of the sort of phenomenon in the Bible that it would study? What is the difference between "tradition history" and "transmission history"? Do the terms overlap?

4. What do anthropologists now know about the character of oral traditions? How does this affect their usability for reconstructing early traditions? How specifically are such oral traditions reflected in Genesis 12–25 or Exodus 1–15?

5. List ways that the Bible's picture of Israel's origins (where Israelites came from, what their religion was, ethnic makeup, political unity) contrasts with the picture developed by archaeologically informed historians. Specify at least three such contrasts.

6. What are two specific reasons that lead scholars to doubt that ancient Israelites took possession of the land by killing all of the Canaanites in a single conquest?

7. (Focus text: Judges 5) Find three verses in this poem that illustrate three different aspects of earliest Israel. What is each aspect and how does it contrast with the picture of Israel's origins found elsewhere in the Bible, like the book of Joshua, or even other parts of Judges, like Judges 4? What is your overall impression about earliest Israel and their conception of God based on this poem in Judges 5?

RESOURCES FOR FURTHER STUDY

Commentaries and other books on Joshua

Hawk, Daniel L. *Every Promise Fulfilled: Contesting Plots in the Book of Joshua.* Louisville, KY: Westminster John Knox Press, 1991.

Nelson, Richard D. *Joshua.* Louisville, KY: Westminster John Knox Press, 1997.

Commentaries and other books on Judges

Hamlin, John E. *At Risk in the Promised Land: A Commentary on the Book of Judges.* Grand Rapids: Eerdmans, 1990.

McCann, J. Clinton. *Judges.* Louisville, KY: Westminster John Knox Press, 2002.

Niditch, Susan. *Judges.* Louisville, KY: Westminster John Knox Press, 2008.

Trible, Phyllis. *Texts of Terror: Literary-Feminist Readings of Biblical Narratives.* Philadelphia: Fortress, 1984. Chapters on the Levite's wife and Jephthah's daughter.

Everyday life in ancient Israel

King, Philip J., and Stager, Lawrence E. *Life in Biblical Israel.* Louisville, KY: Westminster John Knox Press, 2001.

The history of Israelite religion

Keel, Othmar, and Uehlinger, Christoph. *Gods, Goddesses, and Images of God in Ancient Israel*, trans. Allan W. Mahnke. Minneapolis: Fortress, 1997. Difficult, but good.

Beginnings of the Monarchy and Royal and Zion Texts

3

Chapter Overview

Imagining Early Monarchal Israel

The Rise of the Israelite Monarchy and Resistance to It

The Story of David's Succession

Influence of Ancient Empires on Early Israel's Monarchy and Writings

Echoes of Near Eastern Royal Theology in the Royal and Zion Psalms

Chapter Three Review

Resources for Further Study

CHAPTER OVERVIEW

This chapter examines the first steps toward a monarchy in ancient Israel and surveys biblical texts connected to this period. The first part gives a historical reconstruction of the development in Israel of a city-based kingship, a reconstruction that only partially agrees with the much later and highly theological narratives (in Samuel and Kings) about these events. Apparently, David and Solomon borrowed elements of foreign monarchies when they set up their capital in Jerusalem, particularly elements from Egypt, which had dominated the region up until a few centuries prior to their rule. One major element that the first Israelite kings borrowed from earlier monarchies was the use of written texts to reinforce more stable forms of "cultural memory" across their realm, indeed texts that often promoted the value of the monarchy and its capital, Zion. This chapter concludes with a survey of some pro-royal and pro-Zion texts in the Bible that may come from this period, some of which show similarities to older monarchal traditions in Egypt and Mesopotamia. These royal and Zion psalms, whose pro-royal perspective contrasts with the harsh judgments of later authors of Samuel and Kings, are the first of several biblical echoes of ancient empires

The Hebrew Bible: A Contemporary Introduction to the Christian Old Testament and the Jewish Tanakh, Second Edition. David M. Carr.
© 2021 David M. Carr. Published 2021 by John Wiley & Sons Ltd.

to be discussed in this and the next chapter. Read this chapter with an aim to penetrate beyond the later depiction of the monarchy in the stories of Samuel and 1 Kings to hints of an emergent Israelite monarchy. You can find such hints by reading between the lines of those narratives and analyzing biblical texts (especially royal psalms) potentially from that period.

Imagining Early Monarchal Israel

Once again, we start with an imaginary reconstruction of the context in which these biblical traditions were written. Our sources are few, varied, and disputed. Although the Bible describes Israel as a world power at the time of David and Solomon, it is likely that the Bible's picture of their glory is a fictional creation of an Israelite golden age. In developing the *beginnings* of a city-state monarchy, David and Solomon imitated foreign models for kingship. The following reconstruction of these monarchal beginnings is based on a combination of archaeological and biblical evidence.

Our journey takes us back to another hilltop in ancient Canaan, this time Mount **Zion**, a hilltop to the south of the heartland of tribal Israel. Generally speaking, "Zion" and the city associated with it, "Jerusalem," are synonymous in the Bible. What is less well known is that Jerusalem had a long history as a city before David conquered it and made it the capital of his kingdom. In Chapter 2, we discussed a letter from Abdi-heba, a king of pre-Davidic Jerusalem. This letter is but one sign that Jerusalem before David had its own cultural and political traditions. Moreover, David and his successors may have adapted some of the traditions of this ancient city in the process of setting up their fledgling kingdom. For example, the Bible contains a tantalizing suggestion that the pre-Israelite (Jebusite) inhabitants of the city already had a belief in Jerusalem's invulnerability. When David laid siege to Jerusalem, the Jebusites are said to have told David that "you will not come in, even the blind and lame will ward you off" (2 Sam 5:6). Such a claim that Jerusalem was unconquerable parallels later Biblical **Zion theology** – that is, theology about Jerusalem's specialness and invulnerability – that we will see in some of Israel's psalms and other literature.

Let us return now to imagining the Jerusalem of both Davidic and later, Solomonic, times. As it turned out, the Jebusites were wrong. David succeeded in conquering Jerusalem by stealth. He conquered it and made it the capital of his kingdom. Located between David's own clan of Judah in the southern hills and the Israelite tribes toward the north, the small stronghold in Jerusalem was well situated to function as the base for David's role now as leader of Israel, and he solidified this function by moving an object sacred to the Israelites, the ark of Yahweh at Shiloh, to Jerusalem (2 Samuel 6). The later Jerusalem of Solomon's time houses this ark in a new temple for Yahweh (see Figure 3.1), one that stands alongside a new palace for the king.

King Solomon serves in this city/stronghold as both high priest and commander of the army. Below him is a small but expanding class of priestly, royal, and military officials. This is a new form of leadership, showing an evolution under David from tribal structures to foreign models of monarchy, particularly as seen in Egypt. Solomon's court bears a resemblance to the Egyptian royal court, and many of its positions are filled by the sons of officials who served in David's court. Indeed, one of Solomon's scribes may even have had an Egyptian father, David's scribe "Shisha," whose name is quite similar to the Egyptian word for "scribe." These officials and those under them administrated the complex kingdom. They were the glue that held this broad kingdom of varied tribes and territories together.

This fledgling nation developed various provisions for continuity across space and time, building on models from the monarchies of surrounding nations. Previously, tribal culture had charismatic leaders such as Deborah who galvanized the people in a time of crisis. The development of a monarchy under Solomon and his successors allowed the people to achieve political stability through an ongoing royal dynasty. Where tribal culture depended on tribes volunteering to join others in resisting enemies, this monarchy had a standing army. And where groups in tribal culture shared ever-fluid *oral* traditions, this monarchy resembled other such monarchies in beginning to use *written* texts to reinforce and standardize oral memory. These written texts were not accessible to everyone in a largely non-literate society, but they provided an essential way to educate the new ruling class for this more expansive realm. By memorizing a specific collection of written texts, youths preparing to be leaders learned a common worldview that persisted across space and time. The scribes of Israel's early monarchy are the probable authors of the first such collection of longer Israelite writings.

FIGURE 3.1
Artist's reconstruction of Solomon's Jerusalem. The Temple is on the upper right, next down is the palace, and then the citadel of David with a stepped-stone structure supporting it.

INITIAL READING

David's early reign: 2 Samuel 3–6 and then 2 Samuel 8.
Excerpts from a late account of Solomon's Glory: 1 Kings 4–8 and then 9:10–28
(see end of chapter for more on 2 Samuel 9–20; 1 Kings 1–2).

The Rise of the Israelite Monarchy and Resistance to It

Before looking at the earliest Hebrew texts, we need to appreciate the city-state context in which they were created. In Chapter 2, we saw how Israel emerged as a loose association of villages organized into tribes, settled largely in the northern hill country of Palestine. They were a "people," not a city-state. Their limited resources and social organization made it difficult for them to resist raids by neighboring tribes or attempts to dominate them by nearby city-states. Aside from the rise of temporary leaders in times of crisis, "judges" in the Bible, there were no elite classes. The people shared common access to the orally transmitted "cultural memory" that helped identify them as Israelites. The book of 1 Samuel, written hundreds of years after the period it narrates, gives many explanations for why this tribal existence under judges came to an end: the people requested a king because Samuel's sons were corrupt, or because they wanted to imitate other nations, or because they wanted a human king instead of Yahweh as king. These explanations say more about the perspective of much later authors than they do about the true dynamics surrounding kingship. Meanwhile, another, unnamed force probably played a much bigger role in the beginnings of the monarchy: the Israelites accepted kingship under David and his successors because it was the only form of social organization that was centralized enough to repel the Philistine invasions into the hill country of central Palestine. The Bible records clashes between Israelites and Philistines in stories about Samson (Judges 14–16), the time of Samuel (1 Sam 4:1–7:1), Saul (1 Samuel 13–31), and David (2 Samuel 5 and 8). Saul, a member of the tribe of Benjamin, was anointed as king to repel the Philistines. Nevertheless, in some respects Saul was little more than a powerful local military leader. He did not develop a city capital or a professional army, and he achieved only limited success before being killed in battle with the Philistines, along with his heir Jonathan (1 Samuel 31//2 Chronicles 10). Saul's leadership was not the sort of "kingship" needed to repel the Philistines. It was really more of a "chieftainship."

We see more characteristics of kingship with David and especially his heir, Solomon. Within biblical texts, David is remembered as a paradoxical mix. On the one hand, several texts depict him as a king "faithful" to Yahweh (e.g. 1 Kgs 3:6). On the other hand, he is flawed enough to seduce an officer's wife, Bathsheba, and send her husband to certain death in order to be able to marry her (2 Samuel 11–12). In the broader scheme of things, however, David appears to have been an extraordinarily gifted military

Archaeology and Problems of History Surrounding David, Solomon and the Beginning of the Israelite Monarchy

As noted at the outset of this chapter, the Bible's description of David and Solomon's monarchy has been thoroughly shaped by later authors into a picture of a golden age. Those authors do not even seem to have known specific dates for the beginning and ends of the reigns of these two kings. Instead, these later writers assert that both David and Solomon had forty-year long reigns (1 Kgs 2:11; 11:42). The round number forty was widely-used to designate "a very long time." Other aspects of the narrative also seem questionable, such as the idea that Solomon's wisdom was so famous that other kings and queens flocked to Jerusalem with gifts of gold, silver and other valuables to seek his counsel (1 Kgs 4:29-34 [Hebrew 5:9-14]; 10:1-25). There is actually no mention of Solomon in any preserved texts from other nations of the time, and it is unlikely that a leader in a tiny provincial town like Jerusalem would have attracted such attention. Finally, archaeologists have not succeeded in finding much evidence of major construction in Jerusalem during the overall time that the Bible attributes to their two, supposed forty-year reigns when David supposedly built a place and Solomon a temple (approximately 1010 to 930 BCE). Together, these sorts of data have led some to doubt that David and Solomon even existed, or if they did, whether they established much of a centralized monarchy. Nevertheless, we do see mention of "the house of David" in a Syrian inscription (the "Tel Dan Stele") written in the century after David and Solomon. Only discovered in 1993, this apparent reference to the dynasty of David suggests that he founded some kind of political structure, even if his and Solomon's kingdoms were not as grand as later biblical authors made them out to be. For more on archaeology, biblical study and questions surrounding the kingdoms of David and Solomon, see Matthieu Richelle, *The Bible and Archaeology* (trans. Sarah E. Richelle; Peabody, Mass: Hendrickson, 2018).

Not all Israelites were happy with the changes that came with David's and Solomon's rule. Though surely they were glad to see the Philistine threat contained, many perceived David and especially Solomon as Judean versions of the oppressive kings they had just defeated. After all, village-culture Israelites now had a new burden to add to the struggle for everyday existence. Not only did they need to find a way to provide for their kin each year, but they also had to provide substantial resources to the king and his city-state, both a portion of their crops and providing laborers on a rotation for the kings' construction projects. The unhappiness of tribal leaders over this led to several rebellions against David's kingship, mainly centered in the north, where people in the heartland of ancient tribal "Israel" were the least happy with being ruled by Judah. One such rebellion was led by Absalom, David's own son; another was led by Sheba, a leader from the Israelite north; and the final and successful one was led by Jeroboam, who will be discussed more in Chapter 4. What is important for our purposes now is an appreciation that the leaders in this early monarchy had to contend with opponents, particularly those associated with the Israelite north, who doubted the benefits of this new monarchy. The (proto) monarchy was a major new form of communal life, with many foreign elements, that involved many costs as well as benefits.

commander who established the groundwork for a monarchy that would last hundreds of years.

David started as an officer in Saul's Israelite army, and he was so militarily successful against the Philistines that he had to flee Saul's jealous wrath (see 1 Samuel 16–29). Later, when Saul died, David ruled his tribe, Judah, for a few years from the Judean town of Hebron, while Saul's son Eshbaal ruled Israel (2 Samuel 2–3). Then, when Eshbaal was assassinated, the Israelite leaders anointed David as king over them, so that David became king of both Judah and Israel (2 Sam 4:1–5:5). One of the first things he did as ruler of both peoples was to start a series of campaigns against the Philistines that permanently ended their threat to Judah and Israel (2 Sam 5:17–25; 8:1; see also 2 Sam 21:15–22).

Yet David did much more than defeat the Philistines. He introduced societal changes associated with kingship: city-based rule, organization of a professional army, and enforcement of taxes on the people to support the fortified city and army. First, David captured the Jebusite city of Jerusalem, by stealth, and made it the capital of his new kingdom (2 Sam 5:6–16). This was a politically smart move for a Judean king claiming authority over Israel. Jerusalem was not identified with the southern tribe of Judah the way that Hebron was. Second, David solidified Jerusalem's claim as the capital of "Israel" by bringing into it the ark of the covenant, an object sacred to all the Israelite tribes (2 Samuel 6). Third, he achieved additional military success, in particular over the Philistine tribes that had troubled Israel up through the time of Saul (1 Samuel 5). Fourth and finally, he started to build longer-term city-state structures, solidifying ties with neighboring groups through marriage alliances (2 Sam 3:2–5) and developing an effective army (from 1 Sam 22:1–2 to 2 Sam 23:8–39). He even appears to have followed Egyptian models in developing the beginnings of a royal court, eventually one that also included a position for "forced labor" of his citizens to help with fortifying the country (2 Sam 20:23–26; compare with 2 Sam 8:16–18).

David's successor, Solomon, went yet further in developing the beginnings of a city-state monarchy based in Jerusalem. After being put in power by a virtual coup d'état implemented by his mother, Bathsheba (working in concert with several of David's close associates; see 1 Kings 1–2), Solomon started construction projects that would enhance the Jerusalem stronghold's claim to be the center of a Near Eastern city-state such as building a palace for the king and a temple for Yahweh (1 Kgs 6–8). To do this, Solomon required significant resources. The Bible reports that he established a system of forced labor across Israel to support these construction efforts (1 Kgs 5:27–32), building an infrastructure of 12 administrators over the tribal areas of northern Israel (1 Kgs 4:7–19). Especially since elements like forced labor were seen by some biblical authors as a negative aspect of kingship (see, e.g., the sentiments we see attributed to Samuel in 1 Sam 8:11–17), it is unlikely that later authors created such elements in an effort to build up Israel's glorious past. Instead, Solomon appears to have gone beyond his predecessors in implementing a fuller form of kingship in early Israel, even as his accomplishments, and the regions that he and David were said to rule were much embellished and expanded upon by later authors.

Skim 2 Samuel 9–20 and 1 Kings 1–2 (read the introduction below before reading these chapters).

READING

The Story of David's Succession

Though the Bible's story of early monarchs is generally unreliable, there is a good chance that the stories surrounding the succession to David in 2 Samuel 9–20 and 1 Kings 1–2 preserve early materials. A number of scholars have hypothesized that they contain remnants of an early **Succession Narrative** written after Solomon succeeded to the throne. This narrative contains a number of unflattering stories about David and his family:

1. A story of the birth of David's successor, Solomon, from an illicit union that David had with Bathsheba, the wife of one of his warriors (2 Sam 11:1–12:24).

2. A story about how David's oldest son, Amnon, rapes his daughter, Tamar, and then David's third son, Absalom, kills Amnon in revenge and flees (2 Sam 13).

3. David's near loss of his kingdom when Absalom returns (2 Sam 14) and is barely defeated in a revolt he leads against his father (2 Sam 15–19).

4. Another revolt against David's rule, this time led by a figure, Sheba, from the central Hill Country tribe of Benjamin (2 Sam 20).

5. A battle for succession between David's next son in line, Adonijah, and Solomon, which Solomon and his allies win, while Adonijah and his allies die (1 Kgs 1–2).

Scholars continue to debate whether these stories are early and how much they reflect the actual history of David's reign. Nevertheless, if the Bible preserves any early narrative about David and Solomon, these chapters are the best candidates to preserve parts of it. Later authors probably would not have created such an uncomplimentary, yet relatively non-theological, account of David and Solomon. An early scribe working in the court of the Davidic monarchy, however, could have deemed it necessary to compose this highly untypical court history in order to establish Solomon's legitimacy as a true heir of David, especially given the deep divisions surrounding his rise to power (1 Kings 1–2). The reliability of this account would have been underlined by the fact that its sober descriptions of David's and others' actions were recognized as true by contemporaries. At the same time, taken as a whole, these stories disqualify Solomon's older sons from a claim to kingship (Amnon, Absalom, Adonijah) and establish that Solomon was a true son of David, albeit from an illicit union with Bathsheba.

Whatever the date and origins of this Succession Narrative, it contains some of the Bible's most fascinating storytelling. These chapters rarely moralize or theologize. Instead, they provide a nuanced rendering of a series of missteps and tragedies of David and his heirs. In the end, Solomon rises to power amidst a battle between two groups (1 Kgs 1:5–8): one supporting Adonijah that was led by Joab (David's general) and Abiathar (a priest under David before Jerusalem) and a group supporting Solomon that was led by Benaiah (a leader of David's foreign mercenaries), Zadok (a priest, possibly Jebusite), and the prophet Nathan. Read these stories for an account of the moral ambiguities surrounding Israel's earliest kings. In addition, reading between the lines, one can detect Israelite resistance to the monarchy among those supporting various rebellions. It may be that some of the royal hymns discussed in the next section were formulated to address doubts about David's kingship voiced by supporters of Absalom and Sheba.

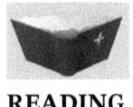

READING

See below for an exercise comparing 2 Sam 23:1–7 with Psalms 2, 21, 72, and 110.

Influence of Ancient Empires on Early Israel's Monarchy and Writings

David and Solomon did not start from scratch when they began to develop the Israelite monarchy and associated Jerusalemite city-state. They were adopting a more ancient social form that was known elsewhere. After all, city-states had been around in Mesopotamia, Syria, Egypt, and even Palestine from the third millennium onward. Indeed, as we have seen, Jerusalem itself was the site of a small, pre-Israelite, Jebusite stronghold that had once been dominated by Egypt. There are numerous signs that David and Solomon drew on older Egyptian and other models in building the monarchy in Jerusalem: the makeup of their royal court, the models used for construction of temple and palace, etc. These are non-textual "echoes of empire" seen in the emergent Davidic monarchy in Jerusalem.

Yet there is another sort of "echo of empire" to be discussed here, and that is the way some biblical texts appear to reflect pre-Israelite texts that were used in the much older empires of Mesopotamia and Egypt. One thing that distinguished many ancient monarchies from the tribal groups surrounding them was their use of written texts, including the sorts of texts found in the Bible: wisdom sayings, psalms, myths, and stories (see Figure 3.2). These written texts were a form of cultural memory like the oral traditions that continued to exist. Nevertheless, there were important differences. Most importantly, the relative firmness of written traditions made them good tools for shaping elites across time and across space. Written texts do not change as readily as oral traditions do. This was important in city-states and empires, which spanned greater distances and joined disparate groups together. An empire or even a centralized city-state could bind together its different parts by making sure that its leaders all learned writing and memorized the same educational texts.

Our best examples of such literary education come from Egypt and Mesopotamia, much larger civilizations whose texts are better preserved (in Egypt because of climate, in Mesopotamia because they used clay tablets). The evidence from Egypt and Mesopotamia shows how students were educated in homes, often learning to read texts from either their own fathers or teachers whom they called "father." Ancient education in Egypt and Mesopotamia followed a similar pattern, a pattern probably common across the ancient world. Students started by learning to write and read basic symbols. The next step was memorizing and reciting basic "wisdom" instructions on how to live, and the final and most advanced stage was internalizing and performing other types of texts, such as royal hymns or stories of creation and flood. Careful analysis of student exercises, such as that seen in Figure 3.3, has allowed scholars to see how students in these cultures were taught to memorize their culture's texts line by line. Only a few in any ancient society had time to acquire such knowledge, but it was an important means by which Egypt, Mesopotamia, and other cultures trained future leaders.

This background from the cultures of Egypt and Mesopotamia is important because their educational-literary systems were used as models for the monarchies of Syria-Palestine in the centuries just before Israel emerged. During the thousand years before Israel's emergence many local city-states had scribes who had learned to read and write Mesopotamian texts, even using Akkadian (a Mesopotamian language) to correspond with rulers in Egypt. In addition, Egypt itself exercised cultural influence in the area, especially in the coastland cities of Phoenicia. The Bible itself records how Solomon was dependent on the Phoenician city of Tyre for supplies and know-how in constructing the Temple (1 Kgs 5:15–25; 7:13–47). We now have ancient inscriptions from the time of David and Solomon – such as the alphabet found at Tel Zayit (see Figure 3.4) – that likewise document the adoption of the 22-letter Phoenician alphabet in Judah, Israel, and surrounding nations. They are precious clues to the adoption, during the early Israelite monarchy, of a major ancient means for uniting broader kingdoms: systems of writing and education (see Figure 3.5).

FIGURE 3.2
Scribe standing before the king of a small neighboring kingdom with a scroll in his hand, dating from about a century after David and Solomon. The image shows the prestige attached to scribal writing even in the small kingdoms of the area.

The kingdom of David and Solomon was far too small to develop its own brand-new counterpart to the massive literatures of those ancient empires. Thus when scribes began writing the first Israelite literary texts in Jerusalem, it seems that they did *not* focus on creating textual versions of earlier Israelite oral traditions about ancestors, exodus, or the like. Instead, the earliest authors of Hebrew literature were dependent on *foreign* models for literary education and imitated *foreign* texts from Egypt and Mesopotamia. Why? Perhaps because in creating Israel's first written literature these early Judean scribes were most interested in adapting earlier examples of such writings (all of which were foreign), and thus drawing on their prestige to buttress new leadership structures, rather than transforming properly oral traditions from the Israelite tribal north. So they started to write Hebrew versions of the sorts of texts used elsewhere to educate leaders for their emergent monarchy: hymns about the king, instructions on proper living, etc.

In this chapter we will look at two types of texts that show particularly close links to the monarchy and some reliance on foreign models as well: royal and Zion psalms. Though some of these texts are attributed to David or Solomon, none were written by those kings personally, and many probably originate from later periods in the monarchy (see the box p. 69). Yet, whether dating from the time of David and Solomon or later, these texts provide another crucial example of how Israel modeled key texts on the traditions of surrounding empires. Comparing Israel's royal psalms with non-biblical hymns can teach us much about how such hymns were used and what made them special.

FIGURE 3.3
Mesopotamian student exercise tablet where the teacher wrote a couple of lines of an educational text on the top half and the student copied below.

Labels (e.g. "Psalm of David"): What They (Don't) Tell Us

As noted above, we must be careful about how much weight we put on associations of psalms and other texts with kings like David or Solomon. Ancient texts could be attributed to authors for a variety of reasons – to continue a stream of tradition associated with a given ancient figure, to gain authority through being associated with an ancient figure, etc.

Therefore, when we see a text such as Psalm 110 assigned to David, this may mean that it was written at the time of David by one of David's scribes, or it may just mean that this psalm was seen as part of a longer tradition of Davidic psalms. Similarly, labels that assign the Song of Songs, Ecclesiastes, and most parts of Proverbs to Solomon do not mean that Solomon wrote these texts. Instead, some may have been written at the time of Solomon, while others may just be part of a broader stream of "Solomonic" tradition extending even to apocryphal texts, such as the Wisdom of Solomon.

That said, the Bible's attribution of texts to figures such as David or Solomon can still be significant. For one thing, they are among the first Judean or Israelite figures in the Bible to have whole biblical texts attributed to them. The attributions of texts to David and Solomon may be recollections, preserved in the Bible, that David and Solomon's *time* was the first phase of the development of Israelite literature.

It should be emphasized that there is no usable historical information in the smaller collection of superscriptions that place certain psalms at particular points in David's life. These include, for example, the superscription to Psalm 51 (a confessional psalm) that locates that psalm in David's life just after Nathan had confronted him about having an affair with Bathsheba and murdering her husband, Uriah, by arranging to have him die in battle (story in 2 Sam 11:1–12:23). Such historicizing superscriptions are marked by their language and theology as later additions to the Psalter and represent examples of early biblical interpretation.

FIGURE 3.4 Letters inscribed into the surface of a stone, with an overlay indicating their shape. The stone was found embedded in a wall from the tenth century BCE.

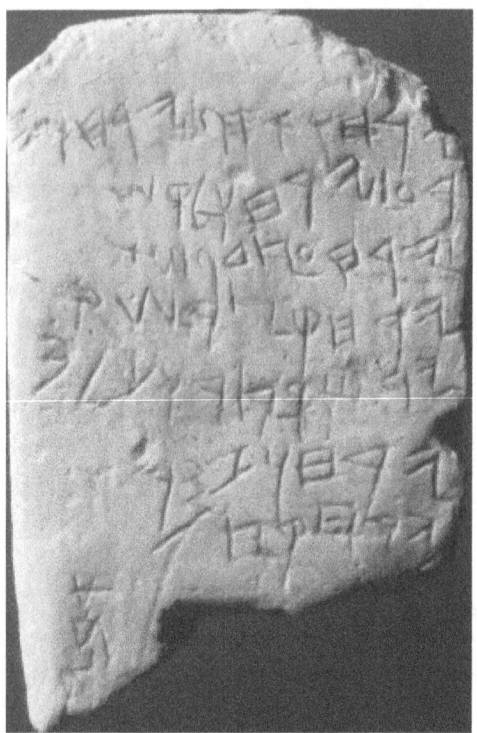

FIGURE 3.5
The "Gezer Calendar." This may be an early educational exercise. It lists what was done in the months of the agricultural year of ancient Canaan.

Echoes of Near Eastern Royal Theology in the Royal and Zion Psalms

One of the main emphases in the literature of ancient empires was the monarchy. For example, Egyptian enthronement texts describe the new king (Pharaoh) receiving a document on which were written his throne names, climaxing with the throne name that marked his status as the only begotten son of the sun god, Re. Temple reliefs show the process by which Re conceived the king, not through intercourse, but through spreading his aroma over the king's mother. By the end of the process, Re equipped the king with all he needed to rule the world in Re's place, proclaiming:

> Son of my body, beloved, lord of the righteousness [Maat] of Re, whose body I have made with me in the palace, I give you all life and wellbeing, to appear as the king of Upper and Lower Egypt on the throne of Horus.

Meanwhile, we also have hymns used in Egyptian education that taught students to celebrate the Egyptian king's power to vanquish wrongdoing and establish prosperity. The following one focuses on the Pharaoh Merneptah:

> Be glad of heart, the entire land! The good times have come. A lord – life, prosperity, health – is given in all lands, and normality has

returned to its place. The king of Upper and Lower Egypt, the lord of millions of years, great of kingship like Horus . . . he who bestows happiness on Egypt, the son of Re, most competent of any king, Merneptah – life, prosperity, health.

All you who are righteous, come that you may see! Right has banished wrong. Evildoers have fallen on their faces. The oppressors are ignored.

(ANET 378, adapted)

Similar themes appear in the royal literature of ancient Mesopotamia. For example, we find the following proclamation to the king in an ancient Babylonian coronation ritual:

May Assur and Ninlil, the lords of your crown, set your crown on your head for a hundred years! May your foot in Ekur and your hands stretched toward the breast of Assur, your God, be pleasing! May your priesthood and the priesthood of your sons be pleasing to Assur, your god! With your straight scepter widen your land! May Assur give you authority, obedience, concord, justice and peace!

(Translation: Livingstone, 472)

Royal texts from both ancient Mesopotamia and Egypt emphasized the choosing of the king by the high god of the pantheon, the king's appointment as the highest authority and priest of the land, his overcoming of all enemies in the name of the god, and his bestowing of justice and peace on the land through his rule. Together, these and other themes comprise what is meant here by **"royal theology."**

Read the following (royal) psalms and make a list of ideas that come up two or more times in them: 2 Sam 23:1–7; Psalms 2, 21, 72, and 110. Include citations in your notes of where each idea occurred. How do these texts form a coherent royal theology that answers the sorts of concerns voiced by Absalom in 2 Sam 15:1–6 or Sheba in 2 Sam 20:1? Now look at some common themes in Pss 9, 15, 46, and 48. These are later psalms that celebrate Zion (//Jerusalem) and articulate what scholars refer to as "Zion theology."

EXERCISE

Many elements of Egyptian and Mesopotamian royal theology are common in the **royal psalms** of the Hebrew Bible (Psalms 2, 18, 20, 21, 45, 72, 89, 110, and 144; along with 2 Sam 23:1–7). These poetic texts feature a distinctive focus on the king and his relationship with God. For example, Psalm 110 opens with a call for the king to sit at the right hand of God (Ps 110:1), a common motif in ancient Egyptian royal art. Its picture of the king subduing his enemies (Ps 110:1–3a) is typical of ancient royal literature, whether Egyptian or Mesopotamian. The latter part of verse 3, however, contains an obscure text whose meaning may be clarified when we look back to Egyptian royal ideology. God proclaims to the king: "from the womb of dawn, I fathered you like dew." Recall that the sun god, Re, in Egypt conceived the king through spreading his aroma over the king's mother. The Egyptian word for "aroma" rhymes with the Hebrew word for "dew." In speaking of Yahweh "fathering" the king "like dew before the womb of the dawn," Psalm 110 seems to apply these ideas to the Judean king. The psalm then hearkens back to the pre-Israelite royal traditions of Jerusalem in reporting God's oath to give the king eternal priesthood "according to the order of Melkizedeq" (110:4), a figure remembered elsewhere in the Bible as one of Jerusalem's kings in the time before David (Gen 14:18). Next come pictures of the king destroying his enemies (Ps 110:5–6) that are quite typical of ancient royal literature, before the psalm concludes with a reference to the king's drinking from Jerusalem's spring (Ps 110:7). Apparently, the Judean king was anointed near the Gihon spring in Jerusalem (1 Kgs 1:33–34, 38–39). Thus Psalm 110 is a good example of a psalm whose obscure references can be understood when we see how it adapts ancient ideas about kingship recalled from pre-Davidic Jerusalem and the yet older royal theologies of Egypt and Mesopotamia. It does not depend on any specific pre-Israelite text, but in a broader way it contains "echoes of ancient empires."

The same can be said of many other biblical royal psalms. Just as the Egyptian king received a written decree from the gods proclaiming his status as the "son of Re," so Psalm 2 has the king report receiving a similar decree from Yahweh:

> I will proclaim the decree of Yahweh.
> He said to me, "You are my son,
> I have fathered you today.
> Ask me, and I will give nations as your birthright,
> The entire world as your possession."
>
> (Ps 2:7–8)

This theme of God offering the king whatever he wants, especially military victory (Ps 2:8), is found in other royal psalms as well (Ps 21:2; see also 1 Kgs 3:5), and is a major feature of ancient Egyptian and Mesopotamian royal theology. Over and over again the texts of these ancient empires emphasize that it is the king who is authorized to call on God for military help. The king, and the king alone, is authorized by God to ask for and achieve military success for his people, and one of the main jobs of the king in ancient Egyptian and Mesopotamian royal texts is to destroy the people's enemies.

This emphasis in royal psalms on the king's violent power can seem harsh to contemporary readers, particularly those in Europe or North America who have not personally experienced the direct threat of military attack. To ancient Israelites, however, such words sounded differently. Though many may have been inclined to follow calls such as Absalom's or Sheba's to reject the monarchy, these royal psalms insist that the king was appointed by God and would protect and defend them against any threat like that of the Philistines. In the process, the psalms draw on older Near Eastern royal imagery – e.g. divine "fathering" of the king, setting the king at God's right hand, the grant of the king's wishes – to justify the Jerusalem monarchy to skeptical Israelites.

One other important theme in these royal psalms is the emphasis on the importance to the kingship of "social responsibility" – Hebrew ***tsedeqah***. This Hebrew word is usually translated into English as "righteousness," but it refers more specifically to the virtue of fulfilling one's social obligations to others, particularly defending those most vulnerable in ancient society: the orphan, widow, and foreign immigrant (the "stranger" or "alien"). For example, 2 Sam 23:3 notes that the king must rule with such "social solidarity" to dawn on his people like the morning light, and virtually all of Psalm 72, a "psalm of Solomon," is a prayer that God may give the king the power to rule his people with such *tsedeqah*:

> Give the king your justice, O God,
> and your social solidarity to the royal son!
> May he judge your people with social solidarity [*tsedeqah*],
> and your poor with justice!
>
> (Ps 72:1–2)

Basics

Book of Psalms: Part 1

(For basics on "Book of Psalms: Part 2," see box on p. 243.)

Multiple levels in the book of Psalms

The book of Psalms was created over a very long period of time. It contains some of Israel's earliest texts. Yet it was still being expanded late into Israel's history. This mix of ancient and later texts in Psalms reflects the fact that these texts were integrally linked to and reflected shifts in the lives of Israelites as they faced ever different individual and national challenges.

Tracking down the earliest psalms

It is impossible to be sure whether a given psalm comes from the pre-exilic period, let alone from the time of David and Solomon. Nevertheless, most scholars agree that some psalms are good candidates for being among Israel's earliest literature. Some hymns, such as the praise of the storm god in Psalm 29, may have originated as pre-Israelite hymns to other gods before being adapted for Israelite use. Some other potentially early psalms mention the king, ark, or Zion, such as the celebration in Psalm 132 of Yahweh's choice of Zion and David's moving of the ark there. It is relatively unlikely that Israelite authors wrote all such references after the destruction of the monarchy and the Zion Temple with its ark.

Other potentially early psalms?

The examples discussed above point to the probable existence of early psalms across the book of Psalms. They stand as potential indicators that *some* of the other psalms that lack such historical references, such as some psalms of lament or trust, may also originate from Israel's early periods. Such texts about individual suffering or rescue are inherently difficult to date. Luckily, such dating is relatively unimportant for their interpretation.

These texts show that Israelite kingship aimed to be an institution that protected the formerly vulnerable peoples of Israel's hill country and provided true justice. As we will see, the monarchy – like all human institutions – did not always live up to its highest aims, and Israelites rebelled against the monarchy several times. Nevertheless, these psalms show how Israel's kingship was meant to be an institution through which God provided both protection and care for the most vulnerable of God's people.

These same values of justice and social solidarity are also prominent in another group of psalms, often termed **"Zion psalms"** because of their common emphasis on the special significance of Zion/Jerusalem, the capital of the new monarchy. For example, Psalm 9 describes how God who dwells in Zion "judges the peoples with social solidarity" (9:8) and is "a stronghold for the oppressed" (9:9). Psalms 15 and 24 are ancient liturgies for those making a pilgrimage to Zion. These psalms bar from Zion those who cannot affirm that they have "clean hands and a pure heart" (24:4) and do not exploit others through lending practices (15:5). Zion, at the heart of ancient Jerusalem, was the mountain where God dwelt. Those who would come there had to hold themselves to a higher standard of behavior. They were expected to be just as the God of Zion is just. Furthermore, these and other psalms repeatedly assert what will be one of the most important claims of Zion theology: that Jerusalem, the dwelling place of God, is invulnerable to foreign attack. See, for example, the description of Jerusalem/Zion in Psalm 46:

> There is a river whose streams bring joy to the city of God,
> The holy dwelling of the most high.
> God is in the midst of her [the city], she shall not fall.
> God will rescue her at the break of day.
>
> (46:4–5)

Though at least some of these royal and Zion psalms were written or revised at later points in the history of the Jerusalem monarchy, they stand as excellent examples of how early Israelites – who had lived for hundreds of years in hilltop villages – made theological sense of this new social form: a new monarchy set in a new capital, Jerusalem. Later Jewish and Christian interpreters, of course, have reinterpreted many of these psalms, so that – for example – the king praised in texts such as Psalm 2 or 110 is understood to be the Messiah. Such reinterpretations can be legitimate, since these texts would not have survived and become part of the Hebrew Bible if later readers had understood them only to be relevant to a monarchy that would eventually perish. Yet these texts should also be understood in their historical context. As such, they are a witness to some of Israel's earliest ideas about power and community, ideas which would prove very important to the later writers of prophecies and histories.

More on Method: Poetic Analysis

Poetry in the Bible does not have the kind of sound rhymes found in much English-language poetry. Instead, it is characterized by a phenomenon called "**seconding**," where the second line of a poetic **couplet** – or pair of lines – builds on the idea or imagery of the first line, but somehow takes it further. Some poems may have a **triplet** (or more). In triplets the stress is on the final, third line, which builds on and advances the idea(s) or imagery of the first two. Take the example of the following triplet from Psalm 110, a royal psalm:

> 2) The LORD sends out from Zion
>   your mighty scepter
>   *Rule in the midst of your foes.*
>
>   (NRSV)

Note how a translation like the NRSV marks a triplet like this through slightly indenting the second and third lines. These indentations of about 2 spaces indicate where the translators locate the Hebrew line breaks.

The example above uses italics for the third and climactic, seconding, line of the triplet. If you are analyzing a couplet or triplet, it is a good idea to write it out this way and underline or highlight the final line. Look at the parallels and differences between this final line and the two lines that precede it. How do the first two lines prepare for the final line and what is the impact of concluding the triplet this way? Can you identify an emotional impact of this poetic couplet in addition to summarizing it?

Take a Bible with the NRSV and try to find and analyze the poetic units in verse 3 of Psalm 110. (Hint: according to the NRSV, there is a triplet and a couplet here.)

For more see Robert Alter, *The Art of Biblical Poetry* (New York: Basic Books, 1985).

CHAPTER THREE REVIEW

For Review

1 Know the meaning and significance of the following terms discussed in this chapter:
   - couplet
   - royal psalms
   - royal theology
   - seconding
   - Succession Narrative
   - triplet
   - *tsedeqah*
   - Zion
   - Zion psalms
   - Zion theology
2 Can you take a translation that marks poetic couplets and triplets (such as the NRSV, NIV, or NAB) and identify couplets and triplets in biblical poems?

3 What was the major reason that scholars think a monarchy arose in Israel? How is this different from other reasons given in the stories of 1 Samuel?

4 What role did writing play in the emergent monarchy? How was this related to orality and memorization?

5 What do the mentions of David in psalm superscriptions tell and not tell us?

For Reflection

6 Some scholars working from a liberation perspective believe that the rise of the monarchy was a "counterrevolution" – a step back from struggle for justice. For them, royal and Zion theology are an oppressive strand of biblical tradition that must be distinguished from liberative strands of biblical theology such as those seen in the exodus story (or biblical prophets such as Amos). Others argue that justice and righteousness stand at the heart of royal and Zion theology and that the survival of Israel and its traditions (including traditions about exodus and justice) depended on the emergence of a monarchy. Which perspective do you find more compelling and why?

RESOURCES FOR FURTHER STUDY

McCarter, P. Kyle. *I–II Samuel*. 2 volumes. Garden City: Doubleday, 1980, 1984.

Interlude: Echoes of Past Empires in Biblical Wisdom, Love Poetry, Law, and Narrative

Chapter Overview

Echoes of Texts from Earlier Empires in Writings Attributed to Solomon

Focus Text: The Speech of Lady Wisdom in Proverbs 8

Echoes of Texts from Earlier Empires Elsewhere in the Bible

Focus Text: The Garden of Eden Story (Genesis 2–3)

Conclusion

Chapter Four Review

Resources for Further Study

CHAPTER OVERVIEW

In this chapter we look at some texts in the Bible that contain strong "echoes" of past ancient empires. Several such texts are associated with Solomon (e.g. Proverbs, Ecclesiastes, Song of Songs), while others are originally anonymous. For example, some of the most interesting echoes of earlier non-biblical texts can be found in anonymous stories of creation and flood in Genesis 1–9. As we will see, the dating of all these texts is quite unclear, even ones that are now associated with Solomon. None were authored by him, and most were written, or at least revised, in later periods. Nevertheless, these texts provide good illustrations of how the Bible echoes very ancient texts from non-Israelite cultures. Also, they illustrate how much we can learn from comparison of biblical texts with their earlier, Near Eastern precursors.

The Hebrew Bible: A Contemporary Introduction to the Christian Old Testament and the Jewish Tanakh, Second Edition. David M. Carr.
© 2021 David M. Carr. Published 2021 by John Wiley & Sons Ltd.

READING

Prov 6:20–8:36; 10:1–32; 22:17–29.
Ecclesiastes 1:1–3:22 and Song of Songs 1:1–2:7.

Echoes of Texts from Earlier Empires in Writings Attributed to Solomon

The previous chapter discussed the rise of a monarchy under David and (particularly) Solomon, a monarchy that began a process of adapting other nations' written traditions into texts that found their way into the Bible. Interestingly, some of the most striking echoes of such foreign texts are found in biblical books attributed to Solomon: Proverbs, Song of Songs, and Ecclesiastes (hereafter usually referred to by its Hebrew name, Qohelet). This does not, of course, mean, that Solomon wrote these books, any more than David was the actual author of the psalms attributed to him (see Chapter 3, box on p. 69). And indeed, the form of the Hebrew language found in Song of Songs and Qohelet resembles the Hebrew that was written centuries after the time of Solomon. Nevertheless, whatever their date, these books were attributed to Solomon partly because they reflect the kind of international wisdom for which he was so famous (1 Kgs 5:9–14; 10). We turn to them now as an extension of the previous chapter's discussion of ways that important biblical texts echo the earlier texts from Egypt and Mesopotamia.

Take, for example, the Song of Songs (otherwise known as Song of Solomon or Canticles), an often overlooked book of passionate love poetry at the heart of the Hebrew Bible. Though early Jewish and Christian communities often read this book as a love dialogue between God and God's beloved community (whether church or synagogue), the book's closest parallels are secular love songs found in Egypt just before the emergence of Israel. Those ancient Egyptian love poems and their parallels in the biblical Song of Songs do not describe the love affairs of gods. The Song of Songs does not ever clearly refer to Yahweh! Instead, like the Egyptian love poetry it most resembles, the Song of Songs is focused on the drama of human physical love: desiring, seeking, losing, and seeking again human passion with one's true love. Moreover, like the love literature that it echoes, the Song of Songs presents a positive, not fearful, picture of female desire. Unlike many other biblical books, the Song foregrounds the words and wishes of a female figure, one who proclaims that she is "black" and "beautiful" (Song 1:4). This woman is a powerful figure, not afraid to ask her lover for what she wants and speaking more than half of the words of the book. Nowhere in the book is she judged for her desire, nor is her lover, even though their love remains frustratingly secret and forbidden (Song 8:1–2).

Basics

Song of Songs

It has proven difficult to find a systematic pattern in the loosely connected love poems that make up the Song of Songs. The following is a rough overview based particularly on the striking set of parallel refrains across the Song (2:7; 3:5; 8:4). These refrains structure a series of love songs spoken by a woman to a man and vice versa, something that is made clear by the distinct male and female pronouns in the original Hebrew of the Song. The student is highly encouraged to consult an English translation that identifies the distinct speeches of these male and female characters.

Outline

I	Introduction of themes	1:1–2:7
	Seeking day/night scenes	2:8–3:5
	Riches and praise	3:6–5:1
	Seeking night scene	5:2–6:3
	Riches and praise	6:4–8:3
II	Concluding statements on themes	8:4–14

Date

Most scholars would date the Song of Songs to the third or fourth centuries BCE, centuries after Solomon, particularly because of late features in its language. A minority see indicators of earlier origins of these materials, such as the way they resemble Egyptian and other early love songs.

Theme: Sex, God, and the Poetics of the Song

Many readers insist that one must decide that the Song is *either* about human desire *or* about divine–human love. The poetry of the Song, however, is more elusive. The dense metaphors and disconnected dialogues invite readers to build their own images of what is happening. The lack of explicit divine references and other features of the Song suggest that the book was meant to evoke the drama of human love. Still, the poetry allows multiple readings, especially now that the Song stands in a Bible that elsewhere depicts God's love for God's people (e.g. the book of Hosea, to be discussed later in this textbook).

> **More on Method: Afrocentric and Womanist Interpretation of the Bible**
>
> Partly because it features a dark-skinned female figure, the Song of Songs has been a focus for a number of African American studies of the Bible. Where the King James version and related translations often translated Song of Songs 1:4 as "I am black, *but* beautiful" [emphasis added] **Afrocentric** interpreters like Kenneth Waters argued persuasively that the Hebrew of the verse supports an affirmation of black beauty, "I am black *and* beautiful" ["The Beauty of Blackness" pp. 56–64 in *Afrocentric Sermons: Beauty of Blackness in the Bible* [Valley Forge, PA: Judson, 1993]). Such **Afrocentric interpretation** foregrounds and celebrates the bodies and cultures of people of African descent, while a **womanist approach** to interpretation more specifically builds on and foregrounds the experience, wisdom, and/or biblical interpretation of African American women. In her commentary on the Song of Songs, womanist scholar Renita Weems argues that the book was authored by a black woman whose body and sexuality were stigmatized in a way similar to the experience of contemporary black women ("Song of Songs" in *The New Interpreter's Bible*, vol. 5 [Nashville: Abingdon, 1997], 361–434). So also, Cheryl Anderson's **womanist** reading of the book lifts up the Song of Songs as an important resource for the Black church confronting the particular impact of the HIV/AIDS epidemic on black women and men. It offers the church a helpful alternative picture of gender and sexual desire that can counter body-denying, patriarchal constructions drawn from other parts of the Bible. See "A Womanist Reading of the Song of Songs in the Age of AIDS" pp. 73–92 in *The Five Scrolls: Texts@Contexts*, eds. Athalya Brenner-Idan, Gale A. Yee, and Archie C. C. Lee (New York: Bloomsbury, 2018). A broader survey and discussion of **womanist** readings of the Bible can be found in Nyasha Junior, *An Introduction to Womanist Biblical Interpretation* (Louisville, KT: Westminster John Knox, 2015).

Scholars are not sure when to date the Song of Songs, though its links to late second-millennium Egyptian love poetry might point to some kind of core of early love songs. Ecclesiastes/Qohelet is similarly difficult to date, and it likewise echoes literature from the ancient Near East. The book, attributed to "the teacher, the son of David in Jerusalem," is a combination of skepticism about wisdom and affirmation of life's small joys. Its main idea is the way all values are called into question by the fact that everyone dies and "you can't take it with you." During ancient Israel's history, there was no belief in a heaven or hell where people would be rewarded or punished for their behavior during life. In light of this, the "teacher" of Ecclesiastes ends up deciding that "emptiness, emptiness, all is emptiness" (Eccl 1:2, 14; 2:1; etc.). Since everyone dies sooner or later, both frantic pleasure seeking (Eccl 2:1–11) and excessive wisdom and righteousness (2:12–23) are pointless, "chasing after wind." Rather than getting too attached to any great project, the teacher of this text urges all to enjoy each day's moderate pleasures:

> Go, eat your food with pleasure, and drink your wine with a happy heart; for God has long approved what you do. Let your clothing always be white, do not let oil be lacking on your head. Enjoy life with the woman you love, all the days of your empty life that you are given under the sun. For that is your portion in life and your work which you work under the sun.
>
> (Eccl. 9:7–9; see also 2:24–25; 5:18–20; 8:15)

This kind of day-to-day living, eating, drinking, and enjoying romantic love, this "imperative of joy" (as one scholar has called it), is the "teacher's" prescription for life lived in a world where "emptiness, emptiness, all is emptiness."

I have not called this "teacher" of Ecclesiastes "Solomon" because historical-critical scholars agree that Solomon was not the author of this enigmatic book. Indeed, most would date it centuries after the time of Solomon, partly because of resemblances they see between the ideas of Ecclesiastes and the Greco-Roman idea of *carpe diem* (Latin for "seize the day"), an idea that might be paraphrased "drink up, for tomorrow you may die." Others, however, see the potential that the present book of Qohelet might be built on an older Israelite wisdom text, one that echoes the Mesopotamian Epic of Gilgamesh. An ancient version of this epic has a scene where its hero, Gilgamesh, is beside himself with grief and despair after seeing his closest friend, Enkidu, die. Having just seen the "fate of all humankind" in the death of his friend, Gilgamesh tells a barmaid, Siduri, of his desperate fear of death and wish that he could be immortal. In response, she speaks words that sound much like the "imperative of joy" of Ecclesiastes:

> Gilgamesh, where are you wandering? You cannot find the life that you seek.
> When gods created humankind, for humankind they established
> death. Immortality they reserved for themselves.
> You, Gilgamesh, let your belly be full. Keep enjoying yourself day and night! Every day make merry, dance and play every night! Let your clothes be clean. Let your head be washed, may you be bathed in water. Gaze on the little one who holds your hand. Let a wife enjoy your repeated embrace! Such is the destiny of mortals.
>
> (Translation: George, vol. 1, 279)

This Gilgamesh text was written about a thousand years before the time of Solomon, yet it was passed down to later times as one of the most commonly used educational texts both inside and outside Mesopotamia. The ancient speech of Siduri in Gilgamesh anticipates Ecclesiastes not only in the response to death through an "imperative of joy," but in the detailed sequence of pleasures it endorses: food, wine and partying, good clothing, good hygiene ("oil" washing), and sexual partnership. It is possible that an author of an early form of Ecclesiastes drew on this part of the ancient Epic of Gilgamesh, rather than later Greco-Roman ideas, in formulating his solution to an empty universe.

> **Basics**
>
> ## Ecclesiastes/Qohelet
>
> **Outline: counter-wisdom instruction**
>
> | | | |
> |---|---|---|
> | I | Introductory royal testament | 1:1–2:26 |
> | II | Instruction in skeptical wisdom | 3:1–12:8 |
> | III | Epilogue with later affirmations | 12:9–14 |
>
> **Major themes: Qohelet's contradictions**
>
> The lead themes through most of Ecclesiastes are the emptiness of all human striving (Eccl 1:2, 14; 2:1; etc.) and the benefits of daily pleasures in life (2:24–25; 5:18–20; etc.). Yet the last verses of the book (12:13–14) as well as isolated sections in its midst (e.g. 2:26; 3:17) affirm the more traditional idea that good eventually is rewarded and evil punished. Many would take these more traditional affirmations to be late additions to the book.
>
> **Date**
>
> Most scholars consider Ecclesiastes/Qohelet to be among the latest books in the Hebrew Bible. The Hebrew in which it is written contains late features, and many would see the book's perspective to be Greek. Certainly, as noted above, the book in its present form contains multiple, identifiable revisions. Nevertheless, as in the case of the Song of Songs, there are some reasons to think some early form of Ecclesiastes may be older, reasons including its resemblance to the old form of the Gilgamesh Epic (see p. 81).

One thing is clear: Ecclesiastes is responding with skepticism to older wisdom of the kind seen in Proverbs, the "Solomonic" book with the best claim to being datable (at least in part) to the time of David and Solomon. This one biblical book actually contains multiple collections, many of which are identified by separate headings: "the Proverbs of Solomon, son of David, king of Israel" (Prov 1:1–9:18), "the Proverbs of Solomon" (Prov 10:1–22:16), "the Proverbs of Solomon that were collected by Hezekiah's men" (Prov 25:1ff.), and so on. What we have in Proverbs, then, is a collection of collections of ancient Israel's educational materials.

This collection of collections in Proverbs contains some of the clearest echoes of foreign educational texts found in the Bible. For example, we find a collection of "words of the wise" in Proverbs 22:17–24:22 whose "thirty sayings" (Prov 22:20) loosely adapt and echo some of the 30 chapters of the Egyptian Instruction of Amenemope (see Figure 4.1). Both collections begin with a call to memorize the following instruction (Amenemope chapter 1; Prov 22:17–21), and continue with similar instructions not to oppress the poor (Amenemope 2; Prov 22:22–23), not to move boundary stones (Amenemope 6; Prov 22:28), not to get tied up in pursuing wealth (Amenemope 7; Prov 23:4–5), to avoid fools

FIGURE 4.1
Copy of the Egyptian Instruction of Amenemope, dated approximately 1200 BCE. The topics of its 30 sayings (cf. Prov 22:20) loosely parallel those found in Prov 22:17–24:22.

(Amenemope 9; Prov 22:24–25), and to take care in eating in front of nobles (Amenemope 23; Prov 23:1–3). To be sure, the author of Proverbs did not translate the ancient Egyptian instruction. The existing parallels between the texts are parallels in general content, and there are many parts of Prov 22:17–24:22 that have no counterpart in the Instruction of Amenemope. Nevertheless, the shared concept of 30 sayings and multiple parallels between these texts are good reasons to conclude that the author of Prov 22:17–24:22 knew of and loosely appropriated parts of the Egyptian Instruction of Amenemope, along with other wisdom traditions, in composing his own version of "30" sayings. In this sense, Prov 22:17–24:22 is an important "echo of ancient [Egyptian] empire" in the Bible.

The book of Proverbs also shows the importance of female wisdom in ancient Israel, an importance reflected in different ways by the Song of Songs and Ecclesiastes. Proverbs starts and continues with calls for students to attend to both the father's *and* the mother's wisdom (Prov 1:8; 6:20; 23:22). The early chapters of Proverbs feature a powerful depiction of wisdom as a female, semi-divine figure (e.g. Prov 1:20–33; 8:1–36, see the Focus text below on Proverb 8). And Proverbs concludes with an instruction attributed to King Lemuel's *mother* (Prov 31:1–9) and an A–Z praise of the "woman of power" which Jewish men often sing to their wives over the table of the Friday evening Sabbath meal (Prov 31:10–31). This broader association of women with wisdom in Proverbs may reflect the prominent role that mothers played in teaching children, both in Israel and in the rest of the ancient Near East. We may see another reflection of women as teachers in the Gilgamesh scene (noted above in relation to Ecclesiastes) where the barmaid teaches Gilgamesh. Note also the teaching voice given to the female lover in Song of Songs, where she makes the daughters of Jerusalem swear not to "awaken or arouse love until she is ready" (Song of Songs 2:7; 3:5; 8:4). In these and other ways, women were viewed as unusually wise in ancient Israel and its surroundings, and this is reflected in the Bible.

> **Basics**
>
> ## Book of Proverbs
>
> ### Outline: compilation of ancient Israelite wisdom
>
> | | | |
> |---|---|---|
> | I | Introductory instruction: seek wisdom! | 1:1–9:18 |
> | II | Additional wisdom collections | 10:1–31:9 |
> | III | A good woman as embodiment of wisdom | 31:10–31 |
>
> ### Date
>
> Most scholars see a great diversity of date in the material of Proverbs. Sections such as Proverbs 1–9 are dated many centuries after Solomon, while parts of other sections, such as Prov 22:17–24:22, are thought to be among the earliest parts of the Bible.
>
> ### Major themes
>
> Since Proverbs is a collection of collections, it is particularly difficult to summarize with a single theme or set of themes. Nevertheless, major features of the book include its prominent focus on female figures toward the beginning (Proverbs 1–9) and end (Prov 31:10–31), and its repeated emphasis on the importance of "fear of Yahweh" (Prov 1:7, 29; 2:5; etc.) throughout.

Alongside all this, there also is a religious element. Both the instructions and the proverbs in the book of Proverbs have a distinctive emphasis on the "fear of Yahweh" as crucial to the successful life (Prov 1:7, 29; 14:26–27; 23:17; etc.). Nevertheless, the collections of educational texts in Proverbs offer broader instruction in how to succeed with both god and human beings. Combined with assertions of the importance of fearing Yahweh (e.g. Prov 14:26) are pragmatic sayings such as the affirmation in Prov 17:8 that bribes often work well. Most materials in Proverbs affirm the basic idea of **moral act-consequence**: the idea that fear of God and/or good actions produce good results, while bad behavior leads to disaster. The task of the student is to walk the path toward success, not toward death.

Returning to Qohelet, the vast bulk of the book directly critiques this idea of moral act-consequence. Where the materials in Proverbs affirm the act-consequence idea that evil is punished, and good rewarded, the author of Qohelet observes that, in actuality, righteous people often die in the midst of their uprightness while evil people prosper despite their wickedness (e.g. Eccl 3:16; 4:1–4; 7:15). In light of this, the author constantly repeats the basic refrain on the basic moral incoherence of the universe, beginning and ending his teaching on that note: "emptiness, emptiness, all is emptiness" (Eccl 1:2; 12:8). But some ancient scribes were apparently not satisfied with leaving the matter there. For we find isolated affirmations of the traditional act-consequence idea across the book (e.g. Eccl 2:26; 3:17), and even the following strange "summary" of Qohelet in the last two verses of the book:

The end of the matter is this. Fear God and observe his commandments ... For God will bring every act to judgment, all that is hidden,
whether good or bad.

(Eccl 12:13–14).

The author who began and concluded his discourse with the affirmation
"emptiness, emptiness, all is emptiness" (Eccl 1:2; 12:8) is hardly likely to have
summarized his book in this way. Instead, this summary in Eccl 12:13–14,
along with similar elements in the book, likely are part of an orthodox revision
of an earlier book of Qohelet. It can be quite important to recognize the distinctive character of such later, potential revisionary texts. A reader who gives
undue attention to them and them alone can be blinded to the unorthodox
counter-wisdom message of the rest of the book.

The Speech of Lady Wisdom in Proverbs 8

FOCUS
TEXT

The speech of wisdom in Proverbs 8 provides an illustration of the complex
way that biblical texts creatively appropriate motifs from non-biblical materials. The "lady Wisdom" figure in Proverbs 8 appears partly to be modeled on
the wise and clever human women, whether clever female trickster types of
the sort discussed in the last chapter or the mother-teachers discussed in this
one. Yet this female Wisdom is also semi-divine. God created her before making anything else (Prov 8:22–26), and she was present to watch God make
the world and delight in the presence of humans (8:27–31). Her presence
from the beginning allows Wisdom to claim to provide many benefits – the
capacity to rule effectively (8:15–16), material wealth (8:18, 21), and the
surpassing benefits of wisdom itself (8:11–14, 19–20). And Wisdom's promises
of various benefits, in turn, grounds her call – at the beginning and end of
the text (8:4–10, 32–36) – for students to *seek wisdom* and thus gain happiness, life, and success. In sum, personified Wisdom in Proverbs 8 goes far
beyond human figures seen elsewhere in Proverbs, even the "father" figure
who elsewhere promises similar benefits to those who seek wisdom. She is a
superhuman female figure vividly symbolizing the benefits of wisdom to the
readership of a wisdom text – Proverbs.

Scholars have long wondered how and why Israelite sages would advertise
wisdom in such a way. To be sure, this "Wisdom" in Proverbs 8 is never called
a goddess. She is a symbol, created to serve a motivational aim. Nevertheless,
the rest of the Bible does not have many good analogies to this remarkable
picture of a semi-divine female figure. Moreover, the features of this figure
of wisdom do not clearly correspond to earlier goddesses of the area, such as
Asherah.

This has led scholars to conclude that parts of this picture may derive from
Israelite adaptation of non-Israelite motifs, whether from goddess worship or
elsewhere. Some have argued that the Egyptian goddess Maat could be a model
for Wisdom in Proverbs 8. She personifies the principle of truth, justice, and
order, and various Egyptian texts praise her as pre-existing creation, caring for

those who love her (cf. Prov 8:17), and providing life and protection to her devotees. Others find the Egyptian goddess Isis to be a better analogy, since she is reported to actually give speeches about her early origins and powers that are analogous to that in Proverbs 8. See for example,

> I, Isis, am ruler of all lands,
> And I was educated by Hermes
> I set down laws for men and legislated that which no one can alter.
> I am the eldest daughter of Kronos.

Later in this text we see some additional elements pertinent to Proverbs 8.

> I have made justice powerful ...
> I have made justice more powerful than gold and silver.
> (Translation: Jan Bergman, *Ich bin Isis* [Uppsala: Universitet, 1968], 301)

Yet there are questions about when and how the authors of Proverbs 8 would have been influenced by either Maat or Isis traditions. Only an Egyptian native could have conveyed the kinds of detailed ideas about Maat that are paralleled in Proverbs 8, perhaps an Egyptian scribe in Solomon's court or a later visitor. Meanwhile, speeches of Isis like the one quoted above were not written until a couple of centuries *after* the latest parts of Proverbs were written.

Ultimately, these parallels do not help us date Proverbs 8 in any particular period. Instead, biblical scholars often prefer one parallel or the other, depending on the dating of Proverbs that they decided on for other reasons. Scholars inclined to date this part of Proverbs to the time of Solomon or a bit later may relate Proverbs 8 to Maat traditions. Meanwhile, scholars who date Proverbs 8 to the Persian period or later are most prone to link Proverbs 8 with later Isis traditions. Whatever the dating, the closest parallels so far seem to point to an Egyptian background to the picture of Wisdom in Proverbs 8. In addition, consideration of Proverbs 8 alongside these traditions about Maat and Isis can sensitize us to the ways that authors of all these ancient texts developed such depictions of symbolic female figures in order to make broader points.

As argued by Carol Newsom in her article "Woman and the Discourse of Patriarchal Wisdom," the depiction of female Wisdom in Proverbs 8 is developed for particular motivational purposes. Within the broader context of the text, the reader is urged to follow the powerful, beneficent figure of female Wisdom while avoiding the seductive lure of the dangerous strange woman described in the previous chapter, Proverbs 7. Proverbs 8 must thus be understood as part of a contrast of "good" and "bad" female figures. On the one side stands semi-divine "Wisdom," symbolizing Proverbs and perhaps modeled in some way on Egyptian female divine figures. On the other side stands the "strange woman," a female figure symbolizing the dangerous attraction of perspectives contrary to Proverbial wisdom.

Echoes of Texts from Earlier Empires Elsewhere in the Bible

Genesis 2–3 and 6–9, Gilgamesh (tablet 11), and Atrahasis (to be found at www.livius.org under "Great flood" and "Atrahasis").

READING

Before reading this section, read Gen 6:5–9:17 and note every place where the same or a quite similar event is narrated twice. An example would be God's announcement of the flood both in Gen 6:13 and in 7:4. Another is Noah's multiple entries into the ark in 7:7 and 7:13. Once you have developed a list of such doubly narrated events, see whether "God" or "LORD" is used to refer to God in any of these doublets. Come up with your own theory about how the biblical flood story ended up this way.

EXERCISE

So far we have found echoes of texts from earlier empires in entire texts (e.g. royal psalms; see Chapter 3) or books (e.g. the Song of Songs) that are associated in different ways with the time of David and Solomon. Nevertheless, other texts from the Bible also contain strong echoes of ancient Near Eastern literature and we can learn much about them through comparison.

For example, scholarship by David Wright (*Inventing God's Law* [New York: Oxford University Press, 2009]) has identified multiple and specific parallels between the ancient Mesopotamian Code of Hammurabi and a collection of biblical laws in Exodus 20:22–23:33 called the **"Covenant Code"** (see Exod 24:7). For over a century scholars have judged that this "Covenant Code" was one of the earliest collections of laws in the Bible, because its laws about topics such as building altars (Exod 20:24–26) and celebrating festivals (Exod 23:14–17) reflect early practices of offering sacrifices all over the land and not just in Jerusalem. Only recently, however, have scholars seen ways that the Covenant Code may be loosely modeled on parts of the Code of Hammurabi (see Figure 4.2), much as Prov 22:17–24:22 was modeled partially on the Instruction of Amenemope. Indeed, it is likely that many of the purity and ritual regulations of Leviticus and Numbers also had ancient precursors, since we have examples of similar sorts of documents about priestly matters found among the remains of the peoples preceding and surrounding ancient Israel. Law, whether royal decree or priestly instruction, was one of the most important forms of ancient writing. And later in this textbook we will discuss in more detail some rather specific parallels between ancient Mesopotamian treaty documents with kings and the covenant with Yahweh depicted in the book of Deuteronomy.

Perhaps the most famous echoes of texts from the ancient Near East are found at the very beginning of the Bible, in the **primeval narrative**

FIGURE 4.2
The Hammurabi stela. The king shows respect before the enthroned Mesopotamian god of justice, Shamash. The text describes his appointment by the gods to give justice and quotes his proclamation of laws that roughly parallel (in topic) parts of the Covenant Code in Exod 20:22–23:33.

(Genesis 1–11), which tells stories about the whole earth and its peoples. Before looking at these echoes, however, it is important to realize that these chapters of Genesis contain *two* parallel sets of stories about the origins of the world. Lots of things are described twice in these chapters. "God" creates plants, animals, and humans (male and female) in Genesis 1, and then "Yahweh God" creates the first man, animals, and then woman in Genesis 2. Genesis 3–4 tell stories about these first humans and their descendants up to the time of Noah, and then Genesis 5 gives a genealogy from Adam to Noah. Then, the flood story of Genesis 6–9 is full of doubly narrated events: two descriptions of God's perception of the problem leading up to the flood (6:5 and 6:12), two assertions that Noah was exceptional in his righteousness (6:8 and 9), and so on. Looking at these duplicate narratives in the flood story and across Genesis 1–11 more generally, it appears as if an Israelite author had two complete, written stories of creation and flood, and that author wove those older written stories, these ancient "sources" of Genesis, together to create the present biblical text. **Source criticism** (see box p. 89) is a method by which scholars use clues in the biblical text, such as doubled narratives of the same event and shifts in terminology, to reconstruct lost, written sources that were combined into the present Bible.

Over the past two hundred years, source critics have reached a high level of agreement on how to untangle these interwoven creation and flood writings (sources) embedded in Genesis 1–11 and beyond. They call one of these sources "**P**" or the **Priestly source**, because its sequence of stories

(Gen 1:1–2:3; 5:1–32; 6:9–22; 7:6, 11, and other parts of the flood up through 9:1–17) links with other parts of the **Pentateuch** (Genesis, Exodus, Leviticus, Numbers, and Deuteronomy) that focus on priests. The other source starts with the Garden of Eden story in Genesis 2:4–3:24, continues with the Cain and Abel story and genealogies of Genesis 4, includes its own flood narrative (Gen 6:1–8; 7:1–5, 10, 12, and other parts up through 8:20–22), and contains an epilogue about Noah and his sons (Gen 9:18–27). In the past this source has been termed the "**J**" or the "**Yahwistic source**" (sometimes spelled "Jahwistic source") since this source uses the holy Hebrew name Yahweh to refer to God. (The German scholars who first discovered the J source two hundred years ago used the letter "j" for their "y" sound and spelled the name Yahwist "Jahwist.") As will be discussed later, in Chapter 10, many scholars see this J source, like P, continuing across the Pentateuch, but there are good reasons to be skeptical of their claims. Instead, any such early J source appears to be limited to some portions of the non-P primeval history. In this textbook the term "non-P primeval history" will be used for this source to avoid confusion of it with the longer "J" source posited in earlier scholarship.

For now, it is just important to recognize the general, centuries-long scholarly consensus on two basic types of material across the Pentateuch – a Priestly source and an earlier source, a non-Priestly one, starting with the Garden of Eden story in Genesis 2–3 (see below: Focus text: The Garden of Eden). This chapter will focus on elements from the earlier, non-Priestly source. We will return to the Priestly source when we come (in Chapter 10) to the Babylonian exile in which it likely was written.

More on Method: Source and Redaction Criticism

The term "**source criticism**" refers to the scholarly attempt to identify previously existing, separate written sources now embedded in the biblical text. We have no manuscripts of these earlier sources. Instead, scholars must examine the biblical text we now have and look for clues to earlier sources, such as doublets, contradictions, and major shifts in language. Sometimes scholars can achieve substantial consensus in reconstructing hypothetical earlier documents, such as the Priestly/P and non-Priestly sources discussed in this chapter.

In addition, scholars speak of editorial additions to ancient sources as **redaction** and often engage in an attempt to identify layers of editorial additions through use of **redaction criticism**. For example, there are signs that the editors who combined the Priestly and non-Priestly primeval narratives added some redactional texts to connect those sources with each other. In other cases, scribes simply expanded on earlier narratives or prophecies with one or more layers of redaction.

Contrasts and Parallels between Biblical and Mesopotamian Flood Narratives

The land of Mesopotamia is prone to floods, especially in the spring. Several Mesopotamian texts describe how the gods of the Mesopotamian pantheon tried to kill humanity through a global flood, but were foiled by a crafty god (Enki or Ea, depending on the version) who told a human of the coming flood and instructed him to build a boat to allow him, his family, and others to survive it. The intertwined biblical flood narratives in Genesis 6–9 merge the roles of these two gods, having the same God bring the flood and instruct the flood hero (Noah) on how he can survive it. Nevertheless, they parallel numerous aspects of the Mesopotamian flood narratives. As indicated in the table below, there is a particularly striking parallel between the biblical scene of Noah sending birds to determine if the flood waters have receded (Gen 8:6–12; part of the non-Priestly flood narrative) and a similar scene in one of the earlier Mesopotamian flood narratives (the Gilgamesh Epic) where the flood hero describes having sent out birds in a similar way (see Figure 4.3 for a picture of one of the tablets of this epic).

Gilgamesh, tablet 11:147–156 (Translation: A. George.)	Non-Priestly flood narrative (Gen 8:6–12)
When the seventh day arrived	**6** At the end of forty days, Noah opened the window of the ark that he had made,
I brought out a dove, setting it free:	**7** and sent the raven out. It went to and fro until the waters dried up from the earth.
Off went the dove ... No perch was available for it and it came back to me.	
I brought out a swallow, setting it free: Off went the swallow ...	**8** Noah sent the dove out to see if the waters had diminished from the surface of the ground,
No perch was available for it and it came back to me.	**9** but it did not find a resting place for its foot and returned to him into the ark because water was still on the surface of the entire earth. He stretched out his hand, took it, and brought it back to him in the ark.
	10 He waited another seven days and again sent out the dove from the ark.
I brought out a raven, setting it free: Off went the raven and it saw the waters receding. It was eating, bobbing up and down, it did not come back to me.	**11** The dove came back in to him at evening time, and a plucked olive leaf was in its mouth.
	Noah then knew that the water on the earth had diminished.
	12 He waited another seven days and sent the dove out, but it did not return to him again.

As is evident above, the parallels are not exact, but they are striking enough to suggest some kind of dependence of the non-Priestly flood narrative on its earlier Mesopotamian counterpart. Take a look for yourself at online versions of the Mesopotamian flood story in the Atrahasis and Gilgamesh epics (see, e.g., "The Epic of Atrahasis" and "Great Flood" at www.livius.org) and compare them with Genesis 6–9. A close comparison will turn up both a list of similarities and some important ways in which the P and non-P flood narratives both resemble and yet diverge from their Mesopotamian precursors.

We do not know how or when biblical authors accessed those Mesopotamian traditions. Nevertheless, we have good reason to think that they knew them in some form. Israelite authors lived in a highland area not prone to floods, and the extensive parallels to the specific form of flood tradition as it is seen in Mesopotamia is excellent evidence that the P and non-P authors adapted foreign traditions in the process of writing stories of creation and flood. We will see other examples of such appropriation of foreign traditions across this textbook.

FIGURE 4.3
Tablet of the Gilgamesh Epic containing the flood narrative.

FOCUS TEXT

The Garden of Eden Story (Gen 2:4–3:24)

We turn next to look more closely at the text that opens the earlier, non-Priestly source discussed above: the Garden of Eden story in Gen 2:4–3:24 (here and elsewhere often referred to as Genesis 2–3). Most people approach this text with presuppositions shaped by its history of interpretation. For example, if asked to name the fruit that Adam and Eve ate in the garden, most would instantly reply "an apple." The Genesis text, however, does not say this. Similarly, though many assume that the snake in the garden was "Satan," that is never specified in the Bible. These and other elements were added to the biblical story by later interpreters (see Figure 4.4).

This history of interpretation of the Garden of Eden text has also influenced what people think the whole story is about. For example, many have understood Paul in Rom 5:18–21 to imply that Genesis 2–3 is a tale of how sin entered the world, putting all humans under the curse of death. In the post-Pauline letter of 1 Timothy, this tragedy is blamed on women, who must now pay the price by bearing children:

> For Adam was formed first, then Eve; and Adam was not deceived, but the woman was deceived and became a transgressor. Yet she will be saved through childbearing, provided they continue in faith and love and holiness, with modesty.
>
> (1 Tim 2:13–15; translation: NRSV)

Later Christian interpreters expanded on this type of interpretation, with the early theologian Gregory Nazianzen talking of how Eve "beguiled the man by means of pleasure" and Tertullian saying to a group of nuns, "Are not each of you an Eve? . . . You are the Devil's gateway." With these and many other interpretations setting the stage for contemporary readings, it is little wonder that many people today assume that this text is an anti-female text blaming Eve for seducing Adam and introducing sin and death into the world.

Yet, particularly thanks to groundbreaking work by Phyllis Trible (*God and the Rhetoric of Sexuality* [Philadelphia: Fortress, 1978]) and others in the mid-1970s, scholars have gradually recognized that there is no more basis for that reading in the text itself than there is for the idea that the fruit that the first humans ate was an "apple" (that word never occurs in Genesis 3). Both of these ideas are later interpretations that have been laid on a text that has very different concerns. Trible and others have pointed out that the text actually celebrates the woman as the culmination of creation. "Sin" is never mentioned in it, and the woman and man share responsibility for the garden crime. Moreover, the consequences for this act that come on them are depicted in the text as tragic, not divinely willed elements of creation. Let us now take a new look at this often-interpreted text.

FIGURE 4.4
Titian's painting of Adam and Eve taking the apple from a snake-tailed cherubic Satan. It well illustrates how later interpretation of Genesis 2–3 influenced people's visions of the scene.

More on Method: Feminist Criticism and history of interpretation/Biblical Reception

History of (biblical) interpretation is study of how a biblical text has been interpreted over time, often with an emphasis on how it was interpreted in Jewish and/or Christian religious contexts. A similar method, **reception history**, focuses particularly on how biblical texts are represented in other media (e.g. painting, film, music; see Figure 4.4) and/or secular interpretations of biblical texts (e.g. in novels, theater). Study of history of interpretation and reception history of biblical texts can be interesting in itself. In addition, it can help the historical-critical reader of the Bible identify interpretive tendencies that might shape their own, unconscious interpretation of the text. For example, study of the history of interpretation of Genesis 2–3 can highlight the particular background and development of readings of the story as an account of "original sin," helping the reader bracket such approaches and take a new look at the text and see if other approaches to it might yield new insights.

One such newer approach is **feminist biblical criticism**. This chapter already noted Phyllis Trible's groundbreaking work on Genesis 2–3, and this kind of research has been done by many others. For example, Carol Meyers' *Rediscovering Eve: Ancient Israelite Women in Context* (New York: Oxford

> University Press, 2013 [original 1988]) gathers archaeological and textual evidence to show the prominent role that women played in the ancient Israelite economy. In this light, she raises the possibility that God's pronouncement over the woman's future in Gen 3:16 is not a prediction of her "pain" in pregnancy (as it's often translated), but instead of her future hard work (Hebrew *itzbon*) along with pregnancy, much like similar toil-labor (*itzbon*) is predicted for the man (Gen 3:17–19). Trible's, Meyers's, and others' work in **feminist biblical criticism** (academic study that analyzes female characters, imagery, and speech) has offered a corrective to predominantly male perspectives in the earlier history of interpretation of Genesis 2–3 (and other texts as well).

The story is organized into three main parts: a description of God's creation of a deeply connected partnership of men and women working the earth (Gen 2:4–25), a crime scene describing their disobedience of God's one prohibition (3:1–6), and an account of the tragic loss of original connectedness to each other and the earth as a result of the crime (3:7–25). The story opens with God creating the first "human" (Hebrew *Adam*) out of the earth (Hebrew *adamah*), and giving him life through breathing the divine breath into him. God sets him in the garden to work and protect it, and the word play on *Adam/Adamah* (much like "human" and "humus") emphasizes the original connectedness of the human to the earth he was destined to work.

Yet God immediately recognizes that there is a problem with this picture: "It is not good for the human to be alone" (Gen 2:18). God then decides to create a partner "corresponding to him." God creates the animals, and brings each to the human for him to name them, but none truly "corresponds" to him (Gen 2:19–20). So God tries a new approach, anesthetizing the first human by putting him to sleep, removing a rib, and "building" the woman out of it. When the human awakens and sees the woman, he sings the first song of creation, one that emphasizes the connectedness they share:

> This one, at last, is bone from my bones, flesh from my flesh!
> This one will be called 'woman' [Hebrew *ishah*]
> Because from man [Hebrew *ish*] this one was taken.
>
> (Gen 2:23)

The text concludes by saying that this is the origin of love and marriage, it is the reason a man leaves his parents and "clings to his wife and they become one flesh." In stark contrast to many other world-creation stories, sex is not initially connected here to having children. Instead, sex is a sign of the original connectedness of the man and the woman created out of a part of him so that they would truly correspond to each other. This is a story of God's will that humans be in close relationship with each other and the earth. In the wake of this creation, both man and woman "were naked and not ashamed" (Gen 2:25). They may work the garden together and eat of its fruit, with one exception: they may not eat of the "tree of knowledge of good and evil" lest they "certainly die" (Gen 2:17).

The scene shifts in Gen 3:1–6 to a new cast of characters, the man, woman, and now a "clever" snake in place of God (Gen 3:1). Again, the history of interpretation has often pictured Satan as the snake, but there is no basis for that in the Hebrew text. Instead, the snake stands as an ancient symbol of wisdom and immortality, and the adjective used to describe him – *arum* ("clever") – is a virtue frequently praised in the wisdom writings of Proverbs. Furthermore, though interpreters have often supposed that the sin of the first humans somehow consisted of sex or desire, there is no hint of that here. As we saw, Genesis 2 already explains the first sexual partnership of humans as the result of God's creation of a woman out of part of a man. Instead, the issue is human acquisition of godlike "wisdom." Not only is the "clever" snake associated with wisdom, but the "tree of knowledge of good and evil" is a symbol of wisdom's fruits. This then is underlined when the snake convinces the woman to consider eating of the tree, and she sees that the "tree was good for food, a delight to the eyes, and good for becoming wise" (Gen 3:6). Performing a role analogous to female wisdom in Proverbs 8, the first woman eats of the fruit of wisdom, gives fruit to her husband; he eats of it as well; and the text says that "the eyes of both were opened" (Gen 3:7). This is a frequent expression for gaining education. Thus Gen 3:1–7 describes the first act of human disobedience as the defiance of God and the gaining of a form of "wisdom" that shows many signs of being associated with the ancient Israelite textual wisdom we have seen in books such as Proverbs.

This then sets in motion a tragic unraveling of much of the connectedness that God had created at the outset. The text already illustrates this when God arrives in the garden, the humans hide, and, when questioned about why they are hiding, begin to blame each other. The man blames both the woman and God who made the woman (3:12), and the woman blames the snake (3:13). In response, God proclaims consequences for all three. The snake will now crawl on the ground and be an eternal enemy of humans. The woman will no longer enjoy idyllic life in the garden, but God will "multiply her toilsome pregnancies" (not "increase pangs in childbearing" as often translated). And the idyllic life of the man likewise will come to an end. His "toil" is to work the ground from which he was made until he dies and returns to it. Where once there was mutual desire, now the woman's desire will be for her husband, and where once there was mutuality between corresponding partners, now the husband will "rule" over his wife (3:16). The story goes on to describe the (hu)man's naming of his wife "Eve" (a name made from the Hebrew word for "life") to reflect her new job of producing children (3:20). God gives the human pair clothes (3:21) – a sign of human civilization that is also seen in ancient non-biblical texts such as the Gilgamesh Epic. Finally, God expels them from the garden for fear that they might gain godlike immortality much as they already gained godlike wisdom (Gen 3:22–24). Now, denied the chance to eat of the tree of life, it turns out to be true that the humans will "certainly die" after eating the forbidden fruit of knowledge (see the prohibition in Gen 2:17).

In this way, the text accurately depicts the non-ideal world that actual Israelites lived in, but with a twist. Most Israelites still lived lives closely tied to the land, working it by the sweat of their brow until they returned to it. The work was hard, famine was frequent, and death came much sooner than it does for people in the developed world today. Women lived in patriarchal marriages, sustaining the household with their work, while undergoing an endless series of pregnancies, many of which were very dangerous. Analysis of female remains has suggested that as many as half of women eventually died in childbirth. In this sense, the realities described in the latter part of Genesis 3 all held true for the ancient Israelite men and women. Yet what is remarkable about this text is its suggestion that this often harsh and patriarchal reality is not what God originally intended for humans. God originally made humans for fruitful farming, long life, and mutual, truly corresponding life and desire between men and women. It was only with the human step toward godlike wisdom that they emerged into the harsh reality that they experience today. "Wisdom" – not women – is the source of the tragic endless labor, patriarchy, and death that characterize the present.

This kind of narrative about human origins is as timeless as many texts discussed above, but it may also stand as a reflection on what "wisdom" was coming to mean in monarchal Israel. Though most still lived in villages, Judah and Israel gradually became increasingly dominated by urban elites who were educated in new literary traditions modeled on non-biblical sources. As this happened, the leaders of Israel during this period underwent a momentous shift in their collective memory. Before the monarchy, tribal villages all had their oral traditions, such as tales of trickster ancestors, the exodus, or military triumph. But, with kingship developing in Jerusalem and Israel, we start to see the emergence of an Israelite literary tradition recited and memorized from *written* texts: royal psalms, stories of royalty, royal wisdom, and stories of primeval origins. Moreover, many of these written texts were based on educational literature from outside Israel, such as Egyptian wisdom and love songs or Mesopotamian traditions about creation and flood. This growing Israelite literary corpus, so difficult to identify and date, was the means by which a small and growing number of literate Israelites gained "knowledge of good and evil" and had their "eyes" "opened."

More on Method: Comparison with Non-Biblical Texts

Biblical scholars learn much through comparing biblical texts with similar texts found elsewhere in the ancient world. Sometimes, as in the case of parallels between Prov 22:17–24:34 and the Egyptian Instruction of Amenemope, scholars are comparing a biblical text with a possible source of that text. As suggested at the outset of the chapter, this can have implications for the dating of that text. At other times, however, such comparison with other ancient texts simply allows a biblical scholar to put a biblical text in a broader cultural context. Through it, we can see distinctive features of the biblical version of a broader Near Eastern tradition and gain possible data on the sorts of social contexts where texts of a given type (e.g. royal psalms, proverbs, or love songs) were produced and used (e.g. education).

Take the example of the Garden of Eden story discussed here. Your reading can be informed by:

- Contrast of God's placement of the human in the lush garden orchard "to work and guard it" with older Mesopotamian traditions of humans being created to take over the hard labor that had been done earlier by lower gods (e.g. the Atrahasis Epic).
- Comparison of the humans' journey from childlike lack of bodily shame to adult "opening of eyes" and acquisition of clothing (Gen 2:25–3:7) with Ancient Near Eastern stories of how humans moved from initial animal-like nakedness to gaining clothing and other marks of civilization (e.g. The Rulers of Lagash, Debate of the Sheep and the Grain; see also the Gilgamesh Epic).
- Placing the story's treatment of human mortality in relation to broader emphases on human mortality in Near Eastern wisdom texts, including some stories of how humans accidentally lost chances to overcome their mortality (the Gilgamesh and Adapa epics).

In this way, interpreting biblical texts like the Eden story in relation to older Near Eastern traditions can help you read more carefully and make sense of key elements that you might otherwise overlook – e.g. themes of nakedness, clothing, mortality, and hard agricultural labor.

Useful resources for comparison

For more translations of non-biblical texts and discussion of them in relation to the Bible: Christopher Hays, *Hidden Riches: A Sourcebook for the Comparative Study of the Hebrew Bible and Ancient Near East*. Louisville: Westminster John Knox, 2014.

For more background on these texts: Kenton L. Sparks, *Ancient Texts for the Study of the Hebrew Bible: A Guide to the Background Literature*. Peabody, MA: Hendrickson, 2005.

Read this way, the Garden of Eden story – itself a highly learned, written text – suggests that wisdom is both an essential part of human growing up and a source of many human ills. On the one hand, it suggests that there is no return to an idyllic life in the garden, munching on fruit and obeying God's one clear command – not to eat of the tree of knowledge of good and evil. On the other hand, this enlightenment, this human journey to mature civilization, has brought many of the ills of adult life with it: endless pregnancies and agricultural work. The marks of original creation persist, such as the way humans still are drawn to "cleave to each other" and "become one flesh." Yet the story recognizes that adult life also has its toil and tragic imperfections. The journey out of the garden has brought a life where humans have work in place of leisure, "wisdom" in place of the single garden command, and male rule over women in place of the connectedness that God originally wished.

Conclusion

As was stressed at the outset of the chapter, this discussion gathers biblical texts of diverse date that have been modeled on earlier Near Eastern texts. These texts illustrate how Israelite scribes, starting with the emergence of kingship in ancient Israel, interacted with earlier Near Eastern myths, laws, and poetry.

Such echoes of non-biblical texts in the Bible can teach us about the context in which ancient Israelites used the sorts of written material now in the Bible. For example, texts like the Instruction of Amenemope, the Gilgamesh Epic, and the laws in the Code of Hammurabi were used in ancient Egyptian or Mesopotamian education. Mesopotamian and Egyptian leaders were qualified for their jobs by learning to read and memorize such texts. When we turn to similar biblical texts, such as the "words of the wise" in Prov 22:17–24:34 that echo Amenemope, it is logical to hypothesize that such biblical texts likewise were used to educate leaders from the beginnings of the Israelite monarchy. Whatever the original function of earlier oral traditions now embedded in such biblical texts, as *writings* they probably helped educate the leadership elite in such an emergent monarchy.

Meanwhile, the differences between biblical texts and their non-biblical counterparts are as important as the similarities. We can learn much about the particular values and perspectives of biblical authors through comparing the Covenant Code with Hammurabi, the "words of the wise" in Prov 22:17–24:34 with the Instruction of Amenemope, the non-Priestly primeval narrative in Genesis 1–11 with Atrahasis, and so on. Biblical authors did not just copy major texts of Mesopotamia and Egypt. They reframed non-biblical traditions in light of their particular values. There is a major difference, for example, between the biblical story of the flood in Genesis 6–9, where just one god brings the flood and rescues a human from it, and the polytheistic tale in Atrahasis, where most of the gods bring the flood while one god rescues a human from it. In this and other biblical texts discussed here, we see ancient Israelite authors building freely on and yet radically adapting more ancient literary traditions from elsewhere. These unknown authors are responsible for writing the first building blocks of what would later become the Hebrew Bible.

In including some texts that likely mix early and late elements (e.g. Song of Songs, Qohelet), this chapter stepped out of the chronological framework of the rest of the introduction. Nevertheless, it may not be so important to determine in which century such texts were written. After all, texts like Proverbs and the Garden of Eden story reflect on timeless aspects of existence, albeit in distinctly different ways, and it is unclear how much one would learn from dating the love poetry of Song of Songs to one century or another. In this way, the texts discussed here are different from the prophetic texts to be discussed in the next and following chapters. Those prophetic texts were addressed to particular historical crises being experienced by the people of Israel and Judah. We turn to those texts now.

CHAPTER FOUR REVIEW

For Review

1. Know the meaning and significance of the following terms discussed in this chapter:
   - Covenant Code
   - moral act-consequence
   - Afrocentric interpretation
   - Womanist interpretation
   - history of (biblical) interpretation
   - reception history
   - source criticism
   - feminist biblical interpretation
2. What are the two basic layers of Qohelet, and why is it important for an interpreter to distinguish them?
3. Know the basic character of the following ancient Near Eastern texts and how they are related by scholars to biblical texts that were discussed in this chapter:
   - Code of Hammurabi
   - Egyptian love songs
   - Instruction of Amenemope
   - Gilgamesh Epic
4. What are two different ways in which comparison of a biblical text with an ancient non-biblical text can be useful? Give two examples of such comparison from this chapter.
5. (Focus texts: Proverbs 8 and Genesis 2–3) Compare the different depictions of feminine figures associated with wisdom/knowledge in Proverbs 8 (feminine Wisdom) and Genesis 2–3 (Eve). Focus especially on the roles of Wisdom and Eve with respect to knowledge. Why do you think the different authors of Proverbs 8 and of Genesis 2–3 chose a feminine figure (rather than a masculine figure) for each role?

RESOURCES FOR FURTHER STUDY

General introduction to wisdom literature

Balentine, Samuel E. *Wisdom Literature*. Core Biblical Studies. Nashville: Abingdon, 2018.

Proverbs

Fox, Michael V. *Proverbs*. 2 volumes. New York: Doubleday, 2000, 2009.

Leeuwen, Raymond C. Van. "Proverbs." *Pp. 17–264 in vol. 5 of the New Interpreter's Bible*, Leander Keck, general ed. Nashville: Abingdon, 1997.

Newsom, Carol A. "Woman and the Discourse of Patriarchal Wisdom: A Study of Proverbs 1–9." Pp. 142–160 in Peggy L. Day (ed.), *Gender and Difference in Ancient Israel*. Philadelphia: Fortress, 1989.

Ecclesiastes

Brown, William. *Ecclesiastes*. Louisville, KY: Westminster John Knox Press, 2000.

Duncan, Julie Ann. *Ecclesiastes*. Nashville: Abingdon, 2016.

Lohfink, Norbert. *Qohelet: A Continental Commentary*, trans. Sean McEvenue. Minneapolis, MN: Fortress, 2003. Translation of a 1980 original.

Song of Songs

Exum, Cheryl. *Song of Songs*. Louisville, KY: Westminster John Knox Press, 2005.

Keel, Othmar. *Song of Songs*, trans. Frederick J. Gaiser. Minneapolis: MN: Fortress, 1997. Translation of a 1986 original.

Weems, Renita. "Song of Songs." *Pp. 361–434 in vol. 5 of the New Interpreter's Bible*, Leander Keck, general ed. Nashville: Abingdon, 1997.

Genesis 1–11

Gowan, Donald. *From Eden to Babel: A Commentary on the Book of Genesis*. Grand Rapids: Eerdmans, 1988.

O'Connor, Kathleen. *Genesis 1–25A*. Macon, GA: Smyth & Helwys, 2018.

Discussion of Song of Songs, Genesis, and other texts relating to sexuality

Carr, David M. *The Erotic Word: Sexuality and Spirituality in the Hebrew Bible*. New York: Oxford University Press, 2003.

Narrative and Prophecy Amidst the Rise and Fall of The Northern Kingdom

5

Chapter Overview

Setting the Stage: The Rise of the Northern Kingdom of Israel and Its Texts

Ancient Near Eastern Prophecy

Amos, Prophet of Justice

Hosea, the Northern Prophet, Calling for Israel's Devotion to Yahweh Alone

Conclusion

Chapter Five Review

Resources for Further Study

CHAPTER OVERVIEW

Previous chapters of this introduction traced echoes of past empires in the Hebrew Bible, while this one focuses on the reverberations of an imperial onslaught. The time to be reviewed here is the ninth and eighth centuries BCE (800s and 700s). The attacking empire was **Assyria**, a Mesopotamian state based in what is now northern Iraq (see Map 1.3, on p. 29). By this point there were two kingdoms in the land of Israel. A kingdom of Israel had risen up in the north, while a southern kingdom of Judah was ruled by descendants of David in Jerusalem. Initially, this northern kingdom (Israel) was stronger than its southern counterpart, and it developed its own corpus of texts that were largely distinct from those used in the south. Yet ultimately the northern kingdom was destroyed by Assyria, and the southern kingdom suffered almost a century of Assyrian domination.

The Hebrew Bible reflects this initial imperial encounter in at least two main ways. First, although the Hebrew Bible is a collection of Judean texts, it preserves some remnants of texts from the destroyed northern kingdom, texts that have been appropriated and adapted by Judean scribes. Second, the Bible's first prophetic books came from this time of imperial encounter. The books of Amos, Hosea, Micah, and Isaiah all contain early prophecies that reflect the crises faced by Judah and Israel leading up to and during the Assyrian onslaught. Knowing more about the origins of these texts – whether northern texts now embedded in the Hebrew Bible (e.g. an early Jacob story) or prophetic writings formed in the crucible of imperial crisis – can help us understand them in new ways.

Setting the Stage: The Rise of the Northern Kingdom of Israel and Its Texts

READING

1 Kings 12; 2 Kgs 14:23–29; 15:17–31; 17:1–6 (from Jeroboam of Israel to the fall of the north). Review Genesis 25–35 and Exodus 2–14.

Our journey toward greater understanding of these texts starts with the story of the emergence of a monarchy in the Israelite north. This monarchy was the ultimate outgrowth of a long process of tribal rebellion. Groups in Israel had tried in the past to gain liberty from the Davidic monarchy, but they did not succeed in breaking free until Solomon's death, around 927 BCE.

According to the description of this event in 1 Kings 12 (//2 Chronicles 10), Solomon's son, Rehoboam, went to the ancient tribal center of Shechem to be anointed by the elders of northern Israel. Instead, they ended up having a confrontation. The elders asked if Rehoboam's "yoke," that is his domination of them, would be as heavy as that of his father. Against the advice of his older advisors, Rehoboam is reported to have said: "I will add to your yoke; my father disciplined you with whips, but I will discipline you with scorpions" (1 Kgs 12:11//2 Chr 10:14). As one might expect, this did not get a good response. The elders called for withdrawal of support of the Davidic monarchy in Jerusalem, saying "To your tents, oh Israel. Look to your own house, David" (1 Kgs 12:16; cf. 2 Sam 20:1). When Rehoboam sent his chief of forced labor to bring the northerners back in line, they stoned him to death (1 Kgs 12:18).

As 1 Kings 12 tells it, the elders of Israel chose a new monarch, rather than returning to the loose tribal grouping they had before kingship. In place of Rehoboam, they anointed as king one of their own countrymen, Jeroboam, who was a man from the tribe of Ephraim. Earlier he had worked for Solomon as chief of forced labor, but rebelled and fled to Egypt when Solomon tried to kill him

(1 Kgs 11:26–27). As a new king of Israel, Jeroboam first established Shechem as his capital, then moved to Penuel, and he established royal sanctuaries at the towns of Bethel (toward the south of Israel) and Dan (in the far north; see Map 5.1). He installed statues of calves at each sanctuary and proclaimed "Here are your gods, Oh Israel, who led you out of Egypt." (1 Kgs 12:28).

MAP 5.1 The neighboring kingdoms of Israel and Judah. Redrawn from Norman Gottwald, *The Hebrew Bible: A Socio-Literary Introduction.* Minneapolis: Fortress, 1985, page 291.

This narrative in 1 Kings 12 represents a perspective by later southern scribes on how awful it was that Israel in the north broke away from Judah. Its depiction of a northern kingdom extending to Dan and its implicit critique of Jeroboam's calves as idolatry are just a couple of the signs that this story is a later creation by Judean (not northern, Israelite) scribes. At the same time, even this unsympathetic narrative preserves a memory of an Israelite northern monarchy that was different from the Davidic monarchy in the south. Having gained liberty, Jeroboam invokes exodus traditions when he sets up his royal sanctuaries in Bethel and Dan ("Here are your gods . . . who led you out of Egypt"). He picks ancient northern cities as bases for his new kingdom, cities such as Shechem and then Penuel. And though Jeroboam's "calves" are viewed negatively in these chapters of the Bible (and in its parallel in the story of Moses, Exodus 32), this critique of them as idols was added by the later (Judean) narrators of the story. Archaeological finds of ancient statues of bulls in Israelite sites suggest that they were one of the most ancient symbols of divinity known in early Israel, and no one in Jeroboam's time would have questioned his use of this revered religious symbol for divinity.

There is one other way in which Jeroboam's scribes and/or other northerners forged a path in founding the northern monarchy: they *appear to have developed a corpus of (Northern) Israelite written texts*. Indeed, this corpus even seems to have been a "counter-curriculum" that contrasted with the perspective of the Jerusalem-centered Zion theology that was central in the Davidic monarchy of the south. This counter-curriculum featured written versions of earlier oral traditions of the north, writings that thus featured northern themes, places, and heroes.

A good example is the story of Jacob found in Genesis (Genesis 25–35). It features Jeroboam's royal sanctuary city of Bethel and early northern capitals such as Penuel (where Jacob wrestles God – Gen 32:22–32). Indeed, the story of Jacob in Genesis counters the claims of the older monarchy in Jerusalem. Where Jerusalem Zion traditions claimed that Yahweh dwelled at Mount Zion (Pss 9:11; 135:21), the Jacob story embedded in Genesis has God (quoted by Jacob) say, "I am the God who dwells in Bethel" (Gen 31:13). These clues suggest that much of the Jacob story now in Genesis was written in the north as a counterpoint to the writings of the Davidic monarchy in the south. To be sure, as we saw in Chapter 2, the Genesis Jacob story builds on more ancient trickster and other oral traditions about Jacob and his family. Nevertheless, most of the *written* story of Jacob probably originates from the northern monarchy of Israel as part of its counter-curriculum. It even seems as if the northern prophet, Hosea, studied this early Jacob story and could refer specifically to it (Hos 12:3-4, 12 [12:4-5, 13 in the Hebrew and some translations]).

It is difficult to know exactly what other biblical texts were composed in the north, but there are many other chapters of the Hebrew Bible that show strong northern connections. Chapter 2 of this textbook discussed one of those chapters, Deborah's victory song in Judges 5, which focuses exclusively on northern tribes. This early song probably was composed (building on earlier oral tradition) in this northern kingdom of Israel. Some form of the book of Deuteronomy may have started in the north as well. It includes a scene of covenant making on northern mountains (Deut 27:1–13) that almost certainly would not have been composed by later Judean scribes. In addition, it is likely that there was some kind of northern version of the exodus-Moses story, whether oral or written. Not only is Jeroboam described as invoking the god of the exodus as the sponsor of his royal sanctuary (1 Kgs 12:28), but the book of the northern prophet, Hosea, contains an unusual density of references to Moses, the exodus, and wilderness.

More on Method: The Joseph Story and Literary Approaches

The Joseph story as a potential early northern text

The Joseph story (Genesis 37–50 minus probable later additions such as Genesis 38, 46, and 48–49) is another good candidate for being a northern text that has been adapted into the present Bible. These chapters tell a tale that starts with a pair of dreams that Joseph has. In one, the sheaves of grain belonging to Joseph's brothers bow down in obedience to Joseph's sheaf. In the other dream, 11 stars and the sun and moon bow down to Joseph. His (11) brothers interpret these dreams as claims by Joseph that he will dominate them, and their murderous resentment about these claims results in Joseph being taken into slavery in Egypt (Genesis 37). There he rises to prominence, is able to provide food for his family when they flee a famine in Israel, and is reconciled with his brothers (Genesis 45 and 50).

Especially since Joseph was seen as the father of Ephraim and Manasseh (Gen 41:50–52; ancestors of the tribes of the heartland of Israel) and thus the ancestor of Jeroboam, an Ephraimite (1 Kgs 11:26), tribal groups of the north could have seen this narrative as an allegory of power. It may have been designed to help them recognize the need for rulers like Jeroboam to rule and provide for "their brothers" much like Joseph's brothers come to recognize his need to rule over and provide for them. As such, an early form of the Joseph narrative that is now embedded in Genesis may have been composed and circulated in Israel (of the northern hill country).

Literary approaches and Joseph

Meanwhile, the Joseph story has been a major focus of literary study of the Bible. No matter when one dates the Joseph story (and there is debate), there is much room for analysis of its characterization of Joseph and his brothers, the contrast between what the storyteller says happened at points and what different brothers report about what happened, and the move of the plot from brotherly resentment to reconciliation. Literary study of biblical narrative draws on the study of modern literature to reach insights about texts like the Joseph story that are not related to particular theories about dating or social context.

Such literary approaches to biblical narrative have grown ever more varied as study of literature in the humanities itself has evolved. For more on diverse literary approaches to narrative, see David Gunn, "Narrative Criticism," pp. 201–29 in S. McKenzie and S. Haynes (eds.), *To Each Its Own Meaning* (Louisville, KY: Westminster John Knox Press, 1999) and Hugh Pyper, "Postmodernism," pp. 117–136 in S. McKenzie and J. Kaltner (eds.), *New Meanings for Ancient Texts* (Louisville, KY: Westminster John Knox, 2013).

It should be no surprise that parts of the Bible would originate from such northern traditions. There is much archaeological evidence that the kingdom of Israel in the north was more powerful and prominent than the kingdom of Judah to the south. In particular, Israel reached a zenith of power during the time of King Omri and his son, Ahab (see Figure 5.1). Omri established a massive new capital in Samaria, made a major marriage alliance with Phoenicia (Ahab's wife, Jezebel, was from the major Phoenician city of Sidon), and dominated the smaller, southern kingdom of Judah, which was still ruled by descendants of David. Though the Omride dynasty was eventually brought down through a coup d'état led by a general Jehu (841 BCE), years afterward, Mesopotamian kings would still refer to the whole area as "the house of Omri." The kingdom of Israel could achieve such prominence during this time partly because it had more land and population than the kingdom of Judah and controlled more central trade routes. Indeed, in many respects the kingdom of Israel represents the first clearly recognizable monarchy for the people of Israel, leaving its mark in the form of a number of urban structures and fortifications in the north that archaeologists date to the time of Omri and afterward. Given this, we can surmise that the kingdom of Israel that was based in the north (ultimately Samaria) is a likely context for multiple writings that came to be included in our present Hebrew Bible.

FIGURE 5.1
One of the ivory carvings found in Samaria, the site of Ahab's famous "ivory palace" (1 Kgs 22:39). Originally covered in gold, these objects illustrate the kind of wealth and power possessed by the northern kingdom, particularly under Omri and Ahab.

FIGURE 5.2
Detail from a wall-sized panorama, in the palace of the Assyrian king Sennacherib, of the defeat of the town of Lachish in Judah. The Assyrians are pushing a siege engine up a ramp to break a hole in the wall of Lachish while the Judean defenders attempt to set the engine on fire by throwing torches down from the wall.

Imperial clouds, however, were on the horizon. In the second half of the eighth century, the Assyrian empire under King Tiglath-Pileser III began extending its reach westward to secure access to resources and trade routes in the area of Israel. The Assyrians had long been a major trading power in the Near East, but by this time they also had assembled an extremely efficient army that was the terror of their neighbors. Figure 5.2 shows an Assyrian depiction of an attack on a Judean city in 701. Other parts of the same set of reliefs show Judean resisters being impaled and inhabitants of the town being led away in chains. Through such attacks, and reports and depictions of them, the Assyrians terrorized the area and enforced their domination. One Assyrian king brags, "Many of the captives . . . I took alive; from some of these I cut off their hands to the wrist, from others I cut off their noses, ears, and fingers; I put out the eyes of many of the soldiers." Another reports, "I fixed up a pile of corpses in front of the gate. I flayed the nobles, as many as had rebelled, and spread their skins out on the piles of corpses." It was in the face of threats like these that central parts of the biblical tradition were formed.

Facing the prospect of possible Assyrian invasion, many countries voluntarily submitted to Assyria and promised to send regular tribute to the Assyrian king. This happened first in the north, perhaps as early as the ninth century with Jehu (as in Figure 5.3), but first in an ongoing way when King Menahem of Israel started paying substantial tribute to Assyria around 738 BCE. But Menahem died, and the kingship was soon taken over around 735 BCE by Pekah, who aimed to join Syria and other nations in rebelling against Assyria and stopping payment of the onerous tribute. In what is called the **Syro-Ephraimite war** (735–734 BCE), this new anti-Assyrian coalition even laid siege to Jerusalem in the south in an attempt to force similar anti-Assyrian policies on Ahaz, who was king of Judah at the time. Ahaz escaped the Israelite and Syrian forces by appealing for Assyrian help, thus defeating those besieging him, but also falling under Assyrian domination himself. Thus began a process by which the northern kingdom was gradually reduced in size and eventually totally destroyed in 722, while Judah barely survived its period of Assyrian rule.

Significant Dates: The Northern Kingdom ("Israel")

Jeroboam, founding kingdom	930–910 BCE
The Omride dynasty (Omri, Ahab, Ahaziah, Joram)	880–841 BCE
Coup d'état by Jehu (Jehu pays tribute to Assyria sometime around 841–814 BCE)	841 BCE
Jeroboam II (relative prosperity)	782–753 BCE
Assyrian domination/destruction of Israel (Menahem, Pekah, Pekahiah, and [King] Hoshea)	745–722 BCE

FIGURE 5.3
Panel from the Black Obelisk of the Assyrian king Shalmaneser III, depicting the Israelite king Jehu offering tribute to and kissing the ground before the Assyrian king. It documents the brief subservience of the northern kingdom to Assyria about a hundred years before Assyria dominated and eventually destroyed the kingdom of Israel in the late eighth century.

This whole process decisively affected the formation of the Hebrew Bible. Whatever texts we now have from the northern kingdom were preserved in the later southern kingdom. Moreover, this drama of Assyrian invasions, anti-Assyrian coalitions, and switching between pro-Assyrian and anti-Assyrian kings forms the backdrop for much of Israel's earliest written prophecy. Prophets such as Hosea are difficult to understand without a sense of the political turmoil their countries were facing. Even the harsh prophecy of Amos, which was delivered prior to the worst of Israel's encounters with Assyria, became as important as it did as an explanation of the disaster that eventually overtook that kingdom.

In sum, much of the Hebrew Bible was formed in the shadow of Assyria's imperial domination of Israel and Judah. The rich literature of the north was destroyed as such, only to be preserved in fragments strewn across Judah's later Bible. In addition, this Assyrian crisis was the starting point for the development of written prophecy in ancient Israel and Judah. Prophets such as Hosea and Amos, Micah and Isaiah, may not have gotten much of a hearing in their own day. Nevertheless, the writings attributed to them became important to later generations of Judeans who had to endure yet more catastrophes like the eighth-century Assyrian onslaught. Let us turn now to look at the phenomenon of such written prophecy.

Ancient Near Eastern Prophecy

Prophecy was a widespread phenomenon in the Near East. The cultures of Egypt, Phoenicia, Syria, and the kingdoms of Mesopotamia all included people, some amateurs and some professionals, who pronounced oracles from the gods. This was part of a broader system by which kings and others tried to predict the future. Much as some people learn to read scrolls, these scholars aimed to learn to "read" clues in the cosmos to the gods' intentions, clues encoded in dreams, omens, parts of special animals sacrificed to divine the future, and other means. Life was unpredictable, and the people of the Near East marshaled every resource they could to understand more about what the gods were doing and what they wished. Verbal prophecies from human mediums were a major way of gaining such information.

Most such prophecies were oral, but sometimes they were written down. The archives at Mari, a Syrian city that became very powerful in the second millennium BCE, contain hundreds of records of prophecies given there, just in case such prophecies might be useful later. Later Mesopotamian archives likewise contain careful records of prophetic oracles and even a few small collections of oracles. Perhaps one of the most interesting written prophecies, however, is an early wall inscription dating from just a few decades before the time of the biblical prophets and found in the Transjordan, just across from Israel, in a crossroads village now known as Deir Alla. Part of the inscription reads as follows:

> This is the scroll of Balaam, son of Beor. He was a seer of the gods. The gods came to Balaam, son of Beor, at night. He beheld a vision in

accordance with an utterance of El. They spoke to Balaam, son of Beor, as follows. "So it will be done, what the brothers have seen. No one has mercy. Make it known. Then Balaam got up the next morning ... he began to fast and to lament bitterly. His people came to him and asked, "Balaam, son of Beor, why do you fast? Why do you weep?" He said to them, "Sit down and let me tell you what the mighty gods have done. [Get] up! See the acts of the gods!

This text is interesting from a variety of angles. The "Balaam, son of Beor" mentioned here is also seen in a biblical text, Numbers 22–24. In Numbers, Balaam is hired to curse Israel, but ends up prophesying Israel's glory instead. In the Deir Alla inscription, however, Balaam's prophecy sounds more like the judgment prophecies of Amos and other biblical prophets. It describes how Balaam saw a vision where the gods announced a devastating drought. A few decades later, Amos, Isaiah, and others would receive divine visions and other messages about devastating judgments about to hit their peoples.

Perhaps yet more interesting, the Deir Alla text may give clues as to how such written prophecies were used. To begin with, the wall inscription shows signs that it once was written on a scroll, much like the books of the biblical eighth-century prophets. In addition, there is a good chance that students were educated at Deir Alla where the inscription was found. An alphabet exercise was found there, and the room where the inscription was found had benches, possibly for students learning texts such as the prophecy of Balaam written there. Perhaps the written prophecies of Amos and other late eighth-century prophets likewise were taught to students, first to the prophets' own children and a few other students, later to many others. Let us turn now for a closer look at their "teachings."

READING Amos 1–2 and 7–9.

Amos, Prophet of Justice

The prophet Amos may be best known right now – insofar as he is known at all – as a prophet of social justice. No other prophet packs so much social critique into so little space. The book starts and finishes with similar divine critiques of elites of northern Israel taking advantage of their power to exploit the poor:

> For the three crimes of Israel and for four,
> I will not turn back the punishment.
> Because they sell the innocent for silver
> And the poor for a pair of sandals.
> They trample the head of the poor into the dust of the earth
> And push the oppressed out of their way.
>
> (Amos 2:6–7; also 8:4–6)

Later, Amos proclaims disaster for the women of the capital city of Samaria, who "oppress the poor and crush the needy" (4:1). He announces disaster for those "who turn justice into wormwood and bring down social solidarity" (5:7). In a passage later echoed by Martin Luther King Jr. and others, he calls for "justice [to] roll down like waters and righteousness like an everflowing stream" (5:24).

This prophecy by Amos does not seem to have been received positively in his own time. To start with, he was an outsider in northern Israel. The Bible records that he came from Judah, having been a shepherd near the small town of Tekoa (Amos 1:1; 7:14). Moreover, most of his prophecies to the north were uncompromisingly harsh, often undermining the ancient traditions most dear to his audience. The Israelites might have thought they were safe because the God of the exodus was on their side, but Amos suggested that this exodus was nothing special:

> Are you not like the Ethiopians to me, Oh Israel?
>> Did I not bring Israel out of Egypt
>> And the Philistines from Caphtor
>> And the Arameans from Kir?
>
> (Amos 9:7)

The Israelites might have thought that God's choosing of them would protect them ("election theology"), but the book of Amos quotes God giving an interesting twist on such northern election theology:

> You only have I known among all the nations of the earth,
> Therefore, I will hold you accountable for all your crimes.
>
> (Amos 3:2)

A later story about Amos in Amos 7:10–17 gives a vivid picture of one response to his message. It starts by telling how Amos went to the royal sanctuary at Bethel and announced that the king of Israel at the time, Jeroboam II, would die by the sword, while his people would go into exile. The high priest at Bethel, Amaziah, sent a message about this to the king and then said to Amos:

> Go away, seer, flee to Judah
> Eat bread there and prophesy,
> But don't ever again prophesy at Bethel because it is the king's
> sanctuary and the temple of the kingdom.
>
> (7:12–13)

Amos in this story responds that he is – or was – not a professional prophet just trying to prophesy anywhere. Instead, God called him from his farmwork in Tekoa to go prophesy to "God's people, Israel" (Amos 7:14–15). But now that Amaziah has told him to stop prophesying in Israel, Amos adds to his former prophecy that the priest's wife will become a city prostitute, his sons will die in battle, and he, a priest, will die "in an unclean land" (7:17).

There is no hint in this and many other prophecies that Amos aimed to change the ways of his Israelite audience. To be sure, there are some isolated calls for the people to change in chapter 5 (Amos 5:4, 6, and 14) and some predictions of hope for Judah added to the end of the book (Amos 9:8b, 11–15). These fragments, however, hardly outweigh the book's general tone of doom. It starts with a set of prophecies where God proclaims that "for three crimes and for four" God will not turn back the punishment (Amos 1–2). It ends with a series of four visions: in the first two Amos turns back God's punishment through his pleas on Israel's behalf (Amos 7:1–6), but in the "third" and "fourth" visions God will not turn back the punishment (7:7–9; 8:1–8). Instead, God has a "plumbline of justice" by which God has measured Israel (7:7–9), and it will be struck by a horrible earthquake (8:8; see also 2:13).

Basics

Book of Amos

Outline: Judean prophetic judgment on Israel

I	Sayings against the nations: setting the judgment of Israel in context	1:1–2:16
II	Elaboration of judgment: the inversion of Israel's election	3:1–9:8a
III	Final qualification: future for "Israel" in a revived Davidic kingdom	9:8b–15

How Amos was adapted for the south

Most specialists in Amos agree that the book of Amos contains numerous additions that adapted his prophecy to the north so that it could speak to the south as well. For example, the oracle of judgment against Judah in Amos 2:4–5 stands out from the other oracles in 1:3–16 and is probably an addition designed to include Judah among the nations judged by Amos. Likewise, the concluding promise that the "booth of David" will be rebuilt (Amos 9:11–15, also introduced by 8b) was probably added to provide a word of hope for Judah (and "Israel" in the wider sense) in contrast to the word of judgment throughout the rest of the book on the northern kingdom of Israel.

More information: Amos and praise

The middle of the book is punctuated by three similar praises of Yahweh: 4:13; 5:8–9; 9:5–6. Read them and see the similarities. These late elements of Amos challenge the reader to praise the awesome God who brings such judgment on Israel and set that judgment in the context of God's creation.

As it turns out, Israel actually was hit by an earthquake around the time of Amos, and this fulfillment of Amos's prophecy was never forgotten (Amos 1:1). Yet his prophecies of disaster proved to be correct in a broader way as well. As Amos had predicted (Amos 2:13–16; 3:11–15; 6:1–7), the northern kingdom was completely destroyed, though not in a way he envisioned. Amos prophesied in a time before the Assyrians' dominance and does not mention them, but in 722 they invaded, destroyed Israel's sanctuaries and palaces, and carried into exile its surviving leaders.

By this time Amos had returned to Judah, and his written prophecy was a form of prophetic "teaching" that Judeans could reinterpret – now in relation to the threat (and later reality) of Assyrian domination. Like teachings seen in Proverbs, these sayings by Amos followed a format of "three and four" (Prov 30:15–31; cf. Amos 1–2; 7:1–9; 8:1–8), rhetorical questions (Amos 3:4–6), and riddles (Amos 3:12; 6:12). Yet this written prophetic teaching of Amos consists of quotations of God, not of a sage like Solomon. And the focus of the teaching is on social acts and their national consequences, not the smaller-scale "moral act-consequence" of an individual student emphasized in Proverbs (see Chapter 4 on moral act-consequence). In the end, this written form of Amos's prophecy had a more lasting effect than any oral words that he delivered. Though he was told to go home by the northern high priest Amaziah, Amos's words are still being read more than two and a half thousand years after they were written.

Hosea, the Northern Prophet, Calling for Israel's Devotion to Yahweh Alone

Hosea 1–2 and 11–12.

READING

The book of Hosea was also addressed to the kingdom of Israel around this time, but it is quite different from the prophecy of Amos. Where Amos emphasized judgment for Israel's injustice, Hosea pleaded for his own people to change, to "sow social solidarity" (10:12) and "protect justice" (12:6 [12:7 in some translations]). Where Amos announced irreversible disaster, Hosea predicted restoration on the other side of God's punishment. And where Amos inverted and critiqued his audience's deep belief in their chosenness (ancient "election theology"), Hosea found new ways of describing that chosenness, ways that emphasized God's love for Israel and God's wish for Israel's devotion. For Hosea, Israel's main failing was a lack of devotion to God and a love of false gods instead.

This is most vividly illustrated at the outset of the book with Hosea's image of God's broken marriage to Israel. The book starts with the story of a rather remarkable and personal act of symbolic prophecy – yet one that we will see also has disturbing overtones. Hosea is called by God to marry and have children by a promiscuous woman, giving these children Hebrew sentence-names that symbolize what God plans to do with Israel, such as "not pitied" and "not my people" (Hos 1:2–9). Then, after the brief insertion of a yet later text reversing this prophecy of judgment (Hos 1:10–2:1), we encounter one of the most powerful passages of the whole book: God's agonized speech to Israel in the wake of Israel's spiritual promiscuity (Hos 2:2–15 [2:4-17 in some translations]). In this speech God, not Hosea, is the husband, and the nation of Israel is the wife. God starts with an address to the children of this "Israel," telling them – in effect – that God has divorced their mother:

> Protest to your mother, protest,
> For she is not my wife
> And I am not her husband.
>
> (Hos 2:2a)

Yet God in Hosea 2 is not as done with this relationship as first appears. God's speech immediately turns toward a plea for the children to get their "mother," their nation, to end her adulterous ways, lest she be subject to the sort of stripping and shaming that wives suspected of adultery had to endure at the hands of their husbands:

> [Tell her to] put away her promiscuity,
> and remove her adultery from between her breasts.
> Lest I strip her naked,
> And display her like the day she was born,
> Make her bare as the desert,
> and make her dry like parched earth,
> And let her die of thirst.
>
> (Hos 2:2b–3)

This Israel, this wife of God, is facing the prospect of drought and famine (the "stripping") because she has gone after "other lovers" in search of love gifts. Yet Yahweh in Hosea's speech insists that she was mistaken about who was providing for her. In actuality, it was really Yahweh, her husband, who was giving her the things a man was to give to his wife: food, clothing, and oil (Hos 2:5, 8).

This list of gifts suggests that Hosea sees Yahweh as betrayed by Israel's worship of other gods, such as Baal (Hos 2:13). According to Hosea, the problem is that Israel sought grain and other benefits from these other gods rather than relying on Yahweh alone. Such worship of multiple gods, of course, was quite common in ancient cultures, and we even see signs (discussed in Chapter 2) that people in earliest Israel worshipped other gods alongside Yahweh (see Figure 5.4). Nevertheless, Hosea proclaims to his people that Yahweh is as offended by such worship of other gods as a husband would be by his wife's adultery. Like a good husband, he provided his wife with good things, and she undermined his manhood by giving her love to others who she thought could provide better.

In response, Yahweh says that he will block Israel's way to her lovers so that – like the woman of the Song of Songs – she will "seek" her lovers and not "find" them (Hos 2:6–7; see Song of Songs 3:1–5). Much of the rest of the speech elaborates on how Yahweh will devastate the land of Israel for its unfaithfulness. Nevertheless, it concludes not with judgment, but with hope –

FIGURE 5.4
Ivory spoon found at Hazor, uniting images of a woman on one side with a tree of life on the other. It illustrates ongoing reverence for a goddess in the form of tree imagery.

in this case Yahweh's plan to seduce Israel and bring back the early times when Israel was in the wilderness and fully in love with God:

> Therefore, look, I will seduce her,
> and I will lead her in the desert,
> And speak tenderly to her.
> I will give her vineyards from there,
> and the valley of Achor as a gate of hope.
> She will respond there as in her youthful days,
> As when she came out of the land of Egypt.
>
> (Hos 2:14–15)

In this way, Hosea's image of marriage between Yahweh and Israel is meant to depict not just Yahweh's pain at what Hosea saw as Israel's betrayal, not just Yahweh's intent to bring consequences, but also Yahweh's enduring love, a love which means that God cannot bear to let Israel go for good and aims to bring her back into relationship with him. As if this were not enough, the book further underscores this point through having Hosea himself describe another act of symbolic prophecy. As a symbol of God's intent to take back Israel despite what "she" has done, God tells Hosea to pay a price to hire a woman known for promiscuity and then specify that she not seek any lovers – not even be with Hosea – for a long time (Hos 3:1–5).

The narratives of symbolic prophecy in Hosea 1 and 3 have led many readers to psychologize Hosea's message, believing that his bold new vision of God was prompted by problems in his personal life, perhaps a propensity to end up with the wrong kinds of women. There are clues elsewhere in the book, however, that suggest a more important background: the power politics surrounding Assyrian domination of Israel going all the way back to the time of King Jehu. In Hos 5:8–6:6 we see Hosea's critique of Israel and Judah's lack of steadfast "love" for Yahweh (6:4). Hosea sees this lovelessness proven when Israel (called "Ephraim" here) pursued "futile" plans (5:11) and even sent away to Assyria to save itself (5:13). In Hos 7:3–7 Hosea condemns as "adultery" (7:4) the constant shifting of kings in Israel, largely in response to the Assyrian threat. In Hos 8:7–10 Hosea likens the kingdom's tribute payments to a case where a prostitute is actually paying her clients ("Ephraim hires its lovers," 8:9). Finally, Hos 9:1–6 mixes images of agricultural plenty and international politics. The prophet tells the people at a harvest festival not to rejoice, because they are like a promiscuous woman who has loved her wages for sex at threshing floor and winepress (9:1–2), and who will soon go into exile in Assyria and Egypt (9:3–6). In these passages, Hosea critiques the multitude of ways that Israel (and Judah) tried to manipulate or buy their way out of oppression by Assyria. According to Hosea, they should have been devoted to and trusted in Yahweh instead of pursuing such power politics.

Basics

Book of Hosea

Outline: prophecy of judgment and hope

| I | Introduction of judgment and hope by way of family imagery | 1–3 |
| II | Elaboration of prophecy of judgment and hope by way of other images | 4–14 |

How Hosea was adapted for the south

Hosea himself may have spoken about Judah in the south (one example is 5:8–15), but there are signs that later Judean scribes adapted Hosea's sayings so that they included Judah in Hosea's judgment (examples are 5:5; 6:4, 11). Still other additions resemble the conclusion to Amos (Amos 9:11–15). Like that conclusion, they see future hope for destroyed "Israel" being located in a broader "Israel" that is centered in Judah and its Davidic monarchy (1:11; 3:5; 11:12).

Hosea's prophecy for the ages

This adaptation of Hosea was but the first step in having the book's images speak to new communities which Hosea had not addressed. Whatever personal or cultic background there once was to Hosea's marriage and other imagery, it gained a symbolic life of its own. Within the present form of the book, the marriage imagery of Hosea 1–3 introduces Hosea's prophecy more generally and then fades into the background. Later, Hosea quotes Yahweh as saying that "by the hand of the prophets I gave analogies" (Hos 12:10; probably mistranslated in the NRSV). These analogies in Hosea – marriage, parent, covenant – have been applied and reapplied by centuries of later readers.

FIGURE 5.5
Pillar figurines of a sort common in archaeological remains of the eighth century. They indicate to many scholars that some kind of goddess worship continued to prevail in the time of Hosea and Amos.

There may be some critique of Israel's cult practices as well, especially given the frequent references to "Baal" throughout Hosea. The people of Israel had worshipped various gods alongside Yahweh, long before Hosea's time, and apparently continued to do so. Indeed, scholars have not been able to reconstruct an early period when the tribes of Israel did not worship other gods. Ancient tribal and later sites have yielded female statues that many interpret to be goddess figurines (see Figure 5.5). Early Israelites appear to have borne names formed from the names of various deities, including "Baal" and "El." And a couple of early inscriptions from around the time of Hosea feature blessings "by Yahweh and his asherah [or Asherah]" (see Figure 5.6). Though there is debate about how to interpret these blessings, many understand them to imply that Yahweh had taken over Asherah, formerly El's wife, as his own. In all these ways, Hosea faced a much more diverse religious landscape than we often picture for early Israel. What was new was that he argued that this religious diversity, this lack of pure worship of Yahweh, was one reason for Israel's ills. He believed that the religious diversity of his time was a falling away from Israel's past pure devotion to Yahweh in the wilderness. That is how most contemporary readers of the present Bible perceive the matter. Yet his audience probably perceived his calls for pure worship of Yahweh alone as something *new*.

Overall, Hosea's main point seems to be that his people are displaying a massive unfaithfulness – whether in international policy or in religious practice. Such unfaithfulness, for Hosea, is like a wife's unfaithfulness to her husband. Yahweh's response is a mix of emotions typical of wronged husbands: agony and jealous wrath at his wife's betrayal combined with a wish to have

FIGURE 5.6
Drawing and inscription found at a desert trading post called Kuntillet Adjrud used by eighth-century Israelites. Interpretation of the drawings is disputed, but note the figure playing a lyre on the upper right. The inscription toward the top is understood by many to refer to "Yahweh and his Asherah."

her back again. In this way, Hosea suggests to his fellow Israelites oppressed by Assyria that Yahweh did not fail or abandon Israel; rather Israel abandoned Yahweh first.

Readers over the years have responded differently to Hosea's picture of God and Israel. For many, the book stands as a powerful picture of God's longing for steadfast love and his willingness to go to any length to bring the people back. Yet others are disturbed by ominous parallels between God's behavior in Hosea's prophecy and the cycle of spousal abuse: a husband's anger at his wife and/or jealous accusations of adultery, physical beating and/or sexual humiliation of the wife, and wooing of the wife back. Hosea used the image metaphorically. Just as – within his time – a husband was seen as justified in punishing, even killing, an unfaithful wife, so also Hosea depicts God as having the right to punish Israel's spiritual promiscuity, starving and stripping her. Most people now would reject this image of God as a husband depriving and beating his sinful, human wife (before taking her back again). Furthermore, such metaphors can be and have been extended to justify literal spouse abuse. Some husbands and religious professionals have taken Hosea's picture to be a biblical endorsement of the right of human husbands to beat or sexually humiliate wives whom they suspect of adultery or other wrongs. Finally, Hosea's use of the image of a sexually promiscuous woman as an image of sin also had consequences. Even though he was critiquing male leaders as much as or more than females, his particular association of feminine sexuality with sin is echoed in several later prophets, the New Testament, and later traditions as well. In light of these concerns, these images in Hosea and later prophets are too painful to serve for many readers as images of a God of love.

There are, however, other images in Hosea that offer alternative ways of envisioning God's agony and passion for reconciliation. Consider, for example, the picture in Hosea 11, where God now is Israel's parent, agonizing over a beloved son's disobedience after God's tender care for him. As before in Hosea, God addresses Israel here as "Ephraim," the main tribal territory that was left after the Assyrians stripped the nation of Israel of its more distant holdings:

> When Israel was a child, I loved him
> From Egypt I called my son.
> They were called that, but they went their own way,
> Sacrificing to baals and making offerings to images.
> But I taught Ephraim how to walk,
> I took them up in my arms.
> They are unaware of my healing care.
> I led them with human ties,
> With cords of love.
> I was like one who takes an infant to their cheeks,
> I bent down to them and fed them.
>
> (Hos 11:1–4)

Yahweh's first response to this son's betrayal after such tender care is threats of exile and destruction. Once again we see distant echoes of Israel's struggles in international politics:

> He will return to Egypt,
> and Assyria will be his king;
> A sword devours his cities,
> and it will consume his limbs.
> It will eat because of his schemes.
>
> (Hos 11:5–6)

Yet for Hosea, unlike Amos, this is not the final word. Like a parent who could never give up a child, God relents:

> How can I give you up, oh Ephraim?
> How can I surrender you, oh Israel? ...
> I have changed my mind.
> My compassion is warm and tender.
> I will not act on my wrath,
> I will not again attack Ephraim.
> For I am God, not a man.
> I am the holy one in your midst.
> I will not come in anger.
>
> (Hos 11:8–9)

Here Hosea draws on the metaphorical power of the parental relationship, yet clearly distinguishes this picture of God from that of a human "man." God here is deeply hurt and angered by the faithlessness of his people. Yet God cannot bear to destroy the child whom he once embraced in Egypt and taught to walk in the wilderness. Even if a father could bear to destroy his son, God here is "not a man" (11:9). For Hosea, God's infinite compassion can be imaged, but only partially so, by the powerful compassion a parent feels for his or her child.

We see one more important image appear in Hosea, again one that is intricately tied to the power politics in which Israel was embroiled: **covenant**. Although this word is sometimes loosely used to designate any relationship of mutual obligation, the word "covenant" (*berit* in Hebrew) had more specific connotations in the world of Hosea's day. A covenant was a contract between political parties that was sealed by oaths and curses. When someone entered into a covenant with another, they would pronounce curses on themselves should they break the agreement. Indeed, the word for "make" a covenant in Hebrew is "cut" (Hebrew *karat*). This may be because the parties to the covenant would cut apart a living animal and walk between the bleeding pieces, proclaiming something like "so may this happen to me and more if I break the words of the covenant." The Assyrians imposed such covenants on the peoples they dominated in the form of **vassal treaties** (a type of international covenant), forcing peoples – their vassals – to act out curses of destruction if

Hosea and the "Book of the Twelve Prophets"

The book of the Twelve Prophets

Hosea is the first in the **book of the Twelve Prophets**, a collection of 12 shorter prophetic books, including the books of Amos and Micah, that is usually placed in bibles after Ezekiel or (Ezekiel and) Daniel. The books are attributed to so-called "**minor prophets**" – Hosea through Malachi. The word "minor" is applied to these prophets not because they are thought to be unimportant, but because the books attributed to them are relatively short. Each of these short books has its own character, but they also show signs of being edited into a larger whole by later scribes.

Hosea 14:9 and prophetic teaching

One possible sign of such editing is the last verse of Hosea, Hos 14:9. It stresses that the "wise" will understand the words of Hosea, and it praises the ways of Yahweh as "right." Such mention of the "wise" is otherwise typical of books such as Proverbs. This verse marks the book of Hosea as a form of prophetic "teaching," much like Solomon's teaching in Proverbs and Ecclesiastes.

At the same time, since Hosea is the first book of the 12 minor prophets, this framing of Hosea's book as a teaching has implications for understanding the 11 books that follow. With this conclusion to Hosea in Hos 14:9, they too stand as prophetic teaching to be understood by the "wise."

they failed to keep the terms of these covenants. Hosea seems to refer to these vassal treaties when he attacks Israel for making a "covenant" with Assyria and sending oil (probably to seal a vassal treaty) to Egypt (Hos 12:2). Hos 6:7 and 8:1 refer to another sort of "covenant," this time a treaty with Yahweh that Israel has broken. If these references come from the prophet, Hosea (and not a later reviser), these are our first datable references to a "covenant" between Yahweh and the people. Hosea may have developed this idea of God's treaty with Israel partly in response to what he saw as false treaties that Israel was making with superpowers such as Egypt and Assyria. If so, Hosea's theological adaptation of the idea of "covenant" or treaty stands as an important early example of the phenomenon of hybridity that will be discussed further in Chapter 7: where an oppressed people takes a cultural form of their oppressor (the vassal treaty) and transforms it so that it can express resistance (a vassal treaty with Yahweh).

Conclusion

This discussion of Hosea is particularly important because his prophecy proved so influential in later biblical writings. We will see elements of his picture of divine–human marriage appear in several other prophets. His development of the picture of God's covenant with Israel also becomes important, especially as Judah and Israel endure decades of oppression under the severe vassal treaties of Assyria and then Babylonia. And his call for exclusive devotion to Yahweh was foundational for later Israelites. Although the present Bible contains much later narratives that project this call for devotion back into earlier periods of Israel's history (such as Exod 20:1–3), the book of Hosea is our earliest datable witness to this idea, and it probably was not well received at first. Nevertheless, this belief in God's exclusive claims on God's people grew in importance, particularly as Israel and Judah had to grapple with Assyrian and Babylonian oppression, destruction, and exile. The people suffering through these experiences asked themselves what they could learn from them. They looked back to traditions such as Hosea, spoken out of the crucible of imperial oppression, and concluded that they needed to learn to be more faithful to Yahweh and Yahweh alone. They believed they must reject any other lord (human or divine) and choose Yahweh's boundless love instead.

Meanwhile, it turned out that Amos's prophecy about the north proved more right than Hosea's, at least regarding the northern kingdom. Readers often find the doom aspect of Amos's prophecy difficult to take. "What," they ask, "is the point of announcing irreversible doom on a people if they cannot do anything about it?" In this respect, Hosea's images of hope on the other side of judgment are attractive. Yet there turned out to be no hope on the other side of judgment for the kingdom of Israel to which Hosea addressed his words. Instead, Amos's words proved "prophetic" in the predictive sense of the term. Though Amos was rejected in his own time, and he may well have judged himself a failure, his prophetic writings were adopted and adapted so that readers now, more than twenty-seven centuries later, are trying to learn the lesson he had to teach.

CHAPTER FIVE REVIEW

For Review

1. Know the meaning and significance of the following terms discussed in this chapter:
   - Assyria
   - book of the Twelve Prophets
   - minor prophet
   - Syro-Ephraimite war
   - covenant
   - vassal treaty
2. Name one or two clues that point to the specifically northern origins of early Jacob narratives in Genesis 25–35, standing as a response to claims for Jerusalem seen in Zion theology. What clues point to similar northern Israelite origins for the Joseph novella across much of Genesis 37–50 or for early traditions about Moses?
3. What was an ancient "covenant," and what did it mean to "cut" it?
4. What was special about a "vassal treaty," and how is it related to a "covenant"?
5. How did Amos and Hosea relate in different ways to the ancient Israelite idea of election?

For Reflection

6. If they were to speak today to the same contemporary community, how would Amos and Hosea address that community differently? Would there be an equivalent in that community to the idea of election theology? How would Amos's and Hosea's different feelings about election theology be reflected in their different contemporary prophecies?
7. Try rewriting one of the following three prophecies so that it now addresses a contemporary community that you know and care about: Amos 2:6–16; 8:1–8; or Hos 11:1–12. Try to match it sentence for sentence, image for image, metaphor for metaphor.

RESOURCES FOR FURTHER STUDY

General works on prophecy and all of the prophets

Heschel, Abraham. *The Prophets*. 2 volumes. New York: Harper & Row, 1962.

Koch, Klaus. *The Prophets*. 2 volumes. Philadelphia: Fortress, 1983.

Commentaries on multiple minor prophets

Birch, Bruce. *Hosea, Joel and Amos*. Louisville, KY: Westminster John Knox, 1997.

Sweeney, Marvin. *The Twelve Prophets, vol. 1. Hosea, Joel, Amos, Obadiah, Jonah*. Collegeville, MN: Liturgical, 2000.

Micah, Isaiah, and the Southern Prophetic Encounter with Assyria

Chapter Overview

The Historical Context for Micah and Isaiah

Micah, a Southern Prophet, Predicting Judgment for Judah and Jerusalem

Isaiah's Vision of Hope for Jerusalem/Zion Embedded in the Book of Isaiah

Focus Text: Contrasting Prophetic Visions of Zion's Future

Chapter Six Review

Resources for Further Study

CHAPTER OVERVIEW

In this chapter we move from the world of the northern kingdom of Israel back to that of the southern kingdom of Judah, but the theme of imperial attack remains the same. The people of Judah faced Assyrian attack with faith in Jerusalem's invulnerability, a faith based in ancient Zion theology and soon deepened by an experience of Assyrian withdrawal from a siege of Jerusalem. Addressing this overall situation, Micah critiqued his audience's faith in Zion's invulnerability and proclaimed doom, while Isaiah offered a vision of God's purging of Zion that combined judgment with hope. Both messages were unpopular at the time they were spoken, but became important later. Indeed, the present books attributed to Micah and Isaiah are a mix of early prophecies actually from Micah and Isaiah and prophecies written centuries later. This chapter focuses primarily on texts from both books that can be traced to the eighth-century prophets, while other chapters will discuss later parts of the book of Isaiah. For now, gain a sense of context from this chapter's historical review and then focus on the assigned readings from Micah and Isaiah to see how the early prophecies in each book represent contrasting visions of Yahweh's plans for Zion.

READING 2 Kgs 15:37–16:20; 18:1–20:21 (Ahaz and Hezekiah).

The Historical Context for Micah and Isaiah

Micah and Isaiah worked in a completely different world of ideas from that seen in Hosea. It is a world similar to that seen in the royal and Zion psalms discussed in Chapter 3 of this textbook. And that should be no surprise, since Micah and Isaiah both prophesied in Jerusalem and Judah, the home of royal and Zion theology. Their audiences were more familiar with ideas that Zion was special and invulnerable than they were with Israelite exodus or wilderness traditions. The tradition of Davidic kingship was deeply rooted there too, along with the hopes in royal theology that the Davidic king would bring justice and blessing to the people.

The Judeans drew on such beliefs in royal and Zion theology as they confronted their own version of threats from the Assyrian onslaught. At first, these threats were indirect. In the Syro-Ephraimite war (735–734), Israel and Syria laid siege to Jerusalem in hopes of forcing King Ahaz (735–715) to join their anti-Assyrian alliance. Ahaz appealed to Assyria for help, and the Assyrian armies eventually arrived, defeated Israel and other allied nations, and imposed tribute on Judah. From this point forward, Judah, along with Israel, was under Assyrian domination. A few decades later, another king was in power, Hezekiah (715–686), and he saw an opening amidst chaos in Assyria to get out from under Assyrian domination. He improved the fortifications of Jerusalem and other major outposts, including building a tunnel to Jerusalem's water supply. Moreover, he appears to have tried to rally the people around Yahweh and ensure Yahweh's support through a religious reform involving purification of the Jerusalem temple (destruction of a bronze snake there) and elimination of competing sanctuaries outside Jerusalem (2 Kgs 18:4; compare with 2 Chr 29:3–19).

Significant Dates: Judah under Assyrian Domination

Ahaz	735–715 BCE
Syro-Ephraimite war	735–734 BCE
Hezekiah	715–686 BCE
Beginning of Hezekiah's rebellion	705 BCE
Attack of Sennacherib	701 BCE
Manasseh	686–642 BCE
Amon	642–640 BCE

Eventually, however, the Assyrian armies came again, laid siege to Jerusalem, and threatened to wipe out the kingdom of Judah much as they destroyed the northern kingdom decades earlier. But here the story takes a different turn. The Assyrian army turned back, apparently to deal with urgent military threats that had developed at home. Subsequent Assyrian and biblical sources talk quite differently about this withdrawal (see box on p. 126 for the Assyrian view), but at least two things are clear. First, after this apparently miraculous deliverance of Jerusalem, the people of the kingdom of Judah had an even deeper and more unshakable belief in Zion theology, particularly the idea that Zion was invulnerable. Second, despite this deliverance, Hezekiah and his successors, Manasseh (686–642) and Amon (642–640), remained Assyrian vassals, suffering under Assyrian domination for several more decades until Assyria's power began to wane.

The prophets to be discussed in this chapter both addressed this situation. Though they came from different parts of Judah, they both probably addressed the citizens of Jerusalem, which at that time was a walled city about the size of a few city blocks. They both prophesied in the last decades of the eighth century and touched on similar themes. This closeness of the two prophets, both geographically and chronologically, makes the contrasts between them all the more striking.

Micah 1-3 and 5-6.

READING

Micah, a Southern Prophet, Predicting Judgment for Judah and Jerusalem

The first prophet to be discussed is Micah, a southern prophet like Amos. Just as Amos spoke to Israel as an outsider from Judah, so Micah spoke to Jerusalem as a Judean refugee coming from an area decimated by Assyria (the town Moresheth). Moreover, both prophets spoke words of judgment to their audiences, attempting to pierce their false sense of security. Yet the differences between these prophets are striking as well, and they point once again to the different traditions held dear by their different audiences. Where Amos undermined northern Israelite ideas of election, Micah attacks southern trust in Zion theology, particularly the idea that Zion/Jerusalem was invulnerable to all attacks, a belief manifest in biblical texts such as Psalm 46: "God is in the midst of the city, it shall not be moved" (Ps 46:5 NRSV).

The book of Micah starts with judgment, as Micah proclaims to the people of Judah that they are not immune from the Assyrian disaster that has hit the north. The first oracle describes an awesome **theophany** (divine appearance)

A View from the Assyrian Imperial Court: The Annals of Sennacherib

The following is a quotation from the text of the prism shown in Figure 6.1, where Sennacherib, king of Assyria, describes his invasion of Palestine and siege of Jerusalem during the reign of Hezekiah, king of Judah.

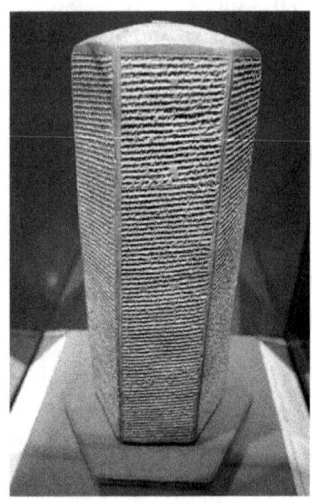

FIGURE 6.1
The Sennacherib prism.

As for Hezekiah of the land Judah, I surrounded and conquered forty-six of his fortified walled cities and smaller settlements in their environs, which were without number by having ramps trodden down and battering rams brought up, the assault of foot soldiers, sapping, breaching and siege engines. I brought out of them 200,150 people, young and old, male and female, horses, mules, donkeys, camels, oxen, sheep, and goats, which were without number, and I counted them as booty. As for him (Hezekiah), I confined him inside the city Jerusalem, his royal city, like a bird in a cage. I set up blockades against him and made him dread exiting his city gate.

I detached from his land the cities of his which I had plundered and I gave (them) to Mitinti, the King of the city Ashdod, and Padi, the King of the city Ekron, (and) to Sillibel, the King of the land Gaza, and thereby made his land smaller. To the former tribute, their annual giving, I added the payment (of) gifts (in recognition) of [my] overlordship and imposed (it) upon them.

As for him (Hezekiah), fear of my lordly brilliance overwhelmed him and, after my departure, he had brought into Niniveh, my capital city, the auxiliary forces and his elite troops whom he had brought inside to strengthen the city Jerusalem, his royal city, and who had provided support, along with 30 talents [420 pounds] of gold . . . as well as his daughters, his palace women, male (and) female singers. Furthermore, he sent a mounted messenger of his to me to deliver this payment and to do obeisance. (Translation adapted from A. Kirk Grayson and Jamie Novotny (eds.), *The Royal Inscriptions of Sennacherib, King of Assyria (704–681 BC), Part 1*. Winona Lake, IN: Eisenbrauns, 2012, 65-66)

Exercise

How does this description compare with Isaiah 36-37 (parallel to 2 Kgs 18:13, 17-19:37)? How about to 2 Kgs 18:14-16 (material not found in Isaiah)?

of Yahweh coming from the Temple (Micah 1:2), yet it quickly becomes clear that this is no cuddly God:

> Yahweh is treading on the sanctuaries of the earth,
> Then the mountains will melt under him,
> And the valleys will burst open
> Like wax on a fire
> Like waters cascading down a slope.

All this, Micah says, is happening because of the "crime of Jacob and the sins of the house of Israel" (1:5). The reader may ask, "What is this crime?" and the text soon answers that it is the capital cities of Samaria and Jerusalem. In a section that sounds much like Hosea, Micah announces that God is about to destroy Samaria, the capital of the northern kingdom, because of its "idols," which he sees as "wages of a prostitute" (1:6–7). But, lest his country-people think they are immune from this disaster, Micah concludes by saying that Judah will be hit by the same destructive power, with the "wound" even reaching the gate of Jerusalem (1:8–9). The next saying (1:10–12) makes a similar point – tracing the path of the invading Assyrian army as it moves from Gath, town by town, to the gate of Jerusalem.

Obviously Micah, like Hosea, is speaking in the context of Assyrian invasion, but he insists that the impending destruction at Assyrian hands is actually caused by God's judgment of the inner ills of the people of Judah. In a social critique reminiscent of Amos, he pronounces a lament over those who:

> plan evil and acts of evil on their beds,
> When morning comes, they do it,
> Because they have the power to do so,
> They covet fields, and seize them
> Houses, and they take them away.
> They defraud others of their homes
> And people of their land.
>
> (2:1–2)

Such critiques continue, as in Micah's attack on those who make women and children homeless (2:9) or in his quotation of God's vivid judgment on the leaders who "devour my people's flesh, flay the skin off them, the flesh off their bones, and . . . breaking their bones to bits, chop them up like soup meat in a pot, like flesh in a caldron" (3:2–3).

Apparently, the powers that be in Micah's time did not like this message. He quotes others as telling him "stop preaching . . . that's no way to preach, shame will not over-take us! Is the house of Jacob really condemned? Is God's patience really so short?" (2:6–7). Apparently there were others proclaiming more hopeful messages, and Micah proclaims Yahweh's judgment on those who "cry 'peace' when they have food in their mouths, but launch war on the one who takes food from them" (3:5). In a climactic message, Micah announces an end to all of the leaders who "build Zion with blood and Jerusalem with malice" (3:10):

> [Jerusalem's] leaders administer justice for bribes,
> Her priests give rulings for a fee,
> And her prophets predict the future for pay.
> And then they rely on Yahweh, saying,
> "Isn't Yahweh in our midst?
> No disaster will come on us!"
>
> (3:11)

For Micah, these leaders and their trust in ancient Zion theology are bringing about the very disaster they consider unthinkable:

> Therefore, because of you,
> Zion shall be plowed as a field
> Jerusalem will become heaps of ruins,
> And the mountain of the house of Yahweh will be a wooded height.
>
> (3:12)

Up to this point, Micah sounds a lot like Amos. He maintains that Jerusalem's corruption is so deep that Yahweh will let the Assyrians destroy it. The book so far explains Judah's oppression by Assyria as a result of its deep-seated iniquity.

Nevertheless, much of the rest of the book, including some of its most famous passages, sounds a much more hopeful note. Micah 4 starts with a famous prophecy (4:1–3), also seen in Isaiah 2:2–4, that God will make Zion/Jerusalem the center of world justice, so that – in a reversal of the usual transformation of farmers into fighters (see Joel 3:10) – nations will "hammer swords into plowshares and spears into pruning hooks" (4:3). The rest of Micah 4–5 contains prophecies of how Yahweh will redeem "daughter Zion," who has endured pain like a woman in labor, bringing her exiles back to her (4:6–7, 8–10). The book goes on to say that when "[Zion] who is in labor has brought forth" (5:3), a powerful ruler will arise from tiny Bethlehem of Ephratah to reign in glory from Jerusalem (5:2–4 [5:1–3 in some translations]). This prophecy, often understood by Christians to be a prophecy of Jesus's birth in Bethlehem, is part of a series of prophecies about how Zion will triumph over the Assyrians and other enemies who dominated her (4:11–5:15).

These words of hope for exiles and promise of victory in Micah 4–5 contrast sharply with the proclamation of absolute doom on Zion in Micah 1–3. Chapters 4 and 5 hardly sound like the words of the prophet who announced that "Zion shall be plowed as a field, and Jerusalem will be heaps of ruins" (3:12). Because of this, most scholars believe that much of Micah 4–5, and likely 6–7 as well (along with a word of hope to later exiles in Micah 2:12–13), was added by later – anonymous – prophets to the book of Micah. To copy and expand an earlier work was an ancient way of recognizing its ongoing importance and applying its message to later times. In this case, these prophets had seen Micah's earlier prophecies of destruction come true, had come to treasure his prophecies, and yet addressed an audience in Babylonian exile who needed new words of comfort to balance Micah's words of judgment. These later prophets declared to their exilic (or post-exilic) audience that Yahweh had a grand future for Zion/Jerusalem and for them. These visionary words of hope – both of a glorious ruler (5:2–4) and of a world where people would not "study war any more" (4:1–3) – have been as important or more important to later communities as the earlier words of judgment on which they were built.

The rest of the book of Micah, however, is not all words of hope. Micah 6:9–16 accuses Jerusalem of succumbing to the same social ills as its northern neighbor: "You have kept the statutes of Omri and the works of the house of Ahab" (6:16). This may be another saying from the same eighth-century prophet (Micah) who proclaimed that the wound of Israel was coming to the gate of Jerusalem (1:9, 12). Most famous of all is the speech in Micah 6:1–8, which responds to people's complaints that God has burdened them (6:3) by saying that God's requirements are simple: "to do justice, love kindness, and walk wisely with your God" (6:8). Soon afterward, the book insists that "it is true wisdom to fear your [God's] name" (6:9), reflecting the fact that the book of Micah, like Amos and Hosea, is prophetic *teaching* or *wisdom*. It is not clear that Micah 6:2–8 came from the same eighth-century prophet who spoke most of Micah 1–3, but it is quite clear that this saying has served for many as a powerful distillation of the long-term significance of the message of the prophets. The saying in 6:2–8 well exemplifies the way the book of Micah has been enriched over time by multiple voices that could be considered "inspired." As a result, the book of Micah now is a powerful mix of Micah's eighth-century words of judgment and later prophetic teachings about hope and God's true wishes for God's people.

Basics

Book of Micah

Outline: cycles of judgment and salvation – Judah

I   Destruction up to the gates of Jerusalem (1:1-2:11) and prediction of the in-gathering of exiles (2:12-13)

II   Destruction of Zion (3:1-12) and its restoration along with the Judean monarchy and people (4:1-5:15)

III   Judgment of Israel (6:1-7:7) and prophetic prayer for restoration (7:8-20)

> **Theme**
>
> Whereas the original prophet, Micah, stressed God's impending judgment on Zion, the book now emphasizes salvation on the other side of such judgment. It was addressed to much later Judeans who had experienced many of the disasters that Micah described. The book encouraged them and later communities to have hope for the future. Though God might destroy everything they held dear, God also could restore them.
>
> **More information**
>
> Micah's words of judgment were not forgotten. A story in the book of Jeremiah, Jeremiah 26, describes how the later, seventh-century prophet Jeremiah was almost executed for proclaiming the destruction of the Temple. At this point, the elders reminded the people of Micah's proclamation of Zion's destruction, a prophecy given a century before the time of Jeremiah (Micah 3:12). In addition, they told a story – not found elsewhere in the Bible – of King Hezekiah listening to Micah's prophecy and repenting (Jer 26:19). Jeremiah's life was spared.

Isaiah's Vision of Hope for Jerusalem/Zion Embedded in the Book of Isaiah

READING

Isaiah 1-11 and 28-32.

The book of Isaiah was one of the first places where scholars recognized this kind of mix of earlier prophecy and later expansion. Isaiah starts with a superscription that identifies what follows as "the vision of Isaiah, son of Amoz, which he saw concerning Judah and Jerusalem during the time of Uzziah, Jotham, Ahaz, and Hezekiah, kings of Judah" (1:1; see also 2:1) – that is, as the revelation given to Isaiah about the southern monarchy during the last few decades of the eighth century. Nevertheless, scholars have found many signs that the book was written over centuries. As early as nine hundred years ago, the Jewish scholar Abraham Ibn Ezra noted that the reference to the Persian king Cyrus in Isa 41:25 seems to indicate that its author not only knew of this king ruling two hundred years after the time of Isaiah, but could describe him to a contemporary audience as one "foretold from the start." Over the last two hundred years, scholars have used these and other observations to distinguish between the words of the eighth-century prophet Isaiah in the book of Isaiah and layer upon layer of prophecies by later writers now in the book as well.

This research has helped scholars see both the complexity and the grandeur of the book of Isaiah. On the one hand, scholars now believe that most sayings actually from "Isaiah ben Amoz" can be found in *parts* of Isaiah 1–11 and 28–32, with *most* of the rest of the book (and all of Isaiah 36–66) coming from later authors. On the other hand, scholars also have an ever increasing appreciation of the insight and artistry of the entire 66-chapter book, later portions included. Certainly, later communities of faith have found inspiration in Isaiah as a whole. Virtually all of the later prophecy in Isaiah 40–66 appears in the cycle of readings used in Jewish synagogues, and the same visions of comfort and restoration have been central to Christianity from the outset. There will be occasion to return to both the design and the interpretation of these portions of the book of Isaiah in Chapters 9 and 12 of this *Introduction*.

For now it is important to recognize that this is another place where modern presuppositions about authorship and "inspiration" can mislead us in reading the Bible. Often modern interpreters assume that the *real* inspiration can only lie with an original author, a prophet in this case, while all later materials must be corruptions of the original, pure message. What emerges, however, from a look at the book of Isaiah and its history of interpretation is that Isaiah – the eighth-century prophet – provided a dynamic and complex vision that was only the start of a much bigger process. Ultimately, the power of his vision *increased* as later authors, addressing quite different times, expanded on and adapted it so that it would speak to those times. The result was a grand book of 66 chapters, the first of the three books of the "**major prophets**" (Isaiah, Jeremiah, and Ezekiel).

Let us turn now to take a closer look at the eighth-century vision of Isaiah ben Amoz. Much of this vision is focused on Yahweh's message amidst threats related to the Assyrian onslaught. The first such major threat was the attempt by Syria and Israel in 735 to force Ahaz of Judah into joining an anti-Assyrian alliance by laying siege to Jerusalem (the Syro-Ephraimite war). The book of Kings describes Ahaz as responding to the siege by asking for help from Assyria (2 Kgs 16:5–9). As we can see in Isaiah 7–8, Isaiah saw this request by King Ahaz as a fatal failure to trust in Yahweh's protection of Zion. In Isa 7:1–9, Isaiah assures Ahaz that the coalition against Judah will not stand and that Ahaz should "not be afraid." Ahaz in 7:10–17 rejects Isaiah's offer of a sign from Yahweh, and Isaiah announces that the result of this rejection will be an imminent attack by the king of Assyria. Finally, Isa 8:1–8 continues these themes, proclaiming disaster on the attackers from Israel and Syria (8:1–4), but also on the people of Judah for refusing to trust in God's protection of Zion (= "the flowing waters of [Jerusalem's spring] Shiloah," 8:6). Each of these stories features a child with a Hebrew name that signifies the core of Isaiah's message: "a remnant shall return" (7:3), "God with us" (7:14), and "speedy comes the booty" (8:1). In light of the rejection of his message, Isaiah tells in 8:10–18 of Yahweh's command to "seal" his prophetic "teaching" in his "students" (8:16), so that these students can serve as a sign for future generations of "Yahweh who dwells in Zion" (8:18). Perhaps some of these students were Isaiah's own, strangely named children, since literate fathers often taught their own children. In this case, Isaiah is passing on to his children a "teaching" and a "witness" that his own generation would not hear. We probably have this process to thank for the initial preservation of Isaiah's words and the beginnings of the book.

The story of Isaiah's commission in Isaiah 6 reflects his experience of rejection during the time of Ahaz. Many readers are well familiar with the beginning of this text, where Isaiah actually sees Yahweh's terrifying presence in the Jerusalem temple, surrounded by "seraphim" (see Figure 6.2 for more on these) – an Egyptian symbol. Awed by the spectacle, he proclaims a lament, "woe upon me, for I am a man of unclean lips in a people of unclean lips, looking onto the king of kings, Yahweh of armies!" (6:5). One of the winged cobras then burns his lips with a fiery coal, saying that this has removed the prophet's sin and bloodguilt (6:6–7). The rest of the passage then describes how Isaiah's people are about to be subjected to a similar burning process, starting with the prophet's commission to deliver a message that will not be heard:

> Go and say to this people:
> "Keep listening, but do not comprehend.
> Keep looking, but do not understand."
> Make the mind of this people senseless,
> And stop up their ears,
> And shut their eyes,
> Lest they see with their eyes,
> And hear with their ears,
> And understand with their mind
> And change their ways and be healed.
>
> (6:9–10)

Isaiah is understandably upset at receiving this commission and asks "how long?" The answer is that Judah is about to be laid waste – again a probable reference to Assyrian attacks. Only after successive invasions is there any sign of hope. It is a "stump," which can regrow (6:13a).

FIGURE 6.2
Judean seals from the time of Isaiah and Micah, showing strong Egyptian influence. Note especially the winged cobras, which probably were the referent for the "seraphim" mentioned in Isaiah 6.

Isaiah 6 and the "Call Narrative"

Many scholars would call Isaiah 6 a "**prophetic call narrative**." Such a narrative is a story, told in the first person by the prophet ("I," "me"), where he tells of how he was authorized by God to be a prophet and deliver God's message. Other examples are Jer 1:4-10 and Ezekiel 1-3.

Here are the typical parts of a prophetic call narrative, with illustrations from Isaiah 6:

1	A divine appearance	1-4
2	An introductory word by God	5-7
3	The call of the prophet (or leader)	8-10
4	An objection from the prophet	11a
5	A divine reassurance/answer	11b-13
6	A sign reinforcing the answer	[not present]

These prophetic call narratives stand toward the outset of a prophetic book (Jeremiah and Ezekiel) or collection in a prophetic book (the Isaiah memoir in Isaiah 6-8) and emphasize God's authorization of the message in that book. They are as different as the books that they authorize, and some scholars dispute the application of the term "call narrative" to some of these texts (particularly since the word "call" has its home in later Christian theology). Sometimes these texts lack one or another part of the typical form. Nevertheless, they share with each other the idea that the prophet's message arose not with him, but with God. The prophet was but a messenger.

Isaiah 6 probably was written as an introduction to his memoir, insisting on God's role in authorizing his prophecy during the Syro-Ephraimite war even though it was rejected. As this text became part of the larger book of Isaiah, it came to authorize the book as a whole.

Other call narratives: an exercise

Judg 6:11-24 and Exod 3:1-4:17 are call narratives for other figures, Gideon and Moses. Compare these texts with Isa 6:1-13. What is similar and what is different about the form of these texts? What is similar or different about the role they play in the biblical books where they occur?

We see this image of the "stump" used elsewhere in Isaiah to communicate that there is hope on the other side of apparent absolute destruction: for an apparently dead stump can have a shoot spring forth from it (see Job 14:8–9). At the end of Isaiah 10, Isaiah describes Yahweh as coming through the whole area, cutting down the tallest trees and chopping off their branches (Isa 10:33–34). Since "trees" were an image for royal dynasties, many understand this to be Isaiah's prediction that Yahweh is about to send the Assyrian army through the area, "cutting off" all of the royal dynasties and thus terminating the monarchies of Judah, Israel, and their neighbors. Yet Isaiah sees a future on the other side of this awful event. Though the Davidic dynasty in Jerusalem might seem like a completely dead stump, Isaiah proclaims that a "shoot shall spring forth from the stump of Jesse [David's father]" (Isa 11:1). This "shoot" will be an ideal king:

> With social solidarity he will judge the poor,
> And he will rule the oppressed fairly.
> He will strike the earth with the rod of his mouth,
> And he will kill the wicked with the breath of his lips.
>
> (Isa 11:4)

Although later Christian interpreters came to see this text as relating to Jesus, it originally stood as an ancient prophecy that a new king would arise over Judah who would fulfill all the promises of royal theology: a king who judges justly and successfully defends his people. The passage then turns to a grand vision of peace centered in Zion:

> The wolf will sojourn with the lamb,
> The leopard will lie down with the calf ...
> They will not hurt or destroy in all my holy mountain,
> For the earth shall be as full of the knowledge of Yahweh
> As waters cover the sea.
>
> (Isa 11:6a and 9)

This whole complex of texts (Isa 10:33–11:9) beautifully displays Isaiah's affirmation of the royal and Zion theology that was so important to Judah, even as he proclaims an awesome, forest-felling destruction of its current leadership. His words, both in Isaiah 6 and Isa 10:33–11:9, helped explain why Judah had undergone such suffering, even as they also offered images of hope that Yahweh eventually would restore Zion and its kingship.

The uniqueness of Isaiah's message is nicely illustrated through comparing Isaiah's words about Zion in Isa 1:21–26 with Micah's proclamation that Zion will be "plowed as a field" (Micah 3:9–12; see the chart at the end of this chapter for a side-by-side comparison with Isa 1:21–26). Where Micah presents God as utterly rejecting Zion (//Jerusalem) as having been built "with blood" (3:10), Isaiah's God sounds more like Hosea's, in agony over how his city – envisioned as female – has been corrupted by violent, corrupt leaders:

> How she has become a promiscuous woman,
> The city that once was faithful!
> She that was full of justice,
> Social solidarity made its home in her,
> And now murderers!
>
> (Isa 1:21)

To be sure, Isaiah does resemble Micah in his understanding of Jerusalem's ills. He, like Micah, criticizes a loss of "justice" (Isa 1:21; see Micah 3:9) caused by its leaders' robbery (1:23, "companions of thieves"; see Micah 2:2), taking of bribes, and perversion of due process owed to the most vulnerable people (Isa 1:23; see Micah 3:11). Yet Isaiah does *not* proclaim a final end to Jerusalem as a result of these misdeeds by its leaders. Instead, in an echo of Isaiah's own burning purification process (Isa 6:6–7), Isaiah announces that God is about to purify Jerusalem as metal alloy is purified in a hot forge (Isa 1:25). This image of a refining fire is Isaiah's way of announcing grand hope for Zion on the other side of painful judgment:

> I will restore your judges as at the first,
> And your counselors as at the beginning.
> Then you will be called "city of social solidarity"
> "The faithful settlement."
>
> (Isa 1:26)

Again, Isaiah contrasts here with Micah. Where Isaiah affirms that Yahweh dwells in Zion and will defend and restore it (Isa 8:18), Micah directly attacks its leadership for saying "Isn't Yahweh in our midst? No disaster will come on us!" (Micah 3:11). It is even possible that Micah had prophets such as Isaiah in mind when he blamed Jerusalem's future destruction on those who would affirm Zion theology in this way (Micah 3:12).

Apparently, Isaiah's message evolved decades later when he prophesied during the time of King Hezekiah, son of Ahaz. This was the time, described in 2 Kings 18–20// Isaiah 36–39 (and 2 Chronicles 29–32), when Hezekiah joined an anti-Assyrian coalition and barely escaped destruction when the Assyrian army of Sennacherib laid siege to Jerusalem (only to withdraw). The narratives about this event found in 2 Kings and Isaiah depict Hezekiah as a positive contrast to his father Ahaz and Isaiah as more affirming of this later king. Where Ahaz refused the sign offered by Isaiah and failed to trust in Yahweh's care for Zion (Isaiah 7–8), Hezekiah actually consulted with Isaiah, and – as a result – the city was rescued (2 Kgs 18–19//Isaiah 36–37; compare with 2 Chronicles 32). The oracles found in Isaiah 28–31, however, show that Isaiah was more critical in this time than these narratives indicate. He repeatedly announces judgment on leaders like Hezekiah who go to Egypt to form anti-Assyrian alliances (30:1–5; also 28:14–22) and rely on military strength for salvation (30:15–16). Yet again, Isaiah seems to have experienced rejection, with people telling him to shut up or preach more comfortable words (30:10–11). This is why, he says, God commanded him to write these prophecies down, preserving them in scroll form as a witness against the people of Hezekiah's time (30:8).

All this suggests that one major impetus for the initial *writing* of prophecies such as those of Isaiah was the experience of rejection. None of the prophets discussed in this or the previous chapter seems to have been a major success in his own time. Yet their words were preserved for a later time by their closest students and/or associates. Moreover, as the words of Isaiah and other prophets appeared to come true over time, the significance of their written prophecies grew. For example, what started as Isaiah's counter-wisdom to the false wisdom of Jerusalem's leaders (see Isa 29:14; 31:1–2) was treasured by later Judeans and expanded in subsequent centuries. Eventually, the smaller groups of sayings seen in Isaiah 1–11, 28–32, and elsewhere grew into the 66-chapter book we now have.

This highlights the multi-layered quality of interpretation of such biblical texts. If the significance of these writings had been exhausted in the time of Amos and Isaiah, we probably would not be reading them now. We have these books because later communities found their sayings so helpful that they copied and expanded them. Moreover, this process of rereading and creative reworking continued in Jewish and Christian communities even after the texts of these prophetic books were fixed. For example, later readers reinterpreted predictions of the imminent arrival of a just Judean monarch (e.g. Micah 5:2–4; Isa 11:1–5) as predictions of a royal messiah who would overcome Rome or some successive oppressive empire. These and other prophecies have retained a lasting significance because problems of injustice and imperial rule did not cease after the Assyrian onslaught in the eighth century.

FOCUS TEXT

Contrasting Prophetic Visions of Zion's Future

Let us conclude with a brief focus on contrasts between the different ways that Isaiah and Micah related to Zion theology and viewed the ultimate future of Jerusalem/Zion. Consider first the summary of Zion theology seen in Psalm 46:

> God is our refuge and strength, a very present help in trouble. Therefore we will not fear though the earth should change, though the mountains shake in the heart of the sea; though its waters roar and foam, though the mountains tremble with its tumult.
>
> There is a river whose streams make glad the city of God, the holy habitation of the Most High. God is in the midst of her, she shall not be moved; God will help her right early. The nations rage, the kingdoms totter; God utters God's voice, the earth melts. Yahweh of armies is with us; the god of Jacob is our refuge.

As we saw in Chapter 3, these kinds of beliefs long preceded prophets like Isaiah and Micah. They were part of the theology that supported the Davidic monarchy with its capital in Jerusalem. In the midst of the Assyrian crisis, Isaiah and Micah present contrasting understandings of the ongoing relevance of such Zion theology. Compare and contrast the following:

Comparison of Micah and Isaiah's Perspectives on Zion/Jerusalem.

Micah 3:9–12	Isaiah 1:21–26
Hear this, you heads of the house of Jacob and rulers of the house of Israel, who abhor justice and pervert all equity who build Zion with blood and Jerusalem with wrong. Its heads give judgment for a bribe, its priests teach for hire, its prophets divine for money; yet they lean upon the Lord and say, "Is not the Lord in the midst of us? No evil shall come upon us."	The faithful city, What a harlot she has become! Zion once full of fair judgment, Where saving justice used to dwell, but now assassins! Your silver has turned to dross, Your wine is watered. Your princes are rebels, Accomplices of brigands. All of them greedy for presents and eager for bribes, They show no justice to the orphan, and the widows' cause never reaches them.
	Hence the Lord Yahweh of armies, the Mighty One of Israel, says this, "I shall get satisfaction from my enemies, I shall avenge myself on my foes.
Therefore, because of you Zion shall be plowed as a field Jerusalem shall become a heap of ruins and the mountain of the house, a wooded height.	I shall turn my hand against you, I shall purge your dross as though with potash, I shall remove your alloy. And I shall restore your judges as at first, Your counselors as in bygone days, After which you will be called 'City of Saving Justice' 'Faithful City'."

The passage in Micah 3:9–12 is an important summation of Micah's prophecy, probably concluding an early collection of his sayings (Micah 4–7 contains material from later times and figures). Notice Micah's critique not only of Zion theology, but of those who trust in such Zion theology. How might Micah have felt about prophecies like that from his contemporary, Isaiah (in the right-hand column)? Meanwhile, note that Isaiah's prophecy is not a mere repetition of Zion theology as seen in Psalm 46. What are both specific similarities and specific differences between Isaiah's message and the affirmations in Psalm 46?

This example provides a specific illustration of how two biblical figures, even prophesying at the same time and place, can have significant differences in perspective. Building on this, use the chapter review questions below to reinforce your sense of the differences between the messages of Isaiah, Micah, and their northern counterparts, Amos and Hosea.

CHAPTER SIX REVIEW

For Review

1. What is a theophany? Where does one occur in Micah? Is it good?
2. What is a "prophetic call narrative," what does it do, and what are its typical parts? Give an example.
3. Which prophets are among the "major prophets," and in what order do these books appear in the Bible?
4. Which chapters in the books of Isaiah and Micah have the largest amounts of material from the eighth-century prophets, and which parts of each book are made up virtually exclusively of texts added by later authors?
5. What differences do you see between the views of these two eighth-century Judean prophets on what is wrong with Jerusalem? What are the main differences in their views of Jerusalem's future? Is either of these identical with Zion theology as seen in Psalm 46? (To help answer this question, use the above chart comparing Micah and Isaiah's perspectives on Zion/Jerusalem.)

For Reflection

6. What differences do you see between Micah (as seen in Micah 1–3) and Amos?
7. What differences do you see between the message of the eighth-century prophet Isaiah (as seen in eighth-century parts of the book) and Hosea?

RESOURCES FOR FURTHER STUDY

Micah

Mays, James Luther. *Micah: A Commentary.* Philadelphia: Westminster Press, 1976.

Isaiah 1–39

Blenkinsopp, Joseph. *Isaiah 1–39.* New York: Doubleday, 2000.

Childs, Brevard. *The Book of Isaiah.* Louisville, KY: Westminster Press, 2001.

Clements, R. E. *Isaiah 1–39.* Grand Rapids: Eerdmans, 1980.

Tull, Patricia. *Isaiah 1–39.* Macon, GA: Smyth & Helwys, 2010.

The history of interpretation of the (whole) book of Isaiah

Sawyer, John. *The Fifth Gospel: Isaiah in the History of Christianity.* Cambridge: Cambridge University Press, 1996.

Torah and History in the Wake of the Assyrian Empire

Chapter Overview

The Seventh Century: Josiah's Reform and the Origins of Deuteronomy

The Deuteronomic Torah of Moses and the Phenomenon of Hybridity

Historical Texts Infused with the Theology and Values of Deuteronomy

   The Book of Joshua

   The Book of Judges

   The Books of 1–2 Samuel

   The Books of 1–2 Kings

Deuteronomistic editing and use of earlier sources in the former prophets

Hybridity and the Traumatic Shaping of History

Focus Text: Deuteronomy 6:4–9

Chapter Seven Review

Resources for Further Study

CHAPTER OVERVIEW

Chapters 5 and 6 featured prophecies responding to Assyrian attack in the eighth century, while this chapter focuses on biblical texts formed in the wake of the collapse of Assyrian domination in the late seventh century (600s). Foremost among these is the first text to be known as a "Torah of Moses." This first "Torah," however, is not Genesis–Deuteronomy, but rather an earlier, seventh-century edition of the book of Deuteronomy. In this chapter of the textbook we will see how Deuteronomy shows the impact of Assyrian oppression even after the Assyrians had lost control of Judah. The same is true of the books that follow Deuteronomy – Joshua, Judges, 1–2 Samuel, and 1–2 Kings. Each of these books reframes earlier traditions about Israel's history in light of Judah's recent experiences of Assyrian oppression. This long experience of imperial domination forms the background for the hostility toward foreigners and foreign influence in Deuteronomy–2 Kings and the emphasis in these books on the importance of exclusive loyalty to Yahweh and Yahweh alone.

The Seventh Century: Josiah's Reform and the Origins of Deuteronomy

The late seventh century was the time when Judah moved from domination by Assyria to eventual domination (and destruction) by Babylonia. At the outset of this period in the 620s BCE the people of Judah already had experienced over seven decades of oppression and humiliation at the hands of the Assyrian empire. During these decades they had been ruled by kings loyal to Assyria, first Manasseh and then (briefly) his son Amon. Then, in the mid-seventh century, cracks began to appear in the once invincible empire. Several regions successfully broke away from Assyria. Amon was assassinated in a palace conspiracy, perhaps by an inner elite hoping to take advantage of the emerging power vacuum. The Bible says that the assassins were themselves killed by the "people of the land," who anointed Amon's 8-year-old son Josiah as king in his place (2 Kgs 21:19–26).

Though he started as a boy king, Josiah reigned for over thirty years (640–609). Important things appear to have happened during his reign, particularly the latter part of it. Thus 2 Kings tells a story of how, in the eighteenth year of his reign, Josiah funded a renovation of the Temple. At some point in the process the priests told him that "the book of the Torah" had been found there (2 Kgs 22:3–10). When it was read to him, Josiah realized his nation faced curses for disobeying the Torah, and he immediately sent to have its authenticity verified by a prophet named Huldah. She prophesied that the words of the book were true, but that King Josiah would die in peace (2 Kgs 22:14–20). Josiah then had the book read to the elders and the rest of the people, and he led the people in making a "covenant" to follow all the words of the book of the Torah that had just been found (2 Kgs 23:1–3). This then started a process that is often described as "**Josiah's reform**" (623 BCE). Josiah commanded the priests to remove the statue of the goddess Asherah from the temple in Jerusalem along with all elements related to Baal and all deities other than Yahweh (2 Kgs 23:4, 6–7). He also destroyed all the sanctuaries ("high places") outside Jerusalem and removed their priests (2 Kgs 23:5, 8–14). In an apparent move to claim lands associated with David and Solomon's kingdom (see Map 7.1), he even desecrated the ancient royal altar at Bethel (2 Kgs 23:15). Finally, he commanded a national Passover in which people from his broader kingdom were to come on pilgrimage to the temple in Jerusalem (2 Kgs 23:21–23). Such a Passover had not been celebrated "from the days of the judges who judged Israel through to the days of the kings of Israel and Judah" (2 Kgs 23:22).

This final note indicates that many elements of Josiah's reform were new. Where the Jerusalem temple had once been the home of worship of various deities alongside Yahweh, now Josiah dedicated it to worship of Yahweh and Yahweh alone. Where the people of Judah and Israel had worshipped in local sanctuaries since the time of the judges, Josiah destroyed those sanctuaries and had them worship in Jerusalem. And where Passover previously had been

MAP 7.1 The Judean kingdom after the fall of the north. Redrawn from Norman Gottwald, *The Hebrew Bible: A Socio-Literary Introduction.* Minneapolis: Fortress, 1985, page 291.

a local festival celebrated by clans in their villages, Josiah required all now to come to Jerusalem, the capital city, in a national pilgrimage festival. Contemporary scholars see an element of political centralization in these moves of religious reform, with Josiah aiming to restore David's Jerusalem-centered kingdom spanning north and south and achieve independence from the Assyrian empire. Nevertheless, the biblical text itself focuses on another rationale for his actions: 2 Kgs 23:24 asserts that all of Josiah's actions were done to implement "the words of the Torah that Hilkiah, the priest, found in the house of Yahweh."

Indeed, scholars have long seen links between Josiah's reform and a book of "Torah" found in the Hebrew Bible. In 1805 the German scholar Wilhelm De Wette noticed that these elements of Josiah's reform are rooted in central emphases of the book of Deuteronomy. The laws in Deuteronomy start with a regulation to destroy all non-Yahwistic worship items and local sanctuaries and worship Yahweh in only one place (Deuteronomy 12). This sounds like an authorization for the temple purification and sanctuary destruction that Josiah implemented. Deuteronomy also includes laws for festivals that require all to come to the central worship place (Deuteronomy 16). This sounds like the background for Josiah's Passover. Deuteronomy concludes with curses that will come upon a people that does not follow its stipulations (Deut 28:15–68). This sounds like the curses that Josiah feared would come upon his people for not obeying the Torah found in the Temple (2 Kgs 22:13). Throughout, the book of Deuteronomy refers to itself as the "Torah" or the "scroll of the Torah" and so on (Deut 1:5; 31:9–12, 24–26; etc.), much as 2 Kings refers to the scroll reported by the priest Hilkiah and implemented by Josiah as "the scroll of the Torah" (2 Kgs 22:8, 10, 13, 16; 23:2–3; etc.). In sum, the biblical story of Josiah's reform implies that the "scroll of the Torah" in Deuteronomy – with its instructions for centralized worship and Passover – is the "Torah" that 2 Kings 22–23 describes Josiah as reading and implementing in his reform.

This narrative in 2 Kings, like other texts to be discussed here, is highly shaped by the theology of its authors. Nevertheless, we have good reason to believe that parts of the description of Josiah's reform in 2 Kings 22–23 reflect actual historical changes that took place during the late monarchy of Judah. Prior to this point, we have tax documents from ancient Samaria and some other early texts that include a proportion of personal names that feature deity names other than Yahweh (e.g. Abibaal "Baal is my father"). After this point, the names found in caches of late Judean letters show virtually exclusive devotion to Yahweh. Archaeologists have found a number of sanctuaries that were used for sacrifice outside Jerusalem from the time before Josiah. In the time of Josiah and afterwards, however, the evidence for such sanctuaries diminishes considerably. Finally, there is a massive shift in the diversity of art around the end of the seventh century. In previous chapters we saw examples of female figurines and images, animals, etc. from earlier periods in Israel and Judah's history. Now our archaeological finds – seen in Figure 7.1 – are heavy on text and light on images. The few images that appear are an isolated human or plant. Thus, not only does the Bible testify to a purification and reform, but the archaeological record confirms that this was a time of significant transformation in how Judeans represented and worshiped their God.

What might have caused such a transformation in the religious and political life of ancient Judah? The first thing to affirm is that this reform was built on older roots. For example, the emphasis on pure worship of Yahweh alone and elimination of Baal worship is a major focus in Hosea's prophecy in the northern kingdom of the eighth century, discussed in Chapter 5. In that chapter we also saw signs that Deuteronomy itself, like Hosea, may have originated as an early northern tradition. Judging from this and similar emphases on cultic purity in narratives about the northern prophets Elijah and Elisha (1 Kings 17–2 Kings 10), it appears that some groups in the Israelite heartland in the north had already strongly advocated pure worship of Yahweh. Moreover, these views may have found expression in an earlier, pre-Josianic version of Deuteronomy, one that found its way into Judah to be discovered in Josiah's time.

Transfers of such northern texts to the south were not uncommon. Late in the eighth century, the northern kingdom was destroyed and the kingdom of Judah became the sole place for the preservation of the values and texts of these groups advocating pure worship of Yahweh. As we have seen, Hezekiah was the king in the south then and instituted some cultic centralization and purification while attempting independence from Assyria as well (see 2 Kgs 18:4 and the later descriptions in 2 Chronicles 29–31). This religious reform by Hezekiah is not explained in the biblical narratives, but may have been

FIGURE 7.1
Seals and other images from the late seventh century. They well illustrate the decline in use of images in Judah and the rise in importance of texts.

motivated by Hezekiah's wish to avoid the mistakes of the northern kingdom as identified by Hosea and other northern traditions. Decades later his religious changes were reversed by his successor, Manasseh (2 Kgs 21:3–7//2 Chr 33:3–7), but they were not forgotten. Indeed, Josiah's reform can be seen as a reinstatement of ancient northern emphases on cultic purity and centralization that had already been introduced to Judah, preliminarily, by Josiah's great-grandfather, Hezekiah.

Even as we recognize the precursors to Josiah's reforms, there are also important new elements. First, the biblical reports are more clear in Josiah's case than in Hezekiah's about how Josiah extended his reforms to encompass some parts of the former northern kingdom – e.g. Bethel – that were closest to Judah (2 Kgs 23:15–20//2 Chr 34:6–7; compare with 2 Kgs 18:4//2 Chr 31:1 on Hezekiah). By the time of Josiah's reform the Assyrian empire had collapsed. This left Josiah room to put his own stamp on the worship of Yahweh in Jerusalem and even extend his power over areas once controlled by northern Israel, such as Bethel, a town about 10 miles north of Jerusalem that had once been the site of Israel's main royal temple. Another mark of Josiah's aspirations may be his institution of a Passover celebration where all came to Jerusalem. Indeed, this is the last major act reported of Josiah (2 Kgs 23:21–23).

This unified celebration of Passover represents one of several ways that Josiah's reign conforms to the regulations of Deuteronomy. Whereas the earlier Covenant Code allowed for Passover to be celebrated at multiple sanctuaries (Exod 23:14–18), the festival calendar in Deuteronomy 16 has Moses instructing Israel to celebrate Passover at just one place, "the place that God will choose" (16:16). So also, the preceding report of Josiah's desecration of the former sanctuary at Bethel (2 Kgs 23:15–20) conforms to the regulations in Deuteronomy 12 about the need to worship Yahweh in one and only one place. Finally, there is an overall parallel between the regulations of Deuteronomy and the above-discussed purifying transformation that apparently took place under Josiah.

All this suggests a final way in which Josiah's reform was distinguished from Hezekiah's: it was connected to a text, in this case a pre-Josiah text sounding much like Deuteronomy (scholars sometimes refer to this pre-Josiah lawbook as "Ur-Deuteronomy"). To be sure, there are signs that some kind of reform was already underway before the "scroll of the Torah of Yahweh" was brought to light. Chronicles suggests that Josiah's purification and centralization preceded the discovery of the scroll (2 Chronicles 34), and even 2 Kings implies that temple renovations were already underway when Josiah was informed about it (2 Kgs 22:3–10). Yet the biblical tradition suggests that this book played an important role in Josiah's reign. This does not necessarily mean that everyone agreed immediately on the authenticity of the book that Josiah put at the center of his reform. Rather, he seems to have felt a need to have it authenticated (2 Kgs 22:14–20//2 Chr 34:22–28), indicating some doubts about its origins (note also a possible critique of this "Torah" in Jer 8:8–9, a potential seventh-century text discussed in the next chapter of this textbook, pp. 169–70, 173, 175). Nevertheless, whatever the origins of the "scroll" announced by the priest, Hilkiah, it appears to have come to play a pivotal role in Josiah's inauguration of a new era in Judah's monarchy.

The present book of Deuteronomy, however, is not the same as the "Ur-Deuteronomy" that preceded Josiah's reform. That earlier Torah book was a more legally focused collection, a lawbook. Yet as that book came to be the center of Josiah's reform, it was supplemented with new elements such as the historical review at its outset (Deuteronomy 1–3) and concluding elements aimed at reinforcing obedience (e.g. Deuteronomy 27–30) that turned the book into a covenant with God. These and other parts of Deuteronomy reflect Judah's experience of oppression by the Assyrians and then their later trauma of exile in Babylonia. Let us turn now to take a look at this complex mix of lawbook and supplements added in light of later oppression.

Comparison: The Covenant Code and Deuteronomy

The laws below cover similar topics, but read a few and see how they treat these topics differently! Though Deuteronomy covers topics not found in the Covenant Code (Exod 20:22–23:33), most topics in the Covenant Code are covered in Deuteronomy. Deuteronomy is thought to be the later of the two.

Topic	Covenant Code	Deuteronomy
Law about altars	Exod 20:22–26	Deut 12:13–28
Slave release laws	Exod 21:1–11	Deut 15:12–18
Cities of Asylum	Exod 21:12–14	Deut 19:1–13
Kidnapping	Exod 21:16	Deut 24:7
Consequences of sex with a virgin	Exod 22:16–17	Deut 22:28–29
Penalty for unlawful religious practices	Exod 22:18	Deut 18:9–14
Penalty for sacrifice to other gods	Exod 22:20	Deut 17:2–7
Prohibition of charging interest	Exod 22:25	Deut 23:19–20
Requirement to return a cloak taken as collateral	Exod 22:26–27	Deut 24:10–13
Requirement of first-born sons and livestock	Exod 22:29–30	Deut 15:19–23
Legal justice rules	Exod 23:2–8	Deut 16:18–20
Returning livestock	Exod 23:4–5	Deut 22:1–4
Prohibition of oppressing foreign workers	Exod 23:9	Deut 24:17–18
Sabbath year rules	Exod 23:10–11	Deut 15:1–11
Sabbath command	Exod 23:12	Deut 5:12–15
Pilgrimage festivals	Exod 23:14–17	Deut 16:1–17
Requirement to bring first fruits	Exod 23:19a	Deut 26:1–10
Not boiling a calf in its mother's milk	Exod 23:19b	Deut 14:21b

The Deuteronomic Torah of Moses and the Phenomenon of Hybridity

READING

Deuteronomy 1–3, 6–7, 12, and 17.

The book of Deuteronomy reveals a remarkable blend of ancient Israelite law and radical adaptation. To start, the book appears to have ancient roots. Not only does it show signs of northern origins (discussed previously), but many of its laws are revisions of older laws seen in the Covenant Code of Exod 20:22–23:33. For example, the altar law in Deuteronomy 12 emphasizes the importance of one altar, while its parallel in Exod 20:24–5 provides instructions for building altars around the land. Similarly, the law about festivals in Deuteronomy 16 parallels the rules about them in Exod 23:14–17 (see box below), making sure that they are celebrated in only one place. In this way and many others, the book of Deuteronomy builds on and revises older legal teachings in Israel. And the Deuteronomic "Torah"-teaching builds on other ancient traditions as well. For example, the law about moving boundary markers in Deut 19:14 builds on a virtually identical teaching in Prov 22:28 (see the box opposite on "Proverbs and Deuteronomy"), which in turn parallels a similar ruling in the Egyptian Instruction of Amenemope. At the same time, Deuteronomy adds a theological rationale not found in the Proverbs teaching.

Overview: The Three Pilgrimage Festivals in the Covenant Code and Deuteronomy

Note the crucial additional note in Deut 16:16 about making a pilgrimage to only one place. Otherwise, the introduction to the pilgrimage festivals in Exod 23:15 and the concluding overview in Deut 16:16 are fairly similar:

Exod 23:15	Deut 16:16
Three times a year you shall make a pilgrimage.	Three times a year every male shall appear before Yahweh your God **in the place that I choose:**
You shall observe the festival of unleavened bread . . .	at the feast of unleavened bread, the feast of weeks, and the feast of booths.
You shall not appear empty-handed before me.	And none should appear empty handed . . .

Comparison exercise

Compare and contrast other parts of Exod 23:14–17 and Deut 16:1–17.

> **Proverbs and Deuteronomy**
>
> Compare and contrast:
>
> | Prov 22:28 | Deut 19:14 |
> |---|---|
> | Do not ever move a boundary marker which your fathers made. | Do not move a boundary marker which earlier generations set |
> | | **In the inheritance which Yahweh your God is giving you to inherit.** |

That said, the biblical book of Deuteronomy is an example of another, quite remarkable form of revision: the revision of an earlier legal document, Ur-Deuteronomy, so that document now forms the core of a biblical **vassal treaty** in Deuteronomy between Israel and Yahweh. During the century that Assyria dominated Israel and Judah, it subjugated many nations through the vassal treaty form. This was a text form that kings under domination and their subjects had to copy and recite. A typical treaty started with a preamble and historical prologue, where the Assyrian king introduced himself and reminded the vassal people of the things he had done on their behalf. Next was the core of the treaty, the requirement by the Assyrian king for the vassal to give exclusive allegiance – "love" – to him. This was followed by a set of instructions on how the vassal king was to express this exclusive allegiance/love. The treaty concluded with elements designed to enforce this set of stipulations: calling of witnesses to the agreement, curses for disobedience, provisions for copying and reading the treaty to the people, etc.

Several biblical texts follow parts of this vassal treaty form, but the book of Deuteronomy follows it almost exactly. Like the other treaties, Deuteronomy starts with a preamble and historical prologue, but now Yahweh, not the Assyrian king, is Israel's sovereign lord who has given Israel its land. Deuteronomy resembles the Assyrian treaties in emphasizing the requirement of allegiance – "love" – that Israel is to offer, but now Israel must offer allegiance to *Yahweh* "with all [its/your] heart, life strength, and might" (Deut 6:4–6). The laws of Deuteronomy include prohibitions of treason against Yahweh (Deuteronomy 13) that resemble Assyrian prohibitions of treason against the Assyrian king. Finally, Deuteronomy, like the Assyrian treaties, concludes with a call for witnesses (now "heaven and earth" 30:19; 31:28), blessings for obedience and curses for disobedience (28 and 29:9–28), and provision for the safekeeping, copying, and regular reading of the treaty (Deut 31:9–13, 24–26; also 17:18–19). Moreover, some of the curses in Deuteronomy 28 are almost exact replicas of curses found in the treaties that the late eighth-century Assyrian king Sennacherib used to ensure loyalty by his vassals to his son and successor, Esarhaddon.

Thus, in the wake of Assyrian oppression, it appears that the authors (or Josianic revisers) of the book of Deuteronomy envisioned Israel as in a vassal treaty relationship with Yahweh, their God. This was what "covenant" (Hebrew *berit*) with Yahweh meant to them. It was a formal relationship, sealed by blessings and curses. Its core was a requirement of exclusive allegiance to a lord. Yet the authors of Deuteronomy made a revolutionary shift vis-à-vis the vassal treaties that they knew: where before Judah had to be exclusively obedient to the Assyrian king, now they were to be exclusively faithful to Yahweh. Where before the Assyrian king was jealous and would tolerate no rivals, now Yahweh is depicted as jealous and intolerant of any rival gods. Before, the people feared the invasion of the massive Assyrian army if they were disobedient. Now they faced direct divine punishment, the "curses of the treaty covenant" (Deut 29:20), if they failed to be faithful to the words of Deuteronomy. Thus when Josiah read some form of Deuteronomy to the people and led them in a covenant ceremony based on it (2 Kgs 23:1–3//2 Chr 34:29–31), he was moving them from one vassal relationship to another. Previously they had known subjugation to Assyria by means of written vassal treaties. Now Josiah was leading them – by means of a Deuteronomy rewritten in light of Neo-Assyrian experience – into a vassal relationship with Yahweh.

We cannot know the precise manner in which some yet older form of Deuteronomy was crafted into an Assyrian-like vassal treaty, but scholars do know analogies to this overall process. In particular, postcolonial theorists have uncovered many examples of writers, artists, and others who appropriate the cultural forms of their former oppressors in the process of trying to develop their own, *post*colonial expressions. For example, even after India achieved independence from Britain in 1947, Indian writers developed a rich tradition of distinctively Indian novels in English. In doing so, they adopted their colonial oppressor's language and an originally non-Indian cultural form, the novel. Yet they used these tools to build a distinctively Indian literature. This is but one example of the way that peoples who must redefine themselves in the wake of oppression often find it helpful to revise and even invert the cultural forms of their former oppressors. Postcolonial theorists refer to this process of adaptation and inversion of oppressors' cultural forms as "**hybridity**." This concept will come up again in this *Introduction* because it is useful in understanding how many biblical texts were formed in a complex response to the cultural forms of Israel's oppressors.

More on Method: Postcolonial Criticism

The term "**postcolonial criticism**" embraces a wide range of approaches that look at how texts and their interpretations are interrelated with structures of colonial domination. Within biblical studies it has taken two main forms.

First, many scholars have taken categories developed in earlier postcolonial studies of contemporary literature and used those categories to

> illuminate the production of ancient biblical literature in relation to imperial domination. This chapter's discussion of Deuteronomy as an example of "hybridity" would be an example of this approach.
>
> Second, other scholars have looked at how the Bible itself has been used as a tool for colonial domination. For more on this approach, see R. S. Sugirtharajah, *Exploring Postcolonial Biblical Criticism: History, Method, Practice* (Chichester: Wiley, 2011).

For now, it is important to recognize that Deuteronomy, this hybrid vassal treaty with God, presents itself as the most important "teaching" Israel could ever have. It bears the label of "Torah," which is the Hebrew equivalent of "teaching," and the book names numerous ways in which the people of Israel are to ensure that this Torah/teaching is foremost in their hearts and minds. They are to memorize this Torah's words (Deut 6:6; 11:18), recite them constantly to their children (Deut 6:7; 11:19), bind copies of Torah commands on the entryways of their houses and on their bodies (Deut 6:8–9; 11:20), make sure that the king reads and obeys this Torah/teaching constantly (Deut 17:18–20), and carefully copy the Torah and read it aloud to the entire community (Deut 31:11–13). As the Assyrian vassal treaty used some of the same means to instill absolute loyalty to the king of Assyria, so also Deuteronomy uses a yet fuller array of these strategies to ensure memorization of this Torah/teaching and loyalty to Yahweh alone.

Apparently, these strictures did lead to later generations reading and rereading Deuteronomy, memorizing its laws, and teaching them to their children. In the following sections of this chapter, we will see how authors of Josiah's time and later infused the theology of Deuteronomy into their telling of the rest of Israel's history in the books of Joshua, Judges, 1–2 Samuel, and 1–2 Kings. In addition, Deuteronomy itself contains additions from times *after* Josiah's reform that show the book's ongoing influence into the exilic period. One of the clearest examples appears toward the end of the book. There we see the addition of an encouragement of later Judeans "exiled to the ends of the earth" (Deut 30:1–10) that now prefaces an earlier section emphasizing the importance of simple obedience (Deut 30:11–20). This addition, one made *after* the period of Assyrian domination, reassures Judean exiles who are in Babylonia that Yahweh will restore them and bring them back to the land if they follow the command of Deut 6:5, loving Yahweh "with all your heart and life strength" (30:6). Contrasting with the threats and promises in Deut 30:11–20, this more reassuring message in Deut 30:1–10 was added to Deuteronomy to show the exiles a way forward amidst apparent total disaster. Through adding such promises, these exilic Deuteronomists gave their people hope, a hope based on return to the Lord and the Lord's Torah.

These and some other such revisions probably played a role in ensuring that Deuteronomy's influence persisted and grew across the exilic and post-exilic periods. We will return in Chapter 9 of this book to consider some comparable exilic revisions to other biblical books.

> **Basics**
>
> ## Deuteronomy (and the Ten Commandments)
>
> ### Outline: farewell teaching of vassal treaty with Yahweh
>
> | | | |
> |---|---|---|
> | I | Introduction of Yahweh's acts, Ten Commandments, and exhortations | 1:1–11:32 |
> | II | Central rules of the treaty with Yahweh (organized by the order of the Ten Commandments) | 12:1–26:19 |
> | III | Means of remembrance and enforcement of the Treaty with Yahweh | 27:1–31:29 |
> | IV | Moses's farewell | 31:30–34:12 |
>
> ### Date(s)
>
> Late pre-exile and exile: Deuteronomy is a combination of an earlier, pre-exilic Deuteronomic lawbook and later, exilic additions to that lawbook. The Deuteronomic lawbook probably includes yet earlier northern materials, but these are impossible to identify precisely.
>
> ### The Ten Commandments and Deuteronomy
>
> The Ten Commandments in Deut 5:6–21 (seen in slightly different form in Exod 20:1–17) are classic teaching materials, short and easily memorized by using your fingers. Their form is similar to the "instruction" form found in Proverbs and other teachings. Like such instructions, the Ten Commandments are difficult to date. They almost certainly do not derive from Moses, but do represent many of Israel's deepest shared values.
>
> The importance of these commandments in the book of Deuteronomy is reflected in the fact that the topics at the center of Deuteronomy (Deuteronomy 12–26) follow about the same order as the topics of the Ten Commandments found in Deuteronomy 5. In this sense, the Ten Commandments form the core of the Mosaic "teaching" given in Deuteronomy.

Historical Texts Infused with the Theology and Values of Deuteronomy

Though Deuteronomy currently stands as the fifth and final book of the Pentateuch/Torah, it actually has as much or more in common with the books that follow it. These are historical narratives that retell and reframe Israel's history from land-conquest to the end of kingship in Judah: Joshua, Judges, 1–2 Samuel, and 1–2 Kings. As we will see, the term "historical" here needs to be understood properly, because these books are not "history" in the modern sense of the word. Instead, they are highly theological presentations of different periods of Israel's life in the land, from the tribal period to exile.

Your challenge in this chapter is to learn to spot signs of that theological slant in these books of the "former prophets" (Joshua to 2 Kings). In particular,

The Books of the Former and Latter Prophets

The books of Joshua, Judges, 1–2 Samuel, and 1–2 Kings are sometimes termed "**the books of the former prophets**" in Jewish tradition. This contrasts them with "**the books of the latter prophets**," which contain oracles and stories connected to prophetic figures (e.g. Isaiah, Amos, Hosea, Micah). As we already saw, these "books of the latter prophets" are not wholly written by the figures with whom they are associated, but instead contain a mix of material by those prophets and later texts. In the case of the "books of the former prophets," none of the material originates from a prophetic figure. Instead, they are originally anonymous narratives about Israel's history that only became associated in later tradition with famous figures (e.g. Joshua, Samuel). Despite this, it is useful to know which books each of these terms ("former prophets" and "latter prophets") refer to.

note the ways that each one connects to ideas in the book of Deuteronomy. For example, the book of Joshua opens with an exhortation for its readers to meditate on the Torah teaching in Deuteronomy (Josh 1:7–8), and the conclusion of 2 Kings includes the above-discussed scene where Josiah makes a covenant based on a book resembling Deuteronomy (2 Kgs 23:24). Moreover, throughout these books we find the repetition of common themes that promote the values seen in Deuteronomy. These include (among other themes) the importance of faithfulness to Yahweh alone, the belief that Yahweh will punish unfaithfulness, the importance of pure worship and sacrifice in only one place, and hostility toward foreigners and/or foreign influence. These are stipulations of the vassal covenant with Yahweh that is presented in Deuteronomy. Because these and other ideas are so characteristic of Deuteronomy, scholars often term these historical books **Deuteronomistic**. Moreover, they apply this adjective, "Deuteronomistic," to particular verses or chapters that have been shaped in light of these values. In the following sections, we look at the Deuteronomistic character of Joshua, Judges, 1–2 Samuel, and 1–2 Kings, seeing how each one presents the history of Israel and its leaders through the lens of Deuteronomistic values and ideas.

The Book of Joshua

Joshua 1, 6, 11

READING

In many ways the connections of the book of Joshua to Deuteronomy are the closest, since Joshua represents the immediate sequel to the covenant with Israel presented in Deuteronomy. Where Deuteronomy presented Moses's speech on the edge of the land, Joshua tells the story of Israel's move into the land. Where

Deuteronomy featured a divine command through Moses to conquer the land and kill all its inhabitants (Deut 7), the book of Joshua then reports how Joshua led Israel to fulfill that command. After some initial chapters reporting Israel's preparations to cross into the land (Josh 1–5), the book reports Israel's complete conquest of the land, starting with the conquering of Jericho (Joshua 6) and continuing until "Joshua took the entire country as Yahweh had commanded Moses" (Josh 11:23) and had also conquered the areas east of the Jordan for the tribes of Reuben, Gad, and Manasseh (Josh 12:1–6). In every respect, Joshua is presented as the true successor to Moses, paralleling him in important ways. Like Moses, he presides over the people crossing water "on dry ground" (Joshua 3–4; compare Exodus 14), and he celebrates a Passover preceded by a circumcision of the new generation of males who were born in the wilderness (Joshua 5; compare Exodus 12). Once the land is conquered, he then distributes it to the 12 tribes (Joshua 12–22). The book then concludes with Joshua's final exhortations to Israel (Joshua 23) and him leading Israel at Shechem to make a final covenant committing to serve Yahweh alone and reject other gods (Joshua 24).

Though the bulk of Joshua presents him as successfully leading Israel in a holy war concluding in the total conquest of the land (Josh 11:23), note that a few parts of the book suggest, in contrast, that the conquest was incomplete (Josh 13:1–7, 13; 15:63; 16:10; 17:12–13), leaving some Canaanite peoples still living in the land. This, then, is the context for Joshua's exhortations to the

The Conquest and Ancient Holy War

The books of Deuteronomy and Joshua describe Israel as conquering all of Canaan and destroying *all* of its inhabitants (Deuteronomy 7; Joshua 1–11). This is a description of an ancient **holy war** (Hebrew *herem*); that is, a sacred war engaged in not for purposes of gaining booty or wives, but at divine command. Biblical rules for the conduct of such holy wars are found particularly in Deuteronomy 20. One gruesome mark of such a war was the destruction of all living beings, human and animal, of the conquered people. The idea behind this was that a holy war was not engaged in for the purposes of profit. Instead, the people and belongings of the conquered land were dedicated to God.

This idea is not unique to Israel. We see this idea in nearby countries too. A main example is found in the ninth-century inscription of King Mesha of Moab. He describes a holy war commanded by his god, Chemosh, against a town in Israel called Nebo.

> Chemosh said to me, "Go, take Nebo from Israel." So I went at night and fought against it from dawn until noon. I seized it and killed all its inhabitants – seven thousand men, youths, women, girls, and even pregnant women. For I had dedicated them [the verb here is related to *herem*] to Chemosh.

One key difference between this inscription and the biblical book of Joshua is that the Mesha text is reporting on a recent killing of people that actually happened. In contrast, Joshua (along with Deuteronomy) draws on the concept of "holy war" to imaginatively depict a conquest centuries before that probably never happened in this way.

> **Basics**
>
> **Book of Joshua**
>
> **Outline: the conquest and settlement of the promised land**
>
> | I | Exodus-like, holy war conquest of the land | 1–12 |
> |---|---|---|
> | II | Distribution of the land | 13–22 |
> | III | Joshua's final exhortations and the covenant at Shechem | 23–24 |
>
> **Date**
>
> Late pre-exilic (especially Joshua 1–12) and exilic/post-exilic (13–24).

people in Joshua 23 and 24, where he urges them to avoid the worship practices of the foreign peoples among them (Josh 23:5–13; 24:14–15). Instead, they should, like Joshua, be devoted to Yahweh and the book of the Torah (Josh 23:6; 24:26; compare Josh 1:7–8). This narrative depiction shows every sign of reflecting the religious challenges of Josiah's and later times, rather than being an accurate depiction of tribal religion. After all, the religion of ancient Israel grew out of Canaanite religion and resembled it in many respects (see Chapter 2). It was only in the wake of Assyrian oppression and Josiah's reform that Israelites saw a need to purify their religion of all foreign influence and thus resist what was now seen as foreign, "Canaanite" elements.

The Book of Judges

Judges 1–5, 21 (Judges 5 already read for Chapter 2).

READING

The book of Judges, to which we now turn, continues this idea that tribal Israel, now in the post-Joshua period, faced the challenge of being faithful to Yahweh and his Torah amidst foreign peoples. In this way, Judges contrasts with large parts of Joshua that depict a total conquest. Where some summary texts in Joshua report that the Israelites engaged in a holy war that killed all Canaanites living in Canaan (e.g. Josh 11:15–16, 23), the book of Judges opens with an emphasis that certain northern tribes in Israel did *not* dispossess certain groups of Canaanites (Judg 1:21, 27–35). This is followed by an angel's judgment on Israel for this failure to fulfill God's commands in Deuteronomy 7 (Judg 2:1–5) and a following report of the death of Joshua and his generation (Judg 2:6–10; compare with Josh 24:28–31). The rest of the book then describes tribal Israel as going through a recurring pattern of punishment and rescue (surveyed in Judg 2:11–22) that is repeated in many of the following chapters:

1. Israel disobeys Yahweh and his commands.
2. Yahweh lets them be conquered by a foreign people.
3. They cry out and Yahweh sends a judge to deliver them.
4. The judge dies, and the people start disobeying again.

The stories in Judg 3:7–16:31 roughly follow this framework, but they also diverge in minor ways, ways that show a spiraling decline of order and obedience in Israel. For example, the judges seen in the book progress from unblemished figures, such as Othniel and Deborah, to less impressive leaders, such as Jephthah and Samson. The final chapters, Judges 17–21, then show how bad things get when the people are without a king and "do what is right in their own eyes" (Judg 17:6; 21:25).

Basics

Book of Judges

Outline: decline of order/obedience in the time of judges

I	Prologue: incomplete conquest and overview of disobedience after Joshua	1:1–3:6
II	Specifics on spiraling chaos:	3:7–21:25
	A Worsening judges: Othniel to Samson	3:7–16:31
	B People on their own with no king	17:1–21:25

Date

Pre-exilic and exilic/post-exilic.

The Books of 1–2 Samuel

1 Sam 8, 12, 15–17; 2 Sam 7–20; 1 Kgs 1–2 (2 Sam 9–20; 1 Kgs 1–2 already read for Chapter 3).

READING

This work is spread over what were once two scrolls (1 and 2 Samuel) and presents an ambivalent picture of the origins of the monarchy. In accordance with its name, the book starts with a report of the birth and commissioning of Samuel (1 Samuel 1–3), who serves as a "judge" in Israel (1 Samuel 7:15) before eventually commissioning Saul and then David as kings.

This story, like those of Joshua and Judges, is a mix of older sources and newer textual elements. The older accounts include, for example, the **Succession Narrative** that was discussed in Chapter 3, one that tells a largely non-theological story of the struggle among David's sons for power and Solomon's eventual triumph (2 Samuel 9–20; 1 Kings 1–2). Scholars also have discerned an older **Story of David's Rise** (to power) behind parts of 1 Samuel 16–31 and 2 Samuel 1–5, and an **Ark Narrative** in 1 Samuel 4–6 (and possibly 2 Samuel 6) telling of Philistine capture and then divine rescue of the ark of the covenant. We do not have actual copies of these earlier sources and cannot know their exact character. Nevertheless, these chapters (1 Samuel 4–6, 16–31; 2 Samuel 1–6, 9–20) are marked by a relative lack of emphasis on Deuteronomistic values, such as the need for the king and people to obey Yahweh's commands and avoid foreign influence.

The present books of 1–2 Samuel, however, reframe earlier materials about Saul and David through a Deuteronomistic lens, largely through placing Deuteronomistic speeches in the mouths of prophetic figures like Samuel and Nathan. For example, earlier traditions about how Saul consolidated power and achieved victory over all of Israel's enemies (e.g. 1 Sam 14:47–48) are preceded by Deuteronomistic chapters where Samuel describes Saul's rule as a rejection of Yahweh's kingship (1 Samuel 8 and 12). Saul's triumph over Amalekites (1 Samuel 15) is critiqued by Samuel as a failure to follow the Deuteronomistic strictures about **holy war** (1 Sam 15:3, 24–28). Earlier stories about David's eventual replacement of Saul as a military hero (e.g. the story of David and Goliath in 1 Samuel 17–18) are now prefaced by a theological scene where Samuel is commissioned by God to anoint David as Saul's successor (e.g. 1 Sam 16:1–13). And the oracle of Nathan to David about his succession in 2 Samuel 7:1–16 provides a Deuteronomistic reaffirmation of God's endorsement of David's dynasty and frames the following **Succession Narrative** (2 Samuel 9–20; 1 Kings 1–2) as the fulfillment of God's promises to him.

Once you recognize this Deuteronomistic recasting of earlier materials, you can make more sense of the multiple perspectives present in the existing text. Saul is both a military hero in earlier materials (e.g. 1 Sam 14:47–48) and a failure by the standards of Deuteronomistic values (e.g. 1 Sam 15:24–28, 34–35). David may have fathered Solomon (through Bathsheba) under questionable circumstances (e.g. 2 Samuel 13–14), but the Deuteronomistic historians present God as endorsing him and his dynasty (1 Sam 16:1–13; 2 Sam 7:1–16). In the end, we will never be able to recover Israel's earliest traditions about figures

---

Basics

Books of 1–2 Samuel

Outline: the beginnings of the Davidic kingship (1–2 Samuel)

I	Transitions to kingship	1 Samuel 1–31
	A Samuel: a judge who anointed kings	1 Samuel 1–8
	B Samuel to Saul: a failed king	1 Samuel 9–15
	C Saul to David: the dynastic founder	1 Samuel 16–31
II	David's reign as Israel's first king	2 Samuel 1–24

Date

Late pre-exile and exile/post-exile with some early pre-exilic sources.

The Books of 1–2 Kings

READING

1 Kgs 3-12 (already read for chapters 3 and 5) and 2 Kgs 17–23.

Like 1–2 Samuel, the books of Kings were divided for space reasons across two scrolls, 1 and 2 Kings. Nevertheless, these two scrolls tell one story of the rise and fall of the monarchy of Israel, from Solomon to the exile. The story starts with the last part of the Succession Narrative, the description of Solomon's successful battle for the throne of David (1 Kings 1–2). Solomon's reign is then narrated in two parts, corresponding to ways that he fulfilled the Deuteronomistic program and yet fell away from it. The first major part describes how Solomon gained wisdom to rightly judge cases (1 Kings 3) and ultimately built and dedicated the temple in Jerusalem (1 Kings 6–8) that became the one place that Israel was allowed to sacrifice, according to the law in Deuteronomy (Deut 12:13–28). The narrative goes on, however, to describe Solomon's fall toward disobedience because of disobeying the Deuteronomic law against marrying foreign wives (1 Kings 11; compare Deut 7:3–4), an episode which is soon followed by the revolt of the northern tribes and their building of their own altars outside Jerusalem (1 Kings 12). From then on, the books of Kings evaluate each king of Israel and Judah by the extent to which he is faithful or disobedient to the commands in Deuteronomy to worship Yahweh alone and to sacrifice at only one place, that place now being Jerusalem. Judged by this standard, the northern kingdom of Israel is doomed from the outset, because its first king, Jeroboam, prevents his people from worshipping in Jerusalem by inaugurating illegitimate sanctuaries at Bethel and Dan and telling his people to worship there (1 Kgs 12:26–33). After this, no Israelite king receives a good evaluation from the Deuteronomistic author of Kings, and the later destruction of Israel by Assyria is explained as resulting from Israel's idolatrous disobedience (2 Kings 17).

The last chapters of 2 Kings then present a mixed picture of the end of David's dynasty. On the one hand, it presents two kings, Hezekiah and Josiah, as fulfilling the commands of Yahweh. They centralize worship in Jerusalem and purify the Jerusalem temple of foreign influence. On the other hand, 2 Kings goes on to explain Judah's subsequent exile in Babylonia as resulting from the fact that Josiah's reform could not appease Yahweh's anger at his grandfather Manasseh's earlier restoration of sanctuaries outside Jerusalem and pollution of the Jerusalem temple (2 Kgs 23:26–27; see 2 Kgs 21:3–15). Both of these perspectives conform to the values of Deuteronomy. The celebration of Hezekiah and Josiah connect with Yahweh's promise of an eternal dynasty in the Deuteronomistic version of Nathan's oracle to David (2 Sam 7:16). Meanwhile, the explanation of exile by way of Manasseh's sins connects with prohibitions against foreign worship in Deuteronomy. In Chapter 9 of this introduction we will return to texts like 2 Kgs 21:10–15 and 23:26–27 that manifest a clearly *exilic* Deuteronomistic perspective. This perspective contrasts at points with potential earlier Deuteronomistic elements like the endorsement of David's dynasty in 2 Samuel 7:1–16.

Basics

Books of 1–2 Kings

Outline: obedience and sin in the history of the monarchies

I	Solomon's rule: devotion and sin	1 Kings 1–11
II	Divided monarchy: northern sin and southern obedience and sin	1 Kings 12–2 Kings 17
III	Decline of Judah: Hezekiah to exile	2 Kings 18–25

Date

Pre-exilic edition and exilic/post-exilic redactions.

Deuteronomistic editing and use of earlier sources in the former prophets

The above discussion has highlighted diverse ways in which the books of the former prophets (Joshua, Judges, 1–2 Samuel, 1–2 Kings) tell their story through the lens of values first seen in the book of Deuteronomy. The stress in Joshua is on Israel's successful completion of the holy war ordered by Moses in Deuteronomy 7, and Joshua concludes with a renewed covenant commitment on the part of Israel (Josh 24). Judges likewise stresses the importance of obedience to Yahweh, but its series of cycles (of disobedience, oppression, and rescue) depicts ways that Israel repeatedly failed to be sufficiently devoted to Yahweh and ultimately descended into social disorder. 1–2 Samuel depict Yahweh's reluctant establishment of kingship in response to the people's ungrateful request for a royal leader in place of Yahweh. Finally, 1–2 Kings evaluate various kings by the standard of the Deuteronomic strictures of centralization and purification, including a mixed evaluation of Solomon as both positive (1 Kings 3–10) and negative (1 Kings 11).

With this background, I encourage you to try the exercise on the next page ("Learning to Recognize..."), where you can see for yourself how certain passages in these books are particularly saturated with Deuteronomistic language, and values. One key skill in reading these books from an academic perspective is learning to recognize the distinctive language and thought of such Deuteronomistic passages and see how they frame the passages around them.

EXERCISE

Learning to Recognize Deuteronomistic Theology and Influence in Biblical Texts

Pick some of the texts assigned above from Deuteronomy, Joshua, Judges, 1–2 Samuel, and 1–2 Kings, and make a list of the chapters and verses in those texts where you see the following themes (from Deuteronomy) appear, such as those listed at the outset of this discussion: (1) the importance of faithfulness to the LORD (Yahweh) alone; (2) the belief that Yahweh will punish unfaithfulness; (3) the importance of pure worship and sacrifice in only one place; and/or (4) hostility toward foreigners and/or foreign influence. These sorts of themes are among the elements that scholars use to identify the addition of Deuteronomistic theology and values to earlier traditions.

Stepping back, one can perceive a certain broader narrative arc in this part of the Bible, one extending from Moses's farewell speech in Deuteronomy to Josiah's rediscovery of the law and implementation of it (2 Kings 22–23) followed by Israel's exile from the land because of the great disobedience of Josiah's father, Manasseh (2 Kgs 23:26–27; 24:3). These kinds of patterns have led many scholars to speak of an overall **Deuteronomistic History**. This hypothesized history began with Deuteronomy and its review of earlier events in Deuteronomy 1–3. It then continued with the story of Israel's life in the land, from Joshua through Judges and the books of 1–2 Samuel and 1–2 Kings. Some theorize that a pre-exilic edition of this Deuteronomistic History originated in Josiah's time, extending from a modified form of his lawbook now found in Deuteronomy to Josiah's implementation of that book in his reform. Others hold that this Deuteronomistic History came together for the first time during the Babylonian exile with which it now concludes.

An increasing number of scholars, however, are not so sure there ever was such a separate Deuteronomistic History beginning in Deuteronomy and ending in 2 Kings. After all, there are some significant differences between these books. For example, the story of total conquest in Joshua does not square with the picture in Judges of the ongoing existence of Canaanites in the land. Moreover, the cycles of judgment seen in Judges express Deuteronomistic values in a different way than the evaluations of kings in 1–2 Kings. Differences like these have led to questions about the existence of a "Deuteronomistic History" as such. Nevertheless, all recognize the particularly strong imprint of various Deuteronomistic ideas across these seven books.

Hybridity and the Traumatic Shaping of History

With this background, we can and should view much of Deuteronomy through 2 Kings as written in the wake of decades of oppression by Assyria and (later) Babylonia. Like Deuteronomy discussed above, the historical books that follow it exemplify the phenomenon of hybridity. For example, the law-oriented history of kingship now in Samuel-Kings resembles the kind of ideological, pro-royal history writing used in the Assyrian empire to instill pro-royal sympathies in leadership near and far. Yet there are differences between those Mesopotamian histories and the Deuteronomistic books in the Bible. Rather than ensuring loyalty to a human king, books like 1–2 Kings were aimed at ensuring complete and exclusive loyalty to the Israelite God, Yahweh. They embodied the values of Josiah's reform, reframing earlier historical traditions through inserting speeches and other texts that echo the language and ideas of the book of Deuteronomy.

Such reframing of history is analogous to the kind of retelling of individual stories that many people do on the other side of a major crisis. A person may tell their own life story one way for a long time, and then something happens – divorce, a near-death experience, struggle with addiction, or another crisis – that makes them realize that some things that they thought were important were not, and other things that they had ignored were very, very important. In light of this experience, that person will tell their life story differently. Building on this analogy, books like Joshua, 1–2 Samuel, or 1–2 Kings can be viewed as ancient Judah's equivalent to this sort of retelling of a personal story. Judah was on the other side of the crisis of Assyrian oppression, and the retelling of its story was aimed at gaining and maintaining freedom from oppression by foreign powers. Like someone retelling their own personal story, this retelling of Israel's story incorporates earlier elements, such as the Succession Narrative or older lists of kings and their years of rule. But the retelling as a whole is now reframed in light of the experience of liberation from Assyria. It is a retelling of the people's history that is completely reoriented toward their new chance to achieve permanent freedom through obedience to Yahweh's Torah.

Each of the Deuteronomistic historical books now reflects central themes of that Torah, from hostility to foreign influence to valuing of pure and centralized worship of Yahweh alone. Much like the memorizing of the Torah in Deuteronomy, this retelling of the people's story in Joshua through 2 Kings was aimed at reshaping the communal soul of Israel. In contrast to the kinds of texts that may have circulated in the time of Judah and Israel's earlier kings, such historical books represented a new form of post-traumatic cultural memory, one aimed at replacing its predecessors. They re-presented memories of Israel's life in the land through a prism of covenantal theology influenced by Assyrian treaty language and the experience of Assyrian oppression.

All this can give us a new perspective on some of the most troubling aspects of these books, such as the report of a divine command to eliminate all foreigners in the land (Deuteronomy 7) and the description in Joshua of the Israelites' fulfillment of that command, killing all Canaanites (Josh 10:40–42; 11:16–23). For many people, these are some of the most disturbing texts in the Bible, and they have been used in destructive ways to justify the killing or displacement of Native Americans and others.

Yet as we read these texts in Joshua, we should realize that they are not historically factual reports of the Israelites' total conquest of the land (as noted previously, the Bible itself contains traditions to the contrary). Rather, these narratives were designed to help the people who were suffering under imperial domination believe in a God who could help them succeed in a battle against all odds. Much like other Deuteronomistic historical narratives, the conquest account in Joshua was written with the idea that Judah's past oppression was caused by its failure to obey Yahweh's Torah and eliminate foreign influence. Writing from this perspective, the authors of Joshua crafted a narrative that could empower later Judeans to eliminate every trace of foreign influence that might cause them to fall back into oppression. Like many disempowered peoples, these authors wanted a God who could fight and fight successfully on their behalf. Of course, contemporary readers who interpret these texts from a position of privilege should recognize their dangers, but should also note how differently such warlike texts can be perceived by people fighting for liberation against more powerful foes.

FOCUS TEXT

Deuteronomy 6:4–9

Having completed an overview, let us turn now to a specific text that exemplifies many of the central dynamics of seventh-century biblical literature, Deut 6:4–9. Many scholars have seen in this text a possible beginning of an early form of Deuteronomy, before later authors added the review of history in Deuteronomy 1–3, the teaching in Deuteronomy 4, and the Ten Commandments in Deuteronomy 5. Whether or not Deut 6:4–9 started an early form of the book, it certainly sums up many of its major themes, along with themes that play a major role in other Deuteronomistic historical books.

The first sentence is marked off in the Hebrew of the Masoretic text tradition by unusually large final letters at the end of its first and last words. Such letters are often used elsewhere in the Bible to mark the outset of a biblical book (examples are found in Genesis, Proverbs, Chronicles) or an important point in a biblical book. Here they mark the beginning of what is known in Judaism as the "Shema," named after the first Hebrew word in the verse: *shema* – "Hear!" The rest of the sentence can be translated in two ways. One could translate it, "Hear, oh Israel, Yahweh is our God, Yahweh alone." This translation emphasizes that Israel should have one and only one God. The other, equally correct translation (in terms of the Hebrew) is, "Hear, oh Israel, that Yahweh, our God, is one Yahweh." We know from earlier inscriptions that earlier Judeans and Israelites worshipped different forms of Yahweh, "Yahweh from Teman" or "Yahweh from Samaria." According to this translation of Deut 6:4, such local manifestations of Yahweh are false. The Yahweh who belongs to Israel is one and only one deity. This would reinforce Josiah's push to centralize and standardize worship of Yahweh. Both translations link with other traditions in Deuteronomy and Deuteronomistic historical books like 1–2 Kings. Perhaps part of the power of this verse was its capacity to express both meanings.

The next verse expresses a core commandment in Deuteronomy and beyond. The people are to "love" God with all that they are and have. The list is often translated as "all your heart, soul and might" (NRSV) or the like, but these English words are a pale reflection of the Hebrew. The first word in the series, *lebab*, is not just the "heart," but also the "mind." For ancient Israel and other ancient Near Eastern peoples, the "heart" and "mind" were connected, not distinct as they so often are in Western culture. The second word that is often translated as "soul," Hebrew *nephesh*, actually refers to the vital life strength that infuses an entire person. It is the power that distinguishes a living person from a corpse, that powers desire, thought, will, and movement. Deut 6:4 calls on all Israel to devote that entire life strength to love of Yahweh. Finally, the word often translated as "might," Hebrew *meod*, refers to power or strength. Most often it appears in the Bible as an adverb, meaning "very." It may serve a similar function in this series in Deut 6:5, emphasizing how very much Israel must "love Yahweh, your God," with all Israel's heart/mind and life strength.

This call to love connects to other texts, both inside and outside the Bible. One of the places in the Bible where we see a similar description of someone "loving" another with their "life strength" (*nephesh*) is the Song of Songs. Several times the woman in the Song of Songs describes her lover as the one whom her "life strength loves" (Song 1:7; 3:1–4). Whether or not one believes that the Song of Songs predates Deuteronomy, the author of this text in Deuteronomy probably expanded on this more general expression for a lover found in ancient love poetry. Where such ancient love poetry spoke of one's love as the one whom one's "life strength" loved, the author of this text speaks of love with one's "whole heart/mind, life strength, and power." Furthermore, similar to Hosea (which also shows possible links to ancient love poetry), this expanded description of love is focused on the people's love of Yahweh, rather than on one human's love for another.

We see this expanded version of the description of love in one other major historical narrative – the description of Josiah at what would have been the conclusion of a Josianic edition of the books of Kings:

> Before Josiah there was no king like him who turned to Yahweh with all his heart/ mind, all his life strength, and all his power, in accordance with the Torah of Moses, and after him there was never another like him.
>
> (2 Kgs 23:25)

This is the highest praise given any king in any part of the books of 1–2 Kings. It marks Josiah as the superlative example of a king who followed the law of the king seen in Deut 17:14–20, which specifies that the king must study and follow the "Torah" as he leads his people in faithfulness. Later authors added material after this text to explain why the exile still happened despite Josiah's virtues (2 Kgs 23:26–27), but that does not appear to be in view here. Nor does Josiah's strange and seemingly pointless death at the hands of the Egyptians fit with the preceding materials about him (2 Kgs 23:29–30). Rather, this final evaluation of Josiah's reign in 2 Kgs 23:25 concludes a narrative arc that began with the call to "love" in Deut 6:4–5.

This call to "love" in Deut 6:5 also connects, however, to yet another discourse, and that is the Assyrian requirement that vassal kings and their people "love" the Assyrian king. In this case, the "love" required was far from the sort of passionate love envisioned in love poetry like the Song of Songs. Rather, the "love" – Akkadian *ramu* – required in Assyrian treaties was faithful obedience to the Assyrian king: paying tribute, not joining alliances with other nations against Assyria, reporting traitors and extraditing them to Assyria, etc. As a hybrid response to this experience of Assyrian domination, Deuteronomy 6:5 and other Deuteronomistic texts reflect this dimension of "love" as well. But now Israel is to show faithful obedience to Yahweh and Yahweh alone. The people must not follow other gods (//alliances), and they must report and try prophets who encourage betrayal of Yahweh (//traitors). Thus the "love" envisioned in Deuteronomy is not a passionate or romantic emotion that one feels at one time and might not feel at another. It is a basic attitude of loyalty and devotion to one far more powerful than one's self; in this case, to Yahweh, the god of Israel. Deut 6:5 represents a basic reorientation of such loyalty and devotion from the Assyrian king to Yahweh in the wake of the collapse of the Assyrian empire.

The rest of the passage, Deut 6:6–9, aims to reinforce that reorientation through making sure that the people internalize the commands of Yahweh that are expressed in the Torah. Wisdom texts, such as the adaptation of the Instruction of Amenemope in Prov 22:17–18 (also Prov 3:3 and 7:3), urged the student to memorize the sayings of the teacher and recite them – "establish them firmly on your lips." The Torah of Moses in Deuteronomy represents a new form of "wisdom," which likewise should be memorized – "put on your heart/mind" (Deut 6:6) – and recited constantly in the presence of one's children, sitting at home, going on one's way, lying down, and getting up (Deut 6:7). This constant repetition of the words of the Torah is not just aimed at reinforcing the loyalty of adult Israelites, but is also intended to teach children the Torah as well, almost like a language that they hear spoken by parents at home. As if this were not enough, the words of Yahweh's commandments are also supposed to be worn on the bodies of Israelites and inscribed on their doorways and gates. Every aspect of their lives is to reflect Yahweh's commands, particularly the call to honor one and only one God, Yahweh, and love Yahweh with all one's heart/mind, life strength, and power (Deut 6:4–5).

Over the long haul, these injunctions appear to have been effective, since this passage ended up being one of the most important texts in both Judaism and Christianity. A version of this command – "you shall love Yahweh, your God, with all your heart, your soul, and your mind/energy" – is named as the greatest commandment of all by Jesus in the Christian Gospel of Mark and later parallels to it in Matthew and Luke (Mark 12:28–29//Matt 22:34–37; Luke 10:25–27). This corresponds to the honoring of this command in Judaism as one of the holiest of all. Jews are required to recite this command and then others in Deut 11:13–21 (more on love and memorization) and Num 15:37–41 (on wearing fringes) twice a day, when rising and when going to bed. The great Jewish rabbi Akiba is reputed to have died at the hands of the Romans with the words of the Shema on his lips, and Jewish martyrs in later centuries have followed his example, reciting Deut 6:4 and the following verses while dying during medieval riots associated with the crusades, in the Spanish inquisition, and in Nazi gas chambers. Ironically and tragically, many of these Jewish martyrs have died at Christian hands while reciting what Christians recognized as the "greatest commandment." Deut 6:4–5 has been important in both traditions, but that has not prevented centuries of deplorable Christian persecution of Jews.

CHAPTER SEVEN REVIEW

For Review

1 Know the meaning and significance of the following terms discussed in this chapter:
   - Ark Narrative
   - books of the former prophets
   - Deuteronomistic
   - Deuteronomistic History
   - hybridity
   - Josiah's reform
   - Ur-Deuteronomy
   - Story of David's Rise
2 In a few sentences, summarize the important role played by Josiah's reform in shaping books like Deuteronomy and introducing important changes in Israelite religion. In addition, note a couple of textual and archaeological clues that have led scholars to perceive the importance of Josiah's reform.
3 What is a vassal treaty and what are its major parts? How is the book of Deuteronomy similar to and yet different from a vassal treaty?
4 What is postcolonial criticism and what are two different ways in which biblical scholars draw on it? What is an example of the use of postcolonial criticism to analyze Deuteronomy and/or Deuteronomistic historical books?
5 What is the ancient concept of "holy war"? How does this concept function in the books of Deuteronomy and Joshua?
6 (Focus text: Deut 6:4–9) Compare the language and ideas of Deut 6:4–9 with the passages assigned above from Joshua, Judges, 1–2 Samuel, and 1–2 Kings. Where do you see echoes of Deut 6:4–9 in these passages? Look also for places where these passages have a different emphasis from Deut 6:4–9. Given this comparison, what do you think about the idea that these books were once united as one long "Deuteronomistic History" that started with Deuteronomy (featuring the Shema in Deut 6:4–9) and extended through these books to the end of 2 Kings? Does it seem plausible? Why or why not?

For Reflection

7 Compare any of the following sets of laws that are parallel between Deuteronomy and the Covenant Code: altar, judges, slavery, pilgrimage festivals. What do the new elements in the laws of Deuteronomy tell us about the book's distinctive values?

RESOURCES FOR FURTHER STUDY

Broader discussion of Deuteronomistic historical books

Nelson, Richard D. *The Historical Books.* Nashville: Abingdon, 1998.

Deuteronomy

Nelson, Richard. *Deuteronomy.* Louisville, KY: Westminster John Knox, 2002.

Tigay, Jeffrey. *Deuteronomy.* Philadelphia: Jewish Publication Society, 1996.

Joshua and Judges

See "Resources for Further Study" in Chapter 2.

1 and 2 Samuel

McCarter, P. Kyle. *I–II Samuel. 2 volumes.* Garden City: Doubleday, 1980, 1984.

Wijk-Bos, Johanna. *The Road to Kingship: 1–2 Samuel.* Grand Rapids: Eerdmans, 2020.

1 and 2 Kings

Nelson, Richard. *First and Second Kings.* Atlanta: John Knox Press, 1987.

Sweeney, Marvin. *1–2 Kings.* Louisville, KY: Westminster John Knox, 2007.

Prophecy in the Transition from Assyrian to Babylonian Domination

8

Chapter Overview
Nahum
Zephaniah
Jeremiah
  The growth of the book of Jeremiah
Focus Text: Jer 31:31–34
Conclusion to the Pre-Exilic Period
Chapter Eight Review
Resources for Further Study

CHAPTER OVERVIEW

In this chapter we continue our look at the seventh century through discussing three prophets from that period. Though two of these prophets, Nahum and Zephaniah, are often overlooked by readers of the Hebrew Bible, they provide helpful insight into Judah just before and during the time of Josiah's reform. The third prophet to be discussed is Jeremiah, another "major prophet," to whom one of the largest books in the Hebrew Bible is devoted. As we will see, this is only partly due to the fact that Jeremiah had a long career, spanning from Josiah's reform until the beginning of Judah's exile in Babylonia. The other reason that his book is long is that it was expanded over time by some of the same scribes who preserved and expanded the Deuteronomistic books discussed in the last chapter. Apparently, Jeremiah's unrelenting message of doom, though unpopular in his day, proved especially powerful to later generations who found it helpful in understanding their experiences of oppression and exile. In contrast, Nahum's and Zephaniah's more comforting messages did not receive the same attention and expansion.

The Hebrew Bible: A Contemporary Introduction to the Christian Old Testament and the Jewish Tanakh, Second Edition. David M. Carr.
© 2021 David M. Carr. Published 2021 by John Wiley & Sons Ltd.

Nahum

READING

Nahum 3.

The first prophet to be discussed, Nahum, gives us a sense of the hostility toward Assyria that was felt by Judeans around the time of Josiah. Where some prophetic books are made up in part by oracles against various nations – examples are Isaiah 12–23, Jeremiah 46–51, and Ezekiel 25–32 – *all* of Nahum is devoted to oracles against *one* nation: Assyria. The book appears to have been written during Josiah's reign. Assyria was in decline and the Babylonians and Medes were about to destroy Assyria's capital, Nineveh, in 612 BCE. The reading from Nahum 3 powerfully expresses the rage against the brutal Assyrian empire after decades of Assyrian oppression. Building on older prophetic uses of the metaphor of the adulterous female (such as in Hosea), Nahum envisions Nineveh as a sexually promiscuous woman about to be punished for her sinfulness through exposure, isolation, and destruction (3:5–7). The impetus behind this vicious imagery is given at the end of the poem:

> There is no easing of your [Nineveh's] pain,
> your wound is fatal,
> All who hear the report of you,
> Clap their hands in celebration.
> For who has escaped your continual cruelty?
>
> (Nah 3:19)

The Assyrian empire had cultivated a reputation for cruelty in an attempt to terrorize its vassals into submission. Here we see the flip side of it. Hav-

---

Basics

Book of Nahum

Outline: proclamation of the end of Assyrian Nineveh

I Hymn: Yahweh, destroyer of oppressors	1
II Taunt song: destruction of Nineveh	2–3

Themes

Though the poem in Nahum 2–3 celebrates the downfall of a specific imperial city, Nineveh, the poem at the outset makes this book into a more general celebration of Yahweh's ability to destroy imperial oppressors and restore the oppressed. For the later revisers of this book, the destruction of Nineveh was but one demonstration of Yahweh's power to destroy oppressive empires.

ing endured such cruelty and terror for so long, dominated nations such as Judah had a deep store of anger toward Assyria that powered the celebration of Assyria's destruction in Nahum. People who have not experienced such long-term oppression by an empire are often baffled by such rage, seen even now in anti-American sentiments in the Arab world and elsewhere. Yet such rage helps explain the deep and persistent anti-foreign sentiment that runs through so much of the Bible.

 Zephaniah 1.

READING

Zephaniah

Our second seventh-century prophet, Zephaniah, is dated to the reign of Josiah and gives us a window into the time before his reform. Zephaniah proclaims Yahweh's irreversible judgment, a "day of Yahweh," against Judah and Jerusalem for impure cultic practices: worship of Baal and heavenly objects, swearing by the god of Ammon (Milkom), and failure to seek Yahweh (Zeph 1:4–6). These are the sorts of practices that Josiah stopped during his reform, but they were popular up to that point. (Indeed, Manasseh, Josiah's grandfather, is said to have restored many of these practices after Hezekiah's earlier reform, and they probably continued during the early years of Josiah's reign as a boy king – he was anointed at age 8.) But Zephaniah proclaims that Yahweh is about to destroy the officials and royalty who promote such impure worship. Echoing the anti-foreign sentiment we saw in Nahum, Zephaniah says that "the officials and king's sons who wear foreign clothes" are about to bear the brunt of Yahweh's judgment. Where others might think of the "**Day of Yahweh**" as a time when Yahweh comes to rescue the people, Zephaniah (Zeph 1:7–18) – echoing Amos (Amos 5:18–20) – proclaims that this "Day of Yahweh" will be a time of great punishment and sorrow.

To be sure, the book of Zephaniah does not just contain judgment prophecies written in the seventh century. Rather, it also includes promises of hope, promises that were probably added by later scribes during the Babylonian exile and later periods. The second chapter is a call to repentance (2:1–3) in light of Yahweh's punishment of other nations (2:4–15), and the third chapter features a series of promises of salvation that much resemble later prophecies (3:9–20). These probable later materials show how later readers of Zephaniah fit his words into a broader picture of hope for exiles and later returnees from exile, while the earlier materials in Zephaniah 1 give us insight into a Judah that stands on the eve of Josiah's reform.

> **Basics**
>
> **Book of Zephaniah**
>
> **Outline: judgment and exhortation to Jerusalem**
>
> | | | |
> |---|---|---|
> | I | Announcement: "Day of Yahweh" against Judah | 1:2–18 |
> | II | Exhortation to repentance | 2:1–3:20 |
> | | A Call for repentance amidst judgment of nations | 2:1–3:8 |
> | | B Reason for repentance: impending restoration | 3:9–20 |
>
> **Themes**
>
> This book provides another example of how an earlier prophet's words of judgment (e.g. Zeph 1:2–18) now introduce words of hope for later Judeans (2:1–3:20). It is difficult to know which words in the book actually addressed people of the time of Josiah and how they were received. What is clear is that Zephaniah's earlier words are now part of a prophetic book relevant to later Judeans. It teaches the need for people in God's holy city, Jerusalem, to repent in light of Yahweh's judgment of other empires.

Jeremiah

READING

Jeremiah 1:1–3:5; 7:1–15 (compare with Jeremiah 26); 20:7–18; 28 and 36.

EXERCISE

Rewrite Jeremiah's prophecy in Jer 7:1–15 so that it addresses a community important to you and its own form of belief in its invulnerability. Match sentence for sentence, image for image, metaphor for metaphor as much as you can. What would it be like to hear this message as a member of that community?

Jeremiah's career probably overlapped those of Nahum and Zephaniah, but it continued well into the time of Josiah's reform and beyond. Like the book of Zephaniah, the book of Jeremiah contains critiques of the sorts of worship of other deities that Josiah eventually eliminated. Yet Jeremiah's early prophecy is distinguished from Zephaniah's in several ways.

First, Jeremiah's prophecy is directed at people in both the north (Israel) and the south (Judah), probably reflecting the push toward unification of north and south that we see in Josiah's reform. For example, in Jer 3:12–14, 19–23, Jeremiah receives a call to prophesy "to the north," and he calls people in the former kingdom of Israel to repent and come to Jerusalem. This northern focus is present in numerous parts of the book of Jeremiah.

Second, the speeches in Jer 2:2–3:11 that precede the Jer 3:12–23 prophecy to the north echo and intensify the husband-and-wife imagery that we saw in the northern prophet Hosea. As in Hosea, Jeremiah's Yahweh fondly remembers early times when Israel was his bride in the wilderness (Jer 2:2; see Hos 2:14–15). Jeremiah, like Hosea, sees the people's seeking of foreign alliances (2:18) and of other gods (2:10–11) as like a woman's sexual promiscuity (2:20–25, 33). Yet Jeremiah goes beyond Hosea, in his pictures of both his people's misdeeds and Yahweh's response to them. For Jeremiah, God's people has been like a woman having sex with anyone anywhere, "on every high hill and under every green tree" (Jer 2:20; also 3:2), like a wild donkey in heat whose lust cannot be contained (Jer 2:24), like a woman so skilled in planning sexual rendezvous that she can teach the most wicked women new tricks (Jer 2:33). In response, Yahweh promises to permanently divorce her (Jer 3:1–5; contrast Hos 2:14–15). "Israel" has not admitted her guilt (3:13), and there is no independent future for her. Instead, addressing Israelites still living in the north under direct Assyrian rule, Jeremiah urges Israel's "children" (literally "sons") to reject their mother's ways and come south to Zion (3:14).

Looking more broadly, Jeremiah has harsh words for the south (Judah) as well as the north (Israel), and these words are directed against false worship, futile political alliances, injustice, and false prophecy of hope. These themes continue throughout the book. The critique of injustice starts in Jer 2:34, where the prophet – in a disturbing extension of the female metaphor for the people – claims that female Israel has "blood" on "her skirts," not menstrual blood but here the "blood of the innocent poor." Finally, a series of prophecies in Jer 23:9–22 attacks fellow prophets for reassuring those who do evil (23:14), announcing hope and security when there is no basis for it (23:16–17), and missing a crucial opportunity to help the people repent of their evil and avoid destruction (23:21–22). Biographical narratives about Jeremiah, such as Jeremiah 28, continue this theme of conflict between him and other prophets.

Jeremiah seems to have grown ever more pessimistic about his people's prospects. Here we should recall that his career spanned the time from the high hopes of Josiah's reform to the total destruction of Jerusalem about thirty-five years later. Early in his career, Jeremiah shared Josiah's focus on the importance of pure worship of Yahweh, and some have found affirmations by Jeremiah of Josiah's program of reunification of north and south in passages such as Jer 3:12–14, 19–23 (discussed above), and 30:18–21. Yet there is a tantalizing hint in a judgment speech in Jer 8:4–13 that Jeremiah rejected the authenticity of the Deuteronomic Torah that came to stand at the center of Josiah's reform:

> How can you say, "we are wise,
> And we have the Torah of Yahweh,"
> When, in fact, the false pen of the scribes,
> has made it into a lie?"
>
> (Jer 8:8)

This text suggests that the Torah of Moses – perhaps some form of Deuteronomy – is the product of contemporary authors, "scribes." It does not represent a truly ancient word. Though Jeremiah recognized Josiah as a king of justice in comparison with his son, Jehoiakim (Jer 22:15–16), in this central respect – the recognition of the authority of a form of Deuteronomy – the Jeremiah seen in Jer 8:8 is skeptical of a crucial part of Josiah's reform.

While Jeremiah may have supported parts of Josiah's program, his relationship with Josiah's successors was resolutely bad. A particularly large number of his prophecies are associated with the time of Jehoiakim, who was appointed over Judah by the Egyptians on their way back from their fight with Babylonia (2 Kgs 23:34–35). Early during Jehoiakim's reign, Jeremiah delivered a sermon against the Jerusalem temple that is described twice in the book of Jeremiah, once in Jer 7:1–15 and again in Jeremiah 26. Both versions of this "Temple sermon" feature a frontal attack on Zion theology, especially the idea that Jerusalem and its Temple were invulnerable. To those who continually affirm "this is the temple of Yahweh, the temple of Yahweh, the temple of Yahweh," Jeremiah proclaims that Yahweh will make it a heap of ruins, much like the ruins of the ancient tribal sanctuary at Shiloh, where the ark of the covenant once was (Jer 7:14//26:6). Such a claim was virtual blasphemy to the people of the time, since the belief in Zion's invulnerability had been reinforced all the more in the wake of the Assyrian king Sennacherib's withdrawal from besieging Jerusalem during the time of Hezekiah. According to Jeremiah 26, the people were ready to kill Jeremiah for speaking such words. Nevertheless, some recalled that Micah had earlier proclaimed that "Zion shall be plowed as a field" (Jer 26:18; see Micah 3:12). Ultimately, Jeremiah was protected by Ahikam, the son of Josiah's former scribe, Shaphan (Jer 26:24).

Another biographical narrative, Jeremiah 36, preserves a fascinating picture of the delivery and writing of Jeremiah's prophecy. It describes how Jeremiah was commissioned by God in Jehoiakim's fourth year to write a scroll containing all of his oracles up to that point in hopes that Judah might hear it and repent (36:1–3). Nevertheless, when the scroll was read to Jehoiakim, he was not pleased with its contents. As each part of the scroll was read, the king cut it off and threw it into the fire. After this, Jeremiah received a commission to write "another scroll." So Baruch, Jeremiah's scribe, produced a new scroll with the words of the original one, along with "many words like them" (Jer 36:27–32). Many scholars believe that much of what is now chapters 1–25 of the book of Jeremiah contains the remnants of that new scroll (see Jer 25:13). Earlier we saw how Isaiah's memoir was compiled a century before Jeremiah in response to the rejection of his prophecy by his contemporaries (Isa 6:1–8:16). Now, this rewriting and expansion of Jeremiah's burnt scroll (36:27–32) stands as an additional example of how the rejection of a prophet's oral prophecies led to them being written down and even (in this case) expanded.

Yet Jeremiah, partly because of his long career, appears to have experienced more than his share of rejection. Chapters 26–45 of Jeremiah contain biographical narratives that chronicle Jeremiah's difficult experiences, starting with his brush with execution after the Temple sermon (Jeremiah 26; cf. Jer 7:1–15), and continuing with episodes such as his battle with Hananiah over falsely hopeful prophecy (Jeremiah 28), the burning of his scroll (Jeremiah 36), his imprisonment during the Babylonian siege of Jerusalem as a possible traitor (Jeremiah 37), his being dumped in a cistern to die by opponents (Jeremiah 38), and finally his being carried off into Egypt by rebels against Babylonian rule (Jeremiah 43). Though these narratives about him postdate the prophet, they probably reflect his increasing isolation as he prophesied judgment throughout Judah's long slide from dreams of glory under Josiah to total destruction by the Babylonians.

The difficulty of Jeremiah's career is also reflected in a set of laments in the book where Jeremiah protests to God about the unfair job that God has given him. For example, in the lament assigned for this section, Jeremiah 20:7–18, the prophet describes being "taken advantage of" by God, who has required him to proclaim a harsh message that leads to his own rejection:

> O Yahweh you have seduced me, and I let myself be seduced.
> You have overpowered me and won.
> I'm a laughingstock all day,
> Everyone makes fun of me.
> For every time I speak, I cry an alarm.
> I call out, "Violence and ruin."
> For the word of Yahweh has become for me
> A cause of embarrassment and criticism all the time.
> (Jer 20:7–8)

Jeremiah goes on to say that he has no choice, because every time he tries to stop speaking God's message, the word becomes "like a burning fire raging in my bones; I cannot keep holding it in" (Jer 20:9). The lament continues and even reaches a fairly hopeful point, where Jeremiah envisions his eventual restoration and praises Yahweh for it (20:11–13), but then we hear another lament, perhaps originally a separate text, where he curses the day he was born and those who announced his birth (20:14–18). These and other laments chronicle the fact that Jeremiah's work was difficult and did not reach a happy ending (see also Jer 11:18–20; 12:1– 6; 15:10–21; 17:14–18; 18:18–23).

The growth of the book of Jeremiah

Though Jeremiah's prophecy was rejected in his own time, his written words became important to later generations of Judeans. His prophecies of disaster appeared in a different light in the wake of the destruction of Jerusalem, removal of the monarchy, and exile of thousands of Judeans to Babylonia. Apparently, Jeremiah's scribe, Baruch, wrote down some of his prophecies, and later authors added biographical accounts about Jeremiah and expanded the book of Jeremiah with numerous additional prophecies, often in the form of prose rather than poetry.

In the case of Jeremiah, we are unusually lucky in having ancient manuscripts that reflect an earlier version of Jeremiah that is quite different from the one now translated in most Bibles. These ancient manuscripts – both old Hebrew manuscripts found near the Dead Sea (at Qumran) and an ancient

> **Basics**
>
> **Book of Jeremiah**
>
> **Outline: of the Jewish (Masoretic) form of Jeremiah: Judah's judgment in broader context**
>
> | | | |
> |---|---|---|
> | I | First scroll: oracles against Judah (and Israel) | 1–25 |
> | II | Biography: Jeremiah's call for submission and hope | 26–45 |
> | III | Oracles against foreign nations | 46–51 |
> | IV | Historical appendix (adapted from 2 Kings 24:18–25:30) | 52 |
>
> **Themes**
>
> The book of Jeremiah aims to make sense of the destruction of Jerusalem (described in the historical appendix, Jer 52) through looking back at Jeremiah's once unpopular prophecy of judgment and call for submission to the Babylonian empire. In addition, it contains words of judgment on other nations and – particularly in the "book of consolation" in Jeremiah 30–31 – words of hope for Judah.

Greek translation of manuscripts much like them, the Septuagint of Jeremiah – reflect a version of Jeremiah that was about one-eighth shorter than the standard Hebrew edition of Jeremiah (the Masoretic text translated in your Bible). Most scholars agree that this shorter version of Jeremiah was an earlier version of the book, before many words, phrases, and even longer passages (e.g. Jer 33:14–26; 39:4–13; etc.) were added to the book by later scribes. Moreover, this older version is quite differently organized from the standard – Masoretic text – version. It proceeds from the scroll of Jeremiah in 1–25 directly to the oracles against the nations (see Jeremiah 46–51 in your Bibles), and only then to the biographical narratives found in Jeremiah 26–45 and historical materials of Jeremiah 52. Apparently, the Hebrew version of Jeremiah now found in the standard Jewish (Masoretic) Bible was produced by moving the oracles against the nations from their original position to a concluding position in the book (46–51). This meant that the biographical narratives about Jeremiah (26–45) now stood close to the sayings attributed to him (Jeremiah 1–25). This reorganization of the book of Jeremiah and the addition of one-eighth of its present material was done centuries after the time of Jeremiah, probably around the third and/or second century BCE.

Unfortunately, we have no manuscripts to help us trace the earlier history of the development of the book, but scholars do think that much of the book (including parts of Jeremiah 1–25) was the creation, not of Jeremiah, but of exilic authors who were heavily influenced by the language and ideas of the book of Deuteronomy. That is why so many passages in Jeremiah, such as the version of the Temple sermon found in Jeremiah 7, sound so much like the Deuteronomic Torah. Ironically, though Jeremiah himself appears to have rejected that Torah (Jer 8:8–9), these post-Jeremiah texts quote him as announcing Yahweh's judgment on those who reject God's "Torah" (e.g. Jer 26:4). Such associations with Deuteronomy have led scholars to speak of a "Deuteronomistic redaction" throughout the book (with "redaction" = "editing"). This exilic redaction starts with the description of Jeremiah's call in Jer 1:4–10 (compare with Isaiah 6 and Ezekiel 1–3) and includes many other texts across the rest of the book. We even see the incorporation into the book of Jeremiah (Jer 39:1–10; 40:7–41:18; 52:1–34) of texts also seen in 1–2 Kings (2 Kgs 24:18–25:30). In sum, when we look at the book of Jeremiah, much of it reflects the words of his scribe, Baruch, and these exilic Deuteronomistic authors rather than the words of Jeremiah himself.

Jer 31:31–34

FOCUS TEXT

As in the case of Isaiah, we should not judge that such later parts of the book of Jeremiah are of little worth. On the contrary, some of the most important texts for Jewish and Christian communities have been ones that scholars have identified as coming from these later "Deuteronomistic" redactors.

One example is Jeremiah 31:31–34, a prose text that builds on multiple parts of Jeremiah's prophecy to give a word of hope to later communities. Like Jeremiah's earlier prophecy, this later text includes both Israel and Judah in its scope, starting with Yahweh's promise to make a "new covenant" with the "house of Israel" and the "house of Judah" (31:31). The text then contrasts this new covenant with the older covenant that Yahweh made with the exodus generation, a covenant which this text asserts was broken. Yahweh in this text is particularly pained by this breaking of the covenant because he had "married" Israel, a subtle reference to earlier images of divine–human marriage in Jeremiah's prophecies (31:32). But this text is moving toward hope, not judgment. The next part, Jer 31:33–34, describes Yahweh's solution. Rather than waiting for the people to memorize teachings as is urged in older wisdom texts (Prov 3:3; 7:3) and the Deuteronomic Torah (Deut 6:4–7; 11:18–19), Yahweh will write these words on the people's hearts himself, so that they no longer will need to encourage each other to be obedient. It will come naturally.

It is impossible to be sure about these things, but the contents and prose form of the text have led most scholars to conclude that it was not authored by Jeremiah, but by a later, anonymous prophet who was addressing later Judeans of the exilic period. As we will see in Chapter 9, the Judeans in exile were in despair over the destruction of their nation and wondered what kind of future Yahweh had in store for them. This addition to the book of Jeremiah in Jer 31:31–34 provides an answer. It insists that Yahweh is making a new covenant with Israel that Yahweh will help them obey.

The history of interpretation shows how this vision of a "new covenant," though an exilic addition, spoke powerfully to later Jewish and early Christian communities. For example, the Jewish community at Qumran who collected the Dead Sea Scrolls saw themselves as a community of the new covenant mentioned in Jeremiah. Just a century or two later, the expression "new covenant" came to play a very important role in the early Christian movement as well. Texts in Paul and Luke quote Jesus as telling his disciples that the wine of the Christian eucharist was the "new covenant in my blood" (1 Cor 11:25; Luke 22:20). In 2 Corinthians 3, Paul goes beyond this, drawing on Jer 31:31–34 to describe how the "Spirit of the living God" has written a "new covenant" on the hearts of the people at his church in Corinth (see especially 2 Cor 3:6). Much as Jer 31:31–34 contrasted the older covenant and the newer one, Paul now contrasts this spiritual writing on "tablets of human hearts" with the writing "on tablets of stone" by Moses. Such language allows Paul to stress God's role in making the Corinthians righteous, rather than their righteousness being anything that they themselves could boast about (2 Cor 3:2–6). By this point in the Christian movement, the "new covenant" of Jer 31:31–34 was reinterpreted as a covenant allowing both Jews and gentiles to be in a relationship with God that revolved around faith in Christ.

Eventually, later Christians applied a derivative of the term "new covenant" – that is, "New Testament" – to the specifically Christian scriptures associated with their movement: e.g. Matthew, Mark, Luke-Acts, John, etc. In addition, they labeled earlier Jewish scriptures with the corresponding term "Old Testament." Read in the light of Jer 31:31–34, this would imply a replacement of the "old testament" with the new, since this passage describes Yahweh's replacement of an older covenant that was broken with a new one. Yet by the point at which these labels – "Old" and "New Testament" – were developed, both sets of scriptures were important in Christianity. Church leaders rejected attempts by some, such as the early theologian Marcion, to have the church authorize only New Testament texts, and theologians found multiple ways in which the texts of the Old Testament pointed toward values and beliefs central to Christianity.

In sum, the words about the "new covenant" in Jer 31:31–34 provided the terms for the later division of scriptures into "Old Testament" and "New Testament," while also defining a major challenge for Christians. Were Hebrew scriptures such as Jer 31:31–34 now themselves to be understood as part of an outdated "covenant?" Or might these scriptures be used to learn more deeply about aspects of the gospel now written on the hearts of Christian believers?

Conclusion to the Pre-Exilic Period

Other chapters in this book have included an imaginary overview of the sorts of texts (and some traditions) that were in circulation at a given time in ancient Israel and Judah. This chapter concludes with a picture of two different groups of texts that probably were prominent in different groups in late seventh-century Judah. On the one hand, many in ancient Judah continued to study older sorts of texts: proverbs and wisdom instructions, royal and other sorts of psalms, love poetry, creation and flood myths, along with assorted traditions with strong northern connections, such as the story of Jacob and Joseph found in Genesis 25–50. On the other hand, the book of Deuteronomy laid claim to be a new kind of "wisdom." Some, such as Jeremiah, seem to have been skeptical of Deuteronomy's claims to be true Torah wisdom (Jer 8:8–9), and our historical evidence suggests that kings after Josiah did not take the Deuteronomic Torah very seriously. Nevertheless, the book of Deuteronomy lays claim to be a potential replacement of older forms of teaching, and the following Deuteronomistic historical books retell the people's history from that perspective. Though Deuteronomy echoes older wisdom texts, it calls on the people to devote all their time to memorizing Moses's Torah teaching (Deut 6:6–9). There is little room in Deuteronomy or the history that follows it for competing claims or texts.

With Josiah's death, many probably dismissed the claims of Deuteronomy and related historical books, but at least one family appears to have continued to treasure and expand those writings: the family of Shaphan. Shaphan was Josiah's scribe, and he is described as very involved in the process leading to the introduction of the Deuteronomic Torah to the king and the people (2 Kgs 22:3–10) and the verification of it through the prophet Huldah (2 Kgs 22:14–20). Shaphan may have been involved in the revision of the Deuteronomic Torah at the time of Josiah and the Deuteronomistic reframing of other historical traditions to bolster Josiah's reform. Furthermore, his family played a particular role in later Judean history. His son, Ahikam, sheltered Jeremiah when people wanted to kill him after his Temple sermon (Jer 26:24), and Shaphan's grandson was the first one to hear Jeremiah's scroll of oracles and make sure it was passed on to officials in the palace (Jer 36:10–13). By this point, the family of Shaphan no longer seems to have been part of the Judean inner circle. Yet one of their members, a grandson of Shaphan's named Gedaliah, is put in power by the Babylonians after the last king is removed (2 Kgs 25:22), and he gives a message of cooperation with Babylonia that sounds somewhat like Jeremiah's prophecy (2 Kgs 25:23–24//Jer 40:7–12). Gedaliah was soon killed (2 Kgs 25:25//Jer 41:1–3), but his family is the most likely group to have cherished and protected the texts discussed in this and the previous chapter. In the twilight of the Judean monarchy, when others may have dismissed texts like Deuteronomy or Jeremiah, they revised and expanded upon both.

Thus the late seventh century is a time when major traditions in the Bible were introduced, but all these texts still had a journey to make before becoming the biblical texts they now are. They do not seem to have been broadly recognized as important until total disaster struck Jerusalem, with the destruction of the Temple and the monarchy. Moreover, Jeremiah along with Deuteronomy and the Deuteronomistic historical books were revised in light of this catastrophe, so that those historical books, for example, now extend up to the first part of exile in Babylonia. Chapter 9 examines the impact of this catastrophe across a broader stretch of biblical traditions.

CHAPTER EIGHT REVIEW

For Review

1. How does Zephaniah understand the "Day of Yahweh" differently from the conventional view? With what other prophet does he share this innovation?

2. What shifts in meaning do you think were produced when the biographical narratives (now in Jeremiah 26–45) were moved from the end of the book to between the words of Jeremiah in 1–25 and the oracles against foreign nations now in Jeremiah 46–51?

3. How was the people's response to Jeremiah's prophecy similar to or different from responses of people to earlier eighth-century prophets?

4. (Focus text: Jer 31:31–34) The prophecy about a new covenant in Jer 31:31–34 illustrates the kind of text in Jeremiah that many scholars believe was *not* written by the original prophet, but instead added by a later author (or authors). Take another look at this passage, review the above discussion of the prophet, and list two things in Jer 31:31–34 that might clue you in to the idea that it was not written by Jeremiah. What are some contrasts between its message and the major themes of Jeremiah's earlier prophecy?

For Reflection

5. Comparing Jeremiah to earlier prophets, such as Hosea or Isaiah, which do you think has more to say to your contemporary community? Why? What would they say now?

RESOURCES FOR FURTHER STUDY

Zephaniah, Habakkuk, Nahum, and other prophets

O'Brien, Julia. M. *Nahum, Habakkuk, Zephaniah, Haggai, Zechariah, Malachi*. Nashville: Abingdon, 2004

Sweeney, Marvin. *The Twelve Prophets, vol. 2. Micah, Nahum, Habakkuk, Zephaniah, Haggai, Zechariah, Malachi*. Collegeville, MN: Liturgical, 2000.

Jeremiah

Carroll, Robert. *Jeremiah*. London: SCM, 1986.

Clements, R. E. *Jeremiah*. Atlanta: John Knox Press, 1988.

Stulman, Louis. *Jeremiah*. Nashville: Abingdon, 2005.

Laments, History, and Prophecies after the Destruction of Jerusalem

9

Chapter Overview

The Sixth Century: The Neo-Babylonian Destruction of Jerusalem and Exile

The Exilic Editions of Biblical Books

Ezekiel

Second Isaiah (also called Deutero-Isaiah)

Focus Text: Isa 52:13–53:12

Chapter Nine Review

Resources for Further Study

CHAPTER OVERVIEW

The Hebrew scriptures were shaped by exiles and their children, and this means that the experience of exile is the central point of biblical history, the period around which all others are oriented. Josiah's reform is a crucial turning point in the pre-exilic period, but already that formulation – "pre-exilic" – shows that the period of the exile is more important still for biblical study. Most discussions of the history of the Hebrew Bible revolve around three periods: the pre-exilic, exilic, and post-exilic, thus adopting the perspective of the exiles (and their descendants) who shaped the Bible. The post-exilic period, as we will see in Chapter 11, is defined particularly by those who returned from exile to Judah. Yet for most others whose families had left Judah, there was no return from "exile" to life in the land, and many Jews have lived away from the land of Judah ever since the exile. Thus, the exile of waves of Judeans, first in 597 and then in 586 (and yet another in 582), introduced a new era in the history of the Israelite people and development of the Bible. From this point onward, they had no nation state. In the wake of the trauma of forced exile and the destruction of Jerusalem, those scriptures now were

The Hebrew Bible: A Contemporary Introduction to the Christian Old Testament and the Jewish Tanakh, Second Edition. David M. Carr.
© 2021 David M. Carr. Published 2021 by John Wiley & Sons Ltd.

scriptures for exiles and returnees living in a land dominated by others. The link between texts and a city-state monarchy was broken. The Bible would never be the same.

This is the first of two chapters focusing on biblical texts that can be linked to the Babylonian exile. In this chapter we look at laments in the wake of Jerusalem's destruction, prophecies addressed to exiles found in Ezekiel and chapters 40–55 of Isaiah, and the rewriting of parts of other biblical books in light of the destruction of Jerusalem. These texts provide clues to the increasing importance during the exile of Israel's traditions about its pre-land origins and the emphasis in many exilic traditions on Yahweh's promise and ability to work with the people, no matter how sinful. We will see these elements again in the next chapter's discussion of Pentateuchal traditions.

The Sixth Century: The Neo-Babylonian Destruction of Jerusalem and Exile

READING

2 Kgs 23:29–25:30.
Exilic laments: Ps 137; Lamentations 1; Isa 63:7–64:12.

EXERCISE

Before reading this section, read the "exilic laments" listed above and then write down five words that these texts from the exile evoke for you.

Despite high hopes during the time of Josiah, the kingdom of Judah never achieved an extended period of independence, nor was its control over the north firm for any length of time. Instead, Josiah was killed in 609 in a confrontation with the Egyptian Pharaoh Necho as Necho was traveling through Israel on his way to assist Assyria in trying to contain a rising military power in Mesopotamia.

That power was the emergent "Neo-Babylonian" state (distinguished from the "Old Babylonian" empire of the early second millennium), a state ruled by a group of Aramean people called "Chaldeans." Thus began a period of Judah and its kings struggling under the shadow of Neo-Babylonian domination. Though the Egyptian Necho appointed one of Josiah's sons, Jehoiakim, as Josiah's successor, Jehoiakim quickly became a Babylonian vassal. A few years later, he sought to get out from under Babylonian domination with Egypt's help, but the Babylonian army eventually came and laid siege to Jerusalem. In an attempt to avert the wrath of the Babylonians, the people of Jerusalem apparently killed Jehoiakim and replaced him with his son, Jehoiachin, but the Babylonians still took young Jehoiachin and several thousand elite Judeans into exile (in 597), the first of several waves of forced resettlement of Judeans in the Babylonian empire. In place of Jehoiachin, the Babylonians appointed as king his uncle, Zedekiah, a son of Josiah. As a Babylonian appointee, Zedekiah was a weak ruler who was not recognized as king by many of his country-people. After about ten years he, like his brother Jehoiakim, tried to get free of Babylonia by joining an anti-Babylonian coalition of nations.

This rebellion by Zedekiah was the final straw for the Babylonians. Nebuchadnezzar marched on Jerusalem in 586 BCE and breached the walls (see Figure 9.1). He destroyed the Temple that Judah had thought was invulnerable, took yet more of Judah's elite into exile (though fewer than in 597), and installed Gedaliah, the grandson of Shaphan, Josiah's scribe, as governor in Mizpah, a town a few miles northwest of Jerusalem. Our last historical records point to the collapse of power structures in the land. In Judah things went from very bad to worse. Gedaliah was assassinated, his assassins fled to Ammon before Gedaliah's forces, and Gedaliah's forces fled to Egypt out of fear of Babylonian reprisals, forcing Jeremiah to come with them (2 Kgs 25:25–26//Jeremiah 41–42). The last we hear of life in Judah, the Babylonians had attacked again and taken a third wave of Judeans into exile in 582 BCE (Jer 52:30; see Map 9.1).

FIGURE 9.1
Ashes and arrowheads left from the Babylonian attack on Jerusalem.

Meanwhile, life went on in Babylonia for the thousands of upper-class Judeans who had been forcibly resettled there. The books of Kings (and Jeremiah) end with a brief account of how the king, Jehoiachin, was taken out of prison during his thirty-seventh year of exile in Babylon, given a place at the Babylonian king's table, and given rations (2 Kgs 25:27–30; appropriated in Jer 52:31–34; cf. Ezek 1:2). This narrative is confirmed by a Babylonian list of rations given to Jehoiachin. It shows the sliver of hope that such exiles found in the elevation of their king. Nevertheless, we never hear of Jehoiachin again, and Davidic kings never regained power. The sun had gone down on the Jerusalem monarchy. The people's future now lay in a life without their own king over them.

With no monarchy left to sponsor the writing of any history, we are in the dark about other specific events during the Babylonian exile. Biblical texts only provide indirect information about what life was like in exile. Certainly it was no picnic. The exiles were forcibly resettled into abandoned areas of central Babylonia where they worked and tried to form a viable communal life hundreds of miles from their homeland. Though the exiles were allowed to settle together and were not all enslaved, exilic texts refer to Babylonian domination as a "yoke" (Ezek 34:27; Isa 47:6; also Jer 30:8) and Babylonia along with its capital city, Babylon, became a symbol of arch-evil throughout the rest of biblical tradition. Multiple traditions suggest that some exiles were in chains

MAP 9.1
The journey to Babylon. Redrawn from Yohanan Aharoni and Michael Avi-Yonah, *The Macmillan Bible Atlas* (revised edition). New York: Macmillan, 1977, map 163.

Forced Labor for Exiles Under Nebuchadnezzar

This is an excerpt from a building inscription by Nebuchadnezzar II about his use of peoples from across his empire to build "Etemenanki," the grand temple for Marduk in the heart of Babylon:

the whole of the races, peoples from far places, whom Marduk, my Lord, delivered to me, I put them to work on the building of Etemenanki. I imposed on them the brick basket. (Translation: D. Smith, "The Politics of Ezra: Sociological Indicators of Postexilic Judaean Society." P. 79 of Philip Davies, ed., *Second Temple Studies*, I, JSOTSup 117. Sheffield: Sheffield Academic Press, 1991.)

(Jer 40:1; the *Antiquities* [10.100–103] by the first-century CE Jewish historian Josephus; see also Nah 3:10), and exilic texts in Isaiah speak of Jerusalem's time of "forced labor" (Isa 40:2), of being confined in prison (Isa 42:7; 49:9) and robbed (Isa 42:22). Meanwhile, one of Nebuchadnezzar's inscriptions boasts of how he forced people from Judah and elsewhere to rebuild the temple in Babylonia (see box above). Babylonia had become their new Egypt (see Figure 9.2).

FIGURE 9.2
Reproduction of part of the magnificent temple of Ishtar located in the heart of the empire of Babylon.

Laments and prophetic quotes from this period give a sense of the inner experience of this exile. Psalm 137 speaks of weeping by the rivers of Babylon where the captors of the Judeans mockingly asked them to "sing one of the songs of Zion." The exiles sing of how they will keep Jerusalem in their memory, though they are far from home.

> If I forget you, O Jerusalem,
> let my right hand wither!
> Let my tongue cling to the roof of my mouth,
> if I do not remember you,
> if I do not set Jerusalem above my highest joy.
>
> (Ps 137:5–6 NRSV)

Lamentations 1 is an alphabet of suffering, where each stanza begins with a different letter of the Hebrew alphabet. After an initial lament over Zion, she cries forth her suffering herself:

> My crimes have been bound into a yoke,
> my misdeeds braided together by [God's] hand.
> They lie on my neck,
> They sap my strength.
> The Lord has given me into the hands of
> Those I cannot overcome.
>
> (Lam 1:14)

Echoing pre-exilic prophets like Hosea and Jeremiah, this Zion figure says, "I called out to my lovers, but they betrayed me. My priests and elders died in the city while seeking food to survive" (Lam 1:19). Meanwhile, in a lament found in Isa 63:7–64:12 (64:11 in some translations), the ancient Judeans cry out to God, "your holy cities have become a wasteland, Zion has become a desert, Jerusalem a heap of ruins" (64:10), and assert to Yahweh, their "father" (64:8), that he has made them "stray from your paths and turn our hearts from fearing you" (64:7). Such laments are part of an ancient literary tradition in Israel of honest crying out to God, even accusing God of being responsible for the people's shortcomings. These laments will be discussed in Chapter 11. For now, it is important to recognize that this type of text, particularly the communal lament, voiced the exiles' mixed feelings of guilt, sadness, fear, and rage as they lived for decades under Neo-Babylonian oppression.

The dynamics of exile can be illuminated through **social-scientific analysis** of the Bible; that is, analysis that draws on contemporary sociological and anthropological studies to provide a more nuanced picture of ancient Israel. For example, Daniel Smith-Christopher's book *Religion of the Landless* (see this chapter's "Resources for Further Study") draws on ethnographic studies of contemporary groups who have experienced displacement from their homelands to try to reconstruct what the experience of Babylonian exile might have been like. He finds that separation from one's homeland inevitably involves major changes for the displaced group. Continuity is not the norm. Transformation is.

> **Basics**
>
> **Book of Lamentations**
>
> **Outline: five-part (= Torah) cry for restoration of Jerusalem**
>
> | | | |
> |---|---|---|
> | I | Four alphabet poems detailing the suffering of Jerusalem and its people | 1–4 |
> | II | Final communal plea for restoration | 5 |
>
> **Theme and purpose**
>
> Other ancient Near Eastern cultures had written and taught laments over the destruction of great cities. These chapters in Lamentations were composed to commemorate the destruction of Jerusalem in 586, particularly on the holiday remembering this event, the Ninth of Av. Over time, however, these poems in Lamentations have come to serve as a cry over Jewish suffering of many kinds, from the destruction of the Second Temple to the genocide of Jews under Hitler and other suffering up to today.

In addition, Smith-Christopher found that displaced communities change in similar ways, reflecting the comparable challenges that many such diaspora communities face. Because they must now live as a minority in a majority culture, family and clan traditions often become more important, while other traditions connected with their old life either disappear or are transformed. For example, Judean traditions about the king's blessing may have been adapted in exile so that they now applied to an ancient ancestor's blessing or God's blessing of a foreign deliverer. Meanwhile, in place of the now defunct royal bureaucracy, the sole means of organization of Judean exiles were family units, "houses of the father," which were ruled by a group of "elders." These elders, along with the remnants of the priesthood, were the leaders in the exiled Judean community.

New practices became important for the Judeans who were in Babylonia, practices that preserved communal identity in a hostile cultural environment. It appears that circumcision (which was not practiced by Babylonians) and Sabbath observance grew in importance. Furthermore, exiles like them had to struggle against the tendency to assimilate into the broader culture, particularly through intermarriage. In the face of this, these exiles, like many contemporary communities in diaspora, sought ways to discourage their children from marrying foreigners. This is but one major way in which peoples in exile, both ancient and contemporary, change in order to survive culturally and build identity.

The violence of the exiles' departure may have been yet another factor leading to the transformation of their traditions. Though it is possible that Judean exiles took some scrolls of ancient texts with them into Babylonia, it is also quite likely that many did not have a chance to pack much up while Jerusalem burned and the Temple – often a storage place for ancient scrolls – was destroyed. Yet the literate elite who went into exile had memorized ancient texts as part of their education. The Deuteronomic Torah, Proverbs, Song of Songs, and other texts were "written on the tablet of their hearts," as Proverbs would put it (Prov 3:3; 7:3). Once in Babylonia, these people could call on their detailed memories of these texts as they produced new copies of them – copies that often reflected the new challenges and hopes of life in exile.

More on Method: Trauma Studies and the Bible

Earlier chapters in this introduction on the history of Israel and Judah under Neo-Assyrian imperialism already have applied the term "**trauma**" to their experiences – including the destruction of Israel in the north and the almost century-long Assyrian domination of Judah in the south. Key themes of prophetic and Deuteronomistic theology were forged amidst such overwhelming experiences of communal defeat, humiliation, and suffering. The exile in Babylonia, however, appears to have been Judah's clearest and most profound experience of what would be described today as "trauma" in a communal form. According to one contemporary definition of trauma (by Cathy Caruth), "trauma is the confrontation with an event that, in its unexpectedness or horror, cannot be placed within schemes of prior knowledge." Another leading theorist, Judith Herman, characterizes traumatic events as those that "overwhelm the ordinary systems of care that give people a sense of control, connection and meaning."

The exile in Babylonia appears to have been just such an event for the inhabitants of Jerusalem, and their texts manifest symptoms often seen in trauma. For example, like many traumatized individuals and communities, the exiles do not seem to have been able to speak much about their experience. Instead, there is a gap in communal memory. Biblical history extends from creation to the exile at the end of 2 Kings, has a blank, and does not pick up again until the conclusion of the Babylonian exile with a Persian king's edict that Judah could return (Ezra 1:1–4//2 Chr 36:22–23). We even see a major gap among the named prophets in the Bible, with a series of prophets extending up to the edge of the exile (Jeremiah, Ezekiel), a gap of more than half a century, and then a series of post-exilic prophets (e.g. Haggai, Zechariah, Malachi). This does not mean that the exiles in Babylonia did not write anything. They just did not write much directly about themselves. (The main exceptions are a brief note in 2 Kgs 25:27–30 and some songs of lament like Psalm 137. The legends about exile in Daniel are dated to much later centuries.)

As we will see in this chapter and the next, biblical texts dated to the exile reflect numerous symptoms seen frequently in traumatized communities. These include a tendency toward self-blame for the community's suffering, growth of us/them thinking that defines an in-group over against outsiders, rage at foreign "others" who are perceived to be responsible for the catastrophe, and an increased communal focus on identities and stories about ancient times before the displacement. This latter tendency is particularly evident in the increasing focus on stories of pre-land ancestors (Abraham, Moses) that is seen during the exile. We will see this focus both in this chapter and in the next chapter's discussion of Pentateuchal texts that were shaped during the Babylonian exile. This illustrates some of the ways that studies of trauma offer insights into the development and/or ongoing use of the Bible amidst situations of trauma.

For more on this approach, see David Carr, *Holy Resilience: The Bible's Traumatic Origins* (New Haven: Yale University Press, 2014).

The Exilic Editions of Biblical Books

Review Deut 30:1–10 (cf. Deut 30:11–20);
Read 2 Kgs 21:2–16; 23:26–28; 25.

READING

One example of such preservation and change of ancient textual traditions is revision and extension of Deuteronomy and other Deuteronomistic historical books in light of the destruction of Jerusalem and its supposedly invulnerable temple.

The book of 2 Kings, for example, appears to have two endings. The first comes at the close of Josiah's reign, where we hear that Josiah surpassed all other kings in fulfilling the greatest command in Deuteronomy (seen in Deut 6:5) by turning to Yahweh "with all his heart/ mind, all his life strength, and all his power, in accordance with the Torah of Moses" (2 Kgs 23:25). This enthusiastic endorsement of Josiah caps a narration in 2 Kings 22–23 of how he showed this loyalty to Yahweh through his reform. Later authors, however, were confronted with a difficult quandary. According to Deuteronomistic theology, Josiah should have been rewarded with long life, and the people who he led in his reform should have enjoyed lasting security. In fact, however, Josiah was killed in an unexplained encounter with Pharaoh Necho (2 Kgs 23:29), and Judah was soon destroyed by the Babylonian empire (2 Kgs 25).

Exilic scribes had to explain why this happened, and we see this explanation immediately after the positive comments about Josiah's righteousness in 2 Kgs 23:25: "there was no king before Josiah who was like him, turning to Yahweh with all his heart, his life breath, and his strength . . . and there was never one after him." The exilic extenders of this history go on to say:

> Yet, the Lord did not turn back from his great anger against Judah and all the awful things that Manasseh [Josiah's predecessor] had done to anger God. The Lord said, "As I banished Israel from my presence, so will I also banish Judah, and I will reject this city that I chose, Jerusalem, and the house where I said my name would live."
>
> (2 Kgs 23:26–27)

This is how one group of exiles, those extending the books of 1–2 Kings into the exile, explained the destruction of the supposedly invulnerable city, Jerusalem, and its sanctuary. The reason they gave was that Manasseh's sin was so grievous that Josiah's virtue could not overcome it. One generation's guilt meant that another generation had to suffer. A proverb quoted by Ezekiel's audience puts it vividly: "the fathers have eaten sour grapes and the children's teeth are set on edge" (Ezek 18:2). As we will see, Ezekiel rejects this idea that a later generation must pay for the sins of their parents. Nevertheless, this passage from 2 Kgs 23:26–27 is a biblical affirmation of this concept. It asserts that later generations of Judah had to suffer the destruction of Judah and Jerusalem because of the sins of Manasseh. Sour grapes indeed.

This is only one example of a range of places where exilic authors seem to have added material to earlier biblical books, much of it influenced to a greater or lesser degree by Deuteronomistic ideology. For example, already in Chapter 7 I discussed a likely addition to Deuteronomy, in Deut 30:1–10, an addition that was shaped to provide comfort and encouragement to people who had been "exiled to the ends of the world" (30:4). And indeed, scholars have found a variety of likely exilic additions in the book of Jeremiah and other prophetic books. Chapter 5 of this *Introduction* included discussion of how the books of Micah (especially chapters 4–5) and Isaiah (chapters 40–55) contain prophecies of hope for Jerusalem/Zion that probably were written to encourage exiles. The promise appended to the end of the book of Amos, Amos 9:11–15, is another place where exiles appear to have added a word of hope to earlier words of judgment. The book of Jeremiah was thoroughly revised during the exile through the addition of passages such as God's promise of a new covenant written on the heart (Jer 31:31–34) that was discussed in Chapter 8. We see our first close analogies to this idea of God actually changing the heart of God's people in the next prophet to be discussed, Ezekiel.

Ezekiel

READING

Ezekiel 1–3, 8–11, 16, 36–37.

Ezekiel is the only prophet in the Hebrew Bible whose prophecy can be dated with certainty to the exilic period. He was a priest who went into exile in Babylonia with King Jehoiachin and thousands of other exiles in 597. There he lived in a Jewish settlement, Tel-abib, located just a few miles from the ancient Sumerian center of learning at Nippur. Though Zedekiah ruled in Jerusalem from 597 until its destruction in 586, all of Ezekiel's prophecies are dated by the years of Jehoiachin's exile. Apparently his career began six years before Jerusalem was destroyed and then continued another 14 years after Jerusalem's destruction (see Ezek 1:2; 40:1). Many divide Ezekiel's book into two major parts, corresponding to the two major periods of his prophecy. Ezekiel 1–32 features oracles of judgment dated to the period before Jerusalem's destruction. These judgments by Ezekiel are roughly contemporary with the last phase of Jeremiah's prophecy but are delivered in Babylonia to Judean exiles there. Then the tone shifts: once Jerusalem is destroyed and the exiles are in despair about their future with God, Ezekiel develops vivid images of hope, and these are stressed in chapters 33–48 of the book.

Like the other books of major prophets, the book of Ezekiel prominently features a story of his commissioning by God, in Ezekiel 1–3. Nevertheless, this commissioning is different in ways that mark the uniqueness of Ezekiel's prophecy. It begins, like Isaiah's, with a vision of God and God's attendants (1:4–28), but Ezekiel's vision is more elaborate: with four strange creatures (1:4–14), each associated with a chariot wheel (1:15–25), and a brilliant blue throne overhead on which God is seated, "an appearance of the likeness of the glory of the LORD" (1:28). Moreover, Ezekiel, unlike Isaiah, sees God outside the Temple (1:2–28; 3:22–23), and the imagery of the wheels in his call narrative anticipates his later "Temple vision," where he sees God leave the Temple and go into exile (Ezekiel 8–11). This focus on God's presence outside the Temple in both Ezekiel 1–3 and 8–11 is the first mark of the radically new, exilic context of Ezekiel's prophecy.

The message that Ezekiel is commissioned to speak, however, sounds like an extreme version of the message seen in Amos, Isaiah, and other prophets of judgment. God tells him to speak to God's people of "rebels," whether they listen or not (2:1–7). Indeed, God predicts that they will not listen, but will reject his message (3:4–9). Nevertheless, like a sentinel on a watchtower who sees an approaching army, Ezekiel must sound the alarm about God's oncoming judgment and let the people make the decision about whether to respond. Otherwise, the blood of his people will be on his hands (Ezek 3:16–21).

When other prophets faced rejection of their prophecy, they had their oracles written down for other generations (e.g. Isa 8:11–18; 30:8–14; Jeremiah 36), and this element of writing is yet more prominent in Ezekiel's call narrative. God offers him a scroll with words of doom written on it and tells Ezekiel to eat it. Ezekiel does eat it, an act signifying his obedient memorization of all that God has told him to prophesy (Ezek 2:8–3:3). Yet the scroll has not lost its purpose. Rather, this narrative implies that its words of doom were included in the book now found in the Hebrew Bible. Though his own generation did not listen, the writing down of his prophecy allowed it to endure and teach future generations.

One central element of Ezekiel's teaching was his proclamation that each generation stood on its own before God: a disobedient generation would be punished for its sins, but if the children of people in that generation were righteous, they would be rewarded. Not everyone agreed on this point. As we saw above, the exilic portions of the books of Kings blamed the suffering of Ezekiel's generation on the sins of an earlier one, especially the evil of Manasseh (2 Kgs 23:26–27). Ezekiel quotes people of his time saying, "the fathers have eaten sour grapes, and the children's teeth are set on edge" (Ezek 18:2), but he decisively rejects that saying. On the contrary, he insists, the fathers will be punished or rewarded for their righteousness, and their children will stand or fall on the basis of their own righteousness as well (Ezek 18:3–24). Many who have read this chapter in the contemporary context of emphasis on the individual have seen here the first emergence in the Hebrew Bible of individual responsibility, but this is mistaken. At issue in every example in the chapter is whether or not later generations must pay for the sins of their parents. The point is to get the exiles to stop saying how "unfair" God is for punishing them on the basis of an earlier generation's sins (18:25, 29). Instead, Ezekiel calls on them to repent of their own past crimes, get a "new heart and a new spirit," and live (Ezek 18:31–32).

> **Basics**
>
> ## Book of Ezekiel
>
> **Outline: judgment and restoration of Jerusalem**
>
> | | | |
> |---|---|---|
> | I | Sentinel announcement of judgment | 1:1–33:20 |
> | II | Restoration of Jerusalem and Temple | 33:21–48:35 |
>
> **Date**
>
> Early to late exile.
>
> **Themes**
>
> The judgment and restoration theme is familiar from other prophets, but Ezekiel, a Zadokite priest, adds a different level of spectacle to his visions (e.g. Ezekiel 1–3 and 37) and a new emphasis on purity, and features a particular focus on the Temple (Ezekiel 9–11) and its restoration (Ezekiel 40–48).
>
> **More information**
>
> Ezekiel is also known for his weird symbolic actions, such as lying on his side for more than a year (Ezek 4:4–8) or not mourning the death of his wife (Ezek 24:15–27). Some in the past have explained these and other aspects of his prophecy as the result of a mental imbalance in Ezekiel. Nevertheless, such attempts to psychologically analyze the prophet on the basis of literature linked to him are extremely risky. Moreover, these approaches miss the emphasis throughout the book on the idea that Ezekiel's words and actions, however unusual, were a message from God for the exiles and later generations.

Ezekiel's imagery for the people and description of their "crimes" sound somewhat like Hosea's, yet things have advanced a long way in the years that separate these prophets. Like Hosea, Ezekiel pictures God's disobedient people as female, and, as in Hosea, Ezekiel uses this image to stress the people's failure to be exclusively faithful to God, both in impure worship (16:15–27) and in playing power politics with other nations (16:28–29). Yet Ezekiel's use of female imagery for God's people(s) is more explicitly degrading and violent than Hosea's, and it is saturated with purity concerns typical of priests like Ezekiel. According to him, Jerusalem is the female offspring of Canaanite peoples and plagued by blood impurity from her birth (16:3–4, 22). Though God cleaned her up and eventually married her, she – and her sister Israel – engaged in the worst form of promiscuity. In response, God promises to offer her up for the stripping and beating that adulterous women receive (16:35–42). Even worse, another chapter that uses this metaphor, Ezekiel 23, promises that both sisters will be brutally killed (Ezek 23:22–49). The first part of the book concludes with God's command to Ezekiel not to mourn the death of his own wife as a sign of the numbness that the people will feel when their beloved city is destroyed (Ezek 24:15–27).

Nevertheless, Ezekiel, like other prophetic books, ends with hope, not judgment. After a series of oracles against foreign nations (Ezekiel 25–32), the book returns to a review of major themes from the first part of the book (33:1–20) before moving to prophecies dated to the destruction of the Jerusalem temple (33:21) or later (40:1). Some of these are words of judgment, such as Ezekiel's oracle against people still in the land who claim Abraham as their ancestor (Ezek 33:23–29) or his condemnation of Judah and Israel's past kings, their "shepherds," for selfishness and injustice (Ezek 34:1–10). Yet these oracles of judgment introduce words of hope to exiles, promising that God will be their shepherd and rescue them from exile and resettle them under a new Davidic king (Ezek 34:11–31). Where Ezekiel prophesied against the mountains of the land in the first part of the book (Ezekiel 6), he offers them hope in this latter part (Ezekiel 36). Where he watched the glory of God leave the temple before (Ezek 11:22–25), he now sees it returning (Ezek 43:1–6). In one of the most powerful visions of all, he imagines Israel as a valley full of "dry bones," bones that symbolize exiles who are convinced that they are completely finished and hope is lost (Ezek 37:11). God calls on Ezekiel to prophesy to this valley of dry bones, this exiled people, and watch their miraculous resurrection (37:12–14).

The restoration imagined in Ezekiel does not depend on the people finding a way to change themselves. His earlier prophecies had already made clear that he thought the people incapable of this. Rather, in this part of the book, Ezekiel reiterates promises given earlier, that God will give the people a new heart and new spirit so that they can obey God's laws (Ezek 36:26–27; 37:14; cf. 11:14–21). Though the exiles might despair that God would ever have anything more to do with them after all that they had done wrong, Ezekiel reassures them that God will do all this "for the sake of [God's] holy name" (Ezek 36:22–23, 32). This idea of "holy name" refers to God's reputation. According to Ezekiel, God's reputation among the nations had suffered when they watched God's chosen people removed from their land (Ezek 36:20–21). Yet God promises to redeem God's own name, God's reputation, through bringing the Israelites back and settling them in the land so that the nations can see this too (36:28–36). In this way, Ezekiel describes a restoration that does not depend on any goodness in the exiles themselves. God's promises of restoration depend on God's wish to look good in front of the nations, not on the people suddenly changing their ways.

Second Isaiah (also called Deutero-Isaiah)

READING

Isaiah 40–55.

Very similar themes appear in the other major prophet that is associated with the exile: the anonymous prophet that wrote chapters 40–55 of the book of Isaiah. Chapter 6 of this *Introduction* mentioned biblical scholarship that has identified this section of Isaiah as coming from a later period of Judah's history than the time of the original Isaiah. This part of the textbook examines how these chapters addressed the fears and hopes of exiles a few decades after the time of Ezekiel. By this point in the exile, this "**Second Isaiah**" (or **Deutero-Isaiah**) can proclaim that the LORD has anointed the Persian king Cyrus as God's shepherd, that is, God's king (Isa 44:28–45:1). We know from other historical documents that this Cyrus would eventually bring down the Neo-Babylonian empire in 539 BCE.

The Divine Council

The people of Israel and surrounding countries believed their god had a royal court of divine beings, a "divine council." Just as human kings had counselors and courtiers, so also the divine king had his. We see reflections of this idea of the divine council across the whole Hebrew Bible: Psalm 89:7 refers to Yahweh's "council of the holy ones." Isaiah 6:8, 40:1, and 40:3 feature commands addressed to an unspecified heavenly group. God debates with a group about whether Job is altruistic in Job 1–2. We may even see a pale reflection of this idea in Genesis where God decides to make humanity "as *our* image" (Gen 1:26) and later fears that humans will be "like *us*" (Gen 3:22 and 11:7).

This exilic portion of Isaiah opens with a commissioning scene in the **divine council** (Isa 40:1–8) that echoes the scene where the earlier prophet, eighth-century Isaiah, was commissioned (6:1–13). The Hebrew of both texts, Isa 6:1–13 and 40:1–8, indicates that God speaks with a *plural* group, probably members of his divine council in the process of deciding who will take God's message to his people (Isa 6:8; 40:1–5). In Isa 6:8 God asks a group of people, "whom shall I send on our behalf?" while Isa 40:1–2 calls a group to go and tell God's people that the exile, the "time of forced labor," is over:

> Comfort my people, comfort them,
> Says your God.
> Speak tenderly to the heart of Jerusalem,
> And call out to her.
> That her time of forced labor is now over,
> That her bloodguilt has been paid for,
> That she has received from Yahweh double for all her sins.
> (Isa 40:1–2)

Isaiah 6, the call narrative for Isaiah of the eighth century, stressed his confrontation with his and his people's "bloodguilt" (Isa 6:5). In contrast, this later exilic text emphasizes God's forgiveness. Isaiah 6 described Yahweh's "glory" as filling the whole earth (Isa 6:3), but this exilic text in Isa 40:5 now has the whole earth actually *seeing* Yahweh's "glory" (Isa 40:3–5). Just as Ezekiel had pictured God's reputation being restored through the nations' witnessing God's rescue of God's people (Ezek 36:28–36), so this exilic "Second Isaiah" imagines God's glory being revealed to the whole world in the exiles' departure from Babylonia (Isa 40:3–5).

Basics

Second Isaiah/Deutero-Isaiah

Outline

I	Exhortation for exiles to join a second exodus out of Babylon	40–48
II	Announcement of hope and return to Jerusalem	49–55

Date
Late exile.

Themes
This part of Isaiah focuses on giving hope to the hopeless. Though possibly written as a separate prophetic collection, it now links in interesting ways with earlier parts of Isaiah (e.g. Isaiah 40:1–9//Isaiah 6). It is also the part of Isaiah that contains the famous "servant songs" (Isa 42:1–4; 49:1–6; 50:4–11; 52:13–53:12) that have been the subject of much religious and scholarly debate.

God's announcement of Jerusalem's liberation is followed by the prophet's call and his objection to the call (40:6), an exchange similar to ones in the call narratives for Isaiah (Isa 6:5) and Jeremiah (Jer 1:6). In this case, however, the exilic prophet is worried about despairing exiles, who wither "like grass" when "the breath of Yahweh blows upon it" (40:6–7). He knows that he must address a discouraged people who have heard many false hopes. Yet a divine presence answers his doubts, first by acknowledging their partial truth, "Yes, the grass withers, and the flower fades," then adding the reassurance that "the word of our God endures forever" (40:8). Though the exiles may feel weak and hopeless, God's word of hope and restoration persists and will prevail.

The rest of Isaiah 40–55 is divided into two main parts: Isaiah 40–48 and 49–55. The first part, Isaiah 40–48, is a passionate call for the exiles to embrace God's plan to take them out of Babylonia. Central to this call is the prophet's reassurance that their God, who might have seemed defeated by other gods in the destruction of Jerusalem, is powerful enough to liberate them. Here "Second Isaiah" invokes creation traditions to affirm that the god who created the world can bring them out of Babylonia (Isa 40:12–27). He reminds the exiles of God's care for their ancestors, both Abraham and Jacob and the people of the exodus generation (41:8–9; 44:1–2; also 51:1–2).

It is in the context of these arguments for Yahweh's power that Second Isaiah makes a monotheistic claim that is new in Israelite religion: he asserts that there is no other god anywhere but Yahweh. All other gods are false idols, worthless pieces of wood and metal (40:18–20; 41:7; 44:9–20). In this way, Second Isaiah reassures the exiles that other nations' gods offer no contest whatsoever for the creator-liberator God of Israel. We have not seen this sort of argument for the non-existence of any other gods in Israelite traditions clearly datable to earlier periods. In Hosea and Deuteronomy we saw calls for Israel not to worship any other gods, yet those calls did not include the assumption that such gods did not exist. Yet here, in the context of Second Isaiah's reassurances to exiles, the prophet argues for just this point of view. Later traditions will take such **monotheism** for granted.

Isaiah 40–48, the first half of Second Isaiah, concludes with an argument from prophecy, an argument that only works if it was directly addressed to exiles and not to an earlier audience. God reminds the exiles of earlier prophecies that have come true, "former things" declared through the prophets. Through seeing the past fulfillment of these prophecies, this text insists, God's "stubborn" people should now be able to trust God's announcement of "new things" (Isa 48:4–6), including God's plans to destroy the sixth-century Neo-Babylonian empire (48:14). Even though it is theoretically possible that an eighth-century prophet, Isaiah, could have accurately predicted the demise of the Babylonian empire, he would not have addressed his eighth-century audience as if his prophecies about Judah lay in the past. Nor would Isaiah of the eighth century have called on his audience, still in Judah, to "go out from Babylon, flee from Chaldea, declare with loud shouts . . . 'God has freed God's servant, Jacob'" (Isa 48:20). These are words addressed by an unknown exilic prophet to a later audience of Judeans exiled in Babylonia, an audience longing to go home.

The second major section of Second Isaiah, Isaiah 49–55, focuses on the task of resettling and restoring Jerusalem. Like 40–48, these chapters start with a commissioning (49:1–6; cf. 40:1–8). This time, God commissions a "**servant**" who is to gather the exiled Israelites back to the LORD and reveal God's glory to the end of the earth (49:5–6). The identity of the "servant" in this and other passages in Second Isaiah has puzzled readers for centuries (see other "**servant songs**" in Isa 42:1–8; 50:4–9; 52:13–53:12 that likewise focus on a distinctive "servant"). In most of Isaiah 40–48, God addresses the whole people of Israel/Jacob as God's servant (Isa 41:8–9; 43:10; 44:1; 48:20). In other cases (e.g. Isa 52:13-53:12), however, the "servant/suffering servant" seems to be separate from the people, serving them (e.g. 49:5–6). Early Christians insisted that the servant of these passages was Jesus Christ. It is highly doubtful, however, that an exilic Judean prophet originally understood himself to be prophesying Jesus Christ. Instead, scholars of the Bible usually conclude that the "servant" in Second Isaiah was either a now unknown individual in the community of the exiles or stood for the community of Israel as a whole. There are grounds for both positions in Isaiah 40–55.

The servant passage in Isa 49:1–6 is followed by a speech where God addresses Jerusalem, personified once again as a woman. Echoing the book of Lamentations, she cries out that "the LORD has abandoned me, my Lord has forgotten me" (Isa 49:14; compare Lam 5:20). God then answers this lament with a remarkable use of parental imagery:

> Can a woman forget her nursing child,
> Or her compassion for the child of her womb?
> Even if these ones forget, I will never forget you.
>
> (Isa 49:15)

The exilic prophet uses mothers as the ultimate example of compassion and then says that God embodies such compassion and more toward the exiles.

More on Method: (Study of) Intertextuality

Recent literary criticism has taught biblical scholars to be ever more aware of **intertextuality** in biblical texts. Intertextuality is a word used to refer to the myriad ways different texts can be related to each other. Literary-critical analysis of biblical intertextuality sometimes takes the form of analyzing ways in which biblical texts allude to or build on earlier texts, such as the echo of Lam 5:20 in the lament by Zion in Isa 49:14. Other times, however, such analysis highlights ways that any reading of a biblical text must now consider that text as part of a broader web of texts, many of which it was not originally connected to. For example, in the next section of this chapter we will look at later readings of the poem about the suffering servant in Isa 52:13-53:12 by Christians and Jews that have been influenced by earlier interpretations of the poem in each faith tradition. As Peter Miscall has put it (echoing John Donne), "no text is an island," whether in its original writing or its subsequent interpretation.

For more: Patricia K. Tull, "Rhetorical Criticism and Intertextuality," pp. 156–179 in S. McKenzie and S. Haynes, *To Each Its Own Meaning: An Introduction to Biblical Criticisms and Their Applications* (Louisville: Westminster, 1999).

Thus begins a series of speeches in Isaiah 49–55 that alternate between speeches of comfort to female Zion (50:1–3; 51:1–52:12; 54:1–17) and speeches by or about God's "servant" (50:4–11; 52:13–53:12). The climax of the songs about the servant is Isa 52:13–53:12, a poem about the shaming and exaltation of a "servant" who has borne the sicknesses of others. The corresponding climax of the songs about female Zion is Isaiah 54, a picture of God's eternal remarriage to Zion after abandoning her "for a brief moment" (54:7). This latter poem is a sharp contrast to Ezekiel's use of marriage imagery earlier in the exile to stress the people's wrongdoing and punishment (Ezekiel 16 and 23). The prophet in Isaiah 54 downplays any past troubles and uses the marriage metaphor to stress God's abiding love for God's beloved city.

The final chapter of Isaiah 40–55 features several distinctive promises to exiles in Babylonia. Where once the Davidic monarchy was promised an eternal covenant (2 Sam 7:12–16; 23:5; Pss 89:3–4, 20–21), now – in the wake of the destruction of the monarchy – God promises an eternal, Davidic covenant with the people themselves (55:3). Echoing the earlier affirmation that "the word of our God endures forever" (40:8), this concluding chapter affirms that God's word "will not return to [God] empty" (55:11). As a result, the exiles should "go out in joy and be led back in peace," watching the mountains and hills break forth in song to greet them on their way home (55:12–13). These extravagant promises, made on the eve of the destruction of the Babylonian empire, were on the minds of many exiles when they returned home with high hopes.

FOCUS TEXT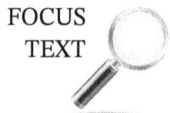

Isa 52:13–53:12

This text about the **suffering servant** is the fourth, longest, and most controversial servant song in Second Isaiah. Of all the texts about Yahweh's servant in Second Isaiah, this one most clearly seems to concern an individual. It starts with Yahweh's proclamation that many nations will be totally surprised by the rise and prosperity of God's "servant," who was once horribly disfigured.

> See my servant will be successful.
> He will rise up, be lifted up, and be very exalted.
> Just as many were aghast at him,
> As his looks were inhuman,
> and his form unlike another mortal,
> So he will startle many nations,
> Kings will shut their mouths because of him.
>
> (52:13–15a)

Looking at the sudden success of the servant, the Judean exiles finally will see "that which they had not been told" before and understand "that which they had not heard" (52:15b; compare with similar terms in Isa 48:6–8). The next part of the text and the heart of the passage, Isa 53:1–11a, is an imagined quoting of that community of exiles, starting with their own astonishment at the sudden rise of this disfigured servant. They say, "who can believe what we just heard? To whom has the arm of Yahweh been revealed?" (53:1). They then go on to describe their realization that the servant they once despised was actually suffering for their own sins (53:2–9), and they conclude that Yahweh both caused the servant's suffering and is now bringing the servant glory (53:10–11a). At this point, Yahweh speaks once again at the end of the passage, affirming that Yahweh will indeed glorify the servant because of his suffering, unto death, for the sins of his people (53:11b–12). This second divine speech echoes the initial divine speech in 52:13–15, enclosing the speech by the people in 53:1–11a in an envelope or **inclusio** structure – that is, a structure where a text begins and ends with similar elements (52:13–15 and 53:11b–12 – the envelope) that enclose a larger middle (53:1–11a). The effect of this envelope structure is to give divine authority to the thoughts of the people in 53:1–11a. There they realize that this disfigured person they thought to be rejected by Yahweh will soon be glorified by Yahweh for suffering on their behalf.

Though, if considered by itself, this text seems to focus on the fortunes of a particular individual known to the text's original audience, it can be read in a broader literary context as concerning the suffering and future glorification of God's servant people. As mentioned before, Yahweh addresses the whole people of Israel as his servant throughout much of Isaiah 40–48. And it appears that the word "Israel" has been added at one point in Isa 49:1–6, namely in Isa 49:3 (disturbing the poetic balance of this verse: "You are my servant, *Israel*, in whom I will be glorified"), so that this passage now describes the commissioning of God's people/servant, "Israel." Such descriptions of all of "Israel" as God's servant in Isaiah 40–48 provide a new context for understanding the speeches about God's servant in Isa 52:13–53:12. Read in light of them, this text can be reinterpreted to describe the suffering and future glorification of Yahweh's entire servant people.

These two levels of understanding the "servant" in Isaiah 52:13–53:12 – individual and collective – are reflected in the different Christian and Jewish understandings of the passage. Most Christian interpreters have asserted that the servant spoken of here is an individual – Jesus Christ. For them, the text predicts his crucifixion and resurrection. For example, in the biblical book of Acts, an Ethiopian eunuch reading the book of Isaiah asks the disciple Philip whether the description of the suffering servant in Isa 53:7–8 is about Isaiah or someone else. Philip then uses this text as the starting point for preaching about Jesus to the eunuch, who converts and becomes one of the first missionaries in the early church (Acts 8:26–40). This illustrates a broader tendency in the New Testament and other early Christian writings to read the story of Jesus's crucifixion and resurrection in light of Isa 52:13–53:12. Apparently, this text helped early Christians understand and cope with Jesus's humiliating death. Where most people of Jesus's time would have seen his life as a failure because of the crucifixion, the first Christians read Isa 52:13–53:12 and saw that such impressions could be deceiving: though Jesus was despised, humiliated, and seemingly rejected by God, he was actually God's faithful, suffering servant as described in Isa 52:13–53:12. With the help of this text, they could affirm that his death was not the end but the prelude to his glorification by God for suffering on behalf of the sins of others.

Meanwhile, Isa 52:13–53:12 did not connect in such a clear way with major ideas or figures in Judaism, so early Jewish interpreters paid much less attention to it. When Jews did interpret this passage, they often understood it as describing all of Israel as Yahweh's suffering servant. Thus the great twelfth-century Jewish interpreter Rashi watched Christian crusaders kill Jews on their way to the holy land and concluded that Isa 52:13–53:12 described Israel's suffering for the sins of others. Another Jewish commentator of the same time, Ibn Ezra, understood the speech in 53:1–11a as quoting what the shamed non-Jewish nations would say one day as they looked back on Israel's suffering at their hands.

Ironically, some Jewish suffering during the medieval period was connected with the reading in Christian churches of this very passage from Isaiah. For this passage – with its frequent use in Christian theology about Jesus's crucifixion – was the traditional scripture reading for the Christian holiday that commemorated the crucifixion: Good Friday. Throughout much of the medieval period, Christians would hear this passage read, hear sermons blaming Jews for crucifying Jesus, and then go on a rampage through the Jewish quarter of their city terrorizing and even killing Jewish men, women, and children. In this way, the Jews of these medieval towns and villages were forced to bear the anti-Jewish iniquity of the Christian people hearing this text. Perhaps partly because such experiences may have led Jews to have bad associations with Isa 52:13–53:12, this passage is far less emphasized in Judaism than others in Second Isaiah. The Jewish holiday of the "Ninth of Av," which commemorates the destruction of the first and second Temples, for example, traditionally includes readings of comfort and hope from virtually every part of Second Isaiah *except* Isa 52:13–53:12.

Today it is impossible to approach this text without this web of associations built up by years of its history of interpretation. Even if Christians realize that the link of this text with Jesus is a later one, many are still preoccupied with finding out exactly who this ancient "suffering servant" of Isaiah was. A closer look, however, reveals that this text is not focused on helping the reader know who the servant is. Instead, it presupposes that the audience already knows this person, and it anticipates that this audience will soon realize that their prejudices about him were wrong. As we have seen, texts already in Isaiah 40–55 have reinterpreted this "servant" to be the people of Israel in exile, and later communities have further reinterpreted the "servant" of this passage, whether as Jesus or the Jewish people. It is too late to read this passage as the original audience would have. Instead, we must read it now in light of its sometimes painful history of interpretation. Christians can choose to continue the ancient tradition of Christological interpretation of the passage, though now knowing that this represents just one in a line of creative reinterpretations. Jews can continue to use this passage to understand the Jewish people's suffering and gain hope for future restoration. And it is possible to reinterpret this passage in relation to other contemporary situations where individuals or groups are despised and/or oppressed, yet might be God's servants bearing, unfairly, the wrongs of others.

CHAPTER NINE REVIEW

For Review

1. Know the meaning and significance of the following terms:
   - Deutero-Isaiah
   - divine council
   - inclusio
   - intertextuality
   - monotheism
   - Second Isaiah
   - servant [in Second Isaiah]
   - servant songs
   - social-scientific analysis
   - suffering servant
   - trauma
   - trauma studies and the Bible
2. What were the differences in the exiles of 597, 586, and 582 and their significance for the destruction of the kingdom of Judah?
3. Where do the exilic edition of the books of Kings (its ending) and the book of Ezekiel disagree? Why was this important in this period?
4. What insights can we gain into the experience of ancient Judeans in exile from survey of contemporary social-scientific studies of people living outside their homelands?
5. What are four symptoms of trauma that are reflected in biblical traditions from the exile?
6. Make a list of the practices and beliefs that became especially prominent in the exile.
7. What elements of earlier prophecy are accentuated in Ezekiel? In which early prophet do they first appear and how are they different in Ezekiel?
8. How does Ezekiel 18 address the particular questions confronting the Judean exiles? What are indicators that it speaks of the question of inter-generational guilt, rather than individual guilt?
9. What can we learn about the unique characteristics of Ezekiel's and Second Isaiah's messages through the different emphases of their two major parts: Ezekiel 1–33/34–48 on the one hand and Isaiah 40–48/49–55 on the other?
10. Why would the "argument from prophecy" in Isaiah 48 not work as well if it were composed by eighth-century Isaiah?
11. What are two types of "intertextuality" studied by biblical scholars? Give two examples of such study from Second Isaiah. Can you think of other potential examples?

For Reflection

12. What would be contemporary analogies, whether individuals or groups, to the anonymous "suffering servant" of Isa 52:13–53:12? Do you see problems with applying this text's picture of "suffering for the sins of others" to these individuals and groups?

RESOURCES FOR FURTHER STUDY

Sociology of exile

Smith-Christopher, Daniel L. *Religion of the Landless: The Social Context of Babylonian Exile*. Bloomington, IN: Meyer-Stone Books, 1989.

Ezekiel

Bowen, Nancy. *Ezekiel*. Nashville: Abingdon, 2010.

Joyce, Paul. *Ezekiel: A Commentary*. New York and London: T & T Clark International, 2009.

Second Isaiah

Blenkinsopp, Joseph. *Isaiah 40–55*. New York: Doubleday, 2002.

Muilenburg, James. "Isaiah 40–66: Introduction and Exegesis." Pp. 381–783 in vol. 5 of *The Interpreter's Bible*. Nashville: Abingdon, 1956.

Torah and Trauma

10

Chapter Overview

The Basic Starting Point: A Century-Old Consensus on Three of the Pentateuch's Prior Sources

Torah and Trauma in the Non-Priestly Narratives about Israel's Early History

Promise to traumatized Judeans in the non-P texts of Genesis

Exilic (L) shaping of the non-P exodus-Moses story

Conclusion on the forging of non-P Pentateuchal materials by L supplements

The Priestly Source (P)

History and Fiction

Focus Text: Gen 12:1–3

Conclusion on the Torah (Pentateuch) and Trauma

Chapter Ten Review

Resources for Further Study

CHAPTER OVERVIEW

In Chapter 9 we saw how the exilic prophecies of Ezekiel and Isaiah addressed the despair of the exiles through promise of Yahweh's salvation. This chapter traces similar themes in the Pentateuch, particularly the books of Genesis through Numbers (Deuteronomy was the focus of Chapter 7 of this introduction). As we will see, these books preserve two earlier versions of the Torah which served as written sources for our present Pentateuch. One is a Priestly source of largely exilic materials starting in the Priestly creation account of Genesis 1 and extending through parts of Genesis to include Priestly materials about priests and other topics in Exodus, Leviticus, and Numbers. In addition, there is a non-Priestly source formed of materials of diverse date that starts with the non-Priestly parts of the Primeval History (Genesis 2–3 and other texts discussed in Chapter 4) and then includes materials about Israel's ancestors and the exodus-wilderness period in non-Priestly portions of Genesis, Exodus, and Numbers. By the end, the basic idea is the following: much as Ezekiel and Isaiah addressed exilic trauma with themes of promise and protection, so also do we find various Priestly and non-Priestly promise-oriented texts in the Pentateuch that were crafted to reassure and give hope to exiled Judeans. That is why we discuss the Pentateuch at this point. The texts of the Pentateuch, whatever their earlier origins, were greatly expanded and reframed through the lens of Judah's experiences of traumatic suffering, especially the exile of Jerusalem's elites to Babylonia in the sixth century BCE.

The Basic Starting Point: A Century-Old Consensus on Three of the Pentateuch's Prior Sources

In Chapter 9 we surveyed texts that are most securely dated to the exile, none of which provided a sustained narrative describing the years spent in Babylonia. Instead, the histories of the Bible have a gap in communal memory surrounding the exile. Much like individuals and groups today who have experienced trauma, it appears that the exiles avoided speaking directly of their traumatic experience.

Instead, they focused more on traditions regarding their distant past, stories of landless ancestors like them: Abraham, Sarah, and their heirs along with Moses and the Israelites of the exodus-wilderness generation. Of course, these figures were not invented, and there were earlier traditions about them, many of them written. Previous chapters of this introduction have discussed some such texts, such as northern Israelite compositions focused on Jacob and Moses. Yet Judah seems to have reframed such precursors amidst later experiences of trauma. Chapter 7 already discussed one stage of that process, where Judean scribes, working in the wake of Neo-Assyrian oppression, created the book of Deuteronomy by revising an earlier law code ("Ur-Deuteronomy") into a vassal treaty with Yahweh. This chapter explores similar dynamics surrounding the exilic reshaping of traditions of Israel's origins now found in the books of Genesis and Exodus–Numbers.

Our starting point is a basic distinction between two sources in Genesis–Numbers: a Priestly source (often called "P") and another, parallel source layer that goes by the term "non-Priestly." The Priestly layer is the agreed-upon orientation point, since scholars have achieved a centuries-long consensus on its contents and largely exilic/post-exilic dating. As we will see, the non-Priestly materials, though overall earlier than P, are more complex than P and their character more debated. The designation "non-Priestly" reflects some of this controversy. While scholars largely agree on what materials are Priestly and when those Priestly texts should be dated, they disagree more about how and when the other materials of the Pentateuch came into their present form. "Non-priestly" points to what scholars agree on about these texts: they are distinct from the Priestly source.

By the end of the chapter, we will refine this picture. But for now, let us start with this basic takeaway: the Pentateuch was formed from at least three blocks of earlier textual material written by different groups – a Priestly layer (by priests), an earlier non-Priestly layer of texts (by lay scribes), and the book of Deuteronomy (by lay scribes, mostly working in the Neo-Assyrian period). It should be noted that the book of Deuteronomy (D) is mostly non-Priestly as well (there are a few Priestly elements). Nevertheless, the term "non-P" or "non-Priestly" is used particularly often for non-P materials aside from Deuteronomy. This can make the often-used term "non-P" confusing and unspecific. Later in this chapter, I will introduce a new letter, L, to more positively designate the character of these non-P/pre-P materials outside Deuteronomy.

These three basic Pentateuchal sources are a given in historical study of Pentateuchal texts. Even though we do not have actual manuscripts of these (or any other) sources of the Pentateuch, these P, D, and other non-P (L) materials are distinct enough from each other to be recognized as having originated from different groups. And this insight alerts the reader to the fact that the Pentateuch is a complex combination of at least three clearly identifiable blocks of pre-existing material, each with their own character.

Traditions that Moses Wrote the Pentateuch

It can be a bit of a shock to learn that the Pentateuch was created out of earlier sources, especially since both Jewish and Christian traditions came to claim Moses as the author of the Pentateuch. This idea, however, is not biblical. Prose narrative texts like the Pentateuch were typically anonymous in the ancient Near East. This seems to be the case with the Pentateuch as well, which is not attributed to any author in ancient manuscripts. At the most, we see references in Deuteronomy to a "Torah" teaching that Moses gave to Israel just before the people entered the land (e.g. Deut 1:5; 31:9), but these references are focused on Moses's role in producing particular parts of Deuteronomy.

We do not see something like the idea of Mosaic authorship of the whole Pentateuch until post-biblical times, when Jews interacted with a more author-focused Greco-Roman culture. During this period, we start to see Jewish writers, such as Josephus and Philo, speak of Moses writing the Pentateuch. We also see mention – within a variety of early Jewish writings of the time (including the New Testament) – of the entire Pentateuch as "the Law of Moses" (the Greek word for law, *nomos*, here taking the place of the Hebrew word for teaching, *Torah*). The tradition developed further from there, with subsequent rabbinic interpretations working to explain how the Pentateuch, even including the report of Moses's death and burial (Deut 34:5–8), might all have been written by Moses himself.

Torah and Trauma in Non-Priestly Narratives about Israel's Earliest History

We begin with a look at the non-Priestly portions of Genesis, Exodus, and Numbers, with a focus on how these stories were shaped during exile into a word of hope for Judeans in Babylonia. This idea can be a challenge to grasp at first: the idea that biblical stories set in a much earlier time (e.g. in the primeval period or time of Abraham, Moses) are a combination of older and newer materials about that early time. Previous chapters of this textbook have discussed some of the older non-Priestly materials about creation and flood (Chapter 4) and northern writings about Jacob, Joseph, and exodus-Moses (Chapter 5). This section now examines how later scribes connected such older writings into a longer, promise-oriented story that would encourage exiles in Babylonia. The key idea here is the following: all of the non-P texts, whether older ones from the pre-exilic period or exilic additions, have been processed through the filter of the experience of exile. Seeing this traumatic background can help us read them better.

The non-Priestly materials of the Pentateuch include texts like the following: the older non-Priestly primeval history (Gen 2:1–4:26; 6:1–4; a flood story starting with 6:5–8; 7:1–5, 10, 12 and concluding with Gen 8:20–22; 9:18–27), a story about Abraham (Genesis 12–16, 18–22), a revised form of the northern Jacob and Joseph compositions (most of Genesis 25–50), and a transformed version of older stories about Moses leading Israel out of Egypt to the wilderness. If you want to imagine this source, try to picture a text up through Numbers that included stories such as the non-P primeval history and most stories about Abraham and other ancestors (e.g. Genesis 12–16, 18–22) along with parts of the Moses story (some of Exodus 1–34; Numbers 11–24), but did not have stories such as the Priestly creation story (Gen 1:1–2:3), the genealogy in Genesis 5, the covenant of circumcision in Genesis 17, etc. We have no separate manuscript of these non-Priestly materials, but scholars have agreed on their basic identification for over one hundred-fifty years.

This non-Priestly strand is highly complex, including within itself a mix of embedded older compositions and newer, exilic additions. An analogy for this kind of composition can be seen in some ancient villages found in the hill country of Israel even today (see Figure 10.1 for a different analogy). Many buildings in such villages are a combination of old and new. The walls beginning at the ground may come from an older building, but then they are continued with newer materials that extend up to the roof. The yard walls may have an old Greek column built into them or another piece of ancient architecture embedded in newer mortar. So also the non-P stories of Genesis and exodus-Moses were built around older literary building blocks such as the non-Priestly primeval history (see Chapter 1 of this *Introduction*), revised forms of the Jacob and Joseph stories originally written in the northern kingdom (see Chapter 5), and (for the exodus-Moses story) a transformed version of the story of Moses written in the early northern kingdom (see Chapter 5). But such building blocks do not make a house. The major shape and emphases of the non-P Genesis and exodus-Moses stories came from those who used these older literary building

FIGURE 10.1
Another analogy for the composition of non-P materials is this conglomerate rock, with larger pre-exilic rocks (such as the non-P primeval history, Jacob-Joseph story) connected to each other by rocky cement (L supplements).

blocks to create a broader story of Israel's earliest origins. Let us turn now to take a closer look at that story, starting with the promise-centered, non-P Abraham narrative that bridges between the primeval history and Jacob-Joseph story.

Promise to traumatized Judeans in the non-P texts of Genesis

Abraham seems to have become a particularly important figure during the exile. Consider, for example, Second Isaiah, where the prophet calls on Judean exiles to look to Abraham for a picture of the kind of divine restoration that they would soon experience:

> Look to the rock from which you were hewn, the quarry from which you were dug. Look to Abraham your father and Sarah who bore you. He was but one person when I called him, but I blessed him and made him numerous. Yahweh will comfort Zion, will bring comfort to her ruins; he will turn her desert into an Eden and her wastelands into the garden of Yahweh. Joy and gladness will be found in her, thanksgiving and the sound of song.
>
> (Isa 51:1–3)

The non-P stories about Abraham in Genesis, though built on earlier traditions about him, can be seen as providing a narrative form of the comfort that Second Isaiah offered exiles. This comfort starts with the following text where Yahweh commissions Abraham to depart from his homeland and promises to multiply, bless, and protect him:

> Go now from your country, your kindred, and your father's house to the land that I will show you. And I will make you a great nation, bless you, and make your name great. Be a blessing! I will bless those who bless you, and I will curse anyone who treats you lightly. And all clans of the ground will bless themselves by you.
>
> (Gen 12:1–3)

This promise text is the lynchpin connecting the non-P primeval history to the following ancestral materials. Its focus on blessing to Abraham stands as a contrast to the curses that occurred across multiple parts of the primeval history (e.g. Gen 3:17–19; 4:11–12; 5:29; 9:25).

The following non-P narratives then tell of Abraham and Sarah's journey to the promised land, reception of Yahweh's promise of that land to them (Gen 12:7), and God's initial fulfillment of promises of protection and blessing as Abraham and Sarah lived among foreigners. In reading these dramatic stories, it is easy to get caught up in the narrative and overlook how much these stories mirror the experience of later Judeans. For the narratives about Abraham and Sarah do not just tell of Yahweh's promises to vulnerable, landless ancestors of Israel. They also vividly depict the struggle of those ancestors to trust and believe in those promises. Immediately after Yahweh's promise of protection in Gen 12:2–3 (see the discussion of this text at the end of the chapter), the story then tells of Abraham's attempt to protect himself in Pharaoh's court by passing Sarah off as his sister (Gen 12:10–20). Moreover, the broader narrative puts the future of the promise in doubt, since it starts with a note about Sarah's infertility (Gen 11:30) and it is thus unclear who will be Abraham's heir. Abraham and Sarah work to solve this problem themselves by having Abraham impregnate Hagar, Sarah's female slave, but she and her son end up receiving promises of their own (Gen 16:10–12; see also 21:13, 18). In the end, Abraham and Sarah do succeed in having a child together, Isaac (Gen 18, 21), but Yahweh then tests Abraham by commanding him to offer Isaac as a burnt offering (Gen 22). This awful command for Abraham to sacrifice the son who represents his future echoes Yahweh's initial command for him to leave his family of the past:

Initial command for Abraham to leave his family of the past	Concluding command for Abraham to sacrifice his family of the future through Isaac
Go now from your country, your kindred, and your father's house	Take your son, your only one, whom you love, Isaac, and go to the land of Moriah, and offer him as a burnt offering
to the land that I will show you. (Gen 12:1)	on a mountain that I will show you (Gen 22:2)

The narrative builds up suspense by slowing down as Abraham prepares to slit Isaac's throat (22:7–10). Yet just before Abraham kills Isaac, a messenger of

Yahweh stays his hand, proclaiming that Abraham has proven to be one who fears God by being prepared to offer up his only son (Gen 22:11–12).

On one level, this is simply a powerful story about human characters that almost anyone in any time could relate to. This helps explain why it has been read and reread in Jewish, Christian, and Muslim contexts. On another level, this story depicts Abraham facing a dire threat to his future that was analogous to that faced by later Judeans under imperial domination. We cannot be sure exactly where an ancient Abraham tradition stops and later reshaping of the story begins. Nevertheless, we can say that non-P stories like these about Abraham are saturated with themes particularly characteristic of later Judean texts. Whatever their earlier background, they have been reshaped into an account of "Abraham your father, Sarah who bore you" that could encourage and instruct later Israelites facing imperial trauma.

As we move to the non-P materials in the latter half of Genesis, we find clear evidence that the theme of promise was added to earlier Jacob and Joseph compositions (on those compositions, see Chapter 5 of this introduction). These earlier compositions generally did not focus on the promise, but on inner-family dramas and dynamics: Jacob's struggles with Esau and then Laban (the Jacob story) and Joseph's drama with his brothers (the Joseph story). Meanwhile, the theme of God's promise only appears rarely in this half of Genesis, usually in evident textual additions that interrupt their context, such as a series of promise-oriented stories about Isaac (Gen 26:1–33) added between stories about Jacob taking Esau's privileges (Gen 25:29–34 and 27:1–45) and a promise scene for Jacob (Gen 46:1–5) that is placed amidst the story of Joseph and his brothers. These sorts of indicators have led many scholars to conclude that the non-P materials about Jacob and Joseph were formed when later scribes expanded earlier Jacob and Joseph narratives, using the theme of promise to connect them back to the preceding, promise-focused Abraham story.

The Story of Jacob at Bethel as an Example of the Addition of Promise to an Older Story

Many scholars now think that God's gift of Abraham's promise to Jacob in Gen 28:13–14 (see the **boldfaced** text and compare with Gen 12:2–3; 13:14–17) was added secondarily into a story about Jacob at Bethel. Originally, that story had focused on Yahweh's promise of protection to Jacob as he fled his homeland (Gen 28:15, 20–22). Try reading the story without the boldface elements. How is it different?

> Jacob came upon a place and spent the night there because the sun was going down. He took a stone and placed his head on it, and lay down in that place. He dreamed, and, look!, a stairway was founded on the earth with its top in heaven. And, behold, divine messengers were going up and down it.

And, look!, Yahweh was standing on it and said, **"I am Yahweh, the god of Abraham, your father and the god of Isaac. The land on which you are lying I will give to you and your children. Your descendants will be as numerous as the dust of the earth, and they will spread out to the west, east, north and south. All clans of the earth shall bless themselves by you and your descendants. [Gen 28:13-14]** Look! I will be with you. I will protect you continually as you go onward and return you to this place. Indeed, I will not abandon you until I have done what I have said to you."

And Jacob woke up from his sleep and said, "Look, Yahweh is in this place, and I did not know it." And he was afraid and said, "how awesome this place is! It is nothing other than the house of God and the gate of heaven." He called that place Bethel [Hebrew: "house of God/ El"]. It had formerly been called Luz.

And Jacob made a vow, "If God is with me, protecting me on this way on which I am going, giving me bread to eat and clothes to wear, and I return in peace to the house of my father, Yahweh will be my God and this stone which I have set as a pillar will be a house of God and I will offer a tithe to you of all that you give me.

(Gen 28:12–22)

Before the addition of the Abraham-promise theme, the older Jacob Bethel story (in regular type) was addressed to Israelites of the north. It connected the northern kingdom's royal sanctuary at Bethel, "the house of God and gate of heaven," with Jacob, the hero of the Israelites. Now, with the addition of the Abrahamic promise, the revised story connects this Jacob to the promise of land and blessing to Abraham (Gen 12:2–3, 7), assuring later Israelites of God's promise ultimately to them.

So what might we call these layers of material that reshaped non-P Genesis and other Pentateuchal materials in a promise-oriented direction? Specialists have not settled on specific terminology for these later non-P layers. The adjective "non-P/non-Priestly" only characterizes what they are not. A more specific term would be helpful to refer more specifically to the supplementary layers, like Gen 28:13–14 or 46:1–4, composed amidst later periods of Assyrian and Babylonian domination.

One possibility is to use the letter "L" as a multi-purpose designation for these multiple layers of later reshaping of non-P materials by lay scribes. Sometimes these L layers are mere supplements to earlier stories, such as the above-discussed expansion of the Bethel story with themes of Abrahamic promise. In other cases, like the Abraham narrative, lay scribes created whole narratives out of earlier (Abraham) traditions. Either way, the designation "L" characterizes the supplementary character of these added layers, the fact that they seem to be written by non-Priestly (lay) scribes, and the dating of them in the relatively late periods, especially the Babylonian exile. For this reason, the designation non-P (L) will be used at points in the following discussion for non-Priestly texts that were composed *or* reshaped by later, lay (L) scribes.

In the end, the point is not to identify and date this or that addition, but to identify ways in which the non-P materials of Genesis have been gradually adapted to address later situations of trauma. To some extent, of course, even the earlier materials of Genesis were preserved by exiles because those stories could be reread through an exilic lens. So, for example, later exiles could see themselves in the early primeval story of humans being expelled from Eden because of disobedience (Genesis 2–3) or in the northern narrative of Jacob fighting for his interests away from home (Genesis 29–33). Nevertheless, non-Priestly lay authors did not just leave such traditions as they were. Instead, they joined such earlier materials into a longer, promise-oriented story that extended from creation to ancestors. In the end, they crafted a story for exiles that extended from non-P primeval narratives like the Eden creation story and flood through to the non-P (L) story of Abraham and new L versions of the Jacob and Joseph compositions.

Exilic (L) shaping of the non-P exodus-Moses story

Exod 19:2–24:14 and 32:1–34:35.

READING

Whereas the first version of Genesis seems to have been built by connecting originally separate building blocks (e.g. a primeval history, Jacob story, Joseph novella), it is more difficult to identify separate early components of the story of Moses and the exodus. Instead, as suggested in Chapter 5, it is likely that some kind of Moses story was composed in the northern monarchy. The exodus tradition was important among early Israelite tribes, and the book of the northern prophet, Hosea, contains a particular density of references to the exodus and wilderness. He speaks, for example, of how "by a prophet Yahweh brought Israel out of Egypt" and quotes God as speaking of having "called my son out of Egypt" (Hos 11:1) and being Israel's God "since the days of Egypt" (Hos 12:10; 13:4; see also Hos 2:17).

Nevertheless, such early back-references to the exodus story leave out a major part of the exodus story as we find it in the book of Exodus: the plagues on Egypt. To be sure, Amos speaks of God afflicting Israel with one of the epidemics that were known to occur in Egypt (4:10), but the references to the exodus in Amos just quote Yahweh who "brought you out of the land of Egypt" (Amos 2:10; see also 3:1; 9:7).

In non-P (L) parts of Exodus, however, the Israelites are able to leave Egypt only after Yahweh has inflicted a series of plagues on Egypt, plagues involving blood (Exod 7:14–18, 23–25), frogs (Exod 7:26–29; 8:4–10), stinging flies (8:16–28), livestock sickness (9:1–7), devastating hail (9:13–35), locust swarms

(10:1–20), and – ultimately – the killing of all of Egypt's firstborn humans and animals (11:4–8; 12:21–27, 29–34). According to Exodus, these disasters were not just about forcing Egyptians to let Israel go. Indeed, Pharaoh is depicted as ready to let Israel leave at several points, but Yahweh "hardens his heart" (Exod 10:20; see also 8:28; 9:7, 34). This entire delayed exodus is explained as occurring for a particular reason, one involving God's need to protect and demonstrate his reputation. Much as Ezekiel and Second Isaiah promised exiles that Yahweh would free them for the sake of his "name" (Ezek 36:20–22; Isa 48:9–11), so Exodus speaks of how God prolonged the exodus under Moses in order that Yahweh's "name" would be spoken throughout the world (Exod 9:16) and Israel would "know that I am Yahweh" (Exod 7:16; 8:18; 10:1). Such a story of *delayed* exodus reassured Judeans frustrated by the delay in their homecoming. They could read this reshaped L narrative and have faith that Yahweh would eventually liberate them and reveal his name, much as Yahweh revealed his name in ages past through the plagues and exodus.

Subsequent parts of the non-P (L) exodus story feature similar projections of exilic themes into Israel's earliest history. For example, the non-P story of Yahweh's covenant with Israel at Sinai (Exodus 19–24, 32–34) reflects themes of self-blame in its picture of ultimate disobedience. Chapter 9 noted that such elements of self-blame are typical of many populations struggling to understand their trauma and prevent future occurrences (see box on p. 184). Texts discussed there blamed the Judeans' for their own oppression under Babylonia. The non-Priestly narrative projects such self-blame back into Israel's early history, suggesting that Israel was disobedient from the beginning and deserving of God's punishment. This starts in Exodus 32 with an account of Israel building a golden calf (Exod 32:1–6) in direct disobedience to the covenant they had just made with Yahweh (Exodus 19–24). Where Yahweh had just led Israel out of Egypt (Exod 19:4), the people now think Moses did (Exod 32:1); where Yahweh specifically prohibited making "gods of gold and silver" (Exod 20:22–23), the people now feel the need to make a golden calf to lead them in the wilderness (Exod 32:1); and where the previous covenant with Yahweh was sealed with a feast, "whole offerings" and "shared offerings" (Exod 24:5), the very same things seal the new covenant that the Israelites, including Aaron, make with the golden calf (Exod 32:5–6). Together, these elements in the non-P narrative depict ancient Israel as engaging in an anti-covenant that threatens to completely destroy them, and indeed this is what Yahweh of this non-P story appears ready to do (Exod 32:7–10). Later Judeans could relate to such stories of disobedience among their ancestors, and they too felt the threat that their exile in Babylonia might completely destroy them.

Yet this non-P (L) story also gave these exiles hope by showing how Yahweh did not destroy the ancient Israelites and thus can be trusted not to give up on them either. For, in Exodus, the Moses of the non-P story changes Yahweh's mind about the destruction by using two arguments relating to themes that become prominent in the exile. He reminds God of the promises to the patriarchs and pleads with God to think about the potential damage to his reputation if the Egyptians hear of Israel's destruction in the wilderness (Exod 32:11–13). Punishment still comes. Moses recruits the Levites – who up until this point in the story are just another tribe – and their first act is to kill every Israelite that their sword can reach (Exod 32:26–29). In addition, Yahweh brings a plague on the people (Exod 32:35). Nevertheless, Yahweh eventually comes back to dwell amidst Israel via the "tent of meeting" (Exod 33:7–17), and makes a new covenant with Israel (Exodus 34).

Scholars have long debated exactly how this non-P account came together. Nevertheless, most recognize that certain parts of it, such as Moses's speech about the patriarchal promise and Yahweh's preservation of his honor/his name (Exod 32:10–14), represent recognizable supplements to an earlier account that did not know of this intervention (see, e.g. Exod 32:30–35). These L elements, like the more hopeful prophecies in Ezekiel and Second Isaiah, stress Yahweh's ability to work with his people *no matter what they do*. To be sure, this reshaped non-P story of Moses insists that God gets angry about disobedience and imposes consequences. Nevertheless, Yahweh's ultimate promise to the people does not depend on their virtue, but rests more on Yahweh's concern for his honor among the nations. On this basis, the exiles can trust that Yahweh will lead them out of Babylonia and back into their homeland, despite the fact that they have not always lived up to Yahweh's expectations for them, do not do so, and will not do so.

These exilic, L-layer affirmations of God's steadfast covenant with Israel in the non-P exodus story now stand at the outset of the Bible that Jews and Christians share, but, ironically, many Christians pay attention to only the judgment on Israel in these stories. For centuries, Christians have used these biblical stories of Israel's shortcomings as ammunition to show why God rejected the Jewish people and started over with the church instead. According to this approach, the shortcomings of Israel described in these biblical texts anticipate Judaism's later rejection of Jesus as the messiah, a rejection which supposedly resulted in God's termination of God's covenant with Jews. Yet the point of the non-P story of the covenant at Sinai is that God has made an unbreakable covenant with Israel, one that can withstand absolutely anything that Israel might do to damage it. Certainly, these stories at the heart of the present Pentateuch decisively stand against any idea that God's covenant with Israel could be ended for any reason, including Israel's refusal to see Jesus as the messiah.

Basics

The Non-P (L) Source

Outline: Yahweh's promise-based, unbreakable covenant

I	Gift of ancestral promise-covenant in the wake of repeated primeval problems	Genesis*
	A Problems with creation and post-flood	Genesis 1–11* (non-P parts)
	B Gift of promise to Abraham and heirs	Genesis 12–50* (non-P parts)
II	Creation + preservation of Moses-led, covenant people	Parts of Exodus*, Numbers*

> **Date**
>
> Exile (building on earlier, pre-exilic compositions).
>
> **Themes**
>
> If we focus on the later L materials within the non-Priestly layer and not probable pre-exilic compositions that the L layers expanded upon, the emphasis seems to be on the gift of Yahweh's covenant despite any shortcomings in the recipients. We see this as early as Yahweh's gift and transmission of the covenant to Abraham, Isaac, and Jacob despite their misdeeds and occasional lack of trust. Then, in the Moses story, Yahweh perseveres in giving a covenant to Israel despite their making of the golden calf (Exodus 32) and lack of trust in the promise of conquest (Num 14:11–25), largely on the basis of the earlier promises to the patriarchs.
>
> **More information: the gap between ancestors and Moses**
>
> Scholars note that the non-Priestly texts in the Pentateuch, aside from a few exceptions such as Genesis 15 or Exodus 32, do not explicitly link the time of the ancestors in Genesis with the time of Moses. This is an indicator to many that writings about the ancestors were not linked with those about Moses until a very late time. Before this time, the stories about Jacob-Joseph, and possibly even those about Abraham and Isaac, stood separately from the Moses story. They were an alternative account of how Israel became related to Yahweh and came into the land.
>
> Thus the exilic (L) link of the primeval, ancestral, and Moses traditions with each other was important. It took what were once competing traditions and put one (the ancestral traditions) before the other (the Moses traditions).

To be sure, there is a lot of judgment on Israel in these texts. Indeed, few other literatures in world history are so brutally self-critical about their people as Israel's is. This may result from the fact that large parts of Israel's literature – both Pentateuchal narrative and prophecy – were shaped by exiles who believed that their exile had been caused by their, and their ancestors', disobedience (//traumatic self-blame). Yet the texts discussed here just as decisively affirm Yahweh's steadfast care for his people. In these stories, Yahweh knows full well that Israel is a "stubborn" and "stiff necked" people (Exod 32:9; 33:5), yet even after they build the golden calf, God proclaims:

> Yahweh, Yahweh, a God merciful and gracious
> slow to anger, and abounding in steadfast love and faithfulness,
> keeping steadfast love for the thousandth generation,
> forgiving bloodguilt and transgression and sin,
> yet by no means clearing the guilty,
> but visiting the bloodguilt of the parents on children and the children's
> children, to the third and fourth generation.
>
> (Exod 34:6–7 NRSV modified)

This affirmation of God's grace, another likely candidate to be an L-supplementary addition to the exodus story, strikes a compromise between the exilic additions to the end of 2 Kings and Ezekiel's prophecy. With exilic parts of 2 Kings (e.g. 2 Kgs 23:26–27), it affirms that children, even grandchildren and great-grandchildren, can pay for the sins of their parents. Yet with Ezekiel (Ezek 18), this text gives despairing exiles and later generations hope by stressing that there is a limit to such intergenerational guilt. Yahweh's ultimate faithfulness to his people is far more permanent and dominant than his anger. This text would have given hope to despairing Judeans in Babylonian exile.

Conclusion on the forging of non-P Pentateuchal materials by L supplements

As stressed at the outset, a key takeaway from the discussion so far should be a growing sense of how some Pentateuchal stories were shaped amidst later trauma, especially exilic trauma, by lay scribes. Sometimes these L supplements are isolated and relatively recognizable, such as the promise to Jacob in Gen 46:1–4. In other cases, L supplements, such as the plague motif in the non-P exodus story, are thoroughly woven into their present non-P context. This is typical of scribal expansions added to earlier documents, since such scribes often shaped such supplements so that they connected with the texts they were meant to reshape.

The authors of these scribal expansions remained anonymous, like other authors of such narrative texts in the ancient Near East. Nevertheless, the non-P exodus narrative may preserve clues to the identity of the group who created and preserved this L/non-P source. It describes 70 "elders of the people/Israel" as getting to see Yahweh at Sinai (Exod 24:1–2, 9–11) and receiving a spirit to lead Israel along with Moses (Num 11:16–17, 24–25). Notably, we see a similar group of 70 elders in the prophecies of Ezekiel (8:11; see also 14:1; 20:1) and in later texts (e.g. Ezra 10:8, 14). These elders seem to have risen to prominence in the wake of the loss of the monarchy, and they constitute the best candidates to have preserved and developed the non-P strand of the Pentateuch, including the later layer of lay materials in it that addressed exilic concerns.

J (the "Yahwistic Source"), E (the "Elohistic Source"), and the Documentary Hypothesis

Throughout the twentieth century, most bible specialists believed that the material discussed here as non-P comprised two long sources from the early pre-exilic period: a **J source** composed in Judah around the time of Solomon and an **E source** composed in (northern) Israel sometime in the eighth century. The J Source or **Yahwistic source** was so called because it frequently used the divine name "Yahweh," which, in the German language of those who pioneered this theory, is spelled with an initial "J." The E source or **Elohistic source** was so called because it more frequently preferred the divine name *Elohim*, which means "god" in Hebrew. For example, earlier scholars maintained that the bulk of Genesis 12–16 and 18–19 came from the hypothesized J source (note the predominance of "LORD" = Yahweh), while parallel stories about Abraham found in Genesis 20–22 were from E (note the predominance of "God" in these chapters).

Problems for the older hypothesis

A number of scholars still find this idea of J and E persuasive. Nevertheless, many specialists in the study of the Pentateuch (including this author) have abandoned this approach, for multiple reasons.

The first problem for the idea of early J and E sources has to do with identifying them in the first place. The non-P material lacks widespread indictors that it was created out of interwoven, parallel sources. For example, we do not see the sorts of extensive doublets and contrasting perspective that allowed scholars to achieve such consensus in distinguishing a Priestly layer from the non-P materials. As a result, aside from the Abraham story and a few other texts, scholars have had a lot of trouble gaining consensus on what might have been the contents of J and E.

The second problem has to do with the early dating often assigned to these hypothesized J and E sources. If such large, tenth- and ninth-century Pentateuchal sources had existed, it is hard to know why we see so few references to the three patriarchs and God's promise to them before the book of Deuteronomy (mostly seventh-century and later) and Ezekiel (sixth century). Hosea, for example, is an early prophet from the north who seems to refer to the Jacob story (Hos 12:3–5, 13) along with the exodus-Moses tradition (e.g. Hos 12:14). But there is no sign that Hosea is familiar with Abraham and the idea of a promise to him, Isaac, and Jacob. Instead, it seems that the demonstrably early material in early prophetic books (e.g. Hosea, Amos, eighth-century Isaiah, Micah 1–3) knows nothing of the broader promise theme that unites the non-P parts of the Pentateuch, while we do see this theme more and more frequently in Deuteronomy, Ezekiel, and Second Isaiah (Isaiah 40–55).

Terminology

Scholars who build on this older approach would call the non-Priestly texts under discussion here "**JE**," a term for the combination of the hypothesized J and E documents. Those specialists who no longer find the J and E hypothesis plausible refer more neutrally to the same group of texts with the term used in this textbook, "non-P" (for non-Priestly). Back when the great majority of scholars thought that D and P were preceded by early J and E sources, this theory was termed the "**Documentary Hypothesis**," and all students were taught that the Pentateuch had four sources – J, E, D, and P. Now J and E have dropped from that scholarly consensus and only **D** and **P** remain as agreed-upon, identifiable sources from the older hypothesis. That is the position adopted in this textbook. For contrasting arguments for a revival of the Documentary Hypothesis in new ("Neo-Documentarian") form, see Joel Baden, *The Composition of the Pentateuch: Renewing the Documentary Hypothesis* (New Haven: Yale University Press, 2012).

The Priestly Source (P)

READING Gen 1:1–2:3; 17:1–27; Exodus 6:2–8 and skim chapters 25–31 and 35–40.

Not everyone in the exile, however, would have appreciated the depiction of Israel's history in the non-P/L source. Alongside the elders, there was another prominent group of exilic leaders – the priests – and they do not come off well in the L Source, especially in the L Source story of the covenant at Sinai. In general, many lower-ranking priests traced their ancestry back to Jacob's son Levi, and the leading priests of the exile and post-exile traced their descent to a particular Levite, Aaron. The non-P (L) Sinai story does not positively portray either Aaron or the descendants of Levi as a group. In it Aaron helps the people make the golden calf (Exod 32:1–6) and later challenges the authority of Moses (Numbers 12). Moreover, the non-P Sinai narrative depicts the Levitical priesthood as being founded in blood, with their first act being to kill as many of their fellow Israelites as their swords could reach (Exod 32:25–29). In sum, the pre-P (L) Sinai narrative depicted the priesthood, particularly the priests claiming descent from Aaron (see e.g. Ezra 7:1–5), as founded in idolatry and the shedding of Israelites' blood – hardly the kind of picture the priests would want to paint of themselves.

These and other concerns helped prompt the leading Aaronide priests in exile to formulate their own story of Israel's history before it had taken possession of the land, a story aimed at replacing the pre-P/L version of events with one more favorable to the priests and their concerns. Although the present Pentateuch now has texts from this **Priestly source** (P) intertwined with the non-P materials, P probably stood separately from its pre-Priestly counterpart when it was originally composed in the exilic period. There are too many repeated narrations of events in these two sources for one of them to have been created as a supplement to the other. Consider, for example, the two creation accounts (non-P Genesis 2–3; P Genesis 1), P and non-P doublets across the flood narrative (Genesis 6–9), two covenants with Abraham (non-P Genesis 15; P Genesis 17), two calls of Moses (non-P Exodus 3:1–4:18; P Exodus 6), and the evident intertwining of P and non-P accounts in the story of the Israelites' exodus through the Red Sea (Exodus 14). A single author would not create so many repeated tellings of the same event. Even an editor of an earlier narrative would not need to repeat it in the process of revising it. Rather, these multiple cases of *doubled* reports of the same events show that the broader Pentateuch originated in two, parallel versions of the Torah: the pre-P (L) version that was discussed above and a later Priestly version that was originally composed to stand separately from it.

This later Priestly version extended from God's creation of the cosmos in Genesis 1 through a series of Priestly texts (e.g. Genesis 17; Exodus 6) including the end of Exodus, where God instructs Moses on creating a tabernacle in which God then comes to dwell amidst Israel (Exodus 25–31; 35–40). It is from this tabernacle that God then gives instructions to Israel about sacrifice and other topics that are key to the ongoing relationship of God to God's people (e.g. Lev 1:1). Because the following book of Leviticus consists exclusively of Priestly materials, I give an overview of that book here (basics on Genesis, Exodus, and Numbers are given in the next chapter).

There are a number of instances where the point of the Priestly version of a story only becomes apparent when it is read apart from its non-Priestly precursors. Consider, for example, the divergent accounts in P and non-P of the reasons for Jacob's departure from Canaan. The non-P version of this story is the old trickster tale about Jacob stealing his father's blessing and fleeing Esau's murderous wrath (Gen 27:1–45). The (later) P version of these events provides a different reason: Esau had married foreign wives (Gen 26:34–35), those wives had been awful to Rebekah (Gen 27:46), and so Isaac blessed Jacob (on purpose!) and sent him homeward to get a proper wife (Gen 28:1–6). Though they are now separated from one another by the older trickster story (Gen 27:1–45),

---

Basics
Book of Leviticus

Outline

I	Establishment of the tabernacle cult		1–10
	A	Instructions for sacrifices	1–7
	B	Establishment of priesthood subject to instructions	8–10
II	Establishment of holy people		11–26
	A	Purity rules	11–15
	B	Holiness Code	16–26
III	Vows		27

Date
Exilic to early post-exilic (building on pre-exilic sources).

Themes
Leviticus now stands at the center of the Pentateuch, and it represents the center of Priestly teaching. Though the book starts with specific instructions for priestly sacrifice (Leviticus 1–7), it concludes with rules for creating a holy, priest-like people (Leviticus 16–26, sometimes termed the "Holiness code"). Many eating and purity rules, once meant only for priests, are extended in Leviticus to the whole people of Israel. These cultic rules are not seen as a burden in the book or difficult to follow. Instead, they are an affirmation of the special, particularly holy character of Yahweh's beloved people.

Which Texts Were Part of the P Source?

We have no separate copy of the hypothesized Priestly source, but scholars have agreed for a long time on which parts of the Pentateuch probably were part of it. The following are some of them. Try reading them together.

P in the Genesis primeval history

Gen 1:1–2:3; 5:1–28, 30–32; major parts of the flood story (such as 6:9–22; 7:13–16a; 8:14–19; 9:1–17); the post-flood genealogy in 11:10–26 (and maybe parts of Genesis 10).

P in the Genesis ancestral history

Birth and journey of Abraham (11:27, 31–32; 12:4b–5; 13:6); birth of Ishmael (16:3, 15–16); covenant of circumcision (Genesis 17); birth of Isaac (21:3–5); death of Abraham and the transition to Isaac and his sons (25:7–21); Esau's marriages and Isaac's sending of Jacob to Padan-Aram for a better wife (26:34–35; 27:46–28:9); Jacob's encounter with God at Bethel (35:9–15); death of Isaac and transition from family of Isaac to Jacob's family (35:22b–37:1); and possible fragments of a P Joseph story (e.g. Gen 37:2; 46:5–7 and 50:12–13).

P in the Moses story

The oppression in Egypt (Exod 1:1–5, 7, 13–14, 23–25); call of Moses and Aaron (Exod 6:2–7:7, also 7:8–13); plagues of blood, frogs, gnats, and boils (7:19–22; 8:1–3, 11–15; 9:8–12; 11:9–10); Passover (12:1–20, 28, 40–51) and Red Sea crossing (parts of Exodus 14, particularly 14:1–4, 8–10, 15–18, 22–23, 26, 28–29); departure for Sinai and giving of manna to eat in the desert (15:22, 27; 16:1–3, 6–27); arrival at Sinai and tabernacle building (Exod 19:1–2a; 24:15–31:18; 35:1–39:43; 40:1–38); all of Leviticus and Num 1:1–10:28; the spying of the land (Num 13:1–17a, 21, 25–26, 32–33; 14:1–3*, 5–10, 26–38); part of the rebellion of Korah story (Num 16:1–11*, 16–24, 27a, 35–50; all of Numbers 17–18); the rebellion at the rock (20:1–13); Aaron's death (20:22–29).

P in Deuteronomy and Joshua

P elements become sparse in the book of Deuteronomy (Deut 34:1*, 7–9), suggesting that they were composed as supplements to their non-P contexts rather than the continuation of an originally separate source. We even find a few examples of such P-like elements in the book of Joshua (e.g. Josh 24:33), suggesting that the work of Priestly scribes extended up to the end of Joshua. After the end of the Hexateuch (Genesis–Joshua), there are no more distinctively Priestly additions.

the P texts that give this alternative explanation connect well together (Gen 26:34–35; 27:46–28:6). They probably originally stood apart from the ancient, northern trickster story in Gen 27:1–45 and were designed to replace its characterization of Jacob.

Thus, we can learn something about this Priestly source when we read it as a separate document. When the overall P source was separate from the non-P/L materials, it chronicled God's involvement with the world in three major stages: (1) creation, (2) the flood and following covenant with Noah, and (3) the covenant with Abraham and eventual creation at Sinai of Israel out of the heirs to Abraham's promise. The first stage, found in Gen 1:1–2:3 along with most of Genesis 5, is God's creation of an orderly and peaceful universe, a cosmos crowned by God's creation of godlike humans to rule earth's other creatures (Gen 1:26–31). The second stage, found in Priestly texts scattered across Genesis 6–9 (such as 6:9–22 and 9:1–17), describes God's actions after this creation was violated by violence: God's destruction of almost all life through a flood, God's rescue of Noah's family and other animals, and God's making of a covenant with Noah and the rest of life not to bring such a flood again. The third and most important stage in P is God's creation of the holy community of Israel. This starts with God's making of a special covenant of circumcision with Abraham (Genesis 17), a covenant in which God gives Abraham and his heirs a special version of the creation blessing given in Genesis 1 (Gen 17:6–8; compare Gen 1:27–28). Other Priestly texts in Genesis show the passing of this blessing on to Jacob (not Esau; Gen 26:34–35; 27:46–28:5; 35:9–15) and trace the genealogies of Abraham's offspring (Gen 25:7–18; 35:22–26; 36:1–43). Jacob in the P source next goes to Egypt, where his descendants multiply into the people of Israel (Exod 1:1–7) and are oppressed by Pharaoh (Exod 1:13–14; 2:23–25). God then calls Moses and Aaron – in Priestly texts – to lead Israel out of Egypt through plagues and the dividing of the Red Sea (Exod 6:2–7:13; etc.). This prepares for the Priestly story of events and instructions given at Mount Sinai (most of Exodus 25 through Numbers 10). There God works through Moses to build a wilderness sanctuary, a "tabernacle," in which God can dwell (Exod 24:15–31:17; 35:1–40:33) and then instructs Israel (through Moses) on how it can become a holy community gathered round the tabernacle (Leviticus and Num 1:1–10:10). The other main narratives that were part of P focus on God's confirmation of Moses's and Aaron's leadership of this new, holy community.

Though the Priestly layer of the Pentateuch sometimes builds on older materials (see Figure 10.2), scholars agree that the bulk of it was written in the exile or early post-exilic period. Some signs pointing to this dating include the following:

- Where Deuteronomy *explicitly calls on Israel* to sacrifice to Yahweh in one and only one place (Deuteronomy 12), the Priestly narratives appear to presuppose this. P does not describe any sacrifice by Noah or the patriarchs before the establishment of the tabernacle at Mount Sinai.
- The P narrative focuses before Sinai on practices that could be carried out in exile and were particularly important then, such as circumcision (Genesis 17), an ancient form of Passover celebration that was celebrated at home (Exod 12:1–20), and Sabbath (Exodus 16).
- Consistent with tendencies of exilic communities to focus on communal boundaries, the P document includes a prominent emphasis on the importance of ethnic purity and the problems with intermarriage, an emphasis seen particularly clearly in the story of Isaac's rejection of Esau because of intermarriage and his sending of Jacob to Haran to get a proper wife (Gen 26:34–35; 27:46–28:9).

Basics

P Source

Outline

I   Expanded genealogy: creation and promise

      A   Elohim: creation–re-creation 11:10–26   Gen 1:1–2:3; 5:1–9:28*

      B   El-Shaddai: the Abrahamic covenant   Gen 11:27–50:26*

II   Yahweh: Moses+Aaron-led pilgrimage to the land

      A   Pilgrimage to Sinai   Exodus 1–19*

      B   Sinai indwelling and instruction   Exodus 20–Numbers 10*

      C   Pilgrimage from Sinai to the land   Numbers 11–36*

* Here and elsewhere, an asterisk indicates that *some parts* of the textual ranges contain relevant (P) texts.

Date

Exile into post-exile (with short pre-exilic sources).

Themes: shifts in the divine name

As indicated in the outline above, some of the shifts in the Priestly source correspond to shifts in the divine designation that it uses for God. In the primeval period, God is known as *Elohim* (Hebrew for "God") and makes with Noah and all life a covenant that is marked by a rainbow. During the ancestral period, God appears to Abraham as *El-Shaddai* (Hebrew for "God Almighty") and makes a covenant with him that is marked with circumcision and passed on by Abraham's heirs, Isaac and Jacob. In the final period, God appears to Moses and the rest of Israel as Yahweh (see the P version of Moses's call in Exod 6:2–8). The centerpoint of this period is Israel's stay at Sinai, where the tabernacle is built, the priesthood of Aaron and his sons is established, and Yahweh's glory comes down to dwell amidst Israel.

More information: P as "redaction" or separate "source"?

The bulk of past and present scholars thinks that a shorter form of this Priestly narrative once existed as a separate source, independent of the non-P texts with which it is now combined. Others, however, believe that the Priestly texts of the Pentateuch were written from the outset as an expansion of the non-P texts and never existed separately. This alternative perspective – P as "redaction" – can make a difference in how one understands the structure and themes of the first Priestly Pentateuch. It becomes another priestly layer (or set of Priestly layers) beyond the "L" layers that were discussed above.

     For your purposes, it is not crucial to resolve this issue one way or the other. To some extent, the Priestly source itself seems to have had some layers, much like non-P. Texts emphasizing the holiness of all Israel in

> Leviticus 17-26, for example, are now seen by many scholars to be part of a distinctive "Holiness" layer of Priestly material found across different parts of the Pentateuch. At the same time, the previously-mentioned doublets of P and non-P stories suggest that some early form of a P source—one with its own narratives of creation, flood, Moses, etc.—originally existed separate from the non-P narratives that it parallels.

- The P document as a whole leads up to the story of God's creation of the wilderness tabernacle with the priests of Aaron at its head. This points to an exilic time when the monarchy is no longer a living institution, and its accoutrements (e.g. a crown; Exod 28:36–38) are assumed by the priests.

The language and concerns of this Priestly document are closest to exilic texts like Ezekiel and Second Isaiah. Like Second Isaiah, the author of the P story encourages exiles to return to the land, in this case through emphasizing God's power in the exodus, the importance of the land in the promise (see Exod 6:2–8), and God's punishment of those who lack enough belief to embrace God's promise and return (Num 13:32; 14:36–37). In these ways and others, the narratives of P show the impact of the Babylonian exile, along with hopes of return, on the Priestly understanding of Israel's history before the conquest.

FIGURE 10.2
Silver amulet, dating to the period around the fall of Jerusalem. It contains a version of the priestly blessing found in Num 6:24–26.

Though P builds on some earlier materials, such as a "scroll of the descendants of Adam" referred to in Gen 5:1 or priestly instructions in Leviticus and Numbers, the broader P layer is a distinctively exilic story for exiles and their children about ancient Israel before the people had a land.

These exilic emphases show up already at the outset of the P source in the creation account with which it opens (Gen 1:1–2:3). The whole structure of this account is oriented around a seven-day scheme that climaxes in God's observance of the Sabbath (Gen 2:1–3). We see a similar emphasis on the Sabbath in Ezekiel (Ezek 20:12–24; 22:8, 26; 23:38). In addition, the text transfers royal traits to non-royal figures, much as in Second Isaiah. In this case, the text builds on ancient ideas in Egyptian and Mesopotamian royal theology that the king was made as the image of God; he was made to serve as the deity's representative among humans, ruling them made to serve as the deity's representative among humans, ruling them (see the box below). The description of the creation of humanity in Gen 1:26–27 takes these ideas and applies them to humanity in general, both men and women. Indeed, many translations overlook the fact that the Hebrew of this passage explicitly connects the creation of humanity as God's image with their destiny to rule creation. God's speech to the divine council (note the plural address) makes this clear, "Let us make humanity as our image, similar to our likeness *so that* they may rule the fish of the sea, the birds of the heavens, the cattle and all the earth, and all the creatures creeping on the earth" (Gen 1:26, emphasis added).

More on Method: Insights from History of Religions

Often we can learn more about the ancient images, metaphors, and ideas in the Bible through looking at other ancient religious ideas and practices studied as part of what is sometimes termed "**history of religions**." An example is the tantalizing reference to humans being made "as the image of God" in Gen 1:26–27.

The king as the image of god in the ancient Near East

Texts in both Mesopotamia and Egypt depict the king as an image of god, representing that god on earth much as a divine statue would. For example, one Mesopotamian letter to the king says:

> The father of the king, my lord, was the image of [the god] Bel, and the king, my lord, is likewise the image of Bel.

Similarly, an Egyptian text has the god Amun proclaim about the king:

> You are my beloved son, who came forth out of my love, my image that I set on earth. I let you rule the land in peace.

How this might inform a reading of Gen 1:26–27

These royal ideas are applied to all of humanity in Gen 1:26–27, both the idea of humans being made as divine images and the idea of this divine image being a mark of their authority to rule others.

According to this radical reapplication of ancient royal theology, there is a reason for the agreement between the human form and human pictures of God in human terms. God had the "human" form first and gave it to humans as a mark of the human destiny to rule creation. According to this text, we are like little god statues walking around the earth, and all the animals of the earth can see in our divine bodily form the stamp of our authority to rule them. In this respect, Gen 1:26–27 may also draw on ancient Near Eastern concepts of divine statues representing deities on earth in a very concrete way. Especially in late periods, Israelites criticized as idolatry the practice of worship of divine images. Genesis 1 may have been written in such a late context, agreeing with such critique of use of such human-made images in worship, yet also implying that God made humans as "divine images" representing god on earth as rulers.

Later interpreters of this text often have been reluctant to see it as affirming an actual bodily similarity between God and humans. Though the text is quite explicit in using multiple terms for physical similarity, both "image" and "likeness," these interpreters have argued that the chapter really means to assert that humans bear a spiritual or intellectual likeness to God. Being "made as the image of God" (sometimes translated "in the image") thus means that humans share God's capacity for relationship or rational thought or the like. Later historical critics have buttressed this approach by arguing that the Priestly narrative has too elevated a picture of God to imagine that God might have a body that humans could resemble. Nevertheless, Ezekiel, a prophet

More on Method: Ecological Biblical Criticism

Ecological biblical criticism (also known as ecological hermeneutics) is a set of approaches that analyze the biblical text and interpretations of it in relation to present ecological crises. In an influential 1967 article in *Science* magazine ("The Historical Roots of Our Ecologic Crisis"), Lynn White argued that texts like Genesis 1 (with its description of humans as divine images) had helped form "the most anthropocentric religion the world has seen" and thus were among the roots of the ecological crisis. A number of biblical scholars responded to White by arguing that Genesis 1 actually depicts a human responsibility to rule *and care* for creation. Nevertheless, such arguments have been undermined by the lack of any emphasis in Genesis 1 on the need for human care for creation and by the presence of elements in Genesis 1 – such as its uncritical affirmation of human population growth (Gen 1:28) – that are ecologically problematic. In more recent years, biblical scholars have looked at a broader range of biblical texts and interpretations of them. Moreover, though the bulk of ecological interpretations of the Bible have attempted to provide earth-affirming rereadings of biblical texts, some scholars also recognize ways that the Bible – shaped for a quite different time – can sometimes be a problematic resource for addressing current environmental challenges.

One good source for more of an overview of past readings of the Bible in relation to ecology and proposals of some new rereadings is Hilary Marlow, *Biblical Prophets and Contemporary Environmental Ethics: Re-reading Amos, Hosea, and First Isaiah* (New York: Oxford University Press, 2009).

with many affinities to the Priestly narrative, has a vision in his call narrative of the divine throne with "something like the appearance of a human" upon it (Ezek 1:26). Apparently, Priestly exiles such as Ezekiel *could* imagine that God had a form that humans could resemble. It is later Biblical interpreters, including historical critics, who have struggled with seeing humans as having a bodily similarity to God.

Read in this way, Gen 1:1–2:3 would have helped Judean exiles understand their situation in a new way. Though they might be relatively powerless vis-à-vis their Babylonian overlords, they shared with the rest of humanity a likeness to God that was seen in their bodies, a likeness that made them "kings" of creation. Moreover, unlike the rest of humanity, the Judean exiles acted out this similarity to God in a particular way: just as God observed a Sabbath after creating the universe, they likewise observed a Sabbath every week. Thus this text takes an ancient practice that became more important during the exile, the Sabbath, and makes it a sign of the exiles' likeness to God.

History and Fiction

By this point many readers may be wondering, "But what about what actually happened with Abraham or at Sinai? Does all this just mean that the exiles made all these stories up?" To this, the answer is both "no" and "yes." The answer is "no," because ancient peoples, including ancient Israel, almost always built new stories out of older ones. Especially with respect to stories about people (rather than gods), ancient authors almost always started with a tradition – whether oral or written – about a given person and then built on that tradition. They did not "make them all up." Yet there is also a sense in which the answer to the question is "yes." Ancient authors did make up certain things. Unlike many contemporary historians, these ancient authors felt free to embellish, modify, and extend the traditions given to them. In light of their experience of imperial trauma, for example, Judean authors found new, promise-centered ways to tell stories about Jacob and Moses, ways that would never have occurred to them before. They saw these stories through the lens of their community's need for resilience and the things they were learning about themselves and God in exile. As a result, they retold, extended, and connected these stories in light of these trauma-forged truths, in light of what they believed "must have happened."

Now we no longer can untangle later "truths" learned in exile or other periods from the kinds of "historical truth" about Israel's early history that contemporary readers often want to know. Through using both data from archaeology and analysis of non-biblical literature, we can affirm that the traditions in the Pentateuch probably have some kind of historical core. Later storytellers would not have made up characters such as Abraham and Sarah. Certainly, exiles would not have created a deliverer figure like Moses with an Egyptian name and foreign wives. Nevertheless, it appears that the stories as we have them now, including almost all their dialogue and other details, reflect their settings in later periods of Israel's history. As a result, they are more useful as sources for the "truths" learned by Israelites in these later periods than in reconstructing historical "truths" about the times of Abraham and/or Moses. We might wish we knew exactly what Sarah said to God or Moses said to Pharaoh, but the biblical texts about them are not good sources for this. They *can* tell us, however, what later Israelites had to say to each other about their identity as a people and God's intentions toward them.

Consider this in relation to a concrete example: the non-P story of covenant at Sinai discussed above (Exodus 19–24, 32–34). Contemporary readers of this story could argue endlessly about whether or not it actually happened. Yet in the end, such arguments miss the larger point of the story. The story that we now have is addressed to Israel of the "thousandth" generation, long after Sinai, an Israel who wonders – as in the laments discussed above – whether God will be eternally angry for past disobedience or will turn and save God's people. The answer given in this story is a decisive affirmation of God's intent to save the people no matter what. This text, with its "yes" to God's mercy, has been absolutely central to Jewish worship and thought, and this affirmation of God's unconditional relationship with Israel can be read by Christians as an anticipation of God's broader unconditional grace toward the world as seen through Jesus Christ. Ultimately, such "truths" about God in Judaism and Christianity are much more central to the ongoing significance of the Bible than specific historical "truths" that could be affirmed or uncovered using modern historical methods. Moreover, these important ideas in ancient biblical texts can be missed if the debates about them all focus on whether or not the events described in them actually happened.

FOCUS TEXT

Gen 12:1–3

We conclude by taking a look at God's first speech to Abraham, still called "Abram" at this point, in Gen 12:1–3. This text, which was discussed above as a linchpin in the initial L layer of non-P Genesis, has two main parts: Yahweh's command to Abram to "go now from your country, your kindred, and your father's house to the land that I will show you" (Gen 12:1), and the following promises that Yahweh will make Abram into "a great nation," make his "name great," and grant him abundant blessing (Gen 12:2–3). These promises echo a more ancient prayer for kings, seen in Ps 72:17, that the king be blessed, have his "name" (reputation) endure forever, and be so fortunate that others "bless themselves by him." This means that the king will be such a paradigm of good luck that others wish on themselves the kind of blessing that the king enjoys (for example, "may God make me as blessed and fortunate as King David of Israel"). Now, in the climactic promise in Gen 12:3, Abram is promised that he, like such kings, will be such an example of blessing that all "clans of the earth" will look to him and bless themselves by him, so that people in other nations might say something like, "may God bless me like Abram and more so."

This promise is echoed in various forms throughout other parts of Genesis (Gen 22:15–18; 26:2–5; 28:13–15), yet Christians and Jews disagree in a basic way on how to interpret the final part about Abram's blessing and other nations: "all the clans of the earth shall . . ." Many Jews follow the lead of

Rashi, one of the greatest Jewish commentators on the Bible, who followed a translation much like that given above: that all clans of the earth shall "bless themselves by" Abram; that is, wish on themselves a blessing as good as the one he has. Understood this way, the rest of the Pentateuch following Gen 12:1–3 is a story of God's (partial) fulfillment of the special promises of blessing on Abraham and his offspring, especially God's blessing and protection of God's chosen people, Israel. In contrast, many Christians follow the lead of Paul in understanding this text as a promise to Abram that "all the gentiles shall be blessed through you" (Gal 3:8), that blessing will flow through Abram – by way of Jesus Christ – to the other nations of the earth. Understood this way, the rest of the Pentateuch following Gen 12:1–3 is focused not on God's blessing and protection of Israel per se, but on the way the people of Israel, Abram's offspring, are a medium of blessing for the other nations of the earth. Thus, these two options for translating the promise in Gen 12:3, both of which are possible in Hebrew, lead to very different understandings of the whole Pentateuch. Rashi's reading remains closest to the emphasis on the people of Israel in the rest of the Hebrew Torah. Paul's reading – reflected in many contemporary translations of Gen 12:3 – reinterprets Abraham's promise in the context of a broader Christian Bible that includes Jesus Christ.

Turning to historical interpretation, Gen 12:1–3 looks quite different depending on whether one thinks it was written by Solomon's scribes or by exilic authors. Some would see Gen 12:1–3 as part of an early continuation of the non-Priestly primeval history, a continuation written to support and endorse Solomon's kingdom. Read this way, God's promises of greatness and blessing to Abram in Gen 12:1–3 anticipate the time when Israel will "become a great nation" under Solomon, and Solomon will enjoy an immense reputation and fabled blessing. If this is correct, Gen 12:1–3 and the rest of the extended J/Yahwistic document thus provide divine sanction to Solomon's mini-empire. This has led some, such as Walter Brueggemann in his influential book *The Prophetic Imagination* (Minneapolis: Fortress, 2001), to criticize texts such as Gen 12:1–3 because they see them as J texts endorsing an oppressive empire.

Things look quite different, however, if one understands Gen 12:1–3 and other promise texts to be words of hope to despairing exiles in the wake of the destruction of Jerusalem and loss of the monarchy. Put in this context, Gen 12:1–3 is a story where a non-royal figure, Abram, receives promises that were once given to kings. We have seen similar exilic gifts of royal promises to other figures in Second Isaiah – to the Persian Cyrus in Isa 44:28–45:1 and to the people in Isa 55:3. Yet the author of Gen 12:1–3 and surrounding texts tells the Abram/Abraham story in a special way, so that Abraham almost sounds like an exile living long before the Babylonian exile. He is made into someone to whom the exiles can relate. Like them, he lives in Babylonia, "Ur of the Chaldees" (Gen 11:28), and, like them, he has been called to go and live as a stranger in a land he does not know (Gen 12:1). In light of this, the promises to Abram become promises of hope to the exiles, much like the prophecies of hope to exiles that we saw in the exilic portions of Isaiah (40–55), Jeremiah, and Ezekiel. Where the exiles longed for a restoration of their nation, they hear in Gen 12:2 that their ancestor Abram, also an exile, was promised that he would "become a great nation." Where we know that the exiles felt "cursed" because of their exile, this text asserts the opposite: they will be so blessed that they will become an example of blessing to other peoples on earth (Gen 12:3). Moreover, there is an additional promise in Gen 12:2–3 that relates specifically to the vulnerability that exiles faced when living as a minority in a larger culture. God reassures Abram of his protection. God will bless those who bless him, and God will curse those who so much as "treat [him] lightly" (Gen 12:3). Exiles would have heard this as a promise that God will provide similar protection to them, as Abraham's children, while living in Babylonia.

Conclusions on the Torah (Pentateuch) and Trauma

In sum, it makes a big difference whether you read Gen 12:1–3 and related texts as endorsing Solomon's (proto)monarchy or as reassuring exiles who had been crushed by the Neo-Babylonian empire. This book has followed recent scholarship that dates Gen 12:1–3 and other L promise texts to times of imperial oppression, especially the exile of Judeans to Babylonia. Yet whatever the original date of the P and non-P texts, it was during later periods, when Judeans needed words of hope, that these writings about God's promises to Abraham's children and God's formation of Israel in the wilderness moved to the center of the Hebrew Bible. In particular, it was during exile that stories of Israel's earliest history started to become the literary foundation on which everything else in the Bible was based.

Up through the exile, however, this literary foundation, this "Torah," was split. On the one hand, there were the non-P/L stories of Genesis and exodus-Moses. On the other hand, there was a P source paralleling numerous parts of its non-P counterpart. Each text features different groups, groups probably responsible for preserving each narrative and expanding it. The non-P/L narrative features the "elders," a major group of lay leaders in the exilic and post-exilic periods. The P narrative features the Aaronide priests, a priestly group that first achieves dominance in the late exile and post-exilic periods. These groups, and their texts, remained separate throughout the exile. There was no unifying political structure in this period to bring them together; the monarchy was gone. We will not see conditions for unifying these P and non-P/L stories until the Persians sponsor the rebuilding of a community of returnee exiles in Jerusalem. We turn next to that important event.

CHAPTER TEN REVIEW

For Review

1 What are the three distinct layers/blocks of material that scholars agree were sources for the present Pentateuch?
2 Know the meaning and significance of the following terms discussed in this chapter:
   - non-Priestly (or non-P) materials (including the question of whether Deuteronomy is included in this designation)
   - L

- The Documentary Hypothesis (know the four posited sources in the older hypothesis, and which ones are no longer part of the scholarly consensus)
  - J (or Yahwistic) source
  - E (or Elohistic) source (be able to link this to the Documentary Hypothesis)
  - JE (be able to link this to the Documentary Hypothesis)
  - P (or Priestly) source
  - H or Holiness Code (//Holiness Layer)
3. What are two major reasons that scholars now doubt whether separate and yet parallel J and E documents once existed and stand behind the non-Priestly materials of the Pentateuch? (Hint: it's *not* because we lack copies of those sources. We lack copies of *all* hypothesized sources.)
4. What are major examples of L supplements in Genesis and where might they be placed historically?
5. What portions of the exodus-Moses story may exemplify later L shaping of an earlier exodus-Moses story? What characteristics help one identify these elements as exilic?
6. What aspects of P reflect later, exilic concerns?
7. What sorts of "history" are best discussed in relation to the Pentateuch? How?
8. Who are the two groups, newly prominent in the exilic period, that may have preserved and developed the separate P and non-P traditions before they were combined?
9. (Focus text: Gen 12:1–3) How do the promises to Abraham in Gen 12:1–3 compare to the wishes for the Davidic king in a royal psalm like Psalm 72 (especially its conclusion in 72:15–19). How might such a story about Abraham be heard differently in a time of exile than in a time when there still was a Davidic monarch? What does the story "do" for the audience in each case?

RESOURCES FOR FURTHER STUDY

More on the formation of the Pentateuch

Carr, David. *Reading the Fractures of Genesis*. Louisville, KY: Westminster John Knox Press, 1996.

Genesis

Brueggemann, Walter. *Genesis*. Atlanta: John Knox Press, 1982.

Sarna, Nahum. *Genesis*. Philadelphia: Jewish Publication Society, 1989.

Exodus

Meyers, Carol. *Exodus*. New York: Cambridge University Press, 2005

Sarna, Nahum. *Exodus*. Philadelphia: Jewish Publication Society, 1991.

Leviticus

Balentine, Samuel E. *Leviticus*. Louisville: Westminster John Knox Press, 2011.

Gerstenberger, Erhard S. *Leviticus*. Louisville, KY: Westminster John Knox Press, 1996.

Levine, Baruch. A. *Leviticus*. Philadelphia: JPS Publication, 2003.

Numbers

Olson, Dennis. *Numbers*. Louisville, KY: Westminster John Knox Press, 1996.

Wenham, Gordon J. *Numbers*. Sheffield: Sheffield Academic Press, 1997.

The Torah, the Psalms, and the Persian-Sponsored Rebuilding of Judah

Chapter Overview

Chapter Overview

History: Persian-Sponsored Building of a Temple and Torah-Centered Judaism

The Formation of the Torah

The Book of Psalms as a Torah-Centered Collection of More Ancient Psalms

Focus Text: The Introduction to Psalms in Psalms 1–2

Chapter Eleven Review

Resources for Further Study

CHAPTER OVERVIEW

This chapter traces how central parts of the Hebrew Bible subtly reflect a *positive* relationship between Judeans and the Persian empire inaugurated by Cyrus. We will see how the Persians played a supportive role at several stages in the restoration of Judah, allowing many exiles to return and helping establish a Temple-centered community of returnees in Jerusalem. In significant ways, the present Hebrew Bible is a collection of Hebrew texts made by former exiles sponsored by the Persian government. This helps explain why so many biblical texts sharply criticize the Assyrian and Babylonian empires but adopt a generally positive tone the few times they mention Persia.

The crowning achievement of this period was the elevation of a combined Pentateuch, a new "Torah of Moses," as a central authority to the community of returnees in Jerusalem. As we will see, there is even some evidence that the relationship with the Persians may have played some role in occasioning the dramatic, artful interweaving of P and non-P that characterizes Genesis–Deuteronomy. Not immediately, but over time, this combined Pentateuch came to play a central and unifying role for Judeans everywhere. One sign of its decisive importance is the way the book of Psalms, a collection of collections of ancient prayer texts used in worship and education, is now introduced by a Torah psalm and divided into five parts that correspond to the five books of the Torah.

FIGURE 11.1
Relief from the Persian capital of Persepolis. It depicts the many subjects of the Persian empire, dressed in the distinctive dress of each country, bearing tribute to the Persian king. The image well illustrates ways that the Persian empire cultivated the support of diverse cultures for its far-flung empire.

History: Persian-Sponsored Building of a Temple and Torah-Centered Judaism

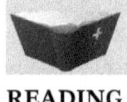

READING

The Nehemiah memoir (e.g. Neh 1:1-7:4; 13:10-14, 30b-31) and Ezra narrative (Ezra 1-10 and Neh 8; compare this with 1 Esdras in the Apocrypha).

EXERCISE

Using the parallel below, compare and contrast the Persian king Cyrus's edict about his anointing by the Babylonian gods (Marduk, Bel, and Nabu) with Ezra 1:1-4.

Cyrus cylinder	Ezra 1:1–4
"I am Cyrus, king of the world, great king, mighty king, king of Babylon, king of the land of Sumer and Akkad, king of the four quarters, son of Cambyses . . . whose rule Bel and Nabu cherish, whose kingship they desire for their hearts' pleasures. . . . I did not allow any to terrorize the land of Sumer and Akkad.	1:2 Thus says King Cyrus of Persia:
I kept in view the needs of Babylon and all its sanctuaries to promote their well being. The citizens of Babylon . . . I lifted their unbecoming yoke . . .	
At my deeds Marduk, the great Lord, rejoiced, and to me, Cyrus, the king who worshipped, and to Cambyses, my son, the offspring of my loins, and to all my troops he graciously gave his blessing, and in good spirit before him we glorified exceedingly his high divinity.	"Yahweh, the God of heaven, has given me
All the kings who sat in the throne rooms, throughout the four quarters, from the Upper to the Lower Sea, those who dwelt in . . . all the kings of the West Country who dwelt in tents, brought me their heavy tribute and kissed my feet in Babylon.	all the kingdoms of the earth,
From . . . to the cities of Ashur and Susa, Agade, Eshnuna, the cities of Zamban, Meurnu, Der, as far as the region of the land of Gutium, the holy cities beyond the Tigris whose sanctuaries had been in ruins over a long period, the gods whose abode is in the midst of them I returned to the places and housed them in lasting abodes.	and he has commanded me to build a house for him in Jerusalem which is in Judah.
I (also) gathered together all their inhabitants and restored to them their dwellings.	1:3 Any of you who are from his people – may his God be with him! – are now allowed to go to Jerusalem in Judah, and rebuild the house of Yahweh, the God of Israel
The Gods of Sumer and Akkad whom Nabonidus had, to the anger of the Lord of the Gods, brought into Babylon, I, at the bidding of Marduk, the great Lord, made to dwell in peace in their habitations, delightful abodes." (Translation: ANET, 316)	– he is the God who is in Jerusalem; 1:4 and let all who remain, wherever they live, be supported by the people of their place with silver and gold, with goods and with animals, besides freewill offerings for the house of God in Jerusalem."

The **Cyrus cylinder** quoted above (see Figure 11.2) marks another major shift of empires in the Near Eastern world. The Persian king, Cyrus, had just conquered Babylon without a fight, aided in part by disgruntled priests in Babylon who violently disagreed with the religious policies of Nabonidus, the last king of Babylon. Nabonidus had elevated the status of the moon god, Sin, over that of traditional Babylonian gods, and he had removed the divine statues of those gods from their sanctuaries across Babylonia. In the Cyrus cylinder, Cyrus uses the Akkadian language and the form of an Akkadian inscription to describe

FIGURE 11.2
The Cyrus cylinder.

how the Babylonian gods chose him to be king over Babylon and restore the divine statues to their proper places. Apparently, Cyrus's self-promotion was at least partially successful. A Babylonian priest wrote another text around the same time, called "the verse account of Nabonidus," that chronicles the religious crimes of Nabonidus, praises Cyrus's restoration of Babylonia's sanctuaries, and concludes by saying that the people of Babylonia now have "a joyful heart" and rejoice "to look upon Cyrus as king."

Though Cyrus never mentions Judah in his cylinder, we know from the Bible that the Judean exiles also celebrated this shift in power. Even before Cyrus had conquered Babylon, Second Isaiah had seen him on the horizon and quoted Yahweh as anointing Cyrus to subdue nations and rebuild Jerusalem (Isa 44:28–45:1). Furthermore, similar texts at the end of the books of Chronicles (2 Chr 36:22–23) and beginning of Ezra (Ezra 1:1–4) give a Judean version of Cyrus's proclamation, this time proclaiming that Yahweh has given him rule over all the earth and appointed him to rebuild Jerusalem. Since there is no Persian copy of such an inscription, we do not know if something like this was issued by the Persian government or whether it was created by Judean scribes on analogy with inscriptions like the Cyrus cylinder. In either case, these texts from Second Isaiah and the beginning of Ezra show an important development among the exiles. Where they hated Babylonia, many fully supported the Persian empire and endorsed the idea that the Persian king, Cyrus, had been appointed by God to save and restore them.

The biblical texts show in turn that the Persians did much for the Judean exiles, supporting their return and rebuilding efforts and thus insuring that there was pro-Persian local leadership in Judah and Jerusalem, a somewhat strategic area for the Persians as they struggled with Greece for control of the Eastern Mediterranean (see Figure 11.1). In sponsoring such local leadership, the Persians were not doing something entirely new, since Mesopotamian empires such as Assyria had used similar tactics to cultivate sympathetic local leaders in areas that were important to them. The difference is that the Hebrew Bible

MAP 11.1
Judah as a province of the Persian empire. Redrawn from Norman Gottwald, *The Hebrew Bible: A Socio-Literary Introduction*. Minneapolis: Fortress, 1985, page 406.

was shaped by former exiles who had been supported by Persia, while it appears that earlier biblical authors did not enjoy such sponsorship by imperial powers.

Our main source for the history of Judah in this period, Ezra-Nehemiah, appears to be another example of the combination of earlier materials. One block of materials appears to have been a Nehemiah memoir, a first-person account by the lay leader, Nehemiah, of how he rebuilt Jerusalem and provided for the Levites (Neh 1:1–7:4; parts of Nehemiah 13 and possibly 12). Another block of materials tells the story of the rebuilding of the temple and prominently features the priestly scribe, Ezra. Within the present form of the book, Ezra arrives and starts his work earlier than Nehemiah (Ezra 7–10), but he does not conclude his work with Israel, including a grand reading of the Torah of Moses, until after Nehemiah has built his wall (Nehemiah 8–10). That is the order of the book of Ezra-Nehemiah, but it is likely that the historical figure of Ezra actually followed that of Nehemiah. The two figures almost never overlap, and several early Jewish sources know their stories separately. So what might explain their present placement in Ezra-Nehemiah? Many scholars have concluded that this arrangement was produced through a misunderstanding by a much later author who confused the order of the two figures, not knowing that there were two different Persian kings named "Artaxerxes." He mistakenly placed Nehemiah, who arrived and rebuilt Jerusalem's walls in the twentieth year of Artaxerxes *the first* (Neh 2:1; 445 BCE), *after* Ezra, who found those walls rebuilt and probably arrived in the seventh year of Artaxerxes *the second* (Ezra 7:7; 397 BCE).

Alongside these materials collected in Ezra-Nehemiah, we also have the words of several prophets dated to this time as sources for learning about the period of the post-exilic restoration of the Jerusalem community. These include Haggai, Zechariah (particularly Zechariah 1–8), and post-exilic portions of Isaiah such as "Third Isaiah" in Isaiah 56–66 (see Chapter 12). Using these sources, scholars have identified four main stages of the restoration, each of which seems to have featured some sort of Persian sponsorship: the return of some exiles to Judah, Zerubbabel and Joshua's rebuilding of the Jerusalem temple, Nehemiah's rebuilding of the walls of Jerusalem, and Ezra's elevation of the Torah of Moses to the center of a Jerusalem community who had just expelled foreign wives and their children. The following paragraphs discuss each stage in turn before briefly considering the situation of Judeans still living abroad in Egypt and Mesopotamia.

The biblical account of Cyrus's decree gives permission to exiles to "go up to Jerusalem which is in Judah and build the house of Yahweh, god of Israel, the god who is in Jerusalem" (Ezra 1:3). This introduces the first of a series of returns of exiles from Babylonia to Jerusalem. The first wave, probably a tiny fraction of the exiles, returned under the leadership of Sheshbazzar, possibly a son of the exiled king Jehoiachin, shortly after Cyrus's defeat of the Babylonians in 539 BCE. The book of Ezra asserts that Cyrus even gave Sheshbazzar the Temple implements stolen by the Babylonians so that he could take them back to Jerusalem (Ezra 1:7–11), and Sheshbazzar is reported to have rebuilt the foundation of the Temple (Ezra 5:16). A few years later, around 520 BCE, one of Jehoiachin's grandsons, Zerubbabel, led another group of exiles back to Jerusalem. Still other exiles appear to have returned to Jerusalem under Ezra 120 years later (397 BCE; Ezra 7:1–7). In sum, not all exiles came back to Jerusalem, and those who did return came back in several waves. Many, if not most, exiles probably did not want to leave Babylonia. Some, such as Sheshbazzar and Zerubbabel, had assimilated enough to Babylonian culture to have Babylonian names, and we know from later documents of a Jewish family in Babylonia (in the Murashu archive) that some exiles remained there in subsequent centuries. This means that the expression "**post-exilic period**" is only accurate in indicating the end of *forced* exile, since many Judeans never stopped living away from their homeland.

In addition to allowing some Judeans to return to Judah, the Persians played a major role in the **rebuilding of the Jerusalem temple** that had been destroyed by the Babylonians. This rebuilding, a centerpiece of Cyrus's decree in Ezra 1:1–4, happened in at least two stages. The first, mentioned above, was Cyrus's giving of the Temple vessels to Sheshbazzar, and Sheshbazzar's delivery of these vessels to Jerusalem and laying of the foundations for this **Second Temple** there. This probably occurred shortly after Cyrus's victory over Babylon, around 538 BCE. The second stage of the temple rebuilding work was not completed, however, until about twenty years later, from 520 to 515 BCE. By this point, Cyrus had died (in 530), his son Cambyses had reigned for eight years (530–522), and Darius, a more distant member of the royal family, had seized power in the wake of Cambyses's death. Darius gained support among peoples of his empire by reversing the harsh policies of Cambyses and rebuilding temples and priesthoods, especially in Egypt (which Cambyses had conquered and subdued). The rebuilding of the Temple in Jerusalem early in Darius's reign probably was part of this broader project. Yet an important shift in Judean leadership seems to have occurred sometime before the Jerusalem temple was finished. Its rebuilding had begun under both the Davidic leadership of Zerubbabel and the priestly leadership of Joshua. Indeed, certain prophecies by Haggai (2:20–23) and Zechariah (the "branch" in 3:6–10; 4:6–10; 6:9–14) indicate that some hoped that Zerubbabel would re-establish the monarchy in Jerusalem, working alongside Joshua. Yet we hear no more of Zerubbabel in traditions after the Temple was completed. No one knows why. From that point forward the Davidic monarchy was completely finished, and the time of Temple-centered Judaism had begun, the time of the Second Temple (515 BCE–70 CE).

The next major step in the restoration that we know much about is Nehemiah's rebuilding of the walls of Jerusalem 70 years later in 445 BCE. According to his memoir, Nehemiah was a cupbearer in the court of Artaxerxes, probably Artaxerxes I, who reigned from 464 to 423 BCE. Having heard reports of the dilapidated state of Jerusalem, Nehemiah convinced Artaxerxes to send him back to Jerusalem to rebuild the city (Neh 1:1–2:8). There he organized the Judean community to rebuild Jerusalem's walls, despite the opposition of neighboring peoples and internal dissenters (Neh 2:17–6:19). His role was that of Persian-appointed "governor" of Judah (Neh 5:14–19), a lay leader alongside the cultic leadership of the priests. His biggest achievement was the re-establishment of Jerusalem as a walled city, an independent political entity. Sometime later, perhaps in a second term as governor, Nehemiah may have taken additional measures, such as the purging of the Jerusalem temple of foreign priests (see Nehemiah 12–13). If so, this was an anticipation of more major purges that were to happen under Ezra.

Ezra took this purging to a new level as part of a more general program of centering Judaism on observance of the Torah of Moses. Like Nehemiah, Ezra was an exiled Judean who was also a highly placed Persian official – some sort of secretary in the Persian court. According to Ezra 7, he was commissioned by king Artaxerxes to bring offerings to the Jerusalem temple and evaluate the extent to which people in the province were obeying "the law of god and the law of the king" (Ezra 7:26). There has been endless debate about what each of these laws contained, but the subsequent narrative of the reading of the "Torah of Moses" in Nehemiah 8 makes clear that something like the present Pentateuch is understood in this narrative to be "the law of god." Nevertheless, on his way to publicly reading and enforcing this holy law, Ezra comes to learn that earlier returnee Judean men have intermarried with foreign women and thus – in his mind – put at risk the whole project of the restoration of the people (Ezra 9:1–3). Many exiles such as Ezra perceived intermarriage with foreigners as a primary reason why Judah had gone into exile in the first place. Seeing this intermarriage among the returnee exiles, Ezra cries out to God:

> God has not forsaken us in our slavery, but has extended to us his steadfast love before the kings of Persia, to give us new life to set up the house of our God, to repair its ruins, and to give us a wall in Judea and Jerusalem.
> And now, our God, what shall we say after this? For we have forsaken your commandments, which you commanded by your servants the prophets, saying, . . . do not give your daughters to their sons, neither take their daughters for your sons, and never seek their peace or prosperity, so that you may be strong and eat the good of the land and leave it for an inheritance to your children forever.
> (Ezra 9:9–12 NRSV)

Ezra sees the whole Persian-sponsored process of the rebuilding of Jerusalem put into question by intermarriage of returnee Judean men with "foreign women," this latter group actually including a mix of actual non-Israelite women *and also* Judean women from families who had not gone into exile. In response, Ezra gets all men to divorce their foreign wives and expel them and their children. This "purification" of Judah is the prelude to his climactic reading of the "Torah of Moses" before all of Judah (Nehemiah 8), a Torah that seems to be much like the present Pentateuch, with P and non-P source materials combined into a single whole. We will return to the issue of intermarriage and the post-exile in the next chapter. For now we should just acknowledge that this report of expulsion of foreign wives represents one of the most difficult parts of the Bible for contemporary readers to understand, even if it may well not have happened (the Ezra narrative was written long after Ezra) and/or represented the response of returnees to exilic trauma.

Meanwhile, the enactment of the "Torah of Moses" by Ezra is a major step in the formation of a Torah-centered Judaism. After this, virtually all groups in Judaism, whatever else they may disagree about, agree on at least one thing: the importance of the Torah of Moses. This makes the reported Persian role in authorizing Ezra's mission all the more interesting. Elsewhere, the Persians are known to have worked with local leaders to authorize local laws as official Persian legislation (**Persian governmental authorization**). The Persians sponsored an Egyptian priest, Udjahorresnet, to collect and publish Egyptian priestly texts, and an inscription found in what is now Turkey shows that indigenous elites secured Persian endorsement of their local sacrificial laws as well. Apparently, such local leaders could seek Persian governmental support for their texts, while the Persians' offering such support strengthened the hand of their local allies and thereby reinforced Persian control over diverse parts of their empire. So why would Ezra have been interested in Persian support? His leadership status in Jerusalem (beginning around 397 BCE) probably was shaky vis-à-vis the several waves of exiles who had already returned over a century earlier under Sheshbazzar (538 BCE) and Zerubbabel (520 BCE). We know from sociological studies that later returnees like Ezra often must fight hard against the entrenched positions of people already in the land. How was he to prevail? Apparently, he was able to present a "Torah of Moses," made up of L and P texts together, as the Hebrew law authorized by king Artaxerxes, which others in the province had to follow. The Ezra traditions present him as having such governmental authorization to bring this law to the people (Ezra 7). After him, this law is valid across virtually all stretches of Judaism.

Significant Dates: The Persian-Sponsored Restoration of Judah

Cyrus's defeat of Babylonia	539 BCE
Wave 1 of returnees to Judah with Sheshbazzar (laying Temple foundation)	~538 BCE (or later)
Another wave of returnees with Zerubbabel	520 BCE
(Completion of) Rebuilding of Second Temple under Zerubbabel	520–515 BCE
Nehemiah's return and governorships	445–425 BCE
Rebuilding wall, purification of priesthood	
Another wave of returnees with Ezra	397 BCE
Divorce of foreign wives	
(Combination of L+P?) Elevation of Torah	

Much of the significance of all these changes can be seen when comparing Jerusalem of Ezra's time with the situation around the time of Ezra in **Elephantine**, a Jewish colony of mercenaries (soldiers for hire) settled in the southern Nile area of Egypt. This colony had its own temple, dating from before the rebuilding of the Jerusalem temple. The members of the community did correspond with leaders in Jerusalem and Samaria about various cultic matters, such as the celebration of Passover and rebuilding of their local temple, but they do not seem to have known the Torah of Moses advocated by Ezra, or to have followed the more stringent rules against foreign religions seen in the book of Deuteronomy. Only after many years did communities like this either die out or conform to the Torah-centered form of Judaism that arose in Jerusalem. Documents such as the Elephantine archives give us a small taste of the broad diversity of Jewish religion and life in the Persian period which supplements the biblical accounts given by Jewish returnees to Jerusalem.

The Formation of the Torah

READING

Gen 1:1-3:24; 26:34-28:7;
Skim/review Exodus 19-40.

The major literary event of this period was the completion of the Torah and its elevation to the center of post-exilic Judaism. This was a work as much or more about combining older texts as it was about the writing of new ones. Building on earlier traditions, Judeans in exile had already written larger stories of Israel's early history in P and non-P sources (non-P here including Deuteronomy and various L revisions connecting and revising earlier materials). These histories were separate from one another and cherished by the two major leadership groups in the exile and afterwards: the priesthood descending from Aaron (celebrated in P) and the elders (featured in non-P/L). Yet at some point an author combined these sources into one, producing a Pentateuch much like the one we have now. The process of Persian governmental authorization described above may have played some role in this, since it would not have helped someone like Ezra to have the Persians authenticate *two* competing local narratives, L and P. Nevertheless, it would be a mistake to see this joining of traditions as a purely political process. Rather, whatever occasion prompted this creation of the combined Lay and Priestly Torah, there is evidence of considerable theological-literary genius in its execution.

One example of this is the combination of the P and non-P primeval narratives so that both human possibilities and human limitations are more fully expressed. Genesis starts with the Priestly narrative of creation, where God crowns the cosmos with the creation of humans "as our own image and likeness" (Gen 1:26–27), blesses humanity, and says that the whole creation is "very good." In our present Pentateuch this is now balanced by the Garden of Eden story (Gen 2:4–3:24; non-Priestly). Placed after the P creation story (Gen 1:1–2:3), this earlier non-P text now tells us more about the sixth "day" on which God created animal and human life (Gen 2:4; cf. 1:24–31). The Eden story ends with curses (Gen 3:14, 17–19) and stresses all of the problems that come from humans' eating the fruit of knowledge and seeking to be "like God" (Gen 3:1–19). In contrast to the P creation story, in which God made humans godlike from the beginning, in this non-P story God is concerned about humans becoming ever more godlike and expels them from the garden so that they will not gain divine immortality (Gen 3:23–24). So goes the beginning of the combined creation and flood story, a story that balances affirmation of human godlikeness (Gen 1:26–27; 5:1–3; P) with stress on God's care to preserve the divine–human boundary (Gen 6:1–4; 11:1–9; non-P). In this way and others, the P and non-P perspectives are put in a creative tension that is more theologically evocative than either one alone would have been.

> **Basics**
>
> ## Book of Genesis
>
> **Outline: the transmission of the Abrahamic promise to Jacob as an answer to the problems of creation**
>
> | | | |
> |---|---|---|
> | I | Story of creation and re-creation of humanity | 1–11:26 |
> | II | Yahweh's response: promise to ancestors | 11:27–50:26 |
> | A | Abraham (and Lot) | 11:27–25:11 |
> | B | The next generation: non-heir and heir | 25:12–35:39 |
> | 1 | Genealogy of Ishmael, the non-heir | 25:12–18 |
> | 2 | Stories of Isaac's family, the heir | 25:19–35:29 |
> | C | The next generation: non-heir and heir | 36:1–50:26 |
> | 1 | Genealogy of Esau, the non-heir | 36:1–37:1 |
> | 2 | Stories of Jacob's family, the heir | 37:2–50:26 |
>
> Note: though the above outline focuses on men who inherit or do not inherit the promise, it is women such as Sarah and Rebekah who play a prominent role in determining who inherits the promise (Isaac, Jacob) and who does not.
>
> **Date**
>
> Post-exilic (building on earlier sources).
>
> **Themes**
>
> Genesis is a grand synthesis of Priestly and non-Priestly texts. The introduction and structure of Genesis come from the Priestly source. The book starts with the Priestly vision of creation in Genesis 1:1–2:3, and the rest of the book is punctuated with Priestly genealogical headings that now structure the whole (Gen 2:4; 5:1; 6:9; 10:1; 11:10, 27; 25:12, 19; 36:1; 37:2). Much of the substance of Genesis, however, is non-Priestly, detailing Yahweh's struggles to interact with fallible humans, from the early primeval account of Adam and Eve (Gen 2:4–3:24) to the (originally northern) story of Joseph and his brothers (Genesis 37–50). The result of this combination is a book that presents both Yahweh's power to produce order and his struggles to effect his designs with humanity in general and Abraham's family in particular.

We see a similarly majestic combination of sources in the Sinai narrative, where the combined P and non-P (L) narrative describes God's overcoming of the divine–human boundary that was so carefully protected in the primeval history. As we saw in Chapter 10, the separate P and non-P sources described events at Sinai quite differently. The non-P (L) Sinai story stressed God's forgiveness in the face of Israel's building of the golden calf, an act of idolatry that signaled the ultimate rejection of the covenant God had just made with them to make them a kingdom of priests (Exod 19:1–24:14; 32:1–34:35). The "elders" stand at the center of this lay-oriented, non-P narrative (Exod 19:7; 24:1, 9), and God only appoints a special priesthood, the Levites, as a measure to punish the disobedient Israelites (Exod 32:26–28). In contrast, the Priestly story says nothing about any disobedience and focuses instead on God's founding of a wilderness sanctuary run by an Aaronide priesthood (Exod 24:15–31:18; 35:1–40:38; Leviticus; Num 1:1–10:10). The emphasis in P is on the creation of a holy people with a sanctuary and proper priesthood to atone for the people's sins.

Basics

Book of Exodus

Outline: pilgrimage of Moses and of Israel from Egypt to Sinai

(See M. Smith, *The Pilgrimage Pattern in Exodus*, Sheffield: Sheffield Academic Press, 1997.)

I	From Egypt	
	A Oppression and journey of Moses to Midian	1:1–2:25
	B Two calls and two confrontations	3:1–15:21
II	To Sinai	
	A Provision on wilderness journey to Sinai	15:22–18:27
	B Two covenants and two sets of tablets	19:1–40:38

Date

Post-exilic (building on earlier sources).

Themes

Many think of the book of Exodus solely in terms of its initial story of Israel's escape from slavery in Egypt. But the climax of the book is Israel's entry into service to a new lord, Yahweh, as a cultic community centered on the wilderness tabernacle (Exodus 19–40). Thus, Exodus is not just a story of getting away. Instead, it is a pilgrimage from painful service to Pharaoh to life-giving service to Yahweh. This exodus journey by Israel now occurs across the Jewish liturgical year, starting at Passover (Exod 12:2, 39–42), with arrival at Sinai at the feast of weeks (Exod 19:1) and building of the tabernacle at the New Year (Exod 40:2, 17).

More information: whose exodus?

Jon Levenson has criticized some liberationist Christians, such as George Pixley, for their claim that the people of Israel was not the actual historical group to leave Egypt in the exodus. Instead, according to Pixley, the actual exodus group was an impoverished group of slaves that would only later join "Israel." For Levenson, this approach is one more example of an all-too-familiar Christian tendency to try to separate the Hebrew Bible from the Jewish people. He argues that the present, canonical form of the book of Exodus emphasizes the idea that Yahweh rescued Israel not because it was poor, but because it was special to Yahweh. Moreover, this exodus did not mean a rejection of slavery in general, but of Israel's slavery to Pharaoh rather than Yahweh. The *Bible's* story of exodus is *Israel*-centered, not a general endorsement of liberation of the poor.

In response, Pixley and others question whether Christians must focus only on the final form of a book like Exodus. They argue that their historical reconstruction should be evaluated on its historical merits, rather than on its theological implications. For these perspectives, see: Alice Ogden Bellis and Joel Kaminsky (eds.), *Jews, Christians, and the Theology of the Hebrew Scriptures* (Atlanta: Society of Biblical Literature, 2000).

Basics

Book of Numbers

(For basics on Leviticus, see box on p. 214.)

Outline

I	Dissolution of the exodus generation	1–25
	A Preparations for departure from Sinai	1:1–10:10
	B Disobedience, death in the wake of Sinai	10:11–25:18
II	Beginning of the conquest generation	26–36

Date
Post-exilic (building on earlier sources).

Themes
Priestly material again provides the introduction (1:1–10:28) and general structure, with the overall book moving from the Priestly counting of the exodus generation (Numbers 1–4) to another Priestly counting of the next generation after their parents have died in the wilderness (Numbers 26). In between, we have P and non-P stories about rebellion against the authority of Moses and Aaron (11–12, 16–17), the failed expedition to spy out the land (13–14), and a final catastrophic rebellion at Baal Peor (25). These stories help explain the destruction of this exodus generation before their children can enter the land. In the post-exilic period, this form of the book would have mirrored the experience of most exiled Judean families, in which the vast majority of parents who went into exile did not survive to take their children back to the promised land.

More information: the book of Numbers in context
The focus of Numbers on the transition between generations provides a context for the book of Deuteronomy that follows. Read after Numbers, Deuteronomy is the story of Moses's review of history and law for a generation that did not experience all these events themselves.

When these two narratives were combined, the Priestly emphasis on the sanctuary for atonement became part of God's answer to the people's sin that was emphasized in the non-P (L) narrative. Thus, our present combined (P and non-P) story in Exodus has two simultaneous scenes follow the non-P story of Yahweh's covenant with the people of Israel (Exod 19:1–24:14). On the mountain (here P material), God gives Moses instructions for creating the sanctuary through which the people can atone for their sin (Exod 24:15–31:18). At the very same time, down below (non-P material), the people build the golden calf and thus prove their desperate need for such a means of atonement (Exod 32:1–6). In the rest of the combined Sinai account, the Priestly story of the building of the tabernacle sanctuary (Exod 35:1–40:38) becomes the crowning moment of the non-Priestly story of Yahweh's gradual forgiveness of Israel and willingness to make a new covenant with them (Exod 32:7–34:35). The non-P text describes God's new covenant with God's "stiff-necked" people (Exod 34:1–28; non-P) before the P text tells of how Moses led that people in building a tabernacle sanctuary through which they could atone for their sins (35:1–40:33; P).

This event is a highpoint of the present Pentateuch, and we see this through parallels between the conclusion of the Priestly creation narrative (Gen 1:1–2:3) and the conclusion of the Priestly tabernacle narrative (Exod 39:42–40:33).

Creation of the cosmos	Construction of the tabernacle
Gen 1:31	*Exod 39:43*
God saw all which God had done And indeed it was very good (Gen 1:31a)	And Moses saw all the work and indeed it was done just as YHWH had commanded (Exod 39:43a)
And the heavens and earth were finished (2:1)	And all the work on the tabernacle of the tent of meeting was finished (39:32a)
And God finished on the seventh day God's work (2:2a)	And Moses finished the work (40:33b)
And God blessed the seventh day (2:3a)	And Moses blessed them (39:43b)

These parallels are between parts of the Priestly narrative, but the completion of the tabernacle means yet more in the combined P and non-P narrative we now have. The story of God coming down to the tabernacle follows non-Priestly stories in Genesis about how God once worked to preserve the divine–human boundary, expelling humans from the garden (Gen 3:22–24), limiting their lifespan after they intermarried with divine beings (6:1–4), and ending their attempt to build a tower up toward heaven in Babel (11:1–9). Within this broader stretch, the Priestly description of the descent of God's glory to dwell in Israel is a crossing of the divine–human boundary described in the non-Priestly primeval narratives. Indeed, it stands as a climax of non-Priestly promises that God would "be with" the patriarchs and their descendants (Gen 26:3; 28:15; 46:4; Exod 4:12).

Though later authors and editors made some additional changes to the Pentateuch, this combination of P and non-P (L) narratives was the most significant stage in the formation of the Pentateuch. It was a daring move, taking a non-Priestly, lay-oriented narrative and combining it with a Priestly narrative that was originally designed to replace it. Turning back to the example of the P and non-P stories of Jacob's gaining his father's blessing (discussed in Chapter 10), we see that parts of the P story are placed before (26:34–35; P) and after (27:46–28:7; P) the non-Priestly trickster story they were meant to replace (27:1–45; early Jacob story). As a result, the P materials provide a new context for Jacob and Rebekah's deceitful actions. In the combined text now in Genesis, Esau marries foreign wives (Gen 26:34–35; P), which provides some justification for Jacob's theft of his father's blessing (Gen 27:1–45; non-P), which in turn provides a context for Isaac's repeated blessing of Jacob and sending him abroad to get a proper wife (Gen 28:1–5; P). Thus, at this place and others, the post-exilic author who combined P and non-P balanced the perspectives of both sources without hiding or homogenizing the contrasts. Enough traces of his work were left that scholars could achieve consensus on the basic contents of the P and non-P sources despite the fact that we have no separate manuscript of either.

The Book of Psalms as a Torah-Centered Collection of More Ancient Psalms

Pss 13, 22, 57, 74, 88 (lament psalms); Pss 8, 29, 33, 104, 117, 145, 150 (hymns); Pss 32, 116, 138 (thanksgiving songs); Ps 1 (a wisdom psalm); Ps 23 (psalm of trust). Read and compare Pss 41:13; 72:18–19; 89:52; 106:48; 150.

READING

As we have seen, Israelites wrote, read, and learned psalm texts from the earliest point of Israelite history onward. Chapter 3 of this textbook discussed royal and Zion psalms in connection with David and Solomon's monarchy. We saw traces of an ancient lament tradition in Jeremiah's complaints to God about his task. In Chapter 9, we studied communal lament psalms, such as Psalm 137 and Lamentations, as a window into the suffering of the exiles. And there are many more texts across the book of Psalms (also known as the **Psalter**) that probably date from the pre-exilic and exilic periods. One sign of the antiquity of this book is the fact that it is made up of yet older collections of psalms, such as a series of psalms used in pilgrimages (Psalms 120–134) or an "Elohistic" collection of psalms in 42–83 that predominantly uses "Elohim" for God and occasionally duplicates psalms found elsewhere (such as Psalm 53 paralleling Psalm 14).

The book of Psalms as a whole, however, is later, and it shows some special emphases that are connected to the post-exilic period. First and foremost, it is a collection oriented toward Torah instruction. It opens with a psalm encouraging its readers to "meditate" day and night on the "Torah of Yahweh" (Psalm 1), and its longest psalm is a praise of God's Torah that is 176 verses long, organized into alphabetic stanzas (Psalm 119). The book of Psalms is divided into five parts by a set of similar calls to praise found at Pss 41:13; 72:18–19; 89:52; 106:48; and a concluding psalm of praise in Psalm 150. The focus on praise in these sections helps explain the name of the book of Psalms in Hebrew, *tehillim* – (book of) praises. At the same time, the fivefold division of the book of Psalms (Psalms 3–41, 42–72, 73–89, 90–106, 107–150) mirrors the fivefold division of the Pentateuch (Pentateuch is Greek for "five scrolls"). The focus of the present, five-part book of Psalms is on praises that are grounded in and flow from meditation on and study of God's Torah.

More on Method: Form Criticism and Genre

Biblical **form criticism** looks at the characteristics, intention, and social setting of typical categories of psalms; that is, it looks at **genres** in biblical texts. For example, the **lament psalm** discussed here is a genre characterized by some or all of the following elements: complaint, plea for help, vow, statement of trust in God's help, and thanksgiving for God's help. One typical intention of such psalms is to gain God's help in a desperate situation. The original social setting for the lament psalm was worship, whether at home, at a local sanctuary, or at the Jerusalem temple.

Form criticism has achieved many of its greatest results in the study of psalm genres and their social settings, but there have been form-critical studies of many other genres in the Bible as well. Some genres already discussed in this textbook include call narratives (Chapter 6), and proverbs and instructions (Chapter 5).

As study of form criticism has progressed, scholars have seen more and more complexity, both in the genres and in their links to particular social settings. Many biblical texts are a mix of genres. Moreover, genres can be inverted, as in Amos's use of the lament form to pronounce doom on the nation of Israel. Finally, some genres, such as the Hebrew short story, may be linked to a set of cultural conventions rather than a particular social setting like worship.

For more: see Marvin Sweeney, "Form Criticism." Pp. 58–89 in S. McKenzie and S. Haynes (eds.), *To Each Its Own Meaning* (Louisville, KY: Westminster John Knox Press, 1999).

The study of Psalms, however, need not focus only on the shape of the book in its final form. Scholars have found in the psalms a rich source of knowledge about the piety and worship of ancient Israel. In particular, a discipline called "form criticism" (see box above) has uncovered several categories of psalms that were used for different purposes in ancient Israelite worship.

The most common type found in the Psalter is often termed a "lament psalm," sometimes called a "**complaint**" or "**supplication**" as well. The word "**lament**" by itself refers to mourning over an irreversible bad event, such as a death (2 Sam 1:18–27) or destruction of a city (Lamentations). In contrast, a lament psalm is a plea for divine help in the midst of dire distress. Indeed, lament psalms such as Psalm 22 go on to include praise for God's help as if it has already arrived. For example, the psalmist in Psalm 22 starts out by saying "my God, my God, why have you abandoned me? . . . I cry by day, but you do not answer; by night and find no rest" (22:1–2). Later in the same psalm, however, the psalmist is thanking God for God's response, saying "God did not despise or detest the suffering of the oppressed. God did not hide God's face from me, but heard when I cried to God" (22:24). Scholars have developed many theories to explain the abrupt change in tone in such lament psalms, but have not reached agreement. Whatever their original function, such literary lament psalms provided a template for ancient Israelites to voice their deepest pain and anger and move toward hope. Some contemporary readers of such lament psalms are put off by their harsh language about enemies and their bargaining with God (see Ps 22:16–21a and 25). Others find that such psalms are a refreshing alternative to highly censored and sanitized prayers that do not really plumb the depths of human suffering and isolation. In the end, these biblical psalms do not encourage the reader to go out and exact vengeance themselves. Instead, through giving speech to suffering and including invitations for others to join in praise, these lament psalms ultimately move toward reintegration into the community. Even now, they give many contemporary readers a more general language to express their deepest and most personal suffering.

Basics

Book of Psalms: Part 2

(For basics on "Book of Psalms: Part 1," see box on p. 73.)

Outline: Torah-centered praise of Yahweh's kingship

I	Torah and king introduction		1–2
II	Five-part collection		3–145
	A	Book 1: concludes with individual praise associated with King David	3–41
	B	Book 2: concluding in prayer for king	42–72
	C	Book 3: concluding with lament about destruction of the Judean monarchy (Psalm 89)	73–89
	D	Book 4: moving toward exile (Psalm 106) and stressing Yahweh's kingship (Pss 93, 95–99)	90–106
	E	Book 5: moving toward restoration	107–145
III		Fivefold concluding praise of Yahweh	146–150

Date
Post-exilic (building on earlier sources).

Themes
In addition to the Torah focus mentioned in the main text, scholars have observed ways that the complex collection of psalms now reflects Israel's journey through history, from monarchy to exile and then post-exilic

restoration. As indicated in the outline, the concluding psalms in the first four books show a movement from focus on the king (Psalms 3-41) and his role vis-à-vis the people (Psalms 42-72), to the collapse of the monarchy (Psalms 73-89) and rise of Yahweh's kingship in exile (Psalms 90-106). This prepares for the final book, which starts with a psalm focusing on return from exile (Psalms 107-145).

More information: another edition of the book of Psalms

Several psalm scrolls found among the Dead Sea Scrolls at Qumran contain collections of psalms that are quite different from the Masoretic edition of Psalms that is used in Jewish tradition and surveyed above. The divergences are particularly striking after Psalm 89. This suggests to some scholars that that Psalms 1-89 (books 1-3 of the Psalter) may have reached their form earlier, while the following Psalms (90-150) may have been organized later into the form we now see them.

There are many other psalm types in the Psalter as well. One is the "**thanksgiving song**," such as Psalm 32, where an individual praises God for deliverance from suffering and calls on others to join in that praise. Another is the **hymn of trust**, such as Psalm 23 ("The Lord is my shepherd"), that expresses trust in God's protection and sustenance. Yet another psalm form is the **hymn of praise**, a praise of God often punctuated by short refrains, such as the praise of creation in Psalm 8 or the praise of God's acts in history in Psalm 136.

Several of these psalm types appear in association with the king, such as the prayer for royal victory in Psalm 20 or the thanksgiving for such victory in Psalm 21 (royal psalms; see Chapter 3). Overall, it appears that the authors of biblical psalms drew freely on these and other psalm genres. They were obviously well versed in the poetic possibilities of such typical psalm patterns. Nevertheless, they did not rigidly adhere to a single template. The psalm patterns were the melodies on which psalm writers could improvise.

Contemporary readers of psalms now can work with them on multiple levels, depending on their interests and their community. Study of the psalms in relation to their original historical contexts has illuminated their diverse types and possible settings in worship, their roots in older pre-Israelite traditions, and their rich imagery (among other topics). Yet, as in the case of biblical prophets whose words were preserved for later generations, the book of Psalms has survived because the texts in it have transcended their original contexts. Many psalms probably originated in some form during the time of Solomon's first temple, but that temple was destroyed and these older psalms (along with newer ones) came down to us as part of a post-exilic, Torah-centered collection. Now, thousands of years later, the book of Psalms is used more consistently in Jewish and Christian worship than almost any other biblical book. Each community places the psalms in a different context. Jews use psalms in a cycle of Torah-oriented worship, while Christians often reread psalms as Christological prophecies. The use and reuse of these ancient, evocative texts, a process already begun in the formation of the book itself, continues even today.

The Introduction to Psalms in Psalms 1–2

FOCUS TEXT

Psalms 1–2, the introduction to the book of Psalms, illustrate the mix of emphases and materials in the book. They are marked as an introduction by the fact that these two psalms lack any kind of superscription and by the ways in which they introduce major themes that occur across the rest of the book of Psalms. The superscriptions of Psalms start in Psalm 3 with a label that places this lament in the context of David's flight from Absalom (see 2 Sam 15:14–17). As discussed in Chapter 3 (box on p. 69), these labels are not historical, but represent an early Jewish attempt to place various "psalms of David" in the context of his life. Psalms 1–2 lack such a label – not even an attribution to David or another figure. Their function lies not in themselves, but in the way they set the other psalms in context. One might view these two psalms as an extended "superscription" to the Psalter as a whole.

Psalm 1 sets the tone for the whole by calling on the readers of Psalms to devotion to the Torah. It is a teaching psalm – often called a "**wisdom psalm**" – but one focused particularly on Torah teaching. The expression that begins the psalm, "happy is the one," is a teaching expression typical of Proverbs, and, like the sayings in Proverbs, this psalm features a sharp contrast between the "way of the wicked" and the "way of the righteous" (Ps 1:1, 6). Unlike Proverbs, however, the thing that distinguishes these two ways is not "fear of Yahweh" in general, but meditation on the Torah day and night (Ps 1:2). The psalm draws on the ancient tree imagery central to Proverbs and ancient Israelite religion (the tree associated with the goddess Asherah) to describe the benefits that the Torah devotee will enjoy: that person will be "like a tree planted by the water . . . everything that person does will succeed" (Ps 1:3). In contrast, the wicked, who lack such devotion to Torah, will perish (Ps 1:4–6).

In this way, the opening of Psalms links both to the Torah itself and to its immediate aftermath as described in the book of Joshua. At the outset of Joshua, just after Moses has died, Joshua is commanded to do exactly what this psalm calls for: recite the Torah constantly and "meditate on it day and night" (Josh 1:8). Through echoing that call here, this psalm calls on its readers to emulate Joshua, the successor to Moses, in constantly keeping before them the teaching of Moses that became ever more central in the post-exilic period.

The introduction to the Psalms does not stop here, however. It also includes Psalm 2. Chapter 3 discussed how parts of this psalm – among several other royal psalms in the Psalter – are good candidates for being among Israel's earliest texts. Royal and Zion psalms like these helped early Israelite people understand how Yahweh was involved in setting up a king in the new capital city, Jerusalem. Now, however, this psalm is linked to Psalm 1 as part of a common introduction to what is a post-exilic Psalter. The rebellious "conspiring" of the peoples at the beginning of Psalm 2 (2:1 NRSV; Hebrew *hagah*) is the opposite of constant "meditating" on the Torah at the outset of Psalm 1 (1:2; again Hebrew *hagah*). Psalm 2 then describes how Yahweh's anointed king at Mount Zion will destroy his opponents (2:4–9) before echoing Psalm 1 again through proclaiming, "*happy are* those who take refuge in Yahweh" (2:12; see 1:1). In sum, within Psalms 1–2 as a whole there are two groups: (1) the "happy" righteous ones who meditate on the Torah and take refuge in Yahweh, and (2) "the wicked" – a.k.a. the rebellious nations of Psalm 2 – who meditate or conspire for nothing and will be destroyed by Yahweh's anointed king.

The emphasis both on the Torah and on Yahweh's anointed king had a special significance in the Torah-focused, post-monarchic context of the Persian period. After all, there was no anointed Davidic king in this time. Rather, Temple and Torah had risen to take the central place in the existing community that the Davidic monarchy once had. As a result, the returnees in Judah now placed their *hope* in ancient royal traditions. They reread royal psalms such as Psalm 2 not as endorsements of existing power structures but as *promises* that God, the cosmic king, would anoint an earthly king who would put the empires of the world in their place. This is the expectation of a royal **messiah**, the Hebrew word for "anointed" (Ps 2:2). It is a late, post-exilic hope that the empire of God, with a Davidic monarch at its head, would destroy the foreign empires dominating the people of Israel.

In this way, the introduction to the Psalter embraces both elements that have been important to centuries of Jewish and Christian interpretation of the Psalms. Psalm 1 anticipates the focus of the rest of the Psalter on the Torah/Pentateuch. This is a major feature in Jewish exegesis of the Psalms. Psalm 2 anticipates the focus of other parts of the Psalter on kingship – both human and divine – and the expectation that God would establish God's kingship and destroy foreign oppressors. Such hope is still found in Judaism, but the emphasis on God's anointed king in the Psalter has been particularly strong in Christianity, a religion whose name is formed from the Greek word for "anointed" – *Christ*. Psalms 1–2, the introduction to the Psalter, show how such hope for God's *messiah* during the post-exilic period was integrally connected to devotion to the Torah of Moses.

CHAPTER ELEVEN REVIEW

For Review

1 Know the meaning and significance of the following terms discussed in this chapter:
- Cyrus cylinder (know similarities to and differences from Ezra 1:1–4)
- Elephantine
- form criticism
- genre
- hymn of praise
- hymn of trust
- lament
- lament psalm
- messiah
- Persian governmental authorization
- Post-exilic period
- Psalter
- rebuilding of the Jerusalem temple (know the date and circumstances)
- Second Temple
- thanksgiving song
- wisdom psalm

2. Know the four major stages in the post-exilic rebuilding of the Judean community:
   - several waves of return
   - rebuilding of the Temple
   - rebuilding of the wall around Jerusalem
   - centering on the Torah
3. Be able to summarize the Persian role in each and other associated circumstances.
4. Why is the Bible's depiction of the Persians so different from its depiction of the Assyrians and Babylonians?
5. What are some problems in using Ezra-Nehemiah as a historical source for this period?
6. What is a way that the documents from the post-exilic Jewish colony at Elephantine are significant?
7. What are two things that the praises of God at Pss 41:13; 72:18–19; 89:52; 106:48; and 150 tell us about the overall emphases of the book of Psalms?
8. What are the main characteristics of the lament psalm? What other terms have scholars used to better characterize this type of psalm?

For Reflection

9. The expulsion of foreign wives is one of the most difficult events for contemporary readers to understand. Are there circumstances in which you can imagine supporting a community's wish to ensure that their children only marry other members of that community, thus agreeing with a perspective akin to that of Ezra? Or are there circumstances where you can imagine a community legitimately needing to protect its identity in other ways? Conversely, in what kinds of circumstances can such tendencies be particularly dangerous, thus supporting a perspective more like that in Isaiah 56:1–8 (or Jonah or Ruth)?

RESOURCES FOR FURTHER STUDY

(Resources for study of Ezra-Nehemiah and of Haggai and Zechariah are listed at the end of Chapter 12.)

Genesis and Exodus

(See p. 100 and 225 for commentaries on these books.)

Psalms

Brown, William. *Seeing the Psalms: A Theology of Metaphor*. Louisville, KY: Westminster John Knox Press, 2002.

Brueggemann, Walter. *Praying the Psalms (revised edition)*. Winona, MN: St. Mary's, 1993.

Clifford, Richard. *Psalms*. 2 volumes. Nashville: Abingdon, 2002, 2003.

Holladay, William. *The Psalms Through Three Thousand Years: Prayerbook of a Cloud of Witnesses*. Minneapolis: Fortress, 1993. History of interpretation of Psalms.

Mays, James L. *Psalms*. Louisville, KY: Westminster John Knox Press, 1994.

Other Texts Formed in the Crucible of Post-Exilic Rebuilding

12

Chapter Overview

Texts Closely Associated with the Rebuilding of the Judean Community

Texts Emphasizing God's Favor Toward Foreigners

Focus Text: Isa 56:1–8

Scriptures in the Post-Exile

Chapter Twelve Review

Resources for Further Study

CHAPTER OVERVIEW

Though Chapter 11 stressed support provided by the Persians for several stages of restoration of Jerusalem, the returnees to Jerusalem faced significant disappointments in the process of rebuilding. Second Isaiah (seen in Isaiah 40–55), a pro-Persian exilic prophet, had promised that the exiles would return in joy and Jerusalem would be grandly rebuilt (e.g. Isa 49:7–26). Yet things were much more difficult. For example, the prophet Haggai has to reassure returnees that the sad, small temple that they have rebuilt will be much greater (Hag 2:2–9). In the wake of such disappointments, biblical writers of this time had different explanations for why things were not better and what needed to change.

In addition, the memory of exile was deep and painful for these returnees, and they disagreed over what needed to be done to prevent another one. As we saw in Chapter 11, worries about incurring another exile were so intense that Ezra is reported to have led all the returnees in Judah to divorce their "foreign" wives to prevent another exile, with "foreign" now defined as any woman not among the returnees from Babylonia (including some Judean women). Meanwhile, in this chapter, we will discuss other biblical texts probably dating from around this period, such as "Third Isaiah"

The Hebrew Bible: A Contemporary Introduction to the Christian Old Testament and the Jewish Tanakh, Second Edition. David M. Carr.
© 2021 David M. Carr. Published 2021 by John Wiley & Sons Ltd.

(Isaiah 56–66) and the story of Ruth, that offer a positive assessment of the benefits of inclusion of foreigners – that is, Torah-observant foreigners – in the community. These texts, along with other, probably late positive depictions of foreigners in books such as Jonah and Job, form an important counter-balance to difficult stories such as the divorce under Ezra. Read this chapter with a particular focus on uncovering the full diversity of post-exilic perspectives preserved in different parts of the Hebrew Bible.

Texts Closely Associated with the Rebuilding of the Judean Community

READING

Zechariah 1 and 4; Haggai 1:1–2:9;
Skim/Review Ezra 1–10; Nehemiah 8.

Basics

Book of Haggai

Outline: blessing + new rulership after Temple rebuilding

I	Oracles around the start of Temple rebuilding	
	A Prophetic-inspired beginning of rebuilding (including promise of blessing for rebuilding 1:2–11)	1:1–14
	B Encouragement: Zerubbabel's future riches	2:1–9
II	Oracles following up on start of rebuilding	
	A Renewed promise of blessing	2:10–19
	B Encouragement: Zerubbabel's future rule	2:20–23

Date

Fifth century BCE (400s, building on prophecies from 520 BCE).

Themes

In his original setting, Haggai promised his discouraged post-exilic community that investing now in rebuilding the Temple would yield returns of agricultural plenty and political independence under Zerubbabel. Amidst the turmoil of Darius's seizure of the throne of Persia in 522 BCE, Haggai may have hoped that Zerubbabel, a descendant of David, would re-establish the Davidic monarchy (2:23). Though this did not happen and the rebuilt Temple was later destroyed by the Romans (70 CE), the book of Haggai still preserves Jewish hope for renewal and restoration on the other side of another temple rebuilding.

This review of post-exilic writings (outside the Pentateuch and Psalms) starts with the prophecies of Haggai and Zechariah. In Ezra 5:1 these two figures provide the impetus for Zerubbabel and Joshua to restart the temple-rebuilding process. And indeed, aside from a later set of prophecies now found in Zechariah 9–14, much of Haggai and Zechariah's prophecy focuses on Zerubbabel and Joshua and on questions surrounding temple rebuilding. Haggai blames the economic hardship of the returnees on their failure to rebuild the Temple (Hag 1:1–11; 2:10–19). He reassures them that the small temple that they have built will one day be much greater (Hag 1:12–2:9), and he announces that God chose Zerubbabel and made him "like a signet ring," an apparent prediction of Zerubbabel's future glorification and possible anointing as king (Hag 2:23). Zechariah 1–8, sometimes referred to as "First Zechariah," includes prophecies about the rebuilding of the Temple along with Zion (1:7–2:17) and God's future glorification of Zerubbabel and Joshua, the Temple builders (3:1–10; 4:1–15; 6:9–15). Together, these two blocks of prophecy are valuable witnesses to events surrounding the temple rebuilding, since at least some of these prophecies seem to come from around the time of the Temple's reconstruction.

Basics

Book of Zechariah

Outline: from Temple restoration to Yahweh's rule

I	Zechariah's visions surrounding Temple rebuilding	1–8
II	Later visions of Yahweh's establishment of rule	9–14

Date

Fifth century BCE (400s) for a form of Zechariah 1–8 (earlier oracles). Fourth century BCE (300s) for whole book (note Greeks in Zech 9:13).

Themes

The book of Zechariah is a combination of an earlier book surrounding eight visions attributed to Zechariah (Zechariah 1–8) and so-called "Deutero-Zechariah" (Zechariah 9–14). The earlier book, like Haggai, was associated with temple rebuilding and the future rule of Zerubbabel and Joshua. Zechariah 9–14, however, lacks the superscriptions and dates of the earlier chapters that link them to Zechariah and the temple-rebuilding process. Divided into two "oracles" (9–11 and 12–14), this latter part of the book envisions Yahweh's dramatic punishment of all Judah's enemies and the lifting up of Jerusalem to be the center of the world.

In contrast, the narrative standing behind Ezra 1–10 and Nehemiah 8 is much further removed from the events it describes. It divides the rebuilding of the community into two major parallel phases, each of which starts with an act by a Persian king, proceeds to separation from foreigners, and climaxes in the celebration of a major festival. The first phase, temple rebuilding, moves from the departure from Babylonia to the rebuilding of the Temple and celebration of Passover. The second phase, Torah centering, moves from Ezra's commission by Artaxerxes for Torah enforcement to his climactic reading of the Torah to the assembled people.

Phase 1: Temple rebuilding	Phase 2: Torah centering
Cyrus's edict to rebuild the Temple (Ezra 1:1–4)	Artaxerxes' commission of Ezra – Torah (Ezra 7)
Exiles' leaving of foreigners in Babylonia (Ezra 1–2)	Returnees' divorce of foreign wives (Ezra 9–10)
Rebuilding of the Temple (Ezra 3–6)	Reading of the Torah (Nehemiah 8)
Celebration of Passover (Ezra 6:19–22)	Celebration of Sukkoth – Feast of Booths (Neh 8)

The parallels between these phases reveal a striking combination of pro-Persian and anti-foreign sentiment. On the one hand, the narrative prominently describes Persian sponsorship at the start of each phase of community rebuilding, and Ezra's prayer in Ezra 9 reinforces this by saying that God has "extended to us his steadfast love before the kings of Persia, to give us new life to set up the house of our God, to repair its ruins, and to give us a wall in Judea and Jerusalem" (Ezra 9:9). On the other hand, this narrative stresses that each stage of rebuilding was preceded by an act where Judeans separated themselves from foreigners: (1) leaving exile among foreigners in Babylonia (before rebuilding the Temple) and (2) divorcing foreign wives and expelling them and their children (before centering on the Torah).

The writers of this narrative probably saw no contradiction here. They believed that the exile had been caused by God's people forsaking God's Torah and falling under the influence of foreigners around and among them. Like contemporary Jews deeply committed to preventing another genocide of Jews like that which happened in twentieth-century Germany, these ancient Judean returnees wanted to do everything possible to make sure that such foreign influence did not send them into exile again. They had no trouble with Persian sponsors who would help them in this project. Their problem, building on their experience of exile, was with foreigners *in their midst*. Therefore much in the Temple/Ezra narrative is organized around these theological themes.

Nehemiah's memoir is a bit more difficult to discuss, since it is less completely preserved than the Temple-rebuilding/Ezra narrative. Nevertheless, it too tells a story of rebuilding in the face of foreign opposition. When Nehemiah starts the process of rebuilding the wall, he is opposed at several stages by leaders in the local area, including and especially the Tobiad family, who were leaders in Samaria (Neh 2:19–20; 4:1–17; 6:1–13). When the wall is finished, he appoints Levites to guard the gates, and he works to repopulate the city with those who had returned from exile (Neh 6:15–7:5). Later on, after another period of service to Artaxerxes (13:6), Nehemiah narrates his confrontation with returnees over their intermarriages with foreigners (13:23–27). He even expels one of the high priest's sons from the Temple because of his intermarriage with a "foreign" woman – a daughter of the Tobiad family of Samaria (13:28). At first glance this would seem close to stories about the divorce of foreign wives in the Ezra narratives (compare especially Neh 13:25 to Ezra 9:2). Yet Nehemiah does not seem to know of Ezra's work, and he focuses in his memoir on purifying the priesthood of those with foreign wives rather than on encouraging any general divorce of such wives (13:28–30). Nehemiah discourages the Judeans from *future* intermarriages but holds the priests to a higher standard because of their holy vocation.

Both of these stories contrast with the material added to join them (Nehemiah 9–11) in their generally positive attitude toward the Persians. Both feature Judean exiles who have achieved high status in the Persian court, and both describe how they are able to convert their connections into substantial and helpful Persian sponsorship of Judean rebuilding: the Temple, the Torah, the walls of Jerusalem. In his prayer, Ezra contrasts the past captivity and utter shame of his people with the opportunities they now have to rebuild under the Persians (Ezra 9:7–9). In contrast, Nehemiah's prayer in Neh 9:6–37, a probable later addition to the Nehemiah story, concludes with the following complaint to God about foreign rulers:

> Today we are slaves, and the land that you gave our fathers to enjoy its fruit and bounty – here we are slaves on it. On account of our sins it yields its abundant crops to kings whom you have set over us. They rule over our bodies and our beasts as they please, and we are in great distress.
> (Neh 9:36–37 NJPS)

These hardly seem the words of the Nehemiah who was cupbearer to Artaxerxes (Neh 1:11) and later returns to work yet further for the king (Neh 13:6). These words and the prayer of which they are a part come from another time and a perspective different from the generally pro-Persian sentiments of both the earlier Ezra and Nehemiah narratives. They will be discussed in the next chapter in connection with a different empire (the Hellenistic empire).

Texts Emphasizing God's Favor Toward Foreigners

Jonah, Ruth, and Isaiah 56, 58, 61, 65–66.
Job 1–5, 38–42.

READING

History may be written by the winners, but, in the case of post-exilic Judah, the prophets and others got a chance to write a rejoinder. Indeed, several texts in the Hebrew Bible appear to respond to the hostility toward foreigners found in

Basics

Book of Job

The book of Job is a post-exilic book that features a foreign sage, but its riches are not to be found in its message about foreigners, but in its reflections on unjust suffering. The book, particularly the poetry at its center, presents different perspectives on this timeless issue, alluding in subtle ways to a wide range of Israel's literature up through the Persian period: proverbs (in the friends' speeches), psalm laments (in Job's speeches), hymns of praise (in God's reply), and much more. Eventually, God appears, rejects the friends' words, and affirms and rewards Job (see Job 42:7–17). Yet this resolution at the end of the book does not do justice to the profundity of the preceding poetic dialogue. Instead, the book has an unresolved quality about it. It is a symphony of voices and perspectives from Israelite tradition up through the Persian period, all marshaled to address a problem of suffering that was as acute as ever then and has never gone away.

Outline: dialogue on disinterested virtue and divine justice

I	Dialogue setting: Job's suffering as a test of whether he is altruistic	1:1–2:13
II	Dialogue between Job, his friends, and God	3:1–42:6
III	Divine affirmation and restoration of Job	42:7–17

Date

Fifth century BCE (400s, possibly building on an earlier prose narrative reflected in Job 1–2).

Important information: the "accuser" not Satan in Job

Many interpreters have believed that the evil figure of Satan is God's dialogue partner in Job. Nevertheless, this interpretation rests on a mistranslation of the Hebrew word *satan* found in Job 1:6–12; 2:1–7. Throughout this text (and also in Zechariah 3), the word *satan* is not a proper name here, but appears with the Hebrew definite article, "the," and thus is equivalent to "the *satan*." Judging from both Job 1–2 and Zechariah 3–4, this *satan* figure is a roaming spy (the word *satan* comes from the Hebrew word "to roam"). This is a formal position in Yahweh's divine council (see 1 Kings 22; Isaiah 6); the figure who fills it is responsible for finding out the misdeeds of Yahweh's people.

More information

The figure of Job is found elsewhere in the Bible and non-biblical literature, but this depiction of him is unique. The book centers on Job's passionate dispute with his friends and God about his unjust suffering. There are other examples of such dialogues about unjust suffering in the Near East, such as the "Babylonian Theodicy" or the Egyptian "Dispute Between a Man and His Ba." This biblical teaching dialogue is prompted by an unusual and disturbing narrative prelude: Yahweh's decision to remove Job's riches, health, and children as part of a test to see whether he is only being good in order to receive divine reward (Job 1:6–12; 2:1–6).

post-exilic traditions such as the Ezra stories. Sometimes the response to the issue takes the form of narrative, as in the story of God's grace toward Assyrians in the book of Jonah, Naomi's evolving attitude toward her Moabite daughter-in-law in the book of Ruth, or the story of an Edomite's unjust suffering in the book of Job. Sometimes, however, the response takes the form of direct prophetic engagement, as in the call in Isaiah 56:3 that the foreigner should not say "Yahweh will separate me from his people," an apparent response to post-exilic efforts to purify Israel through expelling foreigners. Though it is not certain that each of these texts dates from the post-exilic period, they address concerns about foreigners and foreign influence that became prominent in that time. The following section looks at what each of these texts might have said to Judeans of the time of Nehemiah and Ezra.

At first glance, the book of Jonah appears to take us back several centuries to the time of Assyria (the eighth to seventh centuries), but a closer look reveals that it is actually a teaching parable from much later. The book tells a story about God's call of a prophet, Jonah, to preach an Amos-like message of total destruction to the mighty nation of Assyria. Given Assyria's reputation for merciless brutality, the reader is not surprised to hear that Jonah runs in the opposite direction (Jonah 1). This is where God introduces the famous whale to bring Jonah back on track (Jonah 2). He preaches destruction, the Assyrians repent, and Jonah gets very angry with God about God's decision not to destroy the Assyrians after all (Jonah 3–4). The narrative ends with God gently reproving Jonah for his persistent wish to see the destruction of foreigners. God asks Jonah, "should I not care about Nineveh, that great city, in which there are more than a

---

Basics

Book of Jonah

Outline: satire of xenophobic prophet

| I | Initial call, prophetic flight, and mission of Jonah | 1–2 |
| II | Renewed call, prophecy, and anger at repentance | 3–4 |

Date

Whatever the date of this fable, it is far removed from the Neo-Assyrian period that it describes. The Assyrian king is not named.

Themes

The book of Jonah satirically contrasts Jonah with foreigners like the sailors and Assyrians. Jonah repeatedly opposes Yahweh's wishes, fleeing from Assyria when called to prophesy to it (Jonah 1:3) and angrily rejecting Yahweh's decision to have mercy on Assyria (4:1–5). In contrast, the foreign sailors and the Assyrians respond piously to Yahweh's actions (1:7–16; 3:5–9). Whether or not the book was originally intended to speak to issues of foreigners in the post-exilic period, its satiric portrait of Jonah and foreigners now balances the perspective of several other biblical books.

hundred and twenty thousand persons . . . and many animals besides?" (Jonah 4:11). This rhetorical question is but one pointer to the teaching function of the whole. Jonah is not a historical record, set in a specific time of a particular Assyrian king. Rather it is a fable telling of God's ability to have mercy even on such a brutal empire as the Assyrians. The question addressed to Jonah at the end of the book is also a question addressed to the readers: should God care about foreigners like the Assyrians and their animals? In contrast to biblical books such as Nahum or anti-foreign attitudes reflected in Ezra, the book of Jonah implies that the answer to this question about God's care for foreigners is "yes."

The book of Ruth is another narrative that subtly addresses the issue of foreigners, especially the issue of foreign intermarriage. The book opens with the death in Moab of two Judeans, Mahlon and Chilion, about ten years after they married Moabite wives, Orphah and Ruth (1:4–5). Seen through the lens of post-exilic concerns about intermarriage with foreigners, their deaths could be seen as a possible consequence of their intermarriages with foreign women. The character of Naomi, the mother-in-law of these Moabite women, seems to embody such concerns when she urges Orphah and Ruth not to follow her back to Judah (1:8–9). Certainly later post-exilic readers would be able to relate to Naomi when she is silent, rather than thrilled and grateful, when Ruth, the "Moabite" (1:22), passionately declares her intention to follow Naomi to her grave (1:16–18). The rest of the book can be viewed as the education of Naomi in Ruth's importance to her. By the end of the book, Ruth bears a child by Boaz, which Naomi recognizes as her own, and this child becomes one of the ancestors of the great king David (4:13–20). This story, especially the genealogy linking David to a Judean's intermarriage with a Moabite, would have had radical implications in the time of Ezra. Some parts of it may have been written in an earlier time, but the present form of the book would have educated post-exilic Judeans opposed to intermarriage. It would have told them about how Naomi overcame her initial concerns about a Moabite daughter-in-law and ended up becoming the grandmother of an ancestor of Israel's founding king.

Basics

Book of Ruth

Outline: loyalty of all leading to David's line

I	Potential problem: widowed foreign wife in Judah	1
II	Problem into solution: foreign wife produces ancestor of David	2–4

Date

Fifth century BCE (400s, for the present form of the book).

Themes

See the discussion of Ruth in the main text.

Finally, we turn to post-exilic prophecy in Isaiah, particularly the post-exilic prophecies concentrated in chapters 56–66 of the book. Previous chapters of Isaiah also feature texts that are characterized by their positive attitudes toward foreigners. These include the proclamation that peoples of the earth will stream toward Zion to learn God's Torah/teaching (Isa 2:1–4) and the prophecy in Isa 19:19–25 that concludes with Yahweh's blessing on "my people Egypt, my handiwork Assyria, and my very own Israel." Many scholars now think that these and many other parts of Isaiah 1–35 were written in the Persian period or later. When we come to Isaiah 56–66, however, the vast majority of texts come from this period (aside from a possible exilic lament in 63:7–64:12). This section is often called "**Third Isaiah**," and it is distinguished from other parts of Isaiah by the way it applies the prophecies of both Second Isaiah and the eighth-century prophet Isaiah ("First Isaiah") to delays in Jerusalem's rebuilding and other problems of the post-exile.

Second Isaiah contained grand promises that God would "light" the way for the returning exiles (Isa 42:16) and rebuild Jerusalem, but texts in Third Isaiah show that things did not go as well as expected. In Isaiah 59:9 a group cries, "we wait for light and it does not reach us, for brightness, but we walk in gloom," and Isa 58:3 quotes people complaining to God, "why do we fast, but you do not see?" The rest of Isaiah 58 provides a powerful answer to this question: the promises of Second Isaiah have not come true because the fasting and sacrifice of the returnees have not been combined with acts of justice (Isa 58:2–5; also 66:1–4). Like the people of the time of eighth-century Isaiah (1:10–17), they have corrupted their worship practices with oppression of others. Third Isaiah goes on in Isaiah 58 to promise that acts of justice and Sabbath keeping will turn things around. When the returnees share their homes with the poor and stop abusing the Sabbath for profit, the promises of Second Isaiah will come true: God's light will break forth on them like the dawn (58:8, 10) and Jerusalem will be rebuilt from its ruins (58:12). Similar themes arise again at the heart of Third Isaiah, where a speaker – perhaps the anonymous post-exilic prophet that we call "Third Isaiah"? – proclaims that he was commissioned by God to "bring good news to the poor" and "comfort all who mourn in Zion" (Isa 61:1–3). These words of comfort and liberation to the poor will lead to the rebuilding of Jerusalem (61:4).

Basics

Book of Isaiah

Outline: exhortation to repentance

I	Introduction: initial exhortation to repentance	1:1–31
II	Elaboration: restoration of Zion after purging judgment on it and the nations	2:1–64:12
III	Concluding paired oracles: consequences for the disobedient (65:1–66:4) and obedient (66:5–24)	

The above outline builds on scholars' observations of an inclusio in Isaiah, where themes appearing together in the exhortation to repentance in Isa

1:1–31 reappear again in the paired divine speeches to the disobedient and obedient in 65:1–66:24. See the list of parallels between the two halves of the book on the next page. There are other patterns to be observed as well in Isaiah. In this and other cases, books like Isaiah are too complex to be tamed by one outline.

Date

Fifth century BCE (400s, building on earlier materials).

Themes

See the discussion in the main text and of the prophet Isaiah in Chapter 7 and of Second Isaiah in Chapter 10.

For Third Isaiah, the fulfillment of the promises of restoration in Second Isaiah is dependent on people listening to First Isaiah's call for justice and righteousness. This is clear once again in the last four chapters of the book, which include a quotation from an exilic lament (63:7–64:12) and God's response (Isaiah 65–66). The lament concludes with an anguished cry to God that "Zion has become a wilderness" and a following question: "after all this, will you restrain yourself, oh Yahweh? Will you keep silent?" (64:10–12). Yahweh is not silent, but gives conditional words of hope: God will restore Zion for God's righteous "servants," but God will destroy those in Zion who worship in gardens and tombs and then say, "keep to yourself, do not come near me, for I am holy" (Isa 65:3–5; cf. Isa 1:29–31). In this and other ways, the conclusion of Third Isaiah echoes the prophecy in First Isaiah that Yahweh would purge Jerusalem of its corrupt leadership and restore it to its former glory (Isa 1:21–31).

Scholars have found numerous ways in which the book of Isaiah as a whole, though written over centuries, is organized by broader patterns that span its various layers. For example, Isaiah 1:1–2:3 has been seen by many as an introduction to the whole book, introducing themes of judgment and restoration that extend to its end. Isaiah 65–66 serves as a conclusion, echoing many parts of Isaiah 1 in particular. In addition, several parts of the first half of the book, Isaiah 1–33, parallel portions of the second half, Isaiah 34–66:

Isaiah 1–33 (plan for Yahweh's rule from Zion)	Isaiah 34–66 (initial realization of plan)
Introduction: call to hear (Isaiah 1)	Call to hear revenge and restoration (Isa 34–35)
Commission of eighth-century Isaiah (Isaiah 6)	
Isaiah-Ahaz materials (Isaiah 7–8)	Isaiah-Hezekiah narratives (Isaiah 36–39)
	Commission of exilic prophet (40:1–11)
Anti-nations/Babylon (Isaiah 13–27)	Oracle against Babylon (Isaiah 47)
Oracles focused on Zion (Isaiah 28–32)	Oracles on Zion's restoration (49–66)

There is some evidence in the Dead Sea Scrolls that early Jewish communities sometimes copied these two halves of Isaiah on separate scrolls (thus 1 and 2 Isaiah, like 1 and 2 Samuel or Kings), but these and other patterns also bind the book together into a complex unity. It is a chorale of prophetic voices from different centuries, joining in witness to Yahweh, "the holy one of Israel," and his plans for Zion and the nations around it. Let us now focus on one text from Third Isaiah that speaks particularly directly to the issue of Zion and foreigners from "the nations": Isa 56:1–8.

Isa 56:1–8

FOCUS TEXT

Isa 56:1–8 opens the collection of post-exilic prophecies in Isaiah 56–66, prophecies that immediately follow Second Isaiah's words of "comfort" to exiles in 40–55. Second Isaiah had promised that Yahweh would soon bring his salvation and deliverance. This "Third Isaiah" asserts that the fulfillment of these promises requires a prior act by the people themselves: that they "bring about justice and act with social solidarity" (Isa 56:1). The post-exilic prophet adds that only those who "observe the Sabbath" and "keep away from evil" will be "happy" (56:2). These two verses encapsulate Third Isaiah's addition of moral conditions to the promises of Second Isaiah.

Nevertheless, the balance of the passage goes on to address a particular moral concern of the post-exilic community: the status of foreigners and people considered to be cultically impure. A passage in Deuteronomy insists that neither eunuchs (men whose testicles have been removed) nor Ammonites and Moabites (both of these foreign peoples neighboring Judah) should be allowed to enter the worshipping community of Yahweh (Deut 23:1, 3). In Isa 56:3–8, Yahweh addresses the matter of eunuchs and foreigners who are being excluded from the Temple on this basis, despite their observing the Sabbath and keeping Yahweh's covenant:

> Let not a foreigner say,
>   who has joined himself to Yahweh,
>   "Yahweh will surely separate me from his people,"
> And let not a eunuch say,
>   "I am a dried up tree." (56:3)

To these people, the prophet gives a direct word from Yahweh that contradicts the law in Deuteronomy:

> For thus says Yahweh,
>   To the eunuchs who keep my Sabbaths,
> who have chosen that which I desire,
>   And hold fast to my covenant,
> I will give them a monument and name in my house and my walls
>   better than sons or daughters ...
> And to the foreigners joined to Yahweh,
>   to serve him and love the name of Yahweh ...

> I will bring them into my holy mountain,
> > And help them celebrate in my house of prayer;
> > Their burnt offerings and sacrifices will be pleasing on my altar.
> For my house shall be called a house of prayer
> > for all peoples. (56:4–7)

Thus the prophet offers a direct quotation from Yahweh that contradicts a part of the Mosaic Torah. As we know, the Mosaic Torah was ever more prominent in the post-exilic period, and there was an increasing concern to avoid a future exile by "separating" from foreign peoples, as in Nehemiah's and Ezra's initiatives against intermarriage with foreign women. In this case, the focus is not on intermarriage but on foreigners (and eunuchs) who are faithful to Yahweh but find themselves excluded, on the basis of the Mosaic Torah, from the Temple because of their foreign status. Yahweh in this passage contradicts that Torah, assuring them that all who keep his Sabbaths and hold fast to the covenant are welcome in his house.

The basis for this radical contradiction of Mosaic Torah is the message of Second Isaiah. There the exilic prophet described Yahweh as appointing a "servant" for a task that went beyond just bringing Judeans back from exile:

> It is too light a thing that you should be my servant,
> > To establish the tribes of Jacob
> And bring back the survivors of Israel.
> > I will make you a light to the nations,
> To be my salvation to the end of the earth. (49:6)

In this passage in Third Isaiah, a post-exilic prophet echoes this message, saying:

> Thus says Yahweh,
> > Who gathers the scattered of Israel,
> I soon will gather yet others to them,
> > Besides those already gathered. (56:8)

By this point the prophet can look back on an in-gathering of exiles that has already occurred. Both he and the rest of his post-exilic audience know Yahweh now as a God who has proven true to promises to bring back the exiles. Building on this and on Second Isaiah's message, he extends this idea to foreigners, saying that Second Isaiah's message about being a "light to the nations" also holds. Yahweh is about a larger project of in-gathering, one that means that foreigners joined to Yahweh, Yahweh's "servants" (56:6), will have a full place in worship at Yahweh's mountain. This proclamation of including foreigners is later echoed toward the very end of (Third) Isaiah with a prophecy that some foreigners will even become priests and Levites (66:18–23).

These prophecies stand in sharp contrast to the application in the Ezra traditions of messages from the Pentateuch and Second Isaiah. Ezra seems to have modeled his procession from Babylonia to Judah on the exodus from Egypt, departing on the first day of the year (Ezra 7:9; cf. Exod 12:2) and then making sure that his caravan corresponded to Moses's in having Levitical priests and 12 lay leaders (Ezra 8:1–20). Yet he also seems to have understood this second exodus in terms taken from Second Isaiah, praying, for example, that Yahweh would "make [their] way straight" on the way home to Judah (Ezra 8:21; see Isa 40:3). Ezra soon finds out that the people already in Judah have failed to "separate themselves" from foreign peoples, intermarrying with them (Ezra 9:1), and he moves to expel foreign wives as a precondition for leading the people in devoting themselves to the Torah of Moses (Ezra 9–10; Nehemiah 8).

Third Isaiah is not focused on exactly the same issues, but still represents a sharp contrast to Ezra. Ezra aimed for "separation" from foreign peoples (Ezra 9:1–3; 10:11), while Third Isaiah proclaimed Yahweh's reassurance to foreigners who were concerned – perhaps on the basis of initiatives like Ezra's – that "Yahweh will surely separate me from his people" (56:3). Ezra focused on Second Isaiah's message that Yahweh would bring the exiles home in a second exodus. Third Isaiah added an emphasis on the other half of Second Isaiah's message: that this homecoming of exiles was part of a broader plan in which Yahweh's servant would be a light to "the nations." Ezra's narrative climaxes with the reading of the Torah and the people's rededication of themselves to it (Nehemiah 8). Third Isaiah contradicts a part of that Torah that excludes foreigners and eunuchs from God's temple (Deut 23:1, 3), quoting Yahweh as saying, "my house shall be a house of prayer for all peoples" (56:7). Thus, Third Isaiah stands alongside other traditions discussed above, such as Ruth and Jonah, as an important witness to the ongoing diversity of perspectives in Persian-period Judah. Seeing the period purely through the lens of the Ezra and Nehemiah narratives misses an important part of the picture.

Scriptures in the Post-Exile

Ultimately, both the Mosaic Torah and the book of Isaiah were included in the broader scriptural corpus of post-exilic Judaism. But the Mosaic Torah, now in combined P and non-P (L) form, increasingly became the foundation of everything else. Other holy texts were increasingly understood in light of the Torah. For example, ancient collections of psalms were organized into what is now a five-part, Torah- and praise-oriented whole. Shorter prophetic books such as Hosea and Zechariah were combined into a collection of 12 books that concludes with a passage that urges constant memory of the "Torah of my servant Moses" (Mal 4:4). And readers of other texts would have seen this combined L/P Torah in other references to God's "Torah" in Isaiah, Jeremiah, and Ezekiel.

In these ways, the Torah that first started to emerge under Josiah and was affirmed – in P and non-P (L) forms – in the exile became ever more central in the post-exilic Persian period, possibly with help from the Persians themselves. But this process took time. Some early post-exilic texts, such as Third Isaiah and Job, do not yet reflect the dominance of the Mosaic Torah that we see later. The community of Judah evolved significantly from the initial returns of exiles under Davidic descendants (Sheshbazzar, Zerubbabel) to its consolidation around the Torah under Ezra the priest. Only toward the end of this period do we see the clear outlines of a Temple- and Torah-centered Judaism that would persist for several centuries of Hellenistic rule. Next we shall look at that chapter in the history of the people and development of the Bible.

CHAPTER TWELVE REVIEW

For Review

1. Know the meaning and significance of the following terms:
   - (the) *satan* (careful, be sure to note differences of this figure from the later Satan figure!)
   - Third Isaiah
2. How did the authors of the Ezra and Nehemiah traditions reconcile pro-Persian sympathies with their concern about foreign influence?
3. The book of Job can be seen as a staged dialogue between different parts of Israelite tradition up through the early post-exile. Which parts of Job represent what types of literature? Which type of literature does not seem prominently represented in Job?
4. What is "Third Isaiah" and how is it related to earlier parts of Isaiah?
5. (A bit more difficult) What emphases does the Ezra narrative now included in Ezra-Nehemiah have in common with Third Isaiah and where do these two writings diverge?

For Reflection

6. If a prophet like Third Isaiah were to speak today, to what situation would she or he need to address her or his prophecy? The author of Third Isaiah built on earlier Isaiah (and other) traditions. What traditions would this contemporary prophet build on?
7. Try rewriting Isa 56:1–8 for a contemporary audience, matching sentence for sentence, metaphor for metaphor, etc.

RESOURCES FOR FURTHER STUDY

Haggai and Zechariah 1–8

O'Brien, Julia. M. *Nahum, Habakkuk, Zephaniah, Haggai, Zechariah, Malachi.* Nashville: Abingdon, 2004.

Petersen, David. *Haggai and Zechariah 1–8: A Commentary.* Philadelphia: Westminster Press, 1984.

Sweeney, Marvin. *The Twelve Prophets, vol. 2. Micah, Nahum, Habakkuk, Zephaniah, Haggai, Zechariah, Malachi.* Collegeville, MN: Liturgical, 2000.

Ezra, Nehemiah, and Esther

Blenkinsopp, Joseph. *Ezra-Nehemiah: A Commentary.* Philadelphia: Westminster Press, 1988.

Clines, David. *Ezra, Nehemiah, Esther.* Grand Rapids: Eerdmans, 1984.

Williamson, H. G. M. *Ezra, Nehemiah.* Waco, TX: Word Books, 1985.

Jonah

Trible, Phyllis. *Rhetorical Criticism: Context, Method, and the Book of Jonah.* Minneapolis: Fortress, 1994.

Ruth

Fewell, Danna Nolan, and Gunn, David Miller. *Compromising Redemption: Relating Characters in the Book of Ruth*. Philadelphia: Westminster John Knox Press, 1990.

Kates, Gail Twersky, and Reimer, Judith, eds. *Reading Ruth*. New York: Ballentine Books, 1994. Excellent collection of contemporary interpretations by Jewish women.

Job

Janzen, J. *Gerald*. Job. Atlanta: John Knox Press, 1985.

Newsom, Carol. *"Job."* Pp. 319–637 of vol. 4 of The *New Interpreters Bible*. Nashville: Abingdon, 1996.

Isaiah 56–66

Blenkinsopp, Joseph. *Isaiah 56–66*. New York: Doubleday, 2005.

(See also p. 198 for commentaries on Isaiah 40–66.)

Hellenistic Empires and the Formation of Multiple Scriptures

13

Chapter Overview

Judaism and Hellenism before the Hellenizing Crisis

The Crisis over Hellenizing Jerusalem and the Book of Daniel

A Hellenistic-Period Kingdom of Israel: The Hasmonean Revolt and Monarchy

The Hellenistic/Hasmonean Period as the Setting for Hebrew Bible Texts

Focus Text: Daniel 10–12

The Formation of the Jewish Tanakh and Christian Old Testament(s)

Conclusion

Chapter Thirteen Review

Resources for Further Study

CHAPTER OVERVIEW

It is hard to come up with a sharper contrast in the experience of empire than that between the Judeans' experience of Persian support and their later near annihilation by the Hellenistic (Greek) king Antiochus Epiphanes IV. Though Hellenistic rule was not a serious problem in the first 157 years after Alexander the Great's conquest of the area (in 332 BCE), a major confrontation occurred in Judah in 174 BCE when Hellenizers sought to take control of Jerusalem and turn it into a Greek city. This led to an attempt to eradicate Judaism by the Hellenistic king Antiochus IV, successful rebellion led by a family of provincial priests (the Hasmoneans), and their establishment of a priest-ruled kingdom in Jerusalem that lasted 80 years.

The Hebrew Bible: A Contemporary Introduction to the Christian Old Testament and the Jewish Tanakh, Second Edition. David M. Carr.
© 2021 David M. Carr. Published 2021 by John Wiley & Sons Ltd.

This chapter examines writings composed before and after this confrontation. Some writings composed earlier in the Hellenistic period, such as the Ben Sira or some apocalypses now in Enoch, were included in the Old Testament collections of the Roman Catholic and/or Orthodox churches, but excluded from the Jewish Tanakh (and, as a result, the later Protestant Old Testament). Some later writings composed during or after the Hellenistic confrontation, such as the book of Daniel, were included in the Jewish Tanakh (as well as the Old Testament of all churches). Toward its conclusion, this chapter explores the important question of when Jewish communities started to define which texts were included in Hebrew scripture and how the later Jewish Tanakh and Christian Old Testament(s) developed.

Judaism and Hellenism before the Hellenizing Crisis

READING

Enoch 6–11.
Sirach/Ben Sira 1:1–10;
24:1–34; 44–50.

Though early Hellenistic rule was not benign, it was not antagonistic toward the religion and culture of peoples such as the Judeans. From the time of Alexander's conquest (332 BCE) up to initial efforts to Hellenize Jerusalem (174 BCE), Judah was ruled by a succession of Hellenistic rulers without major incident. After Alexander's death in 323 BCE, his kingdom was split among his generals, including Ptolemy in Egypt and Seleucus in Mesopotamia. Judah was ruled first from Egypt by heirs of Ptolemy (323–198 BCE). Then, after a series of major battles, the Seleucids (heirs of Seleucus) took over in 198 BCE and ruled Judah for much of the following half-century. Things were difficult as the two Hellenistic empires struggled for control of the area, but there is no evidence (prior to the ruler Antiochus IV: more on him below) that either the Ptolemaic or the Seleucid rulers interfered with the religion of those they ruled or otherwise tried to Hellenize them.

Nevertheless, Greek cities and people who had Greek education received privileges in these kingdoms, while those lacking Greek culture sometimes faced prejudice. For example, a non-Greek camel driver complains in an inscription that he was treated poorly because "I am a barbarian" and "I do not know how to behave like a Greek." An Egyptian priest complains in another inscription that a person whom he is suing "despises me because I am an Egyptian." Within Hellenistic cultures, Greek-educated children of Greek parents were at the top of the social pyramid, followed by Greek-educated children of non-Greek parents. Those who lacked any Greek education were disadvantaged even if they – like the Egyptian priest mentioned above – had extensive education in local, non-Greek texts, such as Egyptian classics or Hebrew books.

The solution for more and more people was to get a Greek education. Families would either have an in-house teacher for their children or pay someone else to educate them in a small group of private students. Students would start by learning the Greek alphabet and go on to learn practical wisdom such as Aesop's fables. Later they would progress to writings by a select list of authors from the classical period of Greek culture: Euripides, Thucydides, Plato, and others. The focal point of Greek education, however, was to learn the writings of Homer, whose epics were the classics among classics of Greek literature. Students started memorizing selections from the *Iliad* and *Odyssey* early in their education, and they returned to these texts again and again. Of course, some students did not progress very far, especially if they came from families where no Greek was spoken or read. Often a student would learn only enough Greek to do the simplest of scribal tasks. Some non-Greeks, however, achieved very high levels of Greek learning and obtained high positions in Greek government and/or society. Their education made them culturally "Greek," and they were treated differently than others who lacked such education.

This meant that societies under Hellenistic rule had a growing cultural divide. On the one side stood Greek culture, the knowledge of which gave students access to government positions and/or business contacts across the Greek world. On the other side stood the cultures and native texts of peoples in Judah, Egypt, and Mesopotamia. The knowledge of ancient Near Eastern texts was less and less important in the broader Hellenistic culture but was still valued in temple-priestly circles. Therefore, within Judah, the Temple and various priesthoods connected to it became the primary place where people still learned and wrote texts in Hebrew. Otherwise, priests found themselves and their knowledge of ancient texts increasingly marginalized. In earlier times, knowledge of ancient Hebrew texts gave a person privileges in the Hebrew monarchy or Persian empire, but things were different under Hellenism. Now primary political and economic power belonged increasingly to those who could claim on some level to be "Greek."

The Emergence of "Judaism"

This is the time when we can start to talk about the emergence of a "Jewish" identity in addition to and distinct from a "Judean" identity. The word "Jew" comes from the Greek word for Judean, *Ioudaios*. Though it encompassed Judeans living in Judah, it also embraced the ever expanding number of Jews living permanently outside Judah. Such Jews still had deep ties to Judah, but they were best known for their distinctive religion and set of practices.

Judeans and others dealt with this divide in different ways. Some priestly groups in both Egypt and Judah wrote esoteric visionary texts, called "**apocalypses**" after the Greek word for "uncovering." Some of these texts featured detailed tours of heaven ("**heavenly apocalypses**"), while others reviewed past history and then predicted divine intervention to remove Hellenistic rulers and restore native leaders ("**historical apocalypses**"). These apocalypses reflected both the broad scholarship of their priestly authors and their alienation from the surrounding Greek-dominated culture. The book of (first) Enoch, revered as scripture in the Ethiopic church, contains some of Judaism's oldest visionary texts, such as the calendar-focused "Book of the Luminaries" (now in parts of Enoch 72–82) and the earliest portion of the "Book of the Watchers" (in parts of Enoch 6–11), which told an expanded version of the story of divine human marriages seen in Gen 6:1–4. Jewish groups like the Qumran community (see box on p. 282) appear to have revered books like Enoch as much or more than some other books later included in the Hebrew Bible. The early Christian movement also valued the Enoch traditions. Indeed, a verse from Enoch is cited as authoritative in the New Testament book of Jude (Jude 14–15; referring to Enoch 1:9).

The meaning of these often obscure visionary texts is unclear initially to most readers. On one level, they elaborate on biblical narratives and feature many unfamiliar characters and scenes, battles between angels and the like. Yet on another level, these apocalypses in Enoch are coded descriptions of battles between Hellenistic rulers (Enoch 6–11) or crises in the Jerusalem priesthood (Enoch 12–16) and God's plan to intervene and set things right. These texts speak to concerns that were present in the third century BCE about Hellenistic domination and the corruption of the Temple, but they claim as

FIGURE 13.1
Copy of the Hebrew book of Ben Sira found near the Dead Sea.

their author an ancient, pre-Hellenistic sage, Enoch (see Gen 5:21–24). Such attribution of a later text to an ancient author, termed "**pseudepigraphy**," was particularly common in the Hellenistic age, when ancient authorship determined whether or not a given text would be studied in schools. In this case, however, Hellenistic-style pseudepigraphy was used by Jewish authors to provide extra authority to their predictions of liberation from Hellenistic kings and corrupt leaders.

The book of **Ben Sira** (also known as **Sirach**, its Greek name), originally written in Hebrew by Joshua ben Sira around 200–180 BCE, shows a different way to respond to the divide between local and Hellenistic culture (see Figure 13.1). In a possible critique of esoteric apocalypses such as those in Enoch, Ben Sira discourages speculation about heavenly realms (3:21–24) and rejects dreams as generally misleading (34:1–8). Instead, he writes a wisdom instruction to fit (both) the Torah focus and the Hellenistic tenor of his present time. Like older instructions in Proverbs, Ben Sira directly addresses his students, encouraging them to live prudently and put wisdom above other values. Like more recent works from the exile and post-exile, Ben Sira portrays the Torah as the ultimate wisdom, now going so far as to identify the Torah of Moses with the female personified wisdom seen in Proverbs and elsewhere (Ben Sira 24; see Proverbs 8).

Yet Ben Sira also shows influence from Hellenistic culture. At various points, his sayings resemble Greek sayings by the sixth-century BCE Greek poet Theognis that were commonly used early in the process of Greek education. Moreover, the Torah takes on a role in Ben Sira that is similar to that of Homer's epics in Greek education. It, like Homer, is the foundation and end point of the rest of the process of education and study. Finally, the book of Ben Sira concludes with a set of praises that have much in common with the Hellenistic genre of *encomium* (work of praise): a praise of "great fathers" that is divided between figures in the Pentateuch (Ben Sira 44–45) and figures found in all of the rest of the Hebrew Bible (46–49), followed by an extended praise of the high priest in Ben Sira's own time, Simon (50:1–21).

Many scholars rightly have seen in this "praise of great fathers" evidence that virtually all of the books in the Hebrew Bible were known and revered by Ben Sira's time (200–180 BCE). Nevertheless, other parts of the book of Ben Sira show that its author was not yet working with an idea of a closed collection of scriptural books. His own description of what a scribe studies includes "the law of the most high" (probably the Torah), wisdom of the ancients, prophecies, sayings of the famous, parables and proverbs (Sir 39:1–3) as well as foreign wisdom (39:4). The book of Ben Sira, explicitly written in the late second century by a sage of that time, aims to be a new addition to that broader scribal curriculum.

Ben Sira is just one example of a book written in a local language (Hebrew) that reflects Greek learning. But Jews also wrote Greek works and translated into Greek works that originally were in Hebrew. Sometime in the third century the Pentateuch was translated into Greek, and other Hebrew books (including Ben Sira) were translated later on. This group of early Greek translations of Hebrew scriptures is usually referred to with the term "Septuagint." New works written by Judeans in Greek often drew deeply on models and values seen in the Greek literature that they had learned. Some of these are found in the deuterocanonical books of the Roman Catholic and other churches, books such as 2 Maccabees, Judith, and the Wisdom of Solomon. For example, the Wisdom of Solomon is a work in Greek that draws deeply and broadly on Stoicism and other parts of Greek philosophy in the process of retelling the story of Solomon's search for wisdom.

Because of the high prestige of Greek culture, many Jews wrote books in Greek to improve the image of Judaism both among their own people and in the broader Hellenistic world. A second-century Jewish philosopher, Aristobulus, wrote a work attempting to show how Moses was the true source of the best of Greek learning. Another author, Ezekiel the tragic poet, rewrote the story of the exodus in the form of a Greek tragedy. Still others wrote texts with a positive picture of Judaism that they attempted to present as long-lost lines of famous Greek works or as missing works by famous gentile authors. Such works reveal both a respect for Greek culture and a defensiveness about the place of Judaism vis-à-vis that culture.

When we look across the full range of Jewish texts of this time, it becomes clear that all parts of Judaism were deeply affected by Hellenism and Hellenistic culture, even when they opposed elements of that culture. The apocalypses undergird their messages with Hellenistic-style pseudepigraphy. Ben Sira writes in Hebrew, but draws on sayings, ideas, and forms from Greek education. And the author of the Wisdom of Solomon draws on multiple strands of Greek philosophy in its depictions of wisdom. As a result, there is no clear distinction between "Hellenistic Judaism" and other forms, since all of Judaism was touched by Hellenistic culture and ideas. The main distinction that does appear is between forms of Hellenistic Judaism that were neutral or positive about Hellenism and forms of Hellenistic Judaism that were opposed to it. This distinction emerges particularly in the crisis around the attempt to Hellenize Jerusalem, to which we turn next.

The Crisis over Hellenizing Jerusalem and the Book of Daniel

READING

Narratives about the Maccabean crisis: 2 Maccabees 4–8. Apocalyptic writing: Daniel 7–12.

The Seleucids under Antiochus III were initially quite friendly to Jews and Judaism. When Antiochus III took control of Judah from the Ptolemies in 198 BCE, he affirmed more ancient Persian policies toward Judah. He gave tax relief to the city and money for the Temple, and affirmed by royal decree the right of Jews to live "according to [their] ancestral laws." Later on, however, he suffered defeat by the Romans and started to pay heavy tribute to them. He died in the process of trying to raid one of the temples in his kingdom for money, and a similar attempt apparently was made during the reign of his successor, Seleucus IV (see 2 Maccabees 3). By the time Antiochus Epiphanes IV seized the throne from Seleucus IV in 175 BCE, the kingdom had been humiliated by the Romans, and Antiochus needed money to pay them a large annual tribute. At this point, Judah was one of the few Seleucid territories remaining on the Western Mediterranean.

It was under these circumstances that Antiochus IV started to sell the high priesthood in Jerusalem to the highest bidder, a significant move, since the high priest of Jerusalem's temple functioned at this time as the local ruler and tax-collector for the region. First, Jason, who was a brother of the existing high priest, paid money to Antiochus on the occasion of the latter's accession to the throne for two privileges: (1) the office of high priest and (2) the right to turn Jerusalem into a Greek city, complete with its own gymnasium within sight of the Temple (174 BCE). Three years later, another leading figure, Menelaus, outbid Jason, took over the high priesthood, and forced Jason to flee (171 BCE). Menelaus's rule proved highly unpopular, however, and the Seleucids had to intervene twice to restore him to power. The second time, fed up with revolts, Antiochus IV enacted harsh measures aimed at crushing any trace of Jewish culture (in 167 BCE). He imposed the death penalty on Jews for continuing to follow Torah laws such as eating regulations and circumcision, and he set up an altar to Zeus Olympius over the altar to Yahweh in the Jerusalem temple. What had started as a mild attempt by Jason and other Jerusalemites to gain Greek privileges for Jerusalem and its citizens had turned into a life-and-death struggle for the continuance of Torah observance.

The visions in Daniel 7–12 were written to give Judeans hope in this crisis. Like the apocalyptic visions in Enoch, these chapters of Daniel are attributed to an earlier figure, this time the exilic figure of Daniel who is featured in the tales of Daniel 1–2, 4–6. Moreover, like other historical apocalypses, these visions in Daniel give a coded overview of past history before predicting God's intervention to make things right. We can see an example of this in the vision of four beasts coming out of the sea in Daniel 7. These four beasts correspond to four major world empires leading up to the time of Antiochus IV: the Babylonians who destroyed the Jerusalem temple (7:4), the Medes who dominated lands east of Babylonia (7:5), the Persians (7:6), and the Greeks, particularly the 10 rulers – "horns" – of the Seleucid dynasty (7:7), from which a "little horn," Antiochus IV, sprouts (7:8).

After surveying these four empires, the vision moves to the future, predicting the destruction of the fourth, Greek beast and God's gift of eternal dominion to a mysterious "one like a human being" (7:9–14). Many Christians have read this text in light of gospel accounts where Jesus refers to himself as the "son of man," and have understood Daniel 7 as a prediction of the coming of Jesus. Nevertheless, the details of the text, especially the "interpretation" given to Daniel in 7:15–27, indicate that this chapter was originally intended to give hope to Torah-observant Jews under threat from Antiochus. Antiochus is the one who attempted to end sacrifice and forbid Torah observance, to "change the sacred times and the law" (7:25). In his vision, Daniel is told that God will destroy the kingdom of Antiochus and grant eternal rule to those who have remained faithful to the Torah, "the holy ones of the most High" (7:27).

> **Basics**
>
> **Book of Daniel**
>
> **Outline: apocalyptic visions with prologue of stories of deliverance**
>
> | | | |
> |---|---|---|
> | I | Stories about Daniel and other exiles | 1–6 |
> | II | Daniel's four visions | 7–12 |
>
> **Language**
>
> Several chapters of Daniel are in Aramaic (2–7), others in Hebrew (1, 8–12).
>
> **Date**
>
> The Aramaic legends in Daniel 4–6 go back in some form to the late Persian or early Hellenistic period, while the other stories in Daniel 1–6 largely date to the later Hellenistic period before the crisis over Hellenization. The book as a whole, including the visionary chapters in Daniel 7–12, dates from just before 164 BCE and reflects the crisis of that time.
>
> **More information**
>
> The Greek translation of Daniel preserves yet other traditions about Daniel and other figures (e.g. Susanna in Daniel 13). In addition, an Aramaic story about Nabonidus was found in the Dead Sea Scrolls at Qumran and represents a different form of the tradition seen in Daniel 4.

Things did not work out exactly as this or other visions in Daniel 7–12 predicted, but these visions have continued to give hope to generations of Jews and Christians. Jews have read the text as a prediction of God's establishment of God's rule with the future arrival of the messiah. Christians have read it as a prediction of God's transformation of the world with the second coming of Jesus Christ. In each case, people have found numerous ways to coordinate the obscure symbols of Daniel 7–12 with groups and events of their own time. At their best, such interpretations have given much-needed hope to communities facing oppressors as bad as or worse than Antiochus IV. At their worst, these reinterpretations of Daniel have encouraged people to withdraw from the world and wait for God's imminent intervention on their behalf. Certainly it would be a mistake for any community to suppose that their own understanding of the visions in Daniel is the one and only true way to unlock the code of the book. The persistently strange imagery of the book resists this kind of certainty and is part of what has allowed Daniel to be revered and reinterpreted by communities long after the time of the Hellenistic crisis.

A Hellenistic-Period Kingdom of Israel: The Hasmonean Revolt and Monarchy

Ultimately, Antiochus IV was unsuccessful, though not in the ways envisioned in Daniel 7–12. Members of a marginal priestly family in rural Judah, the **Hasmoneans** or **Maccabees**, launched a guerilla war against the Seleucids. They started by destroying pagan altars, killing Jewish collaborators with the Seleucids, and forcibly circumcising males who had been left uncircumcised under Seleucid order. Their effort culminated with the recapture of Jerusalem and purification of the Temple (164 BCE). (Note: **Hanukkah** is the Jewish holiday celebrating this triumph and the purification of the Temple.) In addition, the Hasmoneans were able to negotiate an end to the edict of Antiochus IV against Judaism. Jews were free to observe Torah regulations again, and we hear no more of any attempts to reverse this policy.

All this did not, however, mean an end to Greek domination. Though Antiochus IV died around this time, the Seleucids soon regained control over Judah, killing the leader of the Hasmonean family, Judas Maccabeus ("the hammer"), in battle and forcing the other Hasmoneans and their supporters to flee. Around 152 BCE, however, the Hasmoneans played their cards right in a power struggle over the Seleucid throne, choosing to back the winner of that struggle, Demetrius. In return, Demetrius appointed the Hasmonean Jonathan as high priest and thus ruler of the province of Judah. When Jonathan was murdered a decade later, his brother Simon declared independence from the Seleucid empire (142 BCE). By then the Seleucids did not have the power to bring Judah back under their control.

Thus Judah was free of direct foreign rule for the first time in hundreds of years. For approximately seven decades (142–63 BCE), the Hasmoneans controlled Jerusalem and the high priesthood. Moreover, they gradually expanded their realm to include not only the old heartland of Judah and Israel but also areas that had few Jews and had not been dominated by Jerusalem for centuries: the Phoenician coastland, Edom and the rest of the Transjordan, and Gali-

Significant Dates: The Rise of the Hasmonean Kingdom

Antiochus IV seizes power over Seleucid empire	175 BCE
Jason buys high priesthood and initiates Hellenizing	174 BCE
Menelaus purchases priesthood Unpopular rule, uprisings	171 BCE
Harsh measures by Antiochus IV to eradicate Judaism Beginning of Maccabean rebellion under Hasmoneans	167 BCE
Purification/rededication of Temple End of harsh edicts against Judaism	164 BCE
Independent Hasmonean rule	142–63 BCE
Beginning of Roman rule of Palestine	63 BCE

lee (see Map 13.1). At the beginning of their activity the Hasmoneans fought for Jewish rights to observe the Torah. Now, as rulers, they expelled gentiles from some of the areas they conquered, converted others, and imposed (male) circumcision on their subject populations. Their passion for ancient ways is seen in their promotion of the Torah, their advocacy for the Hebrew language in a now Aramaic-speaking populace, and their use of ancient Hebrew script on the new coins that they minted. The book of 1 Maccabees was originally written in Hebrew to celebrate and support the Hasmonean kingdom. It presents the Hasmoneans as true heirs of the Israelite judges, proponents of the Hebrew heritage, and righteous opponents of the forces of Hellenism.

Nevertheless, the Hasmonean rulers were also influenced in multiple ways by the Hellenistic culture they purported to oppose. The whole practice of issuing coins was a Greek one, and the Hasmonean coins with ancient Hebrew letters also featured images and symbols drawn from older Greek coins of the Ptolemies and Seleucids. In this way, coins, such as the one pictured in Figure 13.2, vividly illustrate the kind of cultural **hybridity** we have seen at other points in Israelite history: the blending of self-determination with elements drawn from the culture of the past oppressor. We see similar hybridity in other cultural products of the Hasmonean period: The Hasmoneans built palaces with Greek columns and friezes but were careful to equip them with baths to preserve ritual purity. Jewish burial tombs from this time are virtually identical with their Greek-pagan counterparts in other countries except for their avoidance of pictorial representation, in obedience to dictates found in Deuteronomy (Deut 4:15–19). The book of 2 Maccabees celebrates heroes who fought for the Torah, using Hellenistic modes of history writing and imitating Greek models of heroic martyrs. In these and other ways the Hasmoneans developed a hybrid culture that promoted anti-Hellenism while adapting Hellenistic features.

Basics

The Book of Judith (as an example of a Hasmonean text)

The **book of Judith** tells a tale of how a Judean female deliverer, Judith, saves her people from a threat posed by an Assyrian general, Holofernes. In a plot reminiscent of the story of Jael and Sisera (Judg 4:17–24; 5:24–27), Judith seductively lures Holofernes into being alone with her in his tent, cuts off his head, and then orders a successful attack on Holofernes's massive army. Though there are signs that the book may be based on an older set of traditions from the Persian period, multiple historical anachronisms mark it as unhistorical, and the story has been updated so that "Judith's" victory anticipates the victory of Judas and other Hasmoneans over Antiochus IV. It and other histories related to the Hasmonean period (e.g. 1, 2, 3, and 4 Maccabees) did not end up being included in the Jewish Tanakh (and thus also not the Protestant Bible). Nevertheless, they were included in early Christian Bibles and are part of many present Christian Old Testaments.

A Hellenistic-Period Kingdom of Israel: The Hasmonean Revolt and Monarchy

MAP 13.1
The expanding kingdom of the Hasmoneans. Redrawn from Norman Gottwald, *The Hebrew Bible: A Socio-Literary Introduction*. Minneapolis: Fortress, 1985, page 407.

FIGURE 13.2
Coin from the time of the Hasmoneans, combining the Greek practice of coinage (with an image!) with an inscription on the other side in archaic Hebrew lettering.

The Hellenistic/Hasmonean Period as the Setting for Hebrew Bible Texts

READING

Writings about life in the diaspora: Esther, Daniel 3.

The Hebrew Bible contains several books that probably were written sometime during this Hellenistic period. We have already discussed the visions of Daniel, which show clear signs of having been written sometime during the Hellenistic crisis of 169–164 BCE. But other books of the Bible also were either written or modified in the years after Alexander conquered the area.

One example is the books of Chronicles, at least in their present form. The genealogies at the outset of the book (1 Chronicles 1–9), for example, include figures who lived during the Hellenistic period (1 Chr 3:17–24). To be sure, parts of the historical overview in 1 Chronicles 10 through 2 Chronicles 36 are parallel to parts of Samuel and Kings, which means that these sections come from the exilic or pre-exilic periods. Indeed, some parts of Chronicles may be earlier than their counterparts in Samuel and Kings, preserving some historical records from the eighth or early seventh century. Nevertheless, the bulk of texts that are unique to Chronicles, both the genealogies in 1 Chronicles 1–9 and portions of the following historical sections, show linguistic and other signs of having been written in the Persian or Hellenistic periods. As such, the books of Chronicles are another witness to the theology and values of late post-exilic priestly groups, particularly the Levites, who are

---

Basics

Books of 1–2 Chronicles

Outline: Temple and priest-centered history of Judah's kings

I	Genealogy: Adam to exile	1 Chr 1–9
II	Reign of David	1 Chr 10–29
III	Reign of Solomon	2 Chr 1–9
IV	Judean kingship until exile	2 Chr 10–36

Date

Fourth century BCE (300s).

More information

Though isolated parts of Chronicles preserve unique historical sources, the vast majority of its differences from Samuel-Kings represent late divergences added in light of Persian or later historical realities.

---

promoted in the book and were responsible for singing and teaching in post-exilic Judah.

The Hellenistic period is also the most likely time for the composition of the books of Ezra-Nehemiah. As discussed in Chapter 12, this set of books was formed through the combination of separate Ezra and Nehemiah traditions probably written in the Persian period. Nevertheless, these older traditions are combined in a very particular way in Ezra-Nehemiah, as seen in the following chart:

Rebuilding/Ezra narrative	Nehemiah memoir	Combined text
Temple rebuilding		Temple rebuilding
Expulsion of foreign wives		Expulsion of foreign wives
	Rebuilding of wall	Rebuilding of wall
Centering on Torah		Centering on Torah
	Opposition to Tobiads	Opposition to Tobiads

Setting the narrative up this way corresponds to the later effort by the Hasmoneans to protect Torah obedience by gaining political power. In this combined Ezra-Nehemiah narrative, Nehemiah builds the wall and thus protects Jerusalem *before* Ezra leads the people in committing themselves to the Mosaic Torah. In addition, the combined Ezra-Nehemiah narrative would have discredited opponents of the Hasmoneans, specifically the Tobiad family, which supported Hellenization and was sponsored by Antiochus IV. This family is prominent among those who opposed Nehemiah's wall building (Neh 2:10, 19–20; 4:1–9; 6:1–19), and the concluding chapter of Ezra-Nehemiah narrates Nehemiah's expulsion of Tobiah from the Temple (13:4–9). Finally, the authors who combined the older Ezra and Nehemiah materials also wrote new texts of their own. One major example is the prayer of Ezra in Nehemiah 9, which describes the people as suffering from slavery to the Persians and "in great distress" (Neh 9:36–37). This negative attitude toward the Persian empire is alien to the older Ezra and Nehemiah traditions, but it is right at home in the Hellenistic period. We see similar negative pictures of the Persians in the visions of Daniel and other Hellenistic-period texts. For example, most scholars would agree that the book of Esther dates from this time, mostly on the basis of its late language. The Hasmoneans and their supporters would have liked the book's celebration of successful Jewish resistance to an attempt by a corrupt Persian official to kill all of the Jews in the empire.

Basics

Books of Ezra-Nehemiah

Outline: the cultic and political establishment of Torah-centered Judean community

I	Return and rebuilding of Temple	Ezra 1–6
II	Torah+Temple-centered community	
	A Preparations	
	1 Ezra's commission and divorce of foreign wives	Ezra 7–10
	2 Nehemiah's building of politically independent Jerusalem	Nehemiah 1–7
	B Ezra and Nehemiah's creation of Torah-centered community	Nehemiah 8–13

Language

Ezra 4:8–6:18 and 7:12–26 are in Aramaic, while the rest is in Hebrew.

Date

The present form of the book may date as late as the mid-second century (160–150s BCE).

More information

The bulk of the book is probably earlier, particularly the sources for Ezra (Ezra 7–10; Nehemiah 8) and Nehemiah (Neh 1:1–7:4; 13:10–14, 30b–31) that were discussed in Chapter 12.

The apocryphal/deuterocanonical book of 1 Esdras is a Greek narrative that parallels Ezra 1–10 and Nehemiah 8 but lacks any of the Nehemiah materials found in Nehemiah 1–7, 9–13. Many scholars think this book is a Greek translation of an earlier form of the Temple-rebuilding/Ezra account (preceded by a fragment from 2 Chronicles 35–36) before it was combined with the Nehemiah memoir. 1 Esdras also includes a late court tale about a debate between three bodyguards concerning whether wine, the king, women, or truth are more powerful (1 Esdras 3:1–5:6).

An even better case can be made for dating the book of Esther to the Hellenistic period, on the basis of both late language and its unflattering portrayal of Persian rule. Finally, the Aramaic court tales found in Daniel 2–6, though earlier than the visions of 7–12, probably date from the late Persian or early Hellenistic periods. They celebrate the survival and triumph of Daniel and other exiles in the hostile environment of the Neo-Babylonian empire.

Basics

Book of Esther

Outline: story of victory behind the holiday of Purim

| I | Esther's rise and saving of her people | 1–8 |
| II | Revenge of Jews and beginning of Purim | 9–10 |

Date

Third century BCE (200s).

More information

The book of Esther in Hebrew is distinguished by its lack of mention of God or traditional piety. The Greek translations of Esther include additions that solve this problem by inserting prayers, references to God, etc. These more pious forms of Esther were preserved in the Christian church.

Meanwhile, Esther has become the central reading within Judaism for the raucous holiday of Purim. This holiday, which happens in late February or early March, features dressing up, candy, gifts for the poor, and audience response during the reading of the Esther scroll.

Overall, many parts of the Hebrew Bible probably reached their present form in the Hellenistic period. This seems to be the case with books such as the Song of Songs and Ecclesiastes, both of which feature late forms of Hebrew typical of Hellenistic-period texts. Though earlier in this textbook I suggested that some part of these books may have been written during the early monarchy (see Chapter 4), they certainly were modified later. For example, a Hellenistic-period scribe appears to have added the following orthodox conclusion to the book of Ecclesiastes:

> The conclusion of the matter:
> All has been heard,
> Fear God and keep God's commandments
> This is the duty of every human.
> For God will bring every deed to judgment
> Even every secret thing, whether good or bad.
>
> (Eccl 12:13–14)

This conclusion shows ideas of Torah obedience and final judgment that are common in the Hellenistic period. They contrast strongly with the skepticism of most of the rest of Ecclesiastes, such as "Do not be too righteous and do not be too evil, for why should you be ruined?" (Eccl 7:16). In this way and many others, the present Hebrew Bible, in Ecclesiastes and many other books, is an intricate blend of old and new.

FOCUS TEXT

Daniel 10–12

The report of a vision in Daniel 10–12 is one of the best examples of a text that is presented as old, but is manifestly new. At the outset we hear that the exilic figure Daniel received this vision in "the third year of king Cyrus of Persia" (Dan 10:1). Nevertheless, the following two chapters make clear that the author knew world history up to the time of the Hellenistic crisis, but not events afterwards. The vision starts with an angelic figure, perhaps Gabriel, appearing to Daniel and anticipating future events in the Hellenistic and Persian periods: the defeat of the Persian empire by Alexander ("the warrior king" in 11:3), the division of his kingdom among his four generals (11:4), various specific events in the history of the Ptolemies of Egypt ("the king[s] of the south," 11:5–12), the conquest of Judah and Egypt by the Seleucid Antiochus III (11:13–16), the attempt to rob the Jerusalem temple under his successor, Seleucus IV (11:20), the rise and initial conquests of Antiochus IV (11:21–28), and his profaning of the Temple and persecution of observant Jews (11:29–39). At this point, however, the text diverges from history, inaccurately predicting further conquests by Antiochus IV (11:40–45) and the time when the Temple would be purified and rededicated (12:11–12). Clearly this vision was written after the onset of the Hellenistic crisis in 169 BCE but before its end and the death of Antiochus IV.

This text is particularly important, however, because it concludes with a vision of resurrection that is unique in the Hebrew Bible. Elsewhere, the Hebrew Bible has little place for an idea of afterlife. There is no belief in heaven and hell. Instead, all who died were thought to go to a shadowy existence in "Sheol" that involved neither reward nor punishment. As Proverbs indicates, the main hope for virtuous reward was prosperity in this life, along with children and a good name to continue after death (e.g. Prov 10:4, 7, 27–28; 12:28). This perspective, however, did not provide much comfort amidst a situation like the Hellenistic crisis. There people (and their children) were being killed for staying faithful to the Torah. This text in Daniel promises that this is not the end for them. Instead, those who have been faithful – that is, "the wise ones" – will be resurrected after the death of Antiochus IV and "shine like the brightness of heaven." Meanwhile, those of their persecutors who have died will also be resurrected, but to shame and continual punishment (Dan 12:1–3).

The Greeks had long believed in some kind of individual afterlife (e.g. the kingdom of Hades), but this Hebrew idea of collective afterlife in Daniel now empowered resistance to Greek oppression. It gave people hope to resist Antiochus IV even if opposition to his decree would cost them their lives. Here again we can see how the cultural traditions of the oppressor could be used by the oppressed to enable resistance. Moreover, this idea of afterlife has continued to empower resistance by people facing difficult odds. The belief in a reward during God's final judgment has helped generations of Jews and Christians remain faithful even when facing powerful oppressors capable of killing them.

Two centuries later, these kinds of beliefs in God's (coming) transformation of the world would be common among the Jews of the first century, among whom Jesus and the earliest Christians should be numbered. By then a new powerful empire, that of the Romans, had taken control of Judah. Soon Judah was hammered by crises at least as severe as, if not more so than, the Hellenistic crisis of the second century BCE. Within this context, visions such as Daniel 10–12 gave Jews hope that death at the hands of the Romans was not the final chapter in their lives. Though it might seem to them as if the political powers of evil were triumphing, texts such as Daniel reassured them that God soon would intervene, destroy evil empires, and resurrect the faithful ones to everlasting glory.

The Dead Sea Scrolls

Starting in 1946, local Bedouin and then archaeologists began to find extremely old Jewish texts that had been stored in caves in the desert hills on the northwest shore of the Dead Sea. The very dry climate and isolation of the area meant that hundreds of these scrolls had been at least partially preserved over thousands of years. They were collected and stored by a community that appears to have had a base in the ruins known as *Khirbet Qumran*. This Qumran community wrote and stored a wide variety of texts, including some written within and for their community, texts now in the Bible, and yet other Jewish texts. The discovery and study of these Dead Sea Scrolls has provided priceless insight into the final formation of biblical texts and the diversity of Jewish literature in the Second Temple period. Thanks to them, we now have increased insight into the different forms of Judaism that existed in the centuries up to and including Jesus. The texts also show how the ancient Jewish community at Qumran, like the early Christians, read and revered a broader range of books than those included in the Jewish Tanakh and Christian Old Testament(s).

For more information

James C. VanderKam, *The Dead Sea Scrolls Today* (2nd revised edition). Grand Rapids: Eerdmans, 2010. For images and information about the scrolls, see also https://www.deadseascrolls.org.il.

The Formation of the Jewish Tanakh and Christian Old Testament(s)

Thanks to the discovery of the Dead Sea Scrolls and other developments (see box above), we now know that there was no authoritative set of Hebrew scriptures up through the period of the Second Temple. To be sure, most Jews shared a reverence for the Torah of Moses (= Pentateuch) and saw themselves as related in some way to the land of Israel and the temple there. Nevertheless, otherwise there was a great variety in Judaism of the period, and this was reflected in a variety of ways that Hellenistic and Hasmonean period Jews related to older texts. Certain groups that were closely related to a temple – such as the Sadducees (linked to the Jerusalem temple) or the Samaritans (linked to a northern temple at Gerizim) – seem to have focused particularly on the Torah/Pentateuch as their authoritative reference text. Many other Jewish groups, like the Jesus movement or the community based at Qumran, affirmed the authority of "The Torah and Prophets," with "prophets" here relating to a broad array of books considered to be prophetically inspired, both books like Isaiah that were put in the later "Prophets" category of the Tanakh, and also other books, like Enoch, that were not included in the later Tanakh at all.

Indeed, at this point it seems that many books now found in the "Writings" section of the Jewish Tanakh, such as Daniel or Psalms, were considered "prophetic" books. So when one sees references to "the law and the prophets" in the Christian New Testament (or also the Dead Sea Scrolls), this pairing refers to the Torah (= "the law") along with other inspired books (= "the prophets"): Isaiah, Enoch, Judges, Ben Sira, and other works revered as holy scripture. At points, early Jewish texts refer briefly to an additional book or books alongside this "Torah and Prophets" grouping, such as a reference in the Christian gospel of Luke to "Torah, prophets and psalms" (Luke 24:44). Nevertheless, the phrase "Torah and Prophets" seems to have been a major way that Jews referred to scriptures up through the Jewish Mishnah of the second century CE.

It is not clear exactly when some Jews started limiting which books were considered "prophetic" so that their scriptures included a single, unchanging set of books: the Torah/Pentateuch and certain specified "Prophetic" books. There is a chance that the Hasmoneans might have begun this process, since one of the histories promoting them, 1 Maccabees, refers to a time when prophecy had ended (1 Macc 9:27). This reference may imply an idea that books written after this point, e.g. an explicitly Hellenistic-period text like Ben Sira, were not "prophetic" and thus not to be included in the "Torah and Prophets." Perhaps this is an indirect reflection of an attempt by the Hasmonean monarchs to limit scripture to the books that would later be included in the rabbinic Tanakh, excluding explicitly Hellenistic texts like Ben Sira. The Hasmonean kings, who built a reputation for themselves as defenders of Judaism against Hellenism, had the power and the motivation to establish such a standardized set of Jewish texts that then could compete with the similarly standardized set of Greek texts valued in the Hellenistic world (e.g. Homer and the classical authors).

Nevertheless, if the Hasmoneans did attempt such a standardization of Hebrew scripture, that standardization was not recognized by a number of Jewish groups. The above-mentioned Jewish community based at Qumran revered a wide range of texts extending beyond the later Jewish Tanakh, and the same was true for the early Christian movement. Indeed, we do not start to see potential references to the particular set of books that now constitute the Jewish Tanakh until well after the Hellenistic period. In the wake of the Roman destruction of the Second Temple, toward the end of the first century CE, the Jewish historian Josephus gives a listing of "Torah and allied documents" that somewhat resembles the Tanakh (Against Apion 1.38–41). Meanwhile, around the same time, the apocalyptic book of 4 Ezra seems to argue against such a limitation of what books are considered revealed (4 Ezra 14:38–47). These references may be pointers toward an increased standardization of scriptures that occurred in the wake of the Roman destruction of the temple. At the same time, they also show that such standardization was still debated.

If this evidence seems confusing to you, it should clarify why scholars profoundly disagree on these questions. There is no royal pronouncement, no meeting of leaders, no identifiable time that one can point to and say "this is when and why the books in the Bible were included and others were left out."

All we can know is that later Jewish and Christian communities each had slightly different versions of these scriptures. Rabbinic writings like the Babylonian Talmud (from the sixth century CE) contain lists of twenty-four books in a three-part Jewish Bible, the Tanakh (Torah, Prophets, Writings). Meanwhile, Christian church councils of the third and fourth centuries produce various lists of books in their "Old Testament." As noted in this textbook's prologue, these latter books of the Christian Old Testament(s) overlap with those in the

Jewish Tanakh, but they also include other books like Ben Sira, Judith, etc. During the Protestant reform of the 1500s, however, Martin Luther and other Protestant leaders decided to conform the contents of their Old Testament to books found in the rabbinic Tanakh. As a result, Christian Old Testaments now vary in contents. The Protestant Bible has the fewest books (parallel in contents to the Jewish Tanakh), while Roman Catholic and various Orthodox Christian Bibles have an Old Testament that includes additional books, often termed "deuterocanonical."

Conclusion

This chapter has focused on biblical texts written (or revised) during the Hellenistic period, but we must remember again that these texts transcended their original historical contexts. The tales of Daniel 1–6 and Esther gave hope to Jewish exiles of later centuries. The book of Ben Sira provided a new fusion of Torah wisdom with Greek learning. The visions of Enoch and Daniel 7–12 reassured Jews and Christians facing persecution. The histories in Chronicles and Ezra-Nehemiah communicated a vision of Temple- and Torah-centered Judaism to later generations, and narratives like Judith celebrated the triumph of underdogs over imperial aggressors. Overall, the Hellenistic and Hasmonean periods were a fruitful time of cultural cross-fertilization and Jewish literary productivity in Hebrew, Aramaic, and Greek.

In addition, as we have seen, the Hebrew Bible as a whole, the "Torah and Prophets," underwent transformations as it became the foundation of two religious movements: Judaism and Christianity. An increasingly Torah-focused Judaism developed the three-part Tanakh, and these older Hebrew scriptures were studied alongside a newer set of rabbinic legal traditions. Christianity gradually separated from its Jewish roots, but it continued to recognize the books of its Jewish heritage as scripture. Yet now Christians arranged those books of Jewish scripture into an "Old Testament" that led into a "New Testament" of specifically Christian books. People of these times valued what was old, so this labeling of Hebrew scriptures as "*Old* Testament" reflected an ongoing reverence for these texts. Yet the naming of specifically Christian scriptures as "*New* Testament" also showed an emphasis within Christianity on the special importance – both in theology and in worship – of Christian writings such as the gospels and Pauline letters.

CHAPTER THIRTEEN REVIEW

For Review

1 Know the meaning and significance of the following terms discussed in this chapter:
    - apocalypse
    - heavenly apocalypse
    - historical apocalypse
    - Enoch (the book of)
    - Ben Sira/Sirach
    - Hanukkah

- Hasmoneans (Maccabees)
- hybridity (as it applies to the Hasmoneans)
- Judith (the book of)
- Dead Sea Scrolls (or Qumran scrolls)

2 Even before the Hellenistic crisis, what was unique about the Jewish encounter with Hellenistic education and literature in comparison to older literary systems that Judah and Israel had experience with?

3 What major empires are reflected in the coded visions of Daniel 7 and 10–12? How is the Persian empire viewed in these visions in comparison with the Nehemiah memoir and the Ezra narrative?

4 How is the phenomenon of hybridity reflected in the works of the Hasmoneans? How might it be reflected in the final formation of the Hebrew Bible?

5 What is older and what is newer in the books of Chronicles? And in Ezra-Nehemiah?

6 What are other major candidates in the Hebrew Bible to be writings from the Hellenistic period, and why?

For Reflection

7 (Focus text: Daniel 10–12) Drawing on this chapter's discussion of the book of Daniel and of Daniel 10–12 in particular, try writing a brief historical apocalypse that would empower a contemporary oppressed group. Use Daniel 10–12 as your overall model, but make up your own imagery and connect your apocalypse to recent history and contemporary crises. Try to incorporate the kinds of features (pseudepigraphy, historical review, and projection of divine triumph) that are seen in texts such as Daniel 10–12, but attribute the apocalypse to a major authoritative figure of the more recent past. Have a friend read and try to decode it. What is similar and different about your twenty-first-century apocalypse and the one found in Daniel 10–12?

RESOURCES FOR FURTHER STUDY

Jewish writings from the Hellenistic and early Roman periods

Collins, John J. *Jewish Wisdom in the Hellenistic Age*. Louisville, KY: Westminster John Knox Press, 1997.

Nickelsburg, George. *Jewish Literature Between the Bible and the Mishnah* (revised edition). Minneapolis: Fortress, 2005.

Daniel

Newsom, Carol. *Daniel*. Louisville, KY: Westminster John Knox, 2014.

Chronicles

Japhet, Sara. *1 and 2 Chronicles*. Louisville, KY: Westminster John Knox, 1993.

Esther

Beal, Timothy. *The Book of Hiding: Gender, Ethnicity, Annihilation, and Esther*. London: Routledge, 1997.

Berlin, Adele. *Esther*. Philadelphia: Jewish Publication Society, 2001.

The Formation of the Jewish Tanakh and Christian Old Testament(s)

McDonald, Lee Martin. *Origin of the Bible: A Guide for the Perplexed*. New York: Continuum, 2011.

Glossary

Each entry includes (in parentheses) reference to the first location where a term is discussed, whether Prologue or chapter number, along with other major location(s). **Boldface** indicates terms that occur elsewhere in this Glossary.

act-consequence (4) – see moral act-consequence.

African American interpretation (2) – forms of critical biblical study whose questions grow out of the experiences of people of African descent. Such study critiques racist interpretations of the Bible, highlights the presence of African characters in the Bible, and/or critically analyzes the diverse ways that scripture has been used in African American religion and culture (see also **womanist** and **Afrocentric interpretation**).

Afrocentric interpretation (4) – forms of interpretation that foreground and celebrate the bodies and cultures of people of African descent (see also **African American interpretation**).

apocalypse (13) – a text commonly attested in the Hellenistic and later periods that describes a heavenly revelation to a human recipient, often a human recipient from Israel's distant past (e.g. Enoch, Levi, etc.; see **pseudepigraphy**). Such apocalypses appear in two main types, the **heavenly apocalypse** and the **historical apocalypse**, frequently show priestly connections, and feature much focus on esoteric knowledge.

apocrypha (Prologue) – Protestant term for **deuterocanonical** books, in this case designating books that are not viewed in the Protestant tradition as fully **canonical**.

Ark Narrative (7) – hypothesized earlier source about the loss and recovery of the ark of the covenant that is thought to be embedded in 1 Samuel 4–6 and possibly parts of 2 Samuel 6.

Asherah (2) – the mother goddess of the Canaanite pantheon, consort of the chief god, **El**.

Assyria (5) – a Mesopotamian state based in what is now northern Iraq.

Baal (2) – a storm god in the Canaanite pantheon.

Babylonian exile (1) – 586–538 BCE, a time when most of the elite living in Judah (especially Jerusalem) were forced to live outside the land in Babylonia (with many never having the chance to return).

beginning of the Roman period (1) – 63 BCE: the end of the **Hasmonean monarchy** and the beginning of rule of Palestine by rulers appointed by Rome.

Ben Sira (13) – a collection of instructional texts authored in the early second century BCE (approx. 200–180 BCE). It is one example of a **deuterocanonical** book included (under its Greek name **Sirach**) in the Old Testament of the Roman Catholic and Orthodox churches, but excluded from the Jewish Tanakh and Protestant Old Testament.

book of the Twelve Prophets (5) – a book in the Jewish Tanakh that includes the 12 **minor prophets** (Hosea through Malachi).

books of the former prophets (7) – the historical books of Joshua, Judges, 1–2 Samuel, and 1–2 Kings.

books of the latter prophets (7) – the prophetic books of Isaiah, Jeremiah, Ezekiel, and the book of the Twelve Prophets.

canon and **canonical** (Prologue) – "canon" is a collection of books that are recognized as divinely inspired scripture by a given religious community. Those books are recognized as "canonical."

complaint (11) – for discussion see **lament psalm**.

conjectural emendation (Prologue) – a correction of the biblical text proposed by scholars that is not based on any **manuscript witness**.

couplet (3) – along with the less common **triplet**, a basic unit in Hebrew poetry, where the first line is paralleled, contrasted, or otherwise **seconded** by the climactic second line. Many translations identify the second line of a couplet by indenting the beginning of the line a few spaces.

covenant (5) – a solemn agreement between two parties, sealed, in the ancient Near East, by oaths and sometimes by ritual acts calling down curses on the parties should one of them break the agreement.

Covenant Code (4) – a set of early laws embedded in Exod 20:22–23:33 that (apart from some late additions) seem to predate later regulations asserting the requirement to worship Yahweh in just one place (e.g. Deut 12; cf. 2 Kings 22–23). The parallels between the topics of these laws and large portions of the Code of Hammurabi are an indicator that some form of this collection may have been composed already in the early monarchal period, e.g. tenth or ninth century BCE.

cultural memory (2) – a common set of memories, taught to each generation and celebrated in common rituals, that help define a group by its shared past.

Cyrus cylinder (11) – a proclamation by the Persian king Cyrus that he was appointed by the Babylonian gods to liberate the Babylonians and rebuild their temples. It shows many parallels to the Cyrus proclamation quoted in Ezra 1:1–4 that Yahweh had appointed him to rebuild the Temple and allow the Judeans to return home.

Day of Yahweh (8) – a term seen in biblical literature that generally seems to have meant a day when Yahweh would rescue his chosen people (thus part of **election theology**), but is often reinterpreted by prophets (e.g. Amos, Zephaniah) as a day when Yahweh will judge that people.

destruction of Jerusalem (1) – 586 BCE: a climactic event in the history of Judah, including the destruction of Solomon's temple and the end of the holy city many thought to be invulnerable.

destruction of the Second Temple (1) – 70 CE: occurred in the wake of a Jewish revolt against Rome and – along with the total destruction of Jerusalem in 135 CE after another revolt – represented the end of the local Jewish temple state and the recentering of much Jewish life in the communities outside the land.

deuterocanonical (Prologue) – books recognized as **canonical** by the Roman Catholic church, but not part of the Jewish Tanakh or Protestant Old Testament.

Deutero-Isaiah (9) – see **Second Isaiah**.
Deuteronomistic (7) – adjective describing biblical texts that feature terminology and/or theology similar to that permeating the book of Deuteronomy.
Deuteronomistic History (7) – a history extending from Moses's speech to Israel on the edge of the land (Deuteronomy) through the books of Joshua, Judges, 1–2 Samuel, and 1–2 Kings to Judah's eventual exile from the land at the end of the books of Kings. Though incorporating potential earlier blocks of tradition (e.g. a possible early "**Succession Narrative**"), this broader history of Israel in the land is dominated by the later theology articulated most clearly in Deuteronomy, and is thought by most scholars to have been composed partly in the late seventh century and completed during the exile.
Documentary Hypothesis (10) – a hypothesis that the Pentateuch was formed out of the combination of a limited number of earlier written sources. In its oldest and most commonly known form, this hypothesis held that the Pentateuch was formed from four source documents: **J, E, D**, and **P**, but many scholars now doubt whether extended, early **J** and **E** sources are identifiable or even existed. This leaves only **D** and **P** as agreed-upon earlier sources of the Pentateuch along with a more debated block of **non-Priestly** material in the Pentateuch whose origins are more debated.
divine council (9) – the idea that the divine world is organized on analogy with a human monarchal court, with a divine king, his consort, his officials, and other parts of his administration. This idea is reflected in many non-biblical texts as well as in the Bible itself.
dynamic equivalence (Prologue) – a term for a translation that aims to produce a meaning-for-meaning translation of a (biblical) text, as necessary diverging from a word-for-word translation to produce a more exact and understandable equivalent meaning.
E (10) – see **Elohistic source**.
ecological biblical criticism (or ecological hermeneutics; 10) – diverse biblical approaches that share a focus on analysis of biblical texts in relation to ecology and current environmental challenges. Some approaches aim to provide more ecofriendly readings of biblical texts, while others focus on ways that biblical texts – written in a quite different time – can prove problematic resources for guiding present action.
El (2) – the name of the head creator god of the Canaanite pantheon, husband of **Asherah**.
election theology (2) – a set of beliefs surrounding God's choosing of and special protection of a people, Israel. Distinguished from **Zion theology** by its focus on God's relationship to a people rather than a place (Jerusalem).
Elephantine (11) – a Jewish colony in Egypt where ancient papyri were found that document the life and religious practices of Jews living outside the land in the **Persian period**.
Elohistic source (10) – a *hypothesized* source of the **Pentateuch** (no separate copies have been found) that many scholars think is preserved in parts of Genesis 20–22 and other non-Priestly parts of the Pentateuch where the divine designation "Elohim" predominates (the **Priestly source** also uses Elohim for God in Genesis, but is seen as distinct from this Elohistic source). According to this hypothesis, this Elohistic source was composed in the

north of Israel sometime in the late ninth or eighth century, thus coming from a later time and different place from the **Yahwistic source (J)**. This textbook is one of a number of recent treatments that has discarded the idea that there is an identifiable **E** source in the Pentateuch, but there are still many references to this hypothesized source in past and some recent scholarship.

empire (2) – as analyzed in this textbook, a form of ancient social organization where a particular monarchal state dominated other states through amassed military power (often drawing on the resources of subject states), creation of interlocking economic networks, and propagandistic use of terror.

feminist biblical criticism (1 and 4) – applied to the Bible; a range of methods aimed at analyzing biblical depictions of women (or lack of these depictions) and biblical use of feminine imagery.

form criticism (11) – the study of different types of texts, **genres**, in the Bible along with their typical social settings and purposes.

formal correspondence (Prologue) – approach that aims to produce a word-for-word translation of a (biblical) text.

former prophets (7) – see **books of the former prophets**.

genre (11) – a type of text, such as a **lament psalm** or **prophetic call narrative**.

H (10) – a designation either for the **Holiness Code** in Leviticus 17–26 or for a broader layer of material in the **Pentateuch** that is characterized by the central emphases of Leviticus 17–26 (e.g. the importance of Israel's holiness).

Hanukkah (13) – the Jewish holiday celebrating the rededication of the **Second Temple** by Judas Maccabee in 164 BCE after it had been temporarily transformed by Antiochus Epiphanes IV into a temple to Zeus Olympius.

Hasmonean monarchy (1) – 142–63 BCE: the period of rule of members of the Hasmonean priestly family descended from Judas Maccabeus, who led a successful rebellion against the Hellenistic rule of Antiochus Epiphanes IV.

Hasmoneans (1 and 13) – a provincial priestly family who led a revolt against Antiochus Epiphanes IV and eventually founded the **Hasmonean monarchy**.

heavenly apocalypse (13) – a type of **apocalypse** that depicts an ancient figure receiving a tour of heavenly realms.

Hebrew Bible (Prologue) – scriptures shared by Jews and Christians.

Hellenistic period (1) – 332–167 BCE: a period when, following the conquest of the Persian empire by Alexander, Palestine was ruled by a succession of Greek kings based in Egypt (the Ptolemies), Anatolia (contemporary Turkey), or Mesopotamia (the Seleucids).

historical apocalypse (13) – a type of **apocalypse** that reviews the past eras of history, often in encoded form, leading up to the present crises and an impending divine intervention. Though written during a given crisis, they often are attributed to a more ancient sage (see **pseudepigraphy**), who is depicted as receiving the revelation in the distant past as a coded prophecy of *future* eras, crises, and eventual intervention (e.g. Daniel 10–12).

historical criticism (1) – a family of historical methods that analyzes how and where the biblical texts (and oral traditions in them) were composed.

history of (biblical) interpretation (1 and 4) – study of how biblical texts have been interpreted, especially in faith communities (e.g. Judaism, Christianity, Islam).

history of religions (10) – a term used in biblical scholarship to refer to the study of ideas and themes relating to gods and ritual in ancient Near Eastern cultures other than Israel so that we might better understand biblical religious ideas and practices.

Holiness Code (10) – a collection of laws in Leviticus 17–26 *hypothesized* to have once existed separately (no separate copies have been found) and characterized by a frequent focus on the need for the people of Israel to preserve its holiness. Many recent scholars believe instead that the language and themes predominant in Leviticus 17–26 are characteristic of a broader layer of **H** material spanning the rest of material in the **Pentateuch** assigned by others to **P**.

holy war (7) – a concept, shared by peoples surrounding Israel, of a war where all of the spoils of conquest – both people and property – are consecrated to the deity and destroyed.

hybridity (7 and 13) – a concept drawn from postcolonial theory that designates the blending of self-determination with elements drawn from the culture of the past oppressor. It is not identical with mere mixing of different cultural elements in identity. Instead, it refers to the complex identity formed in the midst and wake of the experience of domination.

hymn of praise (11) – sometimes referred to just as "hymn," this is a psalm that focuses on praise of God. It often features a focus on creation and/or is characterized by refrains calling for praise of God.

hymn of trust (11) – a type of psalm that expresses trust in God's protection and provision.

ideological criticism (1) – the analysis of ways that biblical texts can be, have been, and should be read in the midst of systemic structures of power. As such it overlaps with other methods (e.g. **history of (biblical) interpretation**), but with a particular accent on analysis of ideology and power.

inclusio (9) – a literary structure where a text begins and ends with similar elements that enclose a larger middle. Also known as an "envelope structure," where the shorter and similar beginning and ending provide the envelope for the middle.

intertextuality (9) – a word used to refer to the myriad ways different texts can be related to each other. It can refer to conscious or unconscious ways that texts draw on the wording of earlier texts, but also to the ways that the readings of any text can be influenced by what the reader (or reading community) knows of other texts, whether texts dated before or after the text being read.

Israel (1) – two meanings: refers more narrowly to the tribal groups settled in the northern highlands of Canaan or more broadly to Judah (in the south) along with those northern groups.

Israelite (1) – a person who was part of ancient Israel, including Judean individuals who identified themselves as the true heirs of ancient Israel. All are to be clearly distinguished from Israelis, who are members of the modern state of Israel.

J (4 and 10) – the one-letter designation of the hypothesized **Yahwistic source**. The prominent use of the divine "Yahweh" in the Yahwistic source is only one indicator used to argue for the existence of the source, but it has led to the frequent designation of the source as "J" (the German letter for the "y" sound at the outset of Yahweh).

JE (10) – a combination of the **J** and **E** hypothesized sources for the **Pentateuch**. The texts included in what some scholars discuss as "JE" are similar to the **non-P** texts discussed in this textbook as part of the **non-Priestly (L)** layer. The main difference is that this textbook does not see this body of texts as having been created out of a combination of J and E sources. Therefore the term **JE** (sometimes "Jehovist"), though found in many commentaries and introductions, is not used in this book or in a number of other recent discussions.

Josiah's reform (7) – approximately 623 BCE: a socio-religious reform that Josiah is said to have undertaken in the wake of the decline of Assyrian influence over the area (2 Kings 23; compare 2 Chronicles 34), eliminating sanctuaries outside Jerusalem and laying claim to some of the territories of the former northern kingdom.

Judith (book of) (13) – a **deuterocanonical** book that tells a story of how a female heroine, Judith, saved the people of Judah by seducing and killing a general of the Assyrian army, named Holofernes. The tale is unhistorical, likely crafted during the Hasmonean period to stress the ability of Judeans to repel powerful foreign enemies.

King James Version (Prologue) – an authorized translation of the Christian Bible completed under royal sponsorship by the Church of England in 1611.

L (10) – a term used in this textbook to designate a **l**ayer of **l**ate (especially exilic) non-Priestly Pentateuchal material written by **l**ay scribes that reshapes earlier traditions about the primeval history, Israel's ancestors, and the Israelites under Moses. This layer adds promise, blessing, and other themes to those traditions in order to address the concerns of later Judeans, especially during the Babylonian exile.

lament (11) – though this term sometimes is used to refer to a **lament psalm**, it applies more properly to cries over irreversible bad events, such as David's mourning over the death of Saul in 2 Sam 1:18–27 or the book of Lamentations.

lament psalm (11) – a type of psalm that is a cry for God's help and typically includes most of the following elements: complaint, plea for help, vow, statement of trust in God's help, and thanksgiving for God's help. Though some refer to such lament psalms simply as "**laments**," the cry for help typical of a lament psalm is distinguished from a lament proper by the fact that it does not mourn something that is already finished (e.g. a death). Instead, it is a plea that things may get better. Because of this difference, some scholars prefer to call these lament psalms **complaints** or **supplications**.

latter prophets (7) – see **books of the latter prophets**.

literary criticism (1) – the use of methods from modern study of literary texts (e.g. attention to plot, characterization, signification) to illuminate the poetic-narrative dynamics of biblical texts.

LXX (Prologue) – an abbreviation for **Septuagint**.

Maccabees (1 and 13) – another word for the **Hasmoneans**.

major prophets (6) – the three larger prophetic books: Isaiah, Jeremiah, and Ezekiel.

manuscript witness (Prologue) – an ancient copy of a biblical book or quotation of a biblical book (in the original language or translation).

Masoretic text (Prologue) – the authoritative version of the Hebrew text of the **Tanakh** or Hebrew Bible produced by Jewish scribes in the medieval period and used as the base text in most translations.

messiah (11) – a Hebrew word meaning "anointed one," which during the **Second Temple** period came to designate a hoped-for anointed king who would deliver Jews from domination and/or a hoped-for anointed priest to replace the priests in Jerusalem, who were perceived by some to be corrupt.

minor prophets (5) – 12 smaller prophetic books (Hosea, Joel, Amos, Obadiah, Jonah, Micah, Nahum, Habakkuk, Zephaniah, Haggai, Zechariah, and Malachi) that follow the three books of the **major prophets** (Isaiah, Jeremiah, Ezekiel) in the Jewish **Tanakh** and appear at the end of the Old Testament of the Christian Bible.

monarchal city-state (2) – a state based in a walled city (and often supported by other fortified settlements) and ruled by a hereditary monarchic dynasty. This ancient form of social organization allowed an amassing of military resources and wealth not possible for more decentralized tribal groups.

monotheism (9) – a term referring to the belief that there is only one god and that all other gods are false. This is to be distinguished from the idea, attested in the late pre-exilic period, that a given people should worship only one god among the various gods that exist, an idea sometimes designated as "henotheism."

moral act-consequence (4) – the idea that the cosmos is morally coherent; that is, morally good actions eventually lead to good results for the doer(s), while morally bad actions lead to disaster.

MT (Prologue) – an abbreviation for the **Masoretic text**.

neighboring monarchies (1) – 930–722 BCE: a time when there were separate, related monarchies in the south (based in Jerusalem and ruled by descendants of David) and the north (ultimately based in Samaria and ruled by a variety of royal dynasties).

non-P and **non-Priestly** (10) – terms used to refer to texts in the **Pentateuch** not assigned to P. It covers many of the same texts included in the older designation **JE** but is used by scholars who no longer posit the existence of the early **J** and **E** sources.

Old Testament (Prologue and 13) – Christian term for the scriptures originating in ancient Israel, each consisting of nearly identical books (with some exceptions) in a different order that culminates in Malachi's prophecy of Elijah (leading into Matthew 3).

oral traditions (2) – traditions important at every stage in the formation of the Bible, especially if one includes the oral aspects of written traditions, since even the latter often were memorized and performed. More specifically, we see some reflections in the written traditions of the Bible of exclusively oral traditions, and these reflections are the typical focus of biblical **tradition criticism**.

P (4 and 10) – see **Priestly source**.

Palestine, Palestinian (1) – "Palestine" is a designation that the Romans came to use for a province including the land of Israel and much of Syria. The word "Palestinian" was used to characterize inhabitants of that province and continues to be used to refer to descendants of non-Jewish people who lived in the region prior to the establishment of the modern state of Israel.

Pentateuch (Prologue and 4) – the first five books of the Bible, namely Genesis, Exodus, Leviticus, Numbers, and Deuteronomy, otherwise known as the (written) **Torah**.

Persian governmental authorization (11) – a practice seen in different parts of the Persian empire whereby local leaders sought and received official recognition from the Persian authorities of their local laws as Persian law. Some scholars think that Judean **post-exilic period** lay and priestly leaders may have sought such Persian recognition for their traditions, and that this process may stand behind the present combination of **Priestly** and non-Priestly strands of the **Pentateuch**.

Persian period (1) – 538–332 BCE: a time of Persian rule of Judah, when the Persians are recorded in the Bible as helping the Judeans who returned to rebuild the temple and walls of Jerusalem and establish the **Torah** as the authoritative law of the returnee community.

philological (Prologue) – pertaining to the study of language (philology) – the vocabulary, grammar, and syntax of a given language. Such study is important for translating the Hebrew, Aramaic, and Greek manuscripts of the Bible.

postcolonial criticism (7) – study that examines ways in which texts such as the Bible were formed in imperial contexts and/or how biblical texts later functioned in colonial or imperial contexts (e.g. missionary efforts).

post-exilic period (1 and 11) – from 538 BCE: the period following the forced exile to Babylonia, starting with the **Persian period**. Often the Persian period is the primary one meant when referring to the post-exilic period. Note: despite the term *post*-exilic, it is clear that many Judeans still lived outside the land after 538 BCE.

pre-state tribal period (1) – 1250–1000 BCE: a time when Israel lived in villages (joined loosely in larger tribal affiliations) in the hill country without any monarch over them.

Priestly source (4 and 10) – a *hypothesized* source of the **Pentateuch** (no separate copies have been found) which most scholars agree contained texts such as the Genesis 1 creation story, genealogies such as Genesis 5, a strand of the flood narrative where no sacrifice happens (e.g. Gen 6:9–22 to 9:1–17), the covenant of circumcision with Abraham (Genesis 17), the second call of Moses (Exod 6:2–8), the whole section about Sinai (Exodus 19 to Num 10:10), and many other texts in Genesis–Numbers with similar language and themes (though not all focusing on priests). Though this layer contains much earlier traditions, most scholars agree that the broader Priestly source was not composed until the **Babylonian exile** or early **post-exilic period**.

primeval narrative (4) – the stories of creation, flood, and other events concerning early humanity in general found in Genesis 1–11.

prophetic call narrative (6) – a story, usually told in the first person, where a prophetic figure tells of how he was authorized by God to be a prophet, usually including some or all of the following elements: an appearance of God, introductory word by God to the one to be called, call of the prophet, objection by the prophet that he is somehow unfit for the task, divine reassurance, and sign reinforcing the divine reassurance. Examples include Isaiah 6; Jer 1:4–10; and Ezekiel 1–3, though some scholars dispute whether some of these texts are proper "call narratives," and disagree about whether "call" (a term whose home is in later Christian theology) is appropriate for these ancient Hebrew narratives.

proto-monarchy (1) – tenth century (900s) BCE: the time when David and Solomon ruled Israel from Jerusalem, beginning to develop the structures (standing army, fortified base) characteristic of an ancient city-state monarchy.

Psalter (11) – another word for the book of Psalms.

pseudepigraphy (13) – attribution of a later text to a more ancient author. This was particularly common in the Hellenistic period, when Judaism came into contact with a Greek culture that was more focused on establishing ancient authorship of authoritative texts.

Qur'an (Prologue) – the holiest text in Islam, seen in that faith as the collected recitations by Muhammad, the prophet, of direct revelations from God. These recitations on ethical and theological matters sometimes refer to biblical traditions, often as filtered through early Jewish and/or Christian interpretation of those traditions.

rebuilding of the Jerusalem temple (11) – 515 BCE (completion), described in the Bible as done over a period of years with Persian sponsorship: this **Second Temple** represented an important center of leadership and social organization in **post-exilic period** Judah in the years after the destruction of the monarchy.

reception history (4) – the study of the complete variety of ways that texts are used over time, in both textual and other (e.g. artistic) media and in various faith community and other contexts. It thus overlaps with **history of (biblical) interpretation**, but focuses more on non-textual media and/or non-religious examples of scriptural use.

redaction (4) – a form of ancient textual revision involving the expansion of an older text and/or the linking of different texts with each other. The word "redaction" can refer both to the process of such revision and to the material that is added.

redaction criticism (4) – the attempt to identify the ways in which the scribal authors or redactors of the present biblical books created those wholes through arrangement, transformation, and extension of earlier source materials. It is a form of **transmission history**.

royal psalms (3) – a set of psalms in the **Psalter** that focus on the king and God's special relationship to him (see **royal theology**).

royal theology (3) – a set of beliefs and images surrounding God's appointing of the king as ruler and high priest, God's equipping of the king with power, justice, and blessing, and God's granting the king anything he wishes, particularly military victory and long life.

(the) **satan** (11) – a Hebrew term referring in Job to an accuser working *for* God, who roams God's realm and checks up on God's subjects. Though this term is translated in Job with a capital "S," thus leading readers to confuse the "satan" or accuser of Job with the demon Satan of later Jewish and Christian theology, the word is not a proper name in Job and does not refer to the prince of darkness.

Second Isaiah (9) – alternatively **Deutero-Isaiah**: term used to refer to chapters 40–55 of the book of Isaiah, a section that shows many signs of being composed during the time of **Babylonian exile** (with parts possibly even later). Almost no scholars today think that the author of these later chapters was named "Isaiah." The term "Second Isaiah" reflects the fact that this portion of the book of Isaiah was the first one to be distinguished from the words of the first "Isaiah," which are now to be found particularly in portions of Isaiah 1–11 and 28–32.

Second Temple (11) – the Temple rebuilt under Persian sponsorship by 515 BCE and eventually destroyed by the Romans in 70 CE, a center for Judean leadership and social organization throughout the intervening period.

seconding (3) – a term coined by James Kugel in *The Idea of Biblical Poetry* (New Haven: Yale University Press, 1981) for the multiple and complex ways that the final line of a **couplet** or **triplet** can build on the meaning of the initial lines of the given poetic unit. Many find this to be a more flexible and accurate designation for this phenomenon in Hebrew poetry than older and more commonly used terms such as "parallelism."

segmentary society (2) – a term designating the kind of decentralized, horizontal social framework that tribal Israel had prior to the onset of the monarchy.

Septuagint (Prologue) – an ancient set of translations of Jewish Scriptural books into Greek.

servant (9) – a term used in parts of **Second Isaiah** that seems to refer to a specific entity or individual, particularly in the **servant songs** of Isaiah. Scholars debate whether this "servant" is a reference to a particular individual or a metaphor in these texts for the people (or sub-group of the people).

servant songs (9) – a set of texts in Isa 42:1–8; 49:1–6; 50:4–9; and 52:13–53:12 that focus on a **"servant"** figure. Some scholars have thought these servant songs might represent a separate literary layer in **Second Isaiah**.

Sirach (13) – see **Ben Sira**.

social-scientific analysis (9) – when applied to the Bible, analysis that draws on contemporary sociological and anthropological studies to provide a more nuanced picture of ancient Israel.

source criticism (4) – the attempt to reconstruct (now lost) written sources used by the authors of the present biblical texts. It is a type of **transmission history**.

Story of David's Rise (to power) (7) – a hypothesized source telling the story of David's rise to power, achieving military success and replacing Saul as king. It is seen as lying behind much of 1 Samuel 16–31 and 2 Samuel 1–5.

Succession Narrative (3 and 7) – a *hypothesized* older narrative (no separate copies have been found) located in 2 Samuel 9–20 and 1 Kings 1–2 describing the process of succession to David. It is thought to have been written around the time of Solomon.

suffering servant (9) – the particular image of the **servant** in **Second Isaiah** found in Isa 52:13–53:12, an image that often has been interpreted by Christians to refer to the crucifixion and resurrection of Jesus Christ.

supersessionism (Prologue) – the idea that Christianity and the Christian church have superseded and thus replaced Judaism and the people of Israel.

supplication (11) – for discussion see **lament psalm**.

Syro-Ephraimite war (5) – a war occurring around 735 BCE in which Syria and the northern kingdom of Israel laid siege to Jerusalem and thus attempted to force Judah, under King Ahaz, to join a coalition of local states resisting Assyrian rule (though Judah was not yet under Assyrian rule). Ahaz appealed for and received help from Assyria in repelling the Syrian–Israelite alliance, but became subject to Assyria in return for the aid.

Tanakh (Prologue) – the Jewish term for the Hebrew scriptures, referring to the three main parts of those scriptures: the **Torah**, Neviiim (Hebrew for "prophets"), and Ketuvim (Hebrew for "writings"). The arrangement of the Jewish Tanakh culminates in Cyrus's promise to rebuild the Temple at the end of 2 Chronicles.

textual criticism (Prologue) – the collection and analysis of different manuscript readings, e.g. different readings in Hebrew manuscripts and early translations of Hebrew manuscripts of books in the Hebrew Bible.

thanksgiving song (11) – a type of psalm that praises God for deliverance from suffering, and calls on others to join that praise.

theophany (6) – a divine appearance. This term also often refers to a text that describes a divine appearance.

Third Isaiah (12) – a designation for chapters 56–66 of the book of Isaiah, a section distinguished from **Second Isaiah** by more explicit indicators that it addressed the situation of **post-exilic period** Judah.

Torah (Prologue) – the first five books of the Bible, namely Genesis, Exodus, Leviticus, Numbers, and Deuteronomy. Jews often distinguish between this "written Torah" and the "oral Torah" given to Moses, transmitted through the sages, and embodied in the Mishnah and other authoritative Jewish writings.

tradition criticism (1) – the attempt to recover, via the written texts of the Bible, the traditions that stand behind them, usually with a particular focus on the **oral traditions** reflected in the written texts.

tradition history (2) – a history of traditions that existed before and often alongside the written texts now in the Bible. Though such traditions can be written as well as oral, the term often refers primarily to the history of pre-biblical **oral traditions** reconstructed through **tradition criticism**.

transmission history (2) – an umbrella term for the study of the different processes leading up to the final composition of biblical books. It can include **tradition criticism**, **source criticism**, and **redaction criticism**.

trauma (9) – an overwhelming, haunting experience of disaster (or ongoing violence) so powerful in its impact that it cannot be directly encountered and influences an individual or group's behavior and memory in indirect ways.

trauma studies and the Bible (9) – utilization of insights from psychological, sociological, and other studies of trauma to illuminate the development and ongoing use of the Bible amidst situations of **trauma**.

trickster (2) – a character whose ability to survive through trickery and even lawbreaking is celebrated in religion, literature, or another part of culture.

triplet (3) – along with the more common **couplet**, a basic unit of Hebrew poetry. In it, the first two lines set the stage for the climactic third line. Many translations identify the second and third lines of triplets by indenting the beginning of the second line a few spaces.

tsedeqah (3) – a Hebrew word often translated as "righteousness," but perhaps better rendered as "social responsibility," fulfilling one's obligations to others in the society, particularly those most vulnerable.

vassal treaty (5 and 7) – a type of ancient **covenant** imposed by a superpower on one or more nations that it dominated. Such a treaty typically required the subject king or nation to pay tribute to the king of the superpower, maintain constant and exclusive allegiance to him, and incur curses if the subject nation failed to be exclusively and constantly loyal to the dominating power.

village (2) – an unwalled settlement inhabited by a few clans (50–300 people total) living in pillared houses in various extended family units. Though this ancient form of social life is introduced in the discussion of pre-state Israel in Chapter 2, it was the most common way for people to live throughout the history of Israel.

wisdom psalm (11) – a psalm particularly characterized by explicit educational elements, often featuring language in common with other explicit teaching literature such as Proverbs.

womanist approach (to interpretation) (4) – builds on and foregrounds the experience, wisdom, and/or biblical interpretation of African American women. As such it is an example of interpretive method linking to the intersection of diverse social identities, in this case gender and race.

Yahweh (1) – the name of the god of Israel, often translated as "LORD" in English translations. This name came to be seen as especially holy in Jewish tradition.

Yahwistic source (4 and 10) – a *hypothesized* early source of the **Pentateuch** (no copies have been found) that some scholars think starts with the Garden of Eden and materials about Abel and Cain (Gen 2:4b–4:26), continues with a version of the flood story parallel to **P** (e.g. Gen 6:1–4; 7:1–5 to 8:20–22), and continues to include the story of Noah and his sons, and large portions of the Abraham story (the bulk of Genesis 12–13, 16–19) along with various **non-Priestly** portions of the rest of Genesis, Exodus, and Numbers where the divine name **Yahweh** is used (translated as "LORD" in most English translations). According to this hypothesis, this source was composed in the early monarchal south, probably sometime during the tenth century. *Within this textbook* the probability of the existence of this broader J/Yahwistic source is denied.

Zion (3) – the name of a holy mountain on which the fortress and temple of Jerusalem stood. It often comes to serve as a synonym for Jerusalem.

Zion psalms (3) – a set of psalms in the biblical **Psalter** that focus on Zion/Jerusalem and emphasize themes of **Zion theology**.

Zion theology (3) – a set of beliefs surrounding the idea that God lives in Jerusalem, holds Jerusalem to a high ethical standard, and will prevent Jerusalem from being destroyed by any enemy. Note: this is *not* "Zionist" theology.

Index

The letter b after a page reference indicates that the topic appears in a textbox. Page numbers in *italics* refer to illustrations.

abbreviations for biblical books 11b
Abraham *see* Genesis Gen 12:1–3, Genesis 12–25
act-consequence 84
AD 28b
African American biblical interpretation 55b
Afrocentric interpretation 80b
Amos 110–13, 112b
apocalypse, genre of 267–8
apocrypha 5
ark narrative 155
Asherah 45–6, *46*, 85, 140, 245
  Yahweh and his Asherah 117, *118*
Assyrian empire *29*, 29–30, 101–2, *107, 108*, 107–9, 124–8, 125b, 131–3, 142–9
Assyrian vassal treaty *see* vassal treaty
Atrahasis, epic of 98

Baal 45, 117
Babylonian empire *29*, 178–81, *181*, 181b
BC and BCE 28b
Ben Sira *268*, 269
Book of the Watchers (Enochic) 268

call narrative 133b
Canaanite origins of Israel 45–6
canons, formation of
  Hebrew 282–4
canon(s) of the Hebrew Bible 3
Canticles *see* Song of Songs
CE 28b
chapters (origins of chapter notations) 11b
Chronicles, 1–2, books of 277b
citation of biblical passages 11b
Code of Hammurabi 87, *88*
conjectural emendation 8b
conquest, history of 40b, 43–5
  and holy war 152b
couplet 75b
Covenant Code 87, 98, 137–8, 145b, 146
covenant, concept of 120–1, 147–8
creation story *see* Genesis, Gen 1:1–2:3, Gen 2:4–3:24
cultural memory 56–7, 66, 159
Cyrus cylinder 229–30, *230*

Daniel, book of 272–3, 272b
Deborah, song of *see* Judges, book of, Judges 5
deuterocanonical (books) 4–5, 269–70, 283–4

The Hebrew Bible: A Contemporary Introduction to the Christian Old Testament and the Jewish Tanakh, Second Edition. David M. Carr.
© 2021 David M. Carr. Published 2021 by John Wiley & Sons Ltd.

Deutero-Isaiah *see* Isaiah,
    Isaiah 40–55
Deuteronomistic history 158
    exilic edition of 185–6
Deuteronomy 145–50, 135b, 146b,
    147b, 150b
    and the Covenant Code 145b, 146
    Deut 6:4–9 160–3
Deutero-Zechariah 251b
divine council 190, 190b
divine name 31b, 189, 217b
dynamic equivalence translation 9

E *see* Elohistic source
Ecclesiastes 80–5, 82b, 280
ecological biblical criticism (eco-
    logical hermeneutics) 220b
economy, village 36–7
Eden, garden of *see* Genesis,
    Gen 2:4–3:24
Education
    using writing 66–8
El 45, 46b, 109–10, 117
election theology 49, 111, 113
Elephantine 235
Elohistic source (E) 211b
empire 38–9
Enoch, book of 268–9
1 Esdras, 279b
Esther, book of 279, 279b
everyday life in ancient Israel 36–7
exile in Babylon 28, 179–82, *179*,
    181b
Exodus, book of 238b
    Exodus 1–15 54–6, 105
    Exodus 19–40 (Sinai narrative)
    208–13, 237–40
exodus, history of 30, 54–5
Ezekiel, book of 186–9, 188b
Ezra-Nehemiah, books of 252–3,
    277–9, 278–9b

family 36–7
feminist criticism 32, 93b
First Testament 5
form criticism 242–4, 242b
formal correspondence
    translation 9
former prophets 151b

gender and translation 9
Genesis 49–51, 52–3b, 88–91,
    104–5, 237b
    Gen 1:1–2:3 (first creation
    story) 22, 216, 219–21, 219b,
    220b, 236
    Gen 2:4–3:24 (second creation
    story/Eden) 92–7, 236
    Gen 12:1–3 (first promise to
    Abraham) 222–4
    Genesis 1–11 (primeval
    narrative) 88–89
    Genesis 12–25 (Abraham
    story) 51, 51b, 52b, 203–5
    Genesis 25–35 (Jacob story) 50–3,
    52b, 104, 205b
    Genesis 37–50 (Joseph
    story) 53b, 105b
geography
    of the ancient Near East 26–7
    of (the land of) Israel 23–5
Gilgamesh epic 81–2, 90–1b, *91*

H *see* Holiness Code
Haggai, book of 250–1, 250b
Hammurabi *see* Code of
    Hammurabi
Hanukkah 273
Hasmoneans and Hasmonean
    monarchy 29, 273–6
heavenly apocalypse *see* apoca-
    lypse, genre of
Hebrew Bible 5

Hellenistic Judaism 270
Hellenistic period 29, 266–76
Hellenization 266–70
Hezekiah's reform 143–4
historical apocalypse *see* apocalypse, genre of
historical criticism 31
history and fiction 43–5, 158–60, 221–2
history of interpretation 32
history of religions 219b
Holiness Code (H) 217–8b
holy war 152b
Hosea, book of 113–21, 116b
hybridity 121, 146–9, 158–60, 274, 276
hymn of praise 244
hymn of thanksgiving 244

ideological criticism 32
intertextuality 193b
Isaiah, book of 130–37, 257–61, 257–58b
  Isa 52:13–53:12 (fourth servant song) 194–6
  Isa 56:1–8 259–61
  Isaiah 40–55 190–6, 190b
  Isaiah 56–66 257–61
Israel 25, 46b
  and education 66–8
  northern kingdom of 102–8
Israelite 25

J *see* Yahwistic source
Jacob, early stories about 50–51; *see also* Genesis, Genesis 25–35
Jebusites 39, 60
Jeremiah, book of 168–74, 172b
Jerusalem
  imaginative reconstruction of 60–61, *61*

pre-Davidic, Jebusite 39, *40*, 60
Job, book of 254b
Jonah, book of 255–6, 255b
Joseph, early story *see* Genesis, Genesis 37–50
Joshua, book of 40b, 43–5, 151–3, 153b
Josiah's reform 140–45, 156, 159
Judith, book of 274b
Judges, book of 40b, 153–4, 154b
  Judges 5 (song of Deborah) 47–9

Ketuvim (writings) 3
King James Version 8–9
Kings, 1–2, books of 156–7, 157b
kingship *see* monarchy, rise of the Judean-Israelite

L layer (of the Pentateuch) 201–6; *see also* non-P
labels of psalms and books 69b
lament psalm 242–3
Lamentations, book of 182–3, 183b
Leviticus, book of 214b
literary criticism and approaches 29, 105b
literary education *see* education
LORD 31b
LXX *see* Septuagint

Maccabees 29, 273
Maccabees, 1, book of 274, 283
Maccabees, 2, book of 274
major prophets 131
manuscript witnesses to the Hebrew Bible 7–8b
Masoretes 7b, 12b
Masoretic text (MT) 7b, 172
memorization of texts 66–7, 96, 149, 150b, 162, 183–4
Merneptah stela 42–3, *43*

Mesha inscription 152b
messiah 74, 136, 245–6
Micah, book of 125–30, 129–30b
minor prophets 120b
monarchal city-state 37–8
monarchy, rise of the Judean-
    Israelite 62–4
  neighboring monarchies 28,
    102–4
  proto-monarchy 62–4
monotheism 192
moral act-consequence *see*
    act-consequence
Mosaic authorship (of the
    Pentateuch) 201b
MT *see* Masoretic text

Nahum, book of 166–7, 166b
Nehemiah, book of *see*
    Ezra-Nehemiah
Nehemiah memoir 231–2, 252–3
Neo-Babylonian empire *see*
    Babylonian empire
Neo-Documentarian
    Approach 211b
Neviim (prophets) 3
non-P *see* non-Priestly source
non-Priestly source (non-P; cf. L
    layer) 200–211, 209b
  non-P and Deuteronomy (D) 201
  non-P and L 206
Numbers, book of 239b

Old Testament 3–5, 174, 283–4
oral tradition 39, 47–57
  accuracy of 39, 41–2
order of biblical books 3–5

P *see* Priestly source
Palestine and Palestinian 25
Pentateuch, definition of 3

Persian empire 229–31
  thesis of Persian governmental
    authorization 234–5
  Persian involvement in rebuilding
    of Judah 230–5
Persian period 28
poetic analysis 75b
postcolonial criticism 148–9b,
    148–9
post-exilic period 28
pre-state tribal period 27–8
Priestly source (P) 80, 195–202,
    215b, 213b, 213–20
primeval narrative *see* Genesis,
    Genesis 1–11
prophecy outside Israel 109–10
prophetic call narrative *see* call
    narrative
prophets *see* Neviim
Proverbs, book of 82–6, 84b
Psalms 73b, 241–6, 243–4b
  different edition of 244b
  history and 69b
  lament *see* lament psalm
  Psalms 1–2
    (introduction) 245–6
  Psalm 137 182
  and Torah 241–2
pseudepigraphy 248–9

Qohelet *see* Ecclesiastes
Qur'an 5

Rashi 223
reception history 93b
redaction criticism 89b
Roman period 29
royal psalms 71–4, 73b
royal theology 70–2, 134, 219–20
Ruth, book of 256, 256b

Samuel, 1–2, books of 65–6, 154–6, 155b
Satan and/or (the) *satan* 92, 93b, 254b
scribal education *see* education
seconding 75b
Second Isaiah *see* Isaiah, Isaiah 40–55
Second Temple, building and destruction of 28, 233
segmentary society 39b
Septuagint (LXX) 8b, 172, 269–70
servant songs 191b, 192–94
servant, suffering 192–94
sex in the Bible 79b, 94
Shaphan, the scribe 170, 175
Shema *see* Deuteronomy, Deut 6:4–9
Sirach *see* Ben Sira
social-scientific analysis 180–2
software for study of the Bible 10, 14
Song of Songs (also Song of Solomon) 78–80, 79b, 280
source criticism 88, 89b
Story of David's Rise 154–5
study Bibles 10
succession narrative 65–6, 154
superscriptions *see* labels of psalms and books
supersessionism 5
Syro-Ephraimite war 124

Tanakh 3
Temple, Jerusalem 60, *61*, 63, 66–7, 141–2
Ten Commandments 150b
textual criticism 6, 6b
thanksgiving song 244
theophany 125
Third Isaiah *see* Isaiah, Isaiah 56–66
Torah and prophets 282–4
Torah, definition of 3
Torah, rise of 233–5
tradition criticism 31
tradition history 41b
translations 6–10
transmission history 41b
trauma 158–9, 202–7, 210–11
trauma studies and the Bible 184b
tribe 37
trickster 41, 48–53, 56
triplet 75b
tsedeqah ("solidarity" or "righteousness") 73
Twelve Prophets, book of 120b

vassal treaty 120–21, 147–50
verses (origins of verse notations) 11b
village
  as image for textual growth 202
  imaginative reconstruction of 36–7

Wisdom
  female figure in Proverbs 85–6
  and the garden of Eden story 95–6
Wisdom of Solomon, book of 270
womanist interpretation 80b
women and female figures in the Bible 47–9, 53b, 78, 83–6, 92–6, 93–4b, 114–19, 166, 169, 188–9, 193–4, 256, 274
writing 61, 98
  and cultural memory 61, 66
writings *see* Ketuvim

Yahweh 30, 31b
  Day of 167

Yahwistic source (J) 89, 211b, 223

Zechariah, book of 251–3, 251b
Zephaniah, book of 167–8, 168b

Zion 60, 73b,
Zion psalms 73–4
Zion theology 55, 73–4, 124–37, 170

www.ingramcontent.com/pod-product-compliance
Lightning Source LLC
LaVergne TN
LVHW080854290525
812424LV00003B/16